Partial Hegemony

Partial Hegemony

Oil Politics and International Order

JEFF D. COLGAN

OXFORD
UNIVERSITY PRESS

OXFORD
UNIVERSITY PRESS

Oxford University Press is a department of the University of Oxford. It furthers
the University's objective of excellence in research, scholarship, and education
by publishing worldwide. Oxford is a registered trade mark of Oxford University
Press in the UK and certain other countries.

Published in the United States of America by Oxford University Press
198 Madison Avenue, New York, NY 10016, United States of America.

Library of Congress Cataloging-in-Publication Data
Names: Colgan, Jeff, 1975– author.
Title: Partial hegemony : oil politics and international order / Jeffrey Colgan.
Description: New York : Oxford University Press, 2021. |
Includes bibliographical references and index. |
Identifiers: LCCN 2021031372 (print) | LCCN 2021031373 (ebook) |
ISBN 9780197546383 (paperback) | ISBN 9780197546376 (hardback) |
ISBN 9780197546406 (epub) | ISBN 9780197546413
Subjects: LCSH: Hegemony—United States. | Power (Social sciences)—
United States. | Petroleum industry and trade—Political aspects—
United States. | United States—Foreign relations.
Classification: LCC JZ1312 .C62 2021 (print) |
LCC JZ1312 (ebook) | DDC 327.101—dc23
LC record available at https://lccn.loc.gov/2021031372
LC ebook record available at https://lccn.loc.gov/2021031373

DOI: 10.1093/oso/9780197546376.001.0001

3 5 7 9 8 6 4

Paperback printed by LSC Communications, United States of America
Hardback printed by Bridgeport National Bindery, Inc., United States of America

Contents

Acknowledgments   vii

1. Introduction   1

PART I OIL POLITICS

2. Rethinking International Order   31
3. The Rise of OPEC   59
4. The Stagnation of OPEC   94
5. Oil and Security   119

PART II BEYOND OIL

6. Using Subsystems beyond Oil   163
7. Climate Change   186

8. Conclusion   214

Bibliography   225
Index   263

Acknowledgments

Book acknowledgments tend to be a lot like Academy Award speeches, but without the tuxedos, gowns, and sexy people—they go on too long and are boring for almost everyone except the insiders. Sorry. If you aren't an academic author yourself, it's hard to fathom just how many debts a person accrues in the process of writing a book like this. In my case, I needed all the help I could get.

Robert O. Keohane is a mentor, coauthor, and friend. He read several large chunks of this manuscript on multiple occasions and made it better each time with his usual mix of kind encouragement and tough critique. I decided on the book's title mostly because it reflected a core concept I wanted to highlight, but happily it also pays homage to Bob's masterwork, *After Hegemony*.

I've never studied or worked at the University of Chicago, so I especially appreciate the generosity its political scientists have shown to me. They hosted me on multiple occasions in the years it took to write this book. John J. Mearsheimer read my work carefully, zeroed in on its weaknesses with brutal precision, saw its promise, and took the time to sharpen my thinking immensely. Paul Staniland, Austin Carson, Paul Poast, Rochelle Terman, Kara Ross Camarena, and Robert Gulotty gave me new ideas, as did some smart graduate students like Alexandra Chinchilla and Gentry Jenkins.

I was lucky to visit Europe and engage with scholars there as part of this project, including Christian Bueger, Eleni Tsingou, Anders Wivel, Rebecca Adler-Nissen, Ann Towns, Adrian Hyde-Price, Jens Mortensen, Ole Jacob Sending, Halvard Leira, Målfrid Braut-Hegghammer, and Dag Harald Claes. My cousin and coauthor William Colgan made my stay there fun and brought me back to the physical sciences, where my education began (in engineering physics, many moons ago).

I owe thanks to a great many people who read early versions of various chapters, including: Peter Andreas, Leonardo Baccini, Hannah Baron, Sarah Bauerle Danzman, Morgan Bazilian, Katherine Beall, Jean-François Bélanger, Andrew Bennett, Robert Blair, Yuna Blajer de la Garza, Mark Blyth, Jordan Branch, Hal Brands, Joshua Busby, Allison Carnegie, Poulomi Chakrabarti, Christine Cheng, Bridget Coggins, Adam Dean, Charles Doran, Jack Donnelly, Alex Downes, Miles Evers, Michel Fournier-Simard, Jeffry Frieden, Giuliano Garavini, Gregory Gause, Charles Glaser, Ilene Grabel, Marc Grinberg, Seva Gunitsky, Randall Henning, Juliet Johnson, Richard Jordan, Tyler Jost, Miles Kahler, Nikhil Kalyanpur, Peter Katzenstein, Rosemary Kelanic, Andrew Kerner,

William Kring, Paasha Mahdavi, Edward Mansfield, Matthias Matthijs, Rose McDermott, Patrick McDonald, Kathleen McNamara, Nicholas Miller, Jonas Nahm, Daniel Nexon, Stephen Nelson, Joseph Parent, Reid Pauly, Krzysztof Pelc, Margaret Peters, Tyler Pratt, Michael Ross, Elizabeth Saunders, Detlef Sprinz, David Steinberg, Alexander Sullivan, Dustin Tingley, Felicity Vabulas, Thijs van de Graaf, Robert Vitalis, Rachel Whitlark, Alex Weisiger, Ayse Zarakol, and probably a dozen others that I really ought to acknowledge.

I'm grateful to participants at seminars at: McGill University, University of Chicago, Georgetown University, Harvard University, Texas A&M (via the Lonestar Security Forum), Princeton University, George Washington University, Johns Hopkins University, NYU–Abu Dhabi, University of Copenhagen, NUPI (Oslo), King's College London, Northwestern University, University of Gothenburg, Stanford University (CASBS), Cornell University, Colorado School of Mines, and the University of Pennsylvania; and meetings of the International Studies Association, the International Political Economy Society, the Peace Science Association, and the European International Studies Association; and also to students in my classes, who provided detailed feedback.

I conducted interviews and archival work during my research. I especially wish to thank staff members at the OPEC Secretariat in Vienna, including Asma Muttawa, Mohamed Mekerba, and Dr. Aziz Yahyai, for helpful in-person discussions, and Nona Schlegel, Iryna Chupikova, and Almudena Gil Franco for their help accessing OPEC historical records. I also thank the staff at the Lyndon B. Johnson Presidential Library in Austin, Texas; staff at the British National Archives in Kew (London) UK; and Lisette Matano and Scott Taylor at Georgetown University for their help accessing the William E. Mulligan Papers.

My editor David McBride and his team at Oxford University Press made this book better than it would have been otherwise. So did Jacquelyn Larson, who reviewed the manuscript for me. Rachel McMahon provided superb research assistance. Thanks.

Chapter 4 is largely based on my 2014 article in *International Organization,* "The emperor has no clothes: The limits of OPEC in the global oil market." I appreciate permission from Cambridge University Press to reuse that article in revised form.

Most of all, I'm grateful to my family. My mother Valerie and my brother Andrew supported me from afar. My wife January supported me at much closer quarters. I'm very grateful to her, and them, for listening to my self-doubts and frustrations along the way, and for knowing when not to listen too carefully.

My daughter Sophie has been a constant source of joy and distraction over the many years it took me to write this book. She was a toddler when I began; now she is showing the kind of intelligence, creativity, and kindness that I hope she has for the rest of her life. I dedicate this book to her.

1

Introduction

The largest peaceful transfer of wealth across borders in all of human history began in 1973. Prior to the 1970s, a small group of companies controlled the vast majority of the world's petroleum. They kept prices low and steady. These Anglo-American companies made decisions about how much oil to produce and in which countries to produce it. That gave them enormous power over government revenues in countries like Iran and Venezuela. So in 1960, five governments got together to create the Organization of the Petroleum Exporting Countries (OPEC). It grew and hummed along for about a decade. Then in 1973, this little organization helped its members turn the tables on the most powerful businesses on the planet. They quadrupled the price of oil, seized decision-making authority, and shifted the global distribution of profits. The political and economic aftershocks reverberated for years.

Half a century later, the history of oil takes on a renewed importance for two reasons. First, oil and energy continue to lie at the heart of international relations, often generating foreign policy failures. In the United States, a recurring quest for various notions of "energy security" or "energy independence" has generated a lot of muddled thinking over multiple decades. That lack of clarity has tangible consequences. Oil is the strategic context for various misadventures in the Persian Gulf region. It is the topic of misguided economic policies within the United States. And it is deeply connected to climate change, a challenge that policymakers have repeatedly failed to adequately address.

The global oil industry finds itself now, as it did in the 1970s, on the threshold of a massive energy transition. This time, the transition is driven by climate change, new technologies, and, possibly, different consumption patterns in the wake of the Covid-19 pandemic. Yet, like the 1970s, geopolitics will guide who benefits and loses from changing market conditions. Powerful governments and firms will seek to make arrangements that drive outcomes according to their preferences. Their success, or failure, will depend on certain fundamentals that have not changed much in the century that oil has been the world's dominant fuel. One purpose of this book is to reveal those fundamentals.

The second reason to revisit the 1970s goes beyond oil politics. In the twenty-first century, many worry that the "liberal international order,"[1] or the US

---

[1] The "liberal international order" eludes easy definition. People typically use it to describe a set of governing arrangements, underpinned by a set of ideas, and manifested by a set of institutions

position within it, is at risk. The threat is partly internal, driven by loss of social cohesion in Europe and North America. The threat is also external. The United States faces a situation of potential relative decline, especially with respect to China. The economic and political rise of China has led to a long-running debate about whether and how international order will change, or perhaps has already changed.[2] Theorists often try to understand that situation by looking at other cases of great power decline, like the British loss of hegemony in the early twentieth century or even the ancient Athenian conflict with Sparta. Yet so much is different about those cases, from different countries and different historical periods, that we can draw only imperfect lessons from them.

I suggest a complementary approach. We can learn a great deal by looking at how the United States itself already lost much of its international dominance, in the 1970s, in the realm of oil. Only now, with several decades of hindsight, can we fully appreciate the nature and implications of that change in status. The experiences of that partial decline in American hegemony, and the associated shifts in oil politics, can teach us a lot about general patterns of international order.

The stakes are high. International order is easy to take for granted, but it shapes our world. Governing arrangements between states, private firms, and international organizations allow us to eat food imported from other countries, live safely from nuclear war, travel to foreign cities, profit from our savings, protect our natural environment, and much else. Yet sometimes those rules break down, lose legitimacy, or fail to solve problems. New arrangements are then needed.

In much of international relations (IR) theory, a leading state, called a hegemon, is seen as shaping and sustaining the rules of international order.[3] In the theory, hegemony is binary: either a state is a hegemon, or it isn't.[4] A hegemon is supposed to be militarily dominant, the largest economy, the most technologically advanced, and it's also supposed to have control over access to key natural resources and capital markets.[5] Theorists abstract away from mixed cases, where

---

like the United Nations, the International Monetary Fund, the European Union, and the World Trade Organization (Ikenberry 2000; Goldgeier 2018; Lake et al. 2021). They sometimes ignore that it was and is often *illiberal* (Goh 2013; Staniland 2018; Porter 2020), that it was not very *international* outside of the North Atlantic until about 1990 (Tang 2018), and that it certainly was not built in an *orderly* fashion at a single moment (Tooze 2019). Yet for all that, the phrase indicates a US- and European-led set of institutions created after World War II that has tried to buttress liberal democracies, promote economic openness, and prevent international discord (Colgan and Keohane 2017).

[2] Steinfeld 2010; Friedberg 2011; Beckley 2012; Edelstein 2017; Goddard 2018; Weiss 2019; Goh 2019; Cooley and Nexon 2020; Weiss and Wallace 2021.
[3] For a review of a large literature on this idea, see Ikenberry and Nexon 2019.
[4] Gilpin 1981: 29 ("hegemonic: a single powerful state controls or dominates the lesser states in the system"); Mearsheimer 2001: 40 ("A hegemon is a state that is so powerful that it dominates all the other states in the system").
[5] See, for instance, Keohane 1984: 32; Cooley and Nexon 2020: 27.

hegemony is not pure. In a sense, they are right to do so: theories must simplify the world to focus on the key points. In practice, however, states can dominate some but not all of the dimensions that characterize a pure hegemon. I call this situation partial hegemony.

The difference between pure and partial hegemony is complicated and significant. If partial hegemony could be plugged into theories about pure hegemony with little difficulty, all would be well, and the abstraction that theorists traditionally make would be justified. Alas, that is not true. Understanding situations of partial hegemony is both tricky and essential. The United States shifted from hegemony to partial hegemony in the global oil system during the twentieth century. In the twenty-first century, it is undergoing a similar shift in other issue areas, potentially including technological innovation, cyber security, financial investment, health, the environment, and even military primacy in certain areas. That shift will not look the same in each case, but it probably will have some recurring features.

The way that most theorists and policy advisors in the United States think about international order depends on hegemony. Hegemonic stability theory, developed in the 1970s, says that a hegemon is needed to create and sustain international order, and when the hegemon's power fades, so too do its governing arrangements.[6] Certain hinge years (like 1815 or 1945) play a big role as a new hegemon sets the basic rules of the game. Starting in the 1980s, some scholars modified hegemonic stability theory, arguing that international institutions manifesting the governing arrangements could survive even after a hegemon declined.[7] These were landmark contributions. Still, under either the basic or modified version of the theory, the idea is that a hegemon typically creates order after victory in a major war.[8] That conceptual model is still with us. It is thought to explain the current order, which includes bodies like the World Bank, NATO, and the World Trade Organization (WTO). It pervades discussions of US-China rivalry in Washington and in academia.[9]

This book's contribution to IR theory, beyond oil politics, is to show how flawed and incomplete that conceptual model is. More sharp changes in international order occur in peacetime than at the end of hegemonic wars. They might be more probable, then, but such wars are rare, and sharp changes in order are not. Furthermore, when those changes occur, they are always variegated. Change

---

[6] Kindleberger [1973] 1986; Gilpin 1981.

[7] Keohane 1984; Martin and Simmons 1998; Ikenberry 2000.

[8] This sentence certainly describes Ikenberry 2000. It is less clear in Keohane's 1984 book, which argues that institutions might persist after hegemonic decline but does not specify when change is expected and partly endorses hegemonic stability theory. Also, Keohane was among the first to highlight the role of non-state actors and non-hegemonic states in shaping order. My approach differs from his primarily because I focus on subsystems, whereas he focuses on issue areas, as I will describe.

[9] Mearsheimer 2001; Schake 2017; Allison 2017; Lind and Press 2018.

is embedded in continuity. There is no single international order; instead, there are multiple governing arrangements, like pixels that form a digital image. A theory of order must explain simultaneous change *and* continuity. Hegemonic decline does not equate to a monolithic loss of governing arrangements; rather, a partial hegemon can sustain and even strengthen some governing arrangements while others weaken. I show how international order operates in pieces, with a common underlying logic of when change occurs. At its best, my approach can help analysts see *change in the midst of continuity*, and *continuity in the midst of change*, that they would otherwise miss completely.

If we think of IR theory as a railroad system, my aim is not to rip up all of the existing track. I will leave most of it untouched. I aim to add just three ideas, analogous to new pieces of track.[10] The first is about *subsystems*: a collection of states and non-state actors orbiting a question of governance within an issue area like trade or finance.[11] Unlike "issue areas," which scholars typically use but rarely define, subsystems are anchored by a single governance question.[12] Those anchoring questions are focused on tasks to be performed, rather than who governs. I will show how subsystems are a fruitful concept for analyzing when and why international order changes. Second, I see actors using *instruments of coercion* to create and sustain international order within these subsystems. I focus especially on three instruments of coercion—military, economic, and leadership selection—and how they relate to partial hegemony. Third, I argue that two factors drive when and why international order changes: how much each of the actors *benefits* from participating in it, and the *punishments* they can expect for noncompliance. While the general framework of carrots and sticks is familiar, I flesh out the concept of *punishments for noncompliance* in ways that differ from existing work in IR. These three ideas work together: the availability of various instruments of coercion affects the punishments for noncompliance in a given subsystem, which in turn shapes international order.

My objectives in this book are threefold. First, I explain global oil politics over the last century, informed by a new theoretical perspective. If this book does nothing else, I hope it does that. Second, I develop some new ideas about international order, which apply quite generally, beyond oil. My third goal is perhaps the most difficult: I seek to apply those new ideas prescriptively to the issue of climate change. Arguably the twenty-first century's greatest global challenge, climate change is intimately tied up with questions of energy and international

---

[10] This analogy owes much to Max Weber, who wrote, "ideas have, like switchmen, determined the tracks along which action has been pushed by the dynamic of interest" (Weber [1905] 2009).

[11] My use of the term *subsystems* is not to be confused with how it is sometimes used in sociology (e.g., Parsons and Platt 1973) or policy studies (Sabatier 2007). My concept bears closer resemblance to "strategic action fields" in Fligstein and McAdam 2012.

[12] Krasner 1983; Keohane 1984; Martin and Simmons 1998; Adler 2019.

order. Three-quarters of the greenhouse gases (GHG) that drive climate change come from oil and other fossil fuels. Climate change is already transforming our world, having increased the size and severity of hurricanes, droughts, fires, and floods.[13] It will get worse.

Only by understanding the political conditions under which international order changes can we hope to establish effective governing arrangements for mitigating climate change and adapting to its effects. If scholars can use lessons from other areas of politics, like oil, to offer policymakers guidance for how to design climate governance, we should do so. My strategy is to move from the particular (oil politics) to the abstract (IR theory), and then back again (to climate change).

Energy Security, Independence, and Hegemony

To see why hegemony as a simple binary concept can be so misleading, start with the vexed idea of "energy security." People often use that term without defining it. I follow the Council on Foreign Relations, which defines it as the "reliable and affordable supply of energy."[14] In this sense, energy security does rank among a country's vital national interests. The reason is simple: countries that are cut off from vital supplies of energy, especially oil, are economically imperiled and militarily crippled. As early as World War I, political and military leaders saw that fuel shortages could prove decisive in battle. World War II drove the point home at pivotal moments like the Battle of Stalingrad or the Gulf of Leyte (see chapter 5). Military officers and strategists took that lesson to heart. Over the last century, great powers like China and the United States have constantly worried about energy security in the form of vulnerability to disruptions to the flow of oil.[15]

Despite this important truth, the concept of energy security is much abused. There is a tendency to take energy security either far too seriously, or not seriously enough. At one end of the spectrum, some people treat almost everything about the economics of oil as a matter of national security. Every US president since Richard Nixon has argued that the United States needs "energy independence." Politicians typically use that term to mean eliminating oil imports by domestically producing as much as or more than consumption. Despite the political rhetoric, the United States has been a major net importer of oil most of the time since 1970, though less so since 2019.

---

[13] Pachauri et al. (IPCC) 2014; Busby 2018; Colgan et al. 2021.
[14] Deutsch et al. 2006: 3; see also Kalicki and Goldwyn 2005; Moran and Russell 2009; Ciuta 2010; Goldthau and Witte 2009; Stokes and Raphael 2010; Rosenberg 2014; Szulecki and Westphal 2018; Lind and Press 2018.
[15] Kelanic 2020.

Arguments about "energy independence," understood as self-sufficiency, are often misleading. They rarely make it clear how energy independence would deliver the political or security benefits to the United States that it supposedly offers. For instance, to address concerns about wartime vulnerability, policymakers might want domestic production to match military consumption. However, the United States military consumes less than 2 percent of total US consumption.[16] Even if that fraction surged because of wartime needs, military consumption is never likely to be large compared to domestic production.[17] In the last century, the United States has always produced at least 33 percent of its total oil consumption domestically, and the average is over 50 percent.[18] These figures do not even take into account reliable oil imports from close allies like Canada, which are unlikely to be interrupted in wartime under even the most extreme scenarios. While it is true that prolonged war fighting requires civilian industry, a country can sustain industrial activity even as it drastically restricts civilian fuel consumption.[19] In short, wartime energy security does not require "energy independence" in the way that most people use the term (i.e., no net importing during peace).

Having no plausible military argument, advocates of US energy independence often fall back on the idea of potential threats to the civilian economy during peace. It is entirely unclear how "energy independence" would help solve this problem, as it would not magically shield American consumers from price shifts so long as the United States trades with global markets.[20] In reality, US oil companies tend to invoke energy security or independence when seeking higher oil prices and fewer regulations, knowing that those policies negatively affect consumers. Scholars recognize this behavior as "securitization," in which something (e.g., oil) is labeled as critical to national security to craft a particular political narrative.[21]

---

[16] US Department of Defense 2018.

[17] A prolonged war effort would require considerable civilian consumption as well as military consumption. Yet the scenario under consideration here—that is, the United States being totally cut off from all imports for a prolonged period of time—is so extreme that this fact is unlikely to change the basic conclusion about energy security.

[18] My calculations using data from *BP Statistical Review of World Energy 2018*.

[19] The Covid-19 pandemic illustrates why: oil consumption temporarily fell massively in many countries with only marginal losses in industrial goods production (through reductions in civilian travel, services, and retail consumption).

[20] Only if the United States was willing to cut itself off from world trade by banning oil exports would it matter for consumer prices whether the country was self-sufficient. That kind of oil export ban is very unlikely because domestic oil companies would have massive financial incentives to lobby against a ban under such circumstances. (The United States did have a nominal ban on crude oil exports prior to 2015, but that ban was largely meaningless: the country was consuming far more oil than it produced, and US oil prices tracked world prices closely; for details, see Colgan and Van de Graaf 2017.)

[21] Wæver 1993; Hayes and Knox-Hayes 2014; Trombetta 2018; Allan 2018.

When oil prices crashed in 2020 due to Covid-19, for instance, the minority leader of the House of Representatives, Kevin McCarthy, objected to Saudi and Russian oil supplies that lowered prices, arguing that it was "essential to America's national security interests" that the secretary of state take steps to address that issue.[22] In other words, he wanted to raise oil prices. McCarthy did not explain how national security interests were at stake, nor acknowledge the negative effect higher prices would have on consumers. Similarly, in the 2008 presidential election, for instance, John McCain embraced the slogan "drill, baby, drill!" as part of his campaign. His campaign, like others before and since, did not explain why energy independence or increased oil production was a national security interest.[23]

This is not to argue that there are *no* political or security benefits to domestic oil production. National self-sufficiency can have political benefits, mostly in quite specific circumstances. Yet, the supposed benefits are often invented or exaggerated. Identifying the real ones requires a sophisticated understanding of how the economics of oil relates to international security. It is precisely this understanding that is often lacking—not only among politicians and policymakers but also among most scholars.

Indeed, many scholars tend to make the opposite mistake: underestimating the degree to which oil is a security issue. Some of the research in international political economy (IPE) makes this mistake. The 1973 oil crisis helped give birth to modern IPE: it obliged IR scholars to take political economy seriously.[24] At the time, most scholars saw the United States as losing its hegemony, and hence its grip over world oil. Just prior to the oil crisis, Charles P. Kindleberger had developed hegemonic stability theory.[25] While there were big debates about what hegemonic decline would mean for international trade or finance, the scholarly consensus was nearly universal about oil: hegemonic stability theory was essentially correct.[26] It seemed to explain why OPEC could upend the oil regime in the 1970s against American wishes. Even Robert O. Keohane, who rebutted parts of hegemonic stability theory in his 1984 masterwork *After Hegemony*, saw oil in this light.

Declining US hegemony, however, describes only one part of the oil picture in the early 1980s. It largely omits oil's military aspects. The United States' military strength in the Middle East actually grew considerably in the decades that followed 1973.[27] As I show in some detail in chapter 5, its military presence is

---

[22] McCarthy et al. 2020 (letter to Secretary of State Pompeo, April 2).
[23] Kurtz 2012.
[24] Hancock and Vivoda 2014.
[25] Kindleberger 1973 [1986]. It was Robert Keohane, however, who later labeled it hegemonic stability theory.
[26] Gilpin 1975: 217–218, 243.
[27] Bacevich 2016.

part of a set of semi-explicit governing arrangements in which the United States forbids some actors control over certain oil reserves while permitting control by others (e.g., Iraq versus Kuwait in 1990). While these arrangements have not prevented various crises and US failures in the region,[28] they do represent a certain kind of international order. Specifically, the order preserves state sovereignty in a way that distributes ownership of the oil fields across many rulers in the Middle East to prevent any one of them from creating an oil monopoly.

The significance of these ongoing military relationships with the Persian Gulf states became especially apparent in 1990–1991, when the United States staged a massive counter-invasion in defense of Kuwait and Saudi Arabia. Writing in the early 1980s in the wake of the oil shocks and the Iranian revolution, Keohane and others were understandably focused on the United States' loss of standing in the region. With the benefit of hindsight, however, it seems only partially correct to characterize oil politics in this period as driven by declining hegemony. Instead, there was also a pattern of protective military relationships that proved remarkably durable, underpinned by US military hegemony. Thus, within this issue area, there was continuity as well as change.

To sharpen the point, imagine what theorists in 1980 would have predicted about the long-term future of Persian Gulf politics. Would the United States withdraw militarily from the Persian Gulf as the United Kingdom had done 1968–1971, or expand its military presence? With hindsight, we know the answer is expansion, but the logic of hegemonic stability theory suggests the opposite. If we see the rise of OPEC in the 1970s as a result of hegemonic decline, as most theorists do, and our concept of hegemony is binary rather than partial, then the logical extension of the theory is that the United States military presence in the Persian Gulf would wither, just as the United Kingdom's did. Yet it did not.

This problem of partial versus pure hegemony might seem simple. If it were true that the world could be neatly divided into security and economic issues, perhaps it would be easy to adapt our current theories by simply separating military hegemony from economic hegemony. Alas, the world is not so simple. Different forms of economic and military power often commingle in issues of energy, commerce, finance, health, and the environment. Oil politics, as I show in this book, is an example par excellence of this commingling. Even issues that initially seem purely security-oriented, like alliances, nuclear politics, or wars, turn out to have significant economic dimensions. In short, the instruments of coercion that a hegemon uses to influence politics do not map in a one-to-one fashion onto the issue areas of world politics. We need some new ideas about how powerful actors' abilities translate into international order.

---

[28] Packer 2005; Kuperman 2013.

Core Argument

This book is about international order and how it changes, especially in oil politics. Change in international order is the dependent variable. The term "international order" has multiple meanings,[29] which deserve some attention in chapter 2. For now, let's start with a conventional definition: "the governing arrangements among a group of states, including its fundamental rules, principles, and institutions."[30] Thinking about order in this way helps us build on existing scholarship and common usage.

My core argument is that we should understand oil politics, like many issues, as being characterized by multiple subsystems. Oil has two main subsystems. Each contains governing arrangements that create a degree of international order within it, independent of the other subsystem to a certain extent. A partial hegemon and other actors can use instruments of coercion to sustain order in these subsystems. The availability of those instruments changes over time. What makes things quite complicated is the fact that instruments of coercion describe relations between actors, whereas order exists within subsystems. Instruments of coercion affect the strategic benefits and punishments for noncompliance specific to each subsystem, and the way they do varies across subsystems.

The previous paragraph packs in a lot of ideas quite densely. Let me unpack three of the central ideas, one at a time. The first is subsystems. It is conceptual rather than explanatory. A subsystem is a collection of states and non-state actors linked by a single question of governance within an issue area like oil, trade, or finance. Subsystems are more fine-grained than the issue areas used in regime theory.[31] Unlike issue areas, subsystems have a central nucleus: a single question of governance about a functional task that actors can directly influence, like the amount of oil produced at a given time. In other words, subsystems center on policy levers that actors can actually pull. Governing arrangements can be made about such questions. Issue areas, by contrast, tend to be ill-defined and are closer to general topics, like "health" or "finance." Multiple subsystems can operate within an issue area, which helps explain why there can be both change and continuity simultaneously within that issue area.

Order exists within subsystems. After all, if order consists of governing arrangements, those arrangements respond to the questions of governance that anchor subsystems. When we refer to the liberal order at the global or

---

[29] See also Tang 2016; Acharya 2018.

[30] Quoted from Ikenberry 2000: 23; for similar definitions, see Gilpin 1981: 111; Mearsheimer 2019: 9. Other definitions exist; see chapter 2.

[31] Scholars use a variety of ideas to try to disaggregate and locate international order, including "regimes" (Krasner 1983; Keohane 1984), "polycentricity" (Ostrom 2010), "regime complexes" (Raustiala and Victor 2004), "multi-level governance" (Hooghe and Marks 2003; Zürn 2010), "heterarchy" (Donnelly 2009), and "assemblage theory" (Sassen 2006).

systemic level, however, we are really talking about a *theme* across a multitude of subsystems. Changes in the governing arrangements of a subsystem are independent of changes in the ordering theme.[32] For example, we might characterize the "liberal" international order as a continuous theme of the post-1945 period without losing sight of the many significant changes in governing arrangements within that time period.

That view of order differs considerably from the standard IR approach, which misses a huge amount of what is actually interesting about politics. Typically, theorists focus on an order's theme as it shifts in key years like 1648, 1713, 1815, 1919, or 1945. Consider, though, that between 1713 and 1815, there was the American Revolution, the French Revolution, the transnational movement to end slavery, the colonization of the Indian subcontinent, the emergence of the Industrial Revolution, and a great deal more.[33] In our own age, treating the post-1945 liberal order as continuous also ignores a great deal of change, like the establishment of US hierarchy over its allies in the Suez Crisis of 1956, the collapse of the Bretton Woods financial system in the early 1970s, the rise of Reagan-Thatcherite neoliberalism in the 1980s, the upheaval in the Soviet Union's sphere of influence 1989–1991, the rise of the Responsibility to Protect principle of humanitarian intervention in the 1990s, the global war on terror after September 11, 2001, and the transnational spread of right-wing populism. From this perspective, the 1973 oil crisis was one of many shifts in international order that we might wish to understand. Seeing the world in subsystems is helpful for doing so.

Events like the ones identified in the previous paragraph matter for international order to the extent that they alter the governing arrangements that constitute order. Prior to the 1973 oil crisis, for example, there was a set of *de facto* governing arrangements led by the so-called Seven Sister oil companies and backed by the British and American governments. The Seven Sisters (the major Anglo-American oil companies, now known as ExxonMobil, Shell, BP, and Chevron, after various mergers) governed global oil production in the 1950s and 1960s as an oligopoly (outside the Communist bloc). In the 1970s, OPEC and national oil companies displaced the Seven Sisters oligopoly as the key governing arrangements over oil production. Thus the 1973 oil crisis, and events like it, mark a shift in international order.

---

[32] Studying an order's theme can be useful. See, for example, Jones et al. 2009; Barma et al. 2013; Brands and Feaver 2016; Brooks and Wohlforth 2016; Wright 2017; Colgan and Keohane 2017; Friedman Lissner and Rapp-Hooper 2018; Jentleson 2018.

[33] This list of events is intentionally Eurocentric, to compare it to a rather Eurocentric conventional conception of international order. A great deal more happened in the eighteenth century outside of the European sphere of influence, of course. On American- and Euro-centric bias in the study of IR, see Tickner and Weaver 2009; Acharya and Buzan 2010; Acharya 2018; Colgan 2019; Feng et al. 2019.

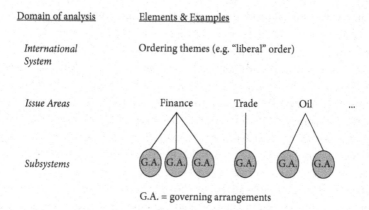

Figure 1.1 Terminology and concepts of international order

Figure 1.1 maps the relationships between themes, governing arrangements, issue areas, and subsystems. Compared to subsystems, issue areas make it difficult to analyze different rates of change within an area. They even make it hard to *notice* that variation in the first place. Treating oil as an issue area might help explain why IR scholars of the 1980s focused on the economic changes in oil, but largely missed the continuity of the governing arrangements associated with the US military presence in the Persian Gulf. As I discuss in chapter 6, that problem is exacerbated in today's IR research by a tendency among scholars to jump straight to causal analysis without investing sufficient time in description and descriptive inference.[34]

Oil politics is better characterized as *two* main subsystems than one issue area. The first is economic (the "oil production" subsystem). The conventional narrative of transformation in the 1970s is basically correct about it. In this subsystem, the actors make decisions about how much oil to produce from which oil fields, largely taking the nationality of those oil fields as fixed. The second has to do with jurisdiction or sovereignty over oil, and it is underpinned by military affairs (the "oil security" subsystem). The distribution of oil fields, especially in the Persian Gulf, is crucial because it affects the global market structure and the distribution of profits. If the market has only a few major sellers, it is an oligopoly that could restrict access to oil supplies. Market structure is so important that great powers have fought wars to ensure that the distribution of oil fields, and access to them, was acceptable. As I will describe, a pattern of external military involvement in the Persian Gulf has remained a consistent context for the global oil industry.

[34] Oatley 2011; Gerring 2012; King 2012; Drezner and McNamara 2013; Chaudoin et al. 2015; Bauerle Danzman et al. 2017; Winecoff 2017.

In other words, the oil production subsystem is different from the security subsystem, and change within them occurs at remarkably different rates.

Powerful states used "oil-for-security" deals to structure their relationships and interventions in the Middle East and North Africa.[35] The deals varied in their details, but essentially they offered military security to oil-producing territories in exchange for a certain amount of economic benefits linked to oil (though not usually oil itself).[36] These deals have a long history, dating back to when the protection of oil assets was an explicit motivation behind the last gasp of British imperialism. As decolonization unfolded, the role of external protector gradually shifted from Britain to the United States.[37] Former colonies and dependencies became legally sovereign, but the basic oil-for-security pattern in many places, like Kuwait or Qatar, stayed the same. Some petrostates, like Iraq, eventually rejected the oil-for-security deals, but many others maintained them into the twenty-first century. Those deals are consequential and help maintain a territorial status quo in the region. In short, many of the same states and individuals involved in OPEC's decision to *upend* the prevailing international order decided, in the case of oil-for-security deals, to *preserve* the prevailing order. The concept of subsystems highlights and helps explain that variation.

Having made my first intellectual move about the existence and nature of subsystems, I then develop a second idea: change in an international order depends principally on the *strategic benefits* and the *punishments for noncompliance* that participating actors face. Strategic benefits are the incentives that actors have to regularize interactions between them in a particular way within a given subsystem. For example, international trade creates mutual gains between the trading nations, which generate strategic benefits for participating in a trade agreement. The punishments for noncompliance are the risks and costs, tangible and intangible, that an actor faces by breaking the rules of an order. Noncompliance with an order creates the risk that one or more powerful actors will impose such costs. For example, the United States and Europe ramped up their economic sanctions on Iran in the period from 2010 to 2013 because of Iran's nuclear program, which they perceived as noncompliance with the Nuclear Nonproliferation Treaty. The costs of punishment are not necessarily economic—they can range from shaming to military violence.

Punishments for noncompliance are not just the flip side of benefits, or the cost side of the equation. The idea of costs for participating in an order is already a part of the concept of strategic benefits, because we should think of

---

[35] The "Middle East and North Africa" is hereafter the "Middle East." The term's meaning has changed over time. I follow a contemporary definition of the Middle East as stretching from Morocco to Iran.

[36] Bronson 2006; Duffield 2007; Yetiv 2011; Kim 2019.

[37] Gause 2009; Jamal 2012.

those benefits in a "net" sense, meaning the degree to which they exceed costs. The punishments for noncompliance are different, because they do not stem from participation in the order. Rather, punishments are imposed for non-participation or defiance. Indeed, sometimes an actor faces the difficult choice of either complying with an order that grants it negative net benefits *or* facing punishments for noncompliance from other actors.

When both the strategic benefits and expected punishments are high, change in an international order is unlikely. Sometimes, however, world events create a shock that increases or decreases the strength of an order's punishments or benefits. If punishments for noncompliance weaken, much then depends on the strategic benefits that an old order offers. Those benefits vary by subsystem. When an order generates more strategic benefits than other potential governing arrangements, it is able to persist even without the threat of punishments from a hegemon or other actor.[38] When an order generates fewer strategic benefits than an alternative governing arrangement, however, change becomes likely unless powerful actors are willing to constantly impose discipline.

Thus, punishments play a key role in the theory.[39] Historically, US leadership has frequently involved tough punishments and coercion. In the Suez Crisis of 1956, for instance, the United States threatened Britain and France with economic disaster if they did not cease their support of Israeli forces in the Sinai Peninsula. (Britain and France backed down.) For decades, the United States fought and harassed various Latin American regimes in the name of anti-communism, from Cuba to Grenada to Nicaragua. Not all coercive actions count as punishments: some of them, like the US intervention in Guatemala in 1954 or Iraq in 2003, were outright violations of liberal order rather than a manifestation of its principles.[40] My point in highlighting US coercion and abuses is not to generate an ideological polemic against it. Despite its significant departures from liberalism, the United States has generally supported an order that was more open and rules-based than its predecessors. The point is to learn how order is actually maintained—even when, or perhaps especially when, that order is normatively more attractive than the feasible alternatives.

My third and final core idea in this book is about the *instruments of coercion* that powerful actors use to shape strategic benefits and, especially, punishments for noncompliance. States and other actors have various instruments of coercion they might be able to use.[41] Governing arrangements link powerful actors'

---

[38] Keohane 1984.
[39] This emphasis differs from some of the liberal institutionalist tradition, as I explain later.
[40] Realist critics of the liberal order sometimes mischaracterize such events as manifestations of liberalism (e.g., Mearsheimer 2019).
[41] Non-state actors that might have such instruments include large corporations, religious groups, and international organizations.

instruments of coercion to their goals. The arrangements must "fit" with available coercive instruments to achieve those goals; otherwise, they stumble, as OPEC frequently does.

I focus on three instruments in this book: military coercion, economic coercion, and leadership selection. Military coercion stems from the credible threat of military force. Economic coercion stems from the ability to open or restrict access to capital, goods, resources, or other economic flows. Leadership selection involves an actor's ability to appoint or remove a political executive in a foreign polity, whether by overt means (e.g., imperial appointment of a colonial governor) or by covert means (e.g., assassination of a foreign leader or coup d'état). These instruments sometimes involve brute force, not just coercion.[42] Of course, other forms of power and influence also exist, like soft power.[43] I focus on these three, however, because they recur at pivotal moments in the history of the global oil industry. I suspect that is true of other issue areas, as well.

The concepts of hegemony and instruments of coercion are related. A pure hegemon has an abundance of all three instruments of coercion. A partial hegemon has the leading ability to use some but not all of these instruments. Partial hegemony is thus closely linked to my argument's independent variables—strategic benefits and punishments for noncompliance—by way of the instruments of coercion. In turn, these factors cause changes in international order.

When a pure hegemon becomes a partial hegemon, it entails the weakening of some of that state's instruments of coercion. Theorists typically treat hegemonic decline as a decline in *all* of the hegemon's instruments of coercion. In reality, some of these instruments might decline while others remain strong or even get stronger. The transition from pure to partial hegemony can undermine some governing arrangements in world politics, while leaving others largely unchanged. We should not expect that partial hegemonic decline corresponds to an equivalent partial collapse in governing arrangements. Instead, a partial hegemon experiencing a shift in its capabilities tends to reach for new or underused instruments of coercion to achieve whichever goals still seem feasible.

Consequently, the effect of hegemonic decline on international order can sometimes be more like squeezing a balloon than popping it. Powerful actors, seeing shifts in the available instruments of coercion, will use whatever instruments they have available to shape governing arrangements according to their preferences. By "shifts in availability," I mean that the cost-effectiveness of

---

[42] Coercion requires credible threats, which means sometimes the threats must be backed with force. Yet even when brute force is applied—by militarily invading a country, for instance, or by assassinating a leader—it is also coercive because it shapes expectations for threats and demands made in future periods.

[43] Nye 2004.

Change in the world (exogeneous) →
Change in available instruments of coercion →
Potential change in benefits and punishments (by subsystem) →
Change in a subsystem's governing arrangements

Figure 1.2 Simplified model of change in international order

an instrument of coercion changes. For instance, the United Kingdom found the threat of military coercion against countries in the Global South much more cost-effective while it was the British Empire in 1900 than it does as a relatively small nation in the twenty-first century. Sometimes a (partial) hegemon's instruments of coercion change because of its internal conditions (e.g., the collapse of the Soviet Union); sometimes they change because of external conditions (e.g., a major technological or normative shift).

I am not the first to notice that power comes in different forms.[44] What is new here is the way that instruments of coercion connect to order. My framework illustrates how changes in an actor's capabilities (e.g., partial hegemonic decline) have a complex, rather than linear, relationship with changes in governing arrangements. It also provides a logic that links changes in capabilities to (possible) changes in governing arrangements.

Figure 1.2 illustrates how international order changes.[45] Some change in the world occurs, exogenous to the theory. That change affects the cost-effectiveness of actors' instruments of coercion. Actors' instruments of coercion shape the punishments for noncompliance and strategic benefits that sustain the governing arrangements in a given subsystem. So changes in instruments of coercion can reverberate through to international order—but the effect varies by subsystem. Empirically, the key step lies in understanding how the instruments of coercion affect the benefits and punishments in a given subsystem.

For modern oil politics, the key exogenous change in the world is twentieth-century decolonization. Decolonization was both a cause and an effect of the reduced power of certain actors, like France and the United Kingdom. Viewed from the colonies' perspective, decolonization was a time of national liberation that gave them new legal and political capabilities for defecting from existing governing arrangements. It did not free them of all constraints, of course, especially economic ones. Still, it increased their scope of action. It also changed ideas in world politics about self-determination and racial equality.[46] Those ideational changes had consequences even for countries that were not formal empires, like

---

[44] Baldwin 1989; Nye 2004.
[45] Making good inferences requires extensive empirical knowledge in any particular subsystem, but the basic causal process that I theorize is simple enough to sketch out.
[46] Crawford 2002; Getachew 2019.

the United States.[47] In Vietnam, for instance, the United States found it next to impossible to militarily impose its will, in part because of postcolonial ideas.

In my theoretical terms, decolonization reduced the cost-effectiveness of some instruments of coercion, especially leader selection by external actors. After decolonization, it was rarer and more costly for great powers to choose who would run the government of distant subordinate territories.[48] It also made economic coercion somewhat harder. Decolonization thus represents, from a theoretical perspective, a system-wide decline in the punishments associated with international order.

Thus, as a matter of research design, this book takes advantage of decolonization as a major shock to one of the two key explanatory variables. That makes variation in the theory's other key variable, strategic benefits, highly important for explaining outcomes following from decolonization. My attention to structural forces and variables does not leave me blind to the role of individuals in history, however. On the contrary, this book describes the role of people like President George H. W. Bush, Shah Reza Pahlavi, Prime Minister Margaret Thatcher, and OPEC visionaries Abdullah Tariki and Juan Pablo Pérez Alfonzo. Individual men and women make choices that guide the course of history.[49] Part of my approach is to show how individuals' agency interacts with, and is conditioned by, the structural forces of world politics.

Lessons for Energy and Climate Change

This book's three core ideas adapt existing IR theory to help make sense of real-world topic areas like energy and climate change. In energy, they help us see how the economics of oil production are related to its security dimensions—and how they are *not* related. A clearer picture helps us understand when governing arrangements will work, and when they won't.

To preview with a concrete example, my research shows why OPEC is a governing arrangement that mostly does not work, contrary to what most news headlines would lead one to believe. I tell a tale of two OPECs in this book. The first OPEC belonged to its early days, from 1960 to roughly 1974. During that time, it operated as a kind of collective bargaining unit, working against the

---

[47] Arguably, the United States acted in a highly imperialistic way toward multiple territories and peoples, including Hawaii, Puerto Rico, and the Philippines. See Go 2012; Morefield 2014; Pepinsky 2015.

[48] The creation of the United Nations also played a role in this shift; see Poznansky 2020.

[49] A large research literature on the role of individual leaders in international relations exists, including Byman and Pollack 2001; Saunders 2011; Mukunda 2012; Colgan 2013a; Croco 2015; Horowitz et al. 2015; Weisiger and Yarhi-Milo 2015; Whitlark 2017; Colgan and Lucas 2017; Fuhrman 2020.

Anglo-American oil companies. OPEC ultimately won that battle, thanks largely to a market shift in the early 1970s that favored OPEC members. Starting in the early 1980s, though, OPEC's effectiveness declined dramatically. Having so thoroughly won against the major oil companies, OPEC tried to control the oil market on its own by acting as a cartel.[50] It has *almost entirely failed* in that task. In theoretical terms, OPEC has no way of imposing punishments for noncompliance on its members, and it offers little in the way of strategic benefits. Unlike the key players prior to the 1970s, OPEC has little in the way of instruments of coercion. Consequently, it is not able to meaningfully constrain its members' oil production, and has almost no long-term impact on the world price for oil. The volatility in oil prices since 1973 is one of many signs of OPEC's ineffectiveness.

Politicians, journalists, and even some scholars wrongly describe OPEC as a cartel, which controls or heavily influences the price of oil.[51] This is a myth. While its member states are important, especially Saudi Arabia, the organization itself is of little consequence today. If the institution ceased to exist tomorrow, not much about the global oil market would change. Its member states would go on producing about as much oil as they did before. The significance of OPEC is not, therefore, in economics but in politics. It operates as a "rational myth"—a fiction that its members help preserve because it increases their status and prestige in international politics. Western policymakers would do well to look past that myth.

Does it still make sense to study oil politics in an age when new technologies are starting to challenge oil's dominance? Absolutely. My work builds on a burgeoning field of research on oil and energy politics.[52] Even if an impending global energy transition were swift and certain, we could still learn a lot about the underlying logic of international order by studying oil over the last century. Petroleum has been a central part of global trade, investment, alliances, wars, migration, and much else. The market for crude oil is worth between USD 1.5 trillion and USD 4 trillion annually, depending on its price.[53] It is the most important commodity on earth, worth more than 100 times the size of the raw diamond

---

[50] A cartel is defined as a group of firms (or states, in this case) that creates agreements about quantities to produce or prices to charge (Mankiw 2011: 351; also see chapter 4).

[51] For various takes on the role of OPEC, see Dahl and Yücel 1991; Claes 2001; Blaydes 2004; Victor 2008; Smith 2009; Goldthau and Witte 2011; Brémond et al. 2012; Jaffe and Morse 2013; van de Graaf 2017; Garavini 2019.

[52] Hertog 2010; Barma et al. 2011; Rudra and Jensen 2011; Ross 2012; Lujala and Rustad 2012; Le Billon 2012; Stulberg 2012; Colgan 2013b, 2013c, 2013d; Hughes and Lipscy 2013; Levi 2013; Liou and Musgrave 2013; Ross and Voeten 2015; Wenar 2016; Lee 2016; Glaser and Kelanic 2016; Kim and Woods 2016; van de Graaf et al. 2016; O'Sullivan 2017; McNally 2017; Stokes and Warshaw 2017; Hendrix 2017; Aklin and Urpelainen 2018; Ashford 2018; Claes 2018; Wald 2018; Toprani 2019; Kelanic 2020; Meierding 2020; Mahdavi 2020; McFarland 2020; Markowitz 2020; Fox-Penner 2020.

[53] Global oil consumption is roughly 98 million barrels per day (International Energy Agency 2018). Prices typically range from USD 40 to USD 100 per barrel.

market, for instance.[54] That economic value alone gives it huge consequences for international politics. To put it in perspective, annual oil sales globally are worth more than the total amount of foreign direct investment (FDI) and the total of bilateral foreign aid, *combined*.[55]

A second reason it still makes sense to study oil politics is that oil is likely to remain hugely consequential for the foreseeable future. Admittedly, some analysts think oil's significance could decline rapidly.[56] Yet, even in the most aggressive scenarios, oil consumption is unlikely to decline to irrelevance.[57] If it declined by 50 percent over the course of decades—which would be a historically unprecedented rate of decline by any major energy source—the world would still be consuming about 50 million barrels per day, leaving oil as probably still the most valuable commodity in the world.

Previous energy transitions offer little reason to believe that oil is about to disappear. When coal became the dominant fuel of the first industrial revolution in the nineteenth century, it swiftly became the largest source of energy, but it did not eliminate traditional fuels like wood and biomass. Globally, those fuels are still in use today at aggregate rates higher than in the year 1800. Likewise, when oil became the lifeblood of modern economies in the twentieth century, it did not eliminate coal. On the contrary, global coal consumption grew massively in the twentieth and early twenty-first century.[58] Wind and solar energy are making great strides in recent years, but to fully displace fossil fuels would require an energy transition of a kind that has never previously occurred in all of history.

I draw lessons from oil to help policymakers better understand climate change and contemporary energy transitions. For instance, global oil politics shows that governing arrangements backed by punishments (e.g., the Seven Sisters cartel) are much more effective than those that are not (e.g., OPEC since 1980). Obvious as that might sound, meaningful enforcement was needed but missing in many climate deals, including the 2015 Paris Agreement. I lay out a path for supplying that enforcement in climate politics. It uses policy linkage and experimentation, both of which have shown success in oil politics.

Briefly, I find that major economies have strong incentives to work together to create an international "climate club," within which all member countries have

[54] Global market for rough diamonds is USD 10 to 15 billion annually. Source: https://www.bain.com/insights/global-diamond-industry-report-2017/.

[55] FDI flows are worth about USD 1.5 trillion annually (World Bank, *World Development Indicators*, 2010). Bilateral foreign aid makes up just USD 0.1 trillion (OECD 2010, "Development Aid Reaches an Historic High in 2010," available at: http://www.oecd.org/dac/stats/developmentaidreachesanhistorichighin2010.htm).

[56] Cherif et al. 2017; Fattouh et al. 2018; Van de Graaf and Bradshaw 2018.

[57] In 2018, the International Energy Agency projected oil consumption to actually increase slightly, from 98 million barrels per day (mbd) in 2017 to 105 mbd in 2040. Source: https://www.iea.org/newsroom/news/2018/february/weo-analysis-a-sea-change-in-the-global-oil-trade.html.

[58] Thurber 2019.

minimum levels of pro-climate policy, and use trade measures such as border adjustment tariffs (BATs) against countries outside of the club. Those tariffs impose punishments on those that refuse to participate, thereby generating meaningful enforcement that has previously been lacking. A climate club is possible with or without domestic carbon pricing. Yet, the strategy depends critically on the size of the economies inside the club. Only a large climate club makes sufficient decarbonization politically sustainable over time—and that means, at a minimum, that Europe, the United States, and China should work together. Subsystems theory is not the only road to this conclusion, but it provides a clear theoretical foundation, and helps identify opportunities for the various climate subsystems to work together.

To create a climate club backed by tariffs, American and European leaders should signal their willingness to take costly climate action, if China will do the same. China has already taken some steps to decarbonize, but as the world's biggest polluter, it must do more if the world is to meet the UN's sustainability goals. If China refuses to join a climate club, the United States and European Union should impose economic costs on China for that choice. They can impose costs by excluding China from access to their economies—*but only if they have not already excluded it, preemptively*. In turn, the pressing need for a climate club carries implications for other parts of American and European foreign policy, particularly with regard to "decoupling" from China. A decoupling strategy would make the job of reducing emissions even harder.

Lessons for IR Theory

Beyond energy and climate change, this book speaks to IR theory. The conventional approach to hegemony has led scholars to debate the extent to which the United States is declining as a hegemon, and the consequences of such a decline. Some scholars see an "exit from hegemony,"[59] while others—especially those looking at global finance—see no significant change.[60] These debates will not, and cannot, be resolved without understanding partial hegemony and its relationship to international order.

The problem is not just explanatory; it is also conceptual. When we refer to *the* international order, we are really referring to a huge complex of governing arrangements. We are not referring to a single object. Nowhere is an order written down in a single document, or manifested in a single organization.[61] At

---

[59] Cooley and Nexon 2020; Haass 2018.
[60] Chaudoin et al. 2017; Norrlof et al. 2020.
[61] Indeed, Elinor Ostrom (2010) argued that for many governance challenges, we would not *want* a single international order.

any given moment, some of those complex arrangements are changing, and some are relatively stable. Even if we bound the scope somewhat, for example, "the order between Western countries in the period 1945–1990," we are still referring to hundreds of governing arrangements. Scholars treat these arrangements as though they aggregate up into order in some fashion, though how they do so is rarely spelled out.[62]

I suggest that it is the principles underlying the governing arrangements in important subsystems that give an international order its theme. Themes arise because powerful actors, especially great power states, participate in many governing arrangements, and heavily influence the ones they participate in.[63] Those arrangements address particular substantive issues, like how to regulate trade or nuclear arms control. A theme exists when those governing arrangements share common underlying principles, like "economic openness" or "multilateralism."[64] Great power states tend to generate themes across multiple governing arrangements to the extent that they have a coherent, consistent view about foreign policy. Studying those systemic themes can be useful.[65] To fully understand order and change, however, we also need to focus on governing arrangements.

Two key implications follow logically from the approach of locating international order at the level of governing arrangements, rather than at systemic themes. First, major power wars are not the only way order changes in a given subsystem, as many hegemonic order theories imply.[66] Change can, and quite commonly does, happen in peacetime. Actors take advantage of structural changes in the conditions that sustain international order in particular subsystems, namely strategic benefits and punishments for noncompliance. Second, when the international order in a subsystem is upended or modified, it is associated with institutional innovation.[67] Existing scholarship shows *why* states create and maintain international institutions: as a way of minimizing transaction and information costs.[68] I focus on *when* actors create or change international institutions.

---

[62] For example, Lake and Powell (1999: 4) say, "the strategic-choice approach . . . *presumes* that strategic interactions at one level aggregate into interactions at other levels in an orderly manner" (emphasis added).

[63] Pratt (2018) shows that powerful states' influence is amplified by institutional deference within a regime complex.

[64] Ikenberry (2020: 18–19) points out that the "liberal" order actually carries two meanings: one is about its characteristics (e.g., what I call its theme); the other is about the liberal democracies around which the order is built. As Ikenberry says, "[US-led] cooperative security does not itself have liberal properties. It is liberal only in the sense that it is an alliance of liberal democracies."

[65] Jones et al. 2009; Barma et al. 2013; Wright 2017; Jentleson 2018; Friedman Lissner and Rapp-Hooper 2018; Rose 2019.

[66] Ikenberry 2000; Lascurettes 2020.

[67] This is a descriptive rather than causal claim, because institutions and order are mutually constitutive. See chapter 2.

[68] Keohane 1984; see also Lipscy 2017.

Looking across a range of subsystems, we can see how strategic benefits and punishments for noncompliance give us clues about when to expect governance arrangements to be effective and durable. Subsystems with strong benefits and punishments, like the anti-conquest rules enshrined in Article 1 of the United Nations Charter, or the Anglo-American oil oligopoly of the 1950s, are the most likely to generate governing arrangements that genuinely modify actors' behavior. Initiatives like the 2017 Treaty on the Prohibition of Nuclear Weapons, which offers very weak strategic benefits to the countries that actually have such weapons and no mechanism to punish them for noncompliance, are very unlikely to alter behavior. Other subsystems, like those involved with controls on capital flow across borders or the Universal Postal Union, are mixed cases. I explore how my theory can be applied to those and other subsystems in chapter 6.

My work does not fall neatly within the confines of any of the three dominant schools of thought in international relations, namely, realism, liberal institutionalism, and constructivism. I borrow from and build on each of them. For instance, my understanding of hegemony, international order, and issue areas follow from debates between liberal institutionalists and realists.[69] My attention to punishments for noncompliance reflects a realist emphasis on power and predation. And I share the constructivist view that change in international order necessarily involves ideas.[70] Constructivists are typically sensitive to "rival collective images," or visions of alternative governing arrangements, in ways that other scholars are not.[71]

Even though I agree with existing scholarship far more than I disagree, it is useful to highlight the disagreements. My argument differs from many liberal institutionalist accounts in two key respects. First, I focus on subsystems rather than issue areas as a way of disaggregating world politics. I have already touched on my reasons for this focus, and will say more in the next chapter. Second, my theory incorporates both strategic benefits and punishments for noncompliance. In that sense, it serves as something of a bridge between liberalism and realism.

Liberal institutionalists, especially American ones, sometimes overlook the role of punishments.[72] John Ikenberry, for instance, argues that in the postwar era, "The United States became a provider of public goods—or at least 'club goods.' It upheld the rules and institutions, fostered security cooperation, led the management of the world economy, and championed shared norms and cooperation

---

[69] Waltz 1979; Gilpin 1981; Krasner 1983; Keohane 1984; Keohane and Martin 1995; Ikenberry 2000, 2020; Mearsheimer 2019.

[70] Including, *inter alia*, Wendt 1999; Finnemore 1996, 2004; Cox and Sinclair 1996; Finnemore and Sikkink 1998; Hurd 1999; Blyth 2002; Buzan 2004; Mattern 2005; Hurrell 2007; Avant et al. 2010; Phillips 2010; Reus-Smit 2013, 2018; Goh 2013; Zarakol 2017; Adler 2019; Matthijs 2020.

[71] Cox and Sinclair 1996; see also Finnemore and Jurkovich 2020.

[72] Gruber 2000; Norrlof 2010; Staniland 2018; Porter 2020. On American blind spots in the study of IR, see Colgan 2019.

among the western-oriented liberal democracies."[73] In this American-led order, states "conduct relations on multilateral platforms—bargaining, consulting, co-ordinating."[74] This description offers a noble vision of the United States' role. There is a hint, in the statement that the United States "upheld the rules and institutions," that a hegemon might use coercion and force, but only in a positive, even heroic, sense. It neglects the extent to which hegemons use coercion and punishment to advance their own interests in ways that other actors oppose and resent.[75] This is especially true outside the North Atlantic region.[76] Realists, too, sometimes overestimate the benign hegemony of the United States.[77] Some de-scribe international order as "Pareto optimal," implying that it rests on voluntary consent.[78]

Compared to liberals, most realists are more likely to pay attention to punishments in international relations. Yet, punishments for noncompliance are not a structural variable that follows mechanically from the distribution of material capabilities, as some realists would suggest.[79] Powerful actors' ability to punish depends significantly on norms and ideas as well as material capabil-ities.[80] For example, racist ideology, social fragmentation among colonial peo-ples, and other intangible factors allowed empires to dominate relatively easily until the early twentieth century.[81] When ideas changed, the colonies' risk of punishment for acts of noncompliance declined substantially. Even if material capabilities were all that mattered, punishments would not be automatic. They depend on choices made by living, breathing people with agency, as well as the nontrivial politics of identifying instances of noncompliance.[82]

A smaller subset of realists suggests that international order is a largely empty concept that describes little more than the interactions between states.[83] They point out, correctly, that international institutions are rarely able to impose hard

[73] Ikenberry 2018: 15.
[74] Ikenberry 2018: 16.
[75] Gruber 2000; Lake 2011.
[76] The North Atlantic area is presumably the closest example of what Ikenberry (2000: 52) described as a constitutional order, in which participants "willingly participate and agree with the overall orientation of the system." It was a special case in that it occurred among relatively like-minded, wealthy, liberal democracies, leading to high strategic benefits and a low need to impose punishments for noncompliance. Even then, coercion, noncompliance, and punishment occurred.
[77] William Wohlforth (1999: 38, quoted in Monteiro 2014: 10), for instance, says, "the existing dis-tribution of capabilities generates incentives for cooperation." It gives the United States the "means and motive to . . . ease local security conflicts" (1999: 8).
[78] Krasner 1991; Lake et al. 2021.
[79] See, for instance, Waltz 1979.
[80] Like Reus-Smit (2018: 216), "I align with those who acknowledge the importance of changing material conditions, as these have enabling and constraining effects on action, but who deny that these are, in themselves, determining."
[81] See Doyle 1986; Abernethy 2002; Spruyt 2005; Wimmer 2012; Lawrence 2013.
[82] Goddard 2018; Carson 2018.
[83] Schweller 2001; Glaser 2019. Other realists see come to very different conclusions: see Gilpin 1981; Mearsheimer 2019.

constraints on powerful states,[84] but that fact hardly means that international order is meaningless or that institutions are irrelevant. The debate between realists and others on this subject is an old one.[85] I do not wish to rehash it, except to make two points. First, international order does not require institutions that can bind powerful states. Instead, governing arrangements can sometimes nudge states' decisions, relative to the counterfactual in which those arrangements did not exist. Governing arrangements work by regulating perceptions, by modifying incentives, and, perhaps, by shaping state preferences or identities through a long-run process of socialization.[86] Much evidence supports this idea.[87] Second, even this limited role for the governing arrangements of an international order can have important consequences. While I illustrate some of those consequences in subsequent chapters, the general point can be made swiftly. Suppose that an international trade regime adds only a small amount of growth to a nation's economy in a given year. Over time, this matters a lot for the same reason that a compound interest rate matters a lot for retirement savings. China's more rapid growth than America's since about 1990 illustrates this point. For all these reasons, I view international order as a question of first-rate importance.

With constructivists, I have few sharp disagreements, but one is fundamental. The liberal-realist definition of international order that I adopt refers to a set of rules or institutions that create or influence a pattern of relationships and behavior between actors, rather than the pattern itself. Rather than an *output*, international order is an *input* to behavior.[88] It is in this sense that scholars and policymakers refer to the UN or the World Bank as part of the international order. Constructivist scholars often dislike this input-output distinction because an order's rules and institutions are not fully separate from behavior, and they matter only to the extent that they shape actors' practices and beliefs.[89] After all, if actors ignore the *de jure* rules, as states did with the 1928 Kellogg-Briand Pact that supposedly outlawed war,[90] then those rules do not constitute international order. Constructivists prefer to see international order as an ever-changing emergent property based on how actors behave. There is real insight there. Unfortunately, constructivists tend to go too far: by obsessively emphasizing agency and change, they lose sight of structure and continuity. Treating order as both input and output simultaneously also creates certain analytical problems, as I describe in chapter 2. I hope to show, instead, that

---

[84] Schweller 2001: 163.

[85] For an introduction, see Mearsheimer 1994; Schweller 2001; Keohane and Martin 1995; Simmons 2000; Phillips 2010.

[86] Keohane and Martin 1995.

[87] In a large literature, see Keohane 1984; Milner 1997; Barnett and Finnemore 2004; Pelc 2010, Davis 2012; Carnegie and Carson 2019.

[88] Mazarr et al. 2016; Glaser 2019. Another common use of "international order" is as a synonym for stability, but that is not helpful if we are looking to explain when and how much change occurs.

[89] Goh 2013; Sending et al. 2015; Reus-Smit 2018; Adler 2019.

[90] The Kellogg-Briand Pact was signed in August 1928, though not ratified until 1929.

Table 1.1   Comparison to Existing Ideas in IR

	Partial Hegemony compared to:		
	Realism	Liberal Institutionalism	Constructivism
Agree on	• Actors usually pursue narrow self-interest • Actors regularly punish and prey upon others	• International order defined as governing arrangements • Actors often seek mutual gains	• Norms, ideas, and identities have causal influence on behavior • Actors create "rival collective images" of political possibilities
Differ on	• Significance of governing arrangements in IR • Punishments depend critically on ideas, norms, and actors' choices	• Subsystems, not issue areas, as key way to disaggregate world politics • Punishments as crucial for sustaining order	• International order as an input to behavior, not an output

studying norms,[91] practices,[92] and fields[93] can enrich and infuse the idea of international order as an input to behavior. Table 1.1 summarizes these points.

Finally, scholars from many parts of the field have been groping toward an understanding of international relations as a complex, adaptive system, rather than as deterministic and Newtonian.[94] Their insight is that generalizable patterns of behavior are recurring but not permanent. The challenge lies in incorporating that insight without destroying the whole basis for social science, namely that we can learn from the past. Subsystems theory offers a way out of that trap by distinguishing the features that are historically specific from those that give a common underlying logic to changes in international order.

Roadmap for the Book

My analysis focuses on global dynamics, rather than particular countries or regions. For oil, the politics of OPEC and the Anglo-American engagement with the Persian Gulf take center stage. Other significant oil producers, including

---

[91] Finnemore and Sikkink 1998; Barnett and Finnemore 2004.
[92] Adler and Pouliot 2011; Bueger 2012; Sending et al. 2015.
[93] Bourdieu 1984; Adler-Nissen 2012; Musgrave and Nexon 2018.
[94] Jervis 1997; Gunitsky 2013; Katzenstein and Seybert 2018; Oatley 2019.

Russia, Norway, Canada, and China, receive little attention. This is not because they are unimportant. But on the scale of the global market, they lack the market share and concentration of oil reserves to shape the main political dynamics. Russia's influence over natural gas markets, for instance, is a useful contrast to its much more limited influence over oil. The world's highly integrated oil market has hinged primarily on the members of OPEC and their most powerful external partners.

The book proceeds as follows. Chapter 2 develops my subsystems theory for analyzing international order. The chapter identifies change in international order as my dependent variable, and shows how the other variables work to explain such changes. It also shows how to use these concepts for the global oil system, to explain why international order was partially preserved and partially upended in the wake of twentieth-century decolonization.

The next three chapters show how the theory can explain oil politics. Chapters 3 and 4 address political economy, while chapter 5 focuses on security. That makes this book somewhat unusual: most IR scholars specialize on either security or political economy, not both.[95] Global oil politics, however, is too intertwined with military and economic dimensions to follow the standard approach.

Chapter 3 follows the rise of OPEC. It returns to the question of how the oil companies known as the Seven Sisters lost control of the world's oil production. The oligopoly consisted of a British company (BP), a British-Dutch company (Royal Dutch Shell), and five American companies. The five later gradually became two companies: Gulf Oil, Texaco, and Standard Oil of California became Chevron, and Standard Oil of New Jersey (Exxon) and New York (Mobil) merged as ExxonMobil. These firms and their governments held the pre-OPEC order together by using both the threat of punishments (quasi-imperial power) and strategic benefits (market incentives). Racism and social hierarchy buttressed those relationships.[96] Eventually, dissatisfied policymakers like Abdullah Tariki of Saudi Arabia and Juan Pablo Pérez Alfonzo of Venezuela created OPEC. They sought an economic sequel to decolonization. They cooperated effectively in the period 1960 to 1974 to shift the structure of the global oil market as first the threat of punishments and then the strategic benefits of the old order declined. A wave of nationalizations manifested the shift: it gave petrostates decision-making authority over production, along with the majority of the industry's profits.

Chapter 4 explains why OPEC has stagnated as an organization. From the early 1980s onward, OPEC has sought to act as a *de facto* cartel that limited world oil supply, stabilized prices, and raised long-term average revenues. It has proved

[95] See Cappella Zielinksi et al. 2020; Colgan 2020a.
[96] Vitalis 2007.

thoroughly ineffective in that effort, because it has no form of punishments for noncompliance. My analysis shows that its members cheat on their commitments 96 percent of the time. Worse still, cheating is only one of OPEC's problems. The members of OPEC agree only to those commitments that reflect what they were going to do anyway (mostly), even in the absence of OPEC. It persists as an organization partly out of inertia and partly because it offers political benefits to its members. National leaders like the late Venezuelan president Hugo Chávez have capitalized on OPEC's prestige and status.

Chapter 5 focuses on international security, which the second subsystem in modern oil politics revolves around. As oil became the preeminent military and economic commodity in the twentieth century, powerful states sought control over global oil production, even in the face of decolonization. Moreover, petrostates faced threats and wanted external protection. The identity of the principal external protector in the Middle East gradually changed from the United Kingdom to the United States as imperialism receded. A meeting between King Abd al-Aziz Al Saud of Saudi Arabia (known in the West as Ibn Saud) and President Franklin D. Roosevelt aboard the USS *Quincy* symbolized the launch of an oil-for-security deal. Later, newly independent states like Kuwait and others developed their own versions of an oil-for-security deal. Some of those deals later ruptured, but many still exist and continue to shape dynamics in the Persian Gulf. Recognizing this second subsystem gives a crisper, clearer understanding of the links between energy and security, and helps us better understand change in international order.

Part II of the book moves beyond oil. Anyone wanting to know how to analyze subsystems in their own area of interest should look to chapter 6. It starts by showing how my subsystems framework lends itself to a particular method or approach to research. That method encourages analysts to really get to know the empirics of their subject before jumping to causal analysis, as is unfortunately common in political science.[97] The chapter then addresses some additional theoretical questions not covered in chapter 2. For example, it identifies the standards of quality by which we can assess subsystems analyses, and considers how changes at the subsystem level aggregate up to a theme at the systemic level (e.g., the liberal order). My goal is to show how others can apply subsystems theory in an analytically fertile way.

Chapter 7 applies my theoretical ideas to climate change. To date, there is only a weak international order for climate. Still, I suggest that there are four emerging subsystems for climate politics, associated with emissions reductions; climate-related capital; negative-emissions technologies; and the climate-trade nexus. My analysis then turns quite prescriptive. I see the

---

[97] Oatley 2011; Gerring 2012; King 2012; Drezner and McNamara 2013.

fourth subsystem as especially important for generating punishments for noncompliance, to be applied to actors who refuse to adopt policies that reduce carbon emissions. A "climate club" of states with relatively green policies could, and should, use trade measures to support a more pro-climate international order.

The final chapter returns to where we began, addressing the general questions of international order. A recurring lesson of the book is that scholars and analysts often look for international order in the wrong place. They focus on the order's theme or its issue areas rather than its governing arrangements. After briefly summarizing the book's argument about a better way—focusing on subsystems—this chapter turns to two additional topics. First, the world is currently experiencing a significant energy transition toward renewables in the context of climate change.[98] I use my subsystems framework to assess what the global energy transition might mean for international order, and vice versa. One lesson that follows from my analysis is that US policymakers should pay careful attention to the benefits of oil-for-security arrangements in the Persian Gulf region before too lightly abandoning them. Those deals have helped avoid wars. While there are some compelling reasons to change the US relationship with various petrostates in the Middle East, we should be mindful of unintended consequences.

The second topic is what the subsystems framework can offer for understanding international order in the twenty-first century. The US-led international order cannot rely too heavily on leader selection or militarily punishing actors for noncompliance. Instead, international order in each subsystem will depend critically on the strategic benefits that it offers. Geopolitical rivalry will matter greatly for these benefits. Actors will evaluate them in a relative sense, especially if China or others create alternative governing arrangements to US-led institutions. My previous research with Nicholas L. Miller showed that in the past, rival great powers used three mechanisms—competitive shaming, outbidding, and international cooperation—to shape the explicit and implicit bargains struck between great powers and other actors in the international system.[99] Those same mechanisms are likely to shape great power rivalry in the twenty-first century.

Ultimately, this book is about how to create and sustain international governing arrangements that actually work. The existential threat of climate change makes the need for improving such arrangements even more urgent

---

[98] Kern and Rogge 2016; Sovacool 2016; O'Sullivan et al. 2017; Jaffe 2018; Van de Graaf and Bradshaw 2018; Goldthau and Westphal 2019; IRENA 2019; Bazilian et al. 2020; Van de Graaf et al. 2020.

[99] Colgan and Miller 2019. On bargains between great powers and other states, see Lake 2011; McDonald 2015.

than it normally is. If policymakers are going to make governing arrangements that work, they must understand international order and what makes sustained, deep cooperation possible. The United States, especially, will have to demonstrate greater restraint and wiser pursuit of its opportunities than it has shown in recent years.

PART I
OIL POLITICS

2

Rethinking International Order

"Our age is insistently, at times almost desperately, in pursuit of a concept of world order."[1]
— Henry Kissinger, former US Secretary of State

"International order is not self-organizing."[2]
— Michèle Flournoy, former US Under Secretary of Defense

How do we make sense of the noisy, turbulent world of oil politics? Wars in the Middle East, international sanctions, terrorist acts, natural disasters, and labor strikes all play a role in making global oil markets highly volatile. On the surface, there doesn't look like there is anything to call international order. Nothing equivalent to Newton's laws exists for oil politics that would make it rational or deterministic—far from it. Yet, there have been times, like a decades-long stretch in the mid-twentieth century, when oil prices were steady and predictable. And despite repeated crises, some political relationships like the US-Saudi partnership are surprisingly durable, even with big differences in values, geography, and regime type within them. Why do certain patterns persist, while others break down?

The answer depends first on having a good grasp of what we mean by international order. In this chapter I clarify and define that concept, and then refine our theories about it. A robust theory of international order can help us understand when and under what conditions it changes over time. I develop three new ideas that work together to explain such changes. The first idea is *subsystems*, within which international order exists. My second idea is about the sources of change in international order: *strategic benefits* and *punishments for noncompliance*. Powerful actors like partial hegemons typically use punishments as a way to sustain international order in a given subsystem. The third idea involves actors' *instruments of coercion*. Changes in the cost-effectiveness of those instruments

---

[1] Kissinger 2015: 2.
[2] Flournoy 2020.

can—but don't always—change the benefits and punishments associated with governing arrangements in a given subsystem.

Collectively, I call these three ideas "subsystems theory," even though only the first deals with subsystems *per se*.[3] In principle, we could use any one of them to amend existing theory because the ideas stand independently. However, they are more powerful together: they challenge the dominance of conventional hegemonic order theories.[4] Jointly, my ideas clarify the relationship between actors' instruments of coercion and their governing arrangements. That clarity reveals when the arrangements are effective. OPEC's failure to function as a real cartel is an example, as we shall see, of a governing arrangement that exceeds the members' available instruments of coercion.

My core hypothesis is that strategic benefits and punishments for noncompliance are specific to a given subsystem. Consequently, change to international order occurs in subsystems, rather than in issue areas or the system as a whole.

I develop and use the theory to explain oil politics over the last century. To preview: twentieth-century decolonization and national liberation made it increasingly hard for great powers like Britain or the United States to use economic coercion and leadership selection to achieve political goals. They occasionally still used these instruments, but those kinds of coercion grew costlier and generally less successful. Thus, the former colonies faced declining risks of punishment for noncompliance with the old imperial governing arrangements. That gave actors in the former colonies new incentives to change governing arrangements in some but not all subsystems. In sum, chapters 3 to 5 focus on the long-term consequences of a single major shift in the punishments from international order: decolonization. With these new concepts in hand, the story of global oil comes into view.

Concepts of International Order

Market watchers might be inclined to equate international order with price stability, and price volatility with disorder. Seen this way, order is an output or outcome. However, people often speak of international order in a second, quite different way: as the *set of rules or institutions* that create or influence behavior, rather than the pattern of behavior itself.[5] When policymakers talk about NATO or the UN or the WTO as part of the international order, they use the term this way. Rather than an outcome, they see order as an input. This approach is

---

[3] In truth, these ideas are grafted onto existing IR concepts, without which they would not constitute a full theory.

[4] For a review, see Ikenberry and Nexon 2019.

[5] Glaser 2019.

useful because it distinguishes the rules of an order (input) from the effectiveness of that order in shaping actors' behavior (output).[6] If we fail to make this distinction—that is, if we treat order as an outcome—then phrases like "the liberal order promotes free trade" have a circular logic. Seeing order as an input is better. In the realm of energy, seeing order as an input allows us to distinguish between different governing arrangements—like the OPEC cartel or the earlier Seven Sister oligopoly—and the effects that they have on prices and markets.

Constructivist scholars tend to dislike this input-output distinction when identifying international order.[7] For example, in "practice theory," theorists see order as an ever-changing emergent property based on what actors do, rather than a set of rules for guiding that behavior.[8] Their approach builds from the insight that the rules and institutions of order matter only to the extent that they shape actors' practices and beliefs. Rules must be upheld (practiced), at least sometimes, to exist at all. In other words, institutions, rules, and principles are tied to the ever-changing practices of actors, rather than wholly separable from those practices. It is a powerful insight.[9]

Still, many constructivists take it too far. We should not confuse "churn" (changes in practices) with "important." While it is true that actors constantly make changes around the margins of core rules and institutions, not everything is in constant flux.[10] Core institutions, rules, and principles do exist that most actors cannot change unilaterally or easily.[11] Once established, even the most powerful cannot change them at any time without significant costs. In fact, much of the ever-changing practices represents actors running to stand still—adjusting governing arrangements to ensure that their implementation reflects the core principles.[12] Those core arrangements

---

[6] An order is based on the *de facto* rules, principles, and institutions. *De jure* rules fail to constitute *de facto* rules if either (1) only peripheral actors make them, without gaining the principal actors' assent, or (2) actors' subsequent behavior thoroughly discredits them. The Kellogg-Briand Pact outlawing war, for instance, was ratified in 1929. Technically it remains in force, although it was thoroughly discredited in the 1930s.

[7] Hurrell 2007; Goh 2013; Reus-Smit 2018; Cooley and Nexon 2020; see also Adler-Nissen 2012; Zarakol 2017; Bueger 2018.

[8] Adler and Pouliot 2011; Sending et al. 2015; Adler 2019; Bueger and Edmunds (unpublished).

[9] This line of thinking produces other insights as well. I strongly agree with the idea, for instance, that there is no single international order, and that it varies considerably across issue areas (Sending 2015; Adler 2019; Cooley and Nexon 2020: 32).

[10] Assemblage theory, for instance, obsesses over change and instability. See Ong and Colliers 2005; Sassen 2006; Bueger 2018.

[11] One way of attempting to square that circle is to claim that structures such as institutions, rules, and principles are actually practices. That might be correct in some sense, but it expands the definition of practices so much that it becomes almost useless. If practices are everything, then claiming that IR is all about practices is reduced to tautology. It then provides no leverage for causal analysis.

[12] Adler (2019) refers to this process as "meta-stability" but fails to see its significance. If continual changes in practices leave a hard core of governing arrangements that are durable over a period of interest, then calling that core "meta-stable" is equivalent to calling it "unchanged" for the period of interest. Thus, everything is *not* in flux. Alternatively, if there is no such hard core, and all is

are durable over periods of interest, and they structure actors' behavior and expectations.[13]

Hence, governing arrangements manifest international order, understood as an input to behavior. Treating governing arrangements as inputs helps avoid certain analytical problems common in the constructivist tradition. For example, treating order as both input and outcome simultaneously can lead to tautological or non-falsifiable explanations, though some of the best constructivist research escapes these problems.[14] Treating order as analytically distinct from its output effects greatly facilitates causal analysis.

I therefore follow a modified version of John Ikenberry's definition of international order as "the governing arrangements among a group of states, including its fundamental rules, principles, and institutions."[15] I broaden this definition to include not only states but also non-state actors, like commercial firms, international organizations, and colonies or imperial territories.[16] As we will see in chapter 3, it is not possible to understand international order in oil politics without including the role of oil companies or international organizations like OPEC. A mountain of research shows how non-state actors matter in other issue areas too.[17]

Governing arrangements, in turn, are defined by the presence (and absence) of principles, norms, rules, and decision-making procedures. Governing arrangements, and hence international order, are meaningful to the extent that they cause states or non-state actors to behave or perceive things differently from how they would in the counterfactual, where those arrangements did

---

continuously in flux, then there is no structure, only agency. This idea of agency is empirically untenable: structures do provide incentives and constraints for actors.

[13] This discussion harks back to the "agent-structure problem" that generated a large literature with a long history, including Archer 1988; Finnemore 1996; Wendt 1999; Wight 2006.

[14] For a wonderful example, see Phillips 2010.

[15] Ikenberry 2000: 23, Gilpin 1981: 111; Mearsheimer 2019. Other definitions exist. Bull (1977: 8) defines international order as "a pattern of activity that sustains the elementary or primary goals of the society of states, or international society." For Reus-Smit (2018: 13), orders are "systemic configurations of political authority." See also Mattern 2005: 30; Cox and Sinclair 1996: 100; Hurrell 2007: 2; Phillips 2010: 5; Goh 2013: 7; Kissinger 2015: 9.

[16] On the need to include non-state actors in a conception of international order, see Reus-Smit 2018: 192–195; Cox and Sinclair 1996.

[17] Keohane and Nye 1972, 1977; Ruggie 1983; Keck and Sikkink 1998; Cameron et al. 1998; Goldstein and Martin 2000; Schultz 2001; Mosley 2003; Nielson and Tierney 2003; Vreeland 2003; Woods 2006; Singer 2007; Busby 2007; Fortna 2008; Weaver 2008; Brooks 2008; Lake 2009; Gutner and Thompson 2010; Copelovitch 2010; Owen 2010; Chenoweth and Stephan 2011; Büthe and Mattli 2011; Scheve and Stasavage 2012; Cammett and Malesky 2012; Branch 2013; Tomz and Weeks 2013; Conrad and Ritter 2013; Green and Colgan 2013; Hyde 2015; Bermeo and Leblang 2015; Bush 2015; Fazal and Green 2015; Hadden 2015; Mattes et al. 2015; Wellhausen 2015; Milner and Tingley 2015; Lightfoot 2016; Cohen 2016; Ripsman et al. 2016; Dean 2016; Matanock 2017; Peters 2017; Nelson and Steinberg 2018; Blair 2020; Jost forthcoming.

not exist. What I call meaningful international order, others have called deep cooperation.[18]

Even when they more or less share this definition, theories of international order often struggle empirically to explain or even identify major shifts in international order. Hegemonic theories, for instance, expect a hegemon to shape international order by setting up institutions in the wake of major power wars.[19] Hegemonic stability theory suggests that a hegemon is needed to sustain international order, and when the hegemon's power fades, so too do its governing arrangements.[20] Liberal theorists, on the other hand, argue that a hegemon might be able to set up institutions that endure even after its power declines.[21] Either way, changes in international order tend to come after big wars, and powerful states drive the changes.

The 1973 oil crisis is a prime example of those theories' limitations. It represented a shift in international order that did not occur in the wake of a major power war, contrary to theoretical expectations. Second, great powers were not the ones leading the change in order; if anything, several of them tried to resist it. Finally, non-state actors like firms, international organizations, and individual leaders played a far larger role in the events than the state-centric theories expect. Other examples of change in international order, like the collapse of the Bretton Woods financial system in the early 1970s or the upheaval in the Soviet Union's sphere of influence between 1989 and 1991, also suggest the limits of seeing order primarily as something great powers establish after major wars.

The chief difficulty of analyzing changes in international order, including those in oil politics, is that the world frequently experiences change and continuity at the same time. Analyzing individual issue areas, like oil or finance, is one way to solve this problem. That is what regime theorists of the 1980s did, and more recently those studying regime complexity.[22] Yet, treating broad topics as monolithic issue areas is still problematic. As I described in chapter 1, the issue area of oil contains security and economic dimensions that can change at vastly different rates and even different directions.

In short, regime theory did not go far enough. It sought to understand order by disaggregating the system down to the level of issue areas, but these were still too broad.

---

[18] Downs, Rocke, and Barsoom 1996.
[19] For a partial definition of a hegemon, see Gilpin 1981: 116; Keohane 1984: 32–35.
[20] Kindleberger 1973; Gilpin 1981; Kennedy 1987; Lascurettes 2020.
[21] Keohane 1984; Ikenberry 2000.
[22] Krasner 1983; Keohane 1984; Raustiala and Victor 2004; Colgan et al. 2012; Henning 2019.

Subsystems in International Politics

To analyze oil politics—and many other topics—we must break down international order from the level of the system or issue area. Disaggregating, however, immediately creates the challenge of knowing when to stop. I propose using subsystems to answer that question because they are where governing arrangements exist. Subsystems are rooted in the types of decisions policymakers and firms can actually make, whereas "issue areas" are ill-defined. There are four advantages of that approach. They come at the price, however, of dealing with the fuzzy boundaries and overlap between subsystems.

I define a *subsystem* as a collection of states and non-state actors linked by a single question of governance within a substantive issue area. For instance, the principal actors in Southeast Asia's 1997 financial crisis included Thailand, South Korea, Indonesia, and Malaysia; the International Monetary Fund; certain global banks; and the US Treasury and Federal Reserve. A subsystem cuts across and combines actors from various levels of analysis.[23] Subsystems are related to, but distinct from, other scholarly ideas like multi-level governance,[24] nested regimes,[25] or regime complexity.[26] Subsystems can be compared to atoms, in which electrons (actors) orbit a central nucleus (governance question).

Each subsystem has only one governance question. This distinguishes subsystems from regimes, which nominally cover whole issue areas.[27] A given issue area can contain multiple questions associated with governance or decision-making, but a subsystem does not. A subsystem's question relates to a functional task, something that actors can directly affect with a specific policy lever or levers. For example, states might not be able to directly affect the spread of disease or the global price of oil, but they can make decisions over how much a national oil company produces or whether to fight militarily for control of certain territories. Governance questions are defined analytically; the actors themselves might not have a clear awareness of the subsystem they operate in.

---

[23] Singer 1961.

[24] On multi-level governance, see Hooghe and Marks 2003; Zürn 2010; Börzel and Risse 2010. Subsystems generally fit the description of "task-specific, intersecting, and flexible jurisdictions" of Type II governance, as opposed to the "general-purpose, non-intersecting, and durable jurisdictions" of Type I governance (Hooghe and Marks 2003: 236–239). Yet whereas "Type II governance is generally embedded in Type I governance," subsystems analysis makes no such assumption and shows how task-specific governance can shape general-purpose jurisdictions (e.g, oil security subsystem).

[25] On nested regimes, see Alter and Meunier 2009. Nested regimes might span multiple subsystems.

[26] On regime complexity, see Raustiala and Victor 2004; Gomez-Mera 2015; Colgan et al. 2012; Henning 2019. As I explore in chapter 6, subsystems theory resists the institutional focus of those studying regime complexity.

[27] Keohane 1984; Krasner 1983.

I treat questions of governance as durable—fixed over the period of interest. That is a useful working assumption for many subsystems, but questions of governance are not eternal. Ultimately, governance questions are shaped by actors' beliefs, expertise, and technology.[28] Still, the degree to which governance questions are fluid varies from subsystem to subsystem. While they might be quite malleable in highly normative areas like humanitarian intervention, they are less malleable in core areas of IR like economic production or military violence, where material constraints almost inevitably render certain questions highly salient. For example, the amount of oil produced in various parts of the world is bound to be significant because of the laws of supply and demand, and the global integration of oil markets. Even for nonmarket economies, oil markets generate massive material incentives that are hard to ignore (as the USSR and China each discovered). Thus, the question, How much oil will be produced in each territory? has been a durable problem of governance since petroleum became central to modern transportation.

The amount of order in a given subsystem depends on the extent to which governing arrangements move actors' behavior away from the counterfactual in which those arrangements did not exist.[29] Mere compliance with governing arrangements is a bad measure of the international order's depth because those arrangements might be so weak that compliance with them is meaningless.[30] Thus, the depth of international order is a variable that ranges from shallow to deep, in proportion to the degree to which the governing arrangements affect actors' behavior. Governing arrangements can take various forms, such as a single regime or a regime complex.[31]

Subsystems analysis does not necessarily differ from regime analysis if there is only one key question of governance in an issue area. International trade, for instance, has only one subsystem (since 1991, at least)[32] because much of the action in trade revolves around a single governance question: To what extent can state governments favor their own producers commercially? States have many ways to favor their own producers—including tariffs, product regulations, and rules of origin—but the basic question is the same.[33] A subsystems approach is best

[28] Fligstein and McAdam 2012; Sending et al. 2015; Seabrooke and Tsingou 2014.
[29] A subsystem is like a petri dish: it is the substrate on which international order can grow. Order consists of governing arrangements, and a subsystem's governing arrangements are the answer to its governance question.
[30] Downs et al. 1996.
[31] Alternatively, order might emerge from informal bilateral agreements between key players. A shallow form of order might even emerge tacitly between hostile parties, such as when warring parties avoid certain barbarous practices (Legro 1995; Tannenwald 2007).
[32] Different regional subsystems can have different governing arrangements over the same governance question, such as the General Agreement on Tariffs and Trade (GATT) and the Council for Mutual Economic Assistance (Comecon) during the Cold War.
[33] Tariffs are a classic method of favoring domestic firms, and the GATT originally focused on lowering tariffs. Since then, the trade regime's scope has expanded to include other policy

for issue areas like energy, finance, or the environment where there are multiple governance questions.

One great advantage of using subsystems is that they help deal with the fact that different types of authority exist in the world. Although governance does not strictly require authority, some form of authority is present in most instances.[34] States typically have supreme authority over the use of force, but often they must share authority over other issue domains (such as health, cybersecurity, or the environment) with firms, churches, international organizations, or other actors.[35] Subsystems help us make sense of different types of authority within circumscribed areas.[36]

This advantage is important because it allows for a more accurate understanding of international order than when we conceive of it as entirely focused on security needs, as realist scholars tend to do. John Mearsheimer, for instance, sees governing arrangements as something that great powers establish to wage security competition with each other, with other social purposes discarded or subordinated to the goal of security.[37] Yet states do not behave in this manner. To claim otherwise is historically tone-deaf. States pursue wealth, for instance, and not just for the purpose of building strong armies. They also pursue other goals.[38] Regardless of whether states *ought* to radically subordinate everything to the goal of security competition, as some realists argue, the fact is that states *do not* focus

---

instruments: product regulations, phytosanitary issues, anti-dumping, rules of origin, dispute-settlement procedures, etc. Yet much or most of these WTO rules and components are still built on the same core issue: keeping a level playing field for commerce across borders. Also, at the WTO, there is a single principal corrective mechanism for noncompliance: tariffs.

[34] Authority is rightful or legitimate rule (Weber 2004 [1919]; Lake 2011: 8). Scholars have previously conceived of different kinds of authority in different "segments" of IR (Hurd 1999: 401) or "specific policy arenas" (Nexon and Wright 2007: 266). On different kinds of social purpose, see also Bull 1977; Ruggie 1982.

[35] Avant 2005; Büthe and Mattli 2011; Green and Colgan 2013.

[36] A state's authority is the most familiar, and might seem like the highest, form of authority. Yet sometimes a non-state actor can compel states, as the Catholic Church sometimes did during the Middle Ages (Donnelly 2009). For instance, Pope Innocent III asserted that the pope was "set between God and man, lower than God but higher than man, who judges all and is judged by no one" (Wheatcroft 1995: 49). More often, a state's authority is just different from that of other actors. For example, if a state tries to conquer a company, it is likely to acquire the firm's physical assets but not its economic productivity or relationships (Frieden 1994). In truth, a state cannot conquer a company, or a religion, or a transnational civil society. These are incommensurable units, with different forms of authority (Keohane and Nye 1972). Authority is not monolithic and comprehensive; it is circumscribed over particular issue domains (Cooley and Spruyt 2009; Lake 2011; Mattern and Zarakol 2016). See also Nexon and Neumann (2017) on how different forms of authority can be purchased or exchanged, even if they are of fundamentally different types.

[37] Mearsheimer 2019: 12–13.

[38] States pursue ideological goals like democracy or communism, sometimes at great expense (Haas 2005; Owen 2011; Jamal 2012; Narizny 2012; Subotic and Zarkaol 2013; Gunitsky 2017). And states pursue other goals like environmental protection, disease eradication, space exploration, and status competition (Bukovansky 2009; Towns 2010; Paul et al. 2014; Dafoe et al. 2014; Renshon 2017; Gilady 2018; Goddard 2018; Musgrave and Nexon 2018).

exclusively on military security. Subsystems allow us to understand this wider variety of international behavior.

Subsystems' second advantage is that they make the question, Has the order changed? much more tractable. Unlike issue areas, each subsystem has only one governance question, over which governing arrangements can be made. Thus, while both change and continuity are possible simultaneously within an issue area,[39] there is only change or continuity in each subsystem at the level of the governing question.[40]

A third advantage is that subsystems make sense of different types of change in order. As I described in chapter 1, changes in governing arrangements are independent of changes in the ordering theme. For example, we might recognize a constant US-led "liberal order" over many decades even as we see changes in various subsystems. The concept of subsystems also suggests a taxonomy for types of change, such as changes in: the actors, the governance question, or the answer to that question. I focus especially on the answer.

The fourth advantage of subsystems is heuristic. The concept of subsystems leads to an analytical approach that emphasizes descriptive inference and avoids reductionism. It requires deep empirical knowledge. As I describe in chapter 6, that requirement can help scholars avoid jumping too quickly to causal inferences, and thereby arriving at misleading conclusions. While identifying the subsystems is a difficult analytic task, it is not simply a matter of taste: its quality can be measured according to standards of accuracy, parsimony, and breadth. A subsystems approach also helps avoid the reductionist fallacy, which is to see a system as merely the sum of its parts.[41] Using subsystems encourages an analyst to be keenly aware that the actors within a subsystem change; that subsystems can split, merge, and interact with each other; and that systemic structure and historical circumstances profoundly affect relations between the units. Thus, seeing international order as intimately tied to subsystems comes with substantial advantages.

Alas, no approach is without disadvantages.[42] For subsystems, the main disadvantage is the question of boundaries. It is not possible to specify the boundaries of subsystems precisely at the level of theory. Instead, the messy empirical world

[39] Cohen, in Krasner 1983; Gowa 1988.

[40] Different policy levers within a subsystem do allow, in a sense, for both change and continuity. But analysts can generally judge the degree of change in the overall answer to a governance question.

[41] On reductionism, see Waltz 1979; Oatley 2011; Drezner and McNamara 2013; Chaudoin et al. 2015; Winecoff 2017; Bauerle Danzman et al. 2017.

[42] Ideally, one could specify precisely the internal logic of subsystems, how they interact with each other, and where the boundaries lie between them. (I am grateful to Stein Eriksen and other participants at a NUPI workshop in Oslo for this formulation.) This chapter offers precision on the first element (how subsystems work internally), and I briefly sketch the second in chapter 6 (how subsystems overlap and interact). The main problem involves boundaries.

defines them.[43] We need bottom-up empirical analysis, rather than top-down deductive reasoning, to define the borders. Theoretically, one can say only that a subsystem's borders are determined by the set of actors who have significant effects on its governance question.[44] Of course, a little common sense goes a long way. The subsystem relating to global oil production, for instance, contains OPEC and oil firms but does not contain actors like the World Health Organization or Microsoft.

The theory's advantages outweigh the disadvantage of having imprecise boundaries between subsystems. At its best, subsystems theory can reveal political change embedded in continuity, or continuity embedded in change, that would otherwise go unnoticed.

Explaining Change in International Order

The concept of order as grounded in subsystems is helpful, but explaining how it changes requires a second key idea. I theorize change in international order as the product of two major independent variables: punishments for noncompliance and the strategic benefits of an order. These independent (or explanatory) variables are shaped by deeper factors like the distribution of power, international norms, and technology.[45]

Defining the Explanatory Variables

The *punishments for noncompliance* are the risks and costs, both tangible and intangible, that an actor faces if they choose to break the rules of the order. An act of noncompliance creates the risk that some powerful actor, often the hegemon, will punish the noncompliant actor. States impose punishments on allies and enemies alike.[46] The "costs" are not just economic: they might be paid in human lives or they might be something else, like political shaming or expulsion from an international organization.[47]

---

[43] The number of subsystems depends on the number of governance questions. That means that an analyst must make empirical judgments about what governance questions are sufficiently significant to constitute a subsystem. See chapter 6.

[44] As Pierre Bourdieu said about fields, "the limit of a field [subsystem] is the point where the effects of its actors and institutions cannot be found." Quoted in Musgrave and Nexon 2018: 15; see also Adler-Nissen 2012; Fligstein and McAdam 2012; Sending 2015; Adler 2019.

[45] Gilpin 1981; Organski and Kugler 1981; Kennedy 1987; Katzenstein 1996; Ruggie 1998; Crawford 2002; Bukovansky 2009; Phillips 2010; Reus-Smit 2013; Goh 2013; Monteiro 2014; Horowitz et al. 2016; Getachew 2019.

[46] Henke 2019; Poast 2019.

[47] von Borzyskowski and Vabulas 2019; Hafner-Burton 2008; Murdie and Davis 2012; Hendrix and Wong 2013; Colgan and Miller 2019.

Noncompliance is always risky and sometimes costly. The strength of a punishment depends on its magnitude, the probability that it is imposed, and actors' perceptions about the punishment. When an actor (like North Korea, in the nuclear realm) chooses noncompliance, it does not know for sure the probability or magnitude of imposed punishment. One way to distinguish punishments from strategic benefits is that punishments are not generally automatic. An actor that wishes to sustain the international order makes a political decision to impose them.

While IR theorists are familiar with the general idea of punishments, some scholars tend to gloss over the role of coercion and force in sustaining an international order. Other scholars are more likely to see punishments for noncompliance as following automatically from the distribution of material power or capabilities.[48] This is wrong. Instead, punishments depend on the ideas and norms that are prevalent at a particular time, and on choices people make.[49] New technology, too, can alter the ability to punish, such as when advanced naval capacity facilitated global power projection.

Punishments are also partly a function of a hegemon's desire to impose them. Three key factors shape the motivation to enforce compliance. First, motivation varies with the benefits that a hegemon (or other enforcing actor) receives from the order. Large benefits make the effort of imposing punishments worthwhile. For example, the United States benefits from a global oil system that is not dominated by a hostile state, so in 1990–1991, the United States had incentive to lead a military coalition to reverse Iraq's invasion of Kuwait.[50] Second, actors have to decide that noncompliance has occurred, which is sometimes less obvious than it might seem. Covert action can complicate it.[51] For example, noncompliance might be unclear when a country is suspected of developing a nuclear program. Even when the facts are public, actors interpret events differently in light of their beliefs and perceptions.[52] The various justifications for the Iraq war are an example.[53] Third, the motivation to enforce varies with the degree to which the order reinforces a hegemon's domestic political narrative. To a certain extent, all hegemons try to externalize their own values.[54] When domestic politics change, it can ripple outward to international politics.[55] For example, America's

---

[48] Structural realists also tend to emphasize the capabilities of great powers, paying little attention to weak states or other actors. See Waltz 1979; Gilpin 1981; Mearsheimer 2001.

[49] See Lawrence 2013; Spruyt 2005; Abernethy 2002; Doyle 1986.

[50] Colgan 2013b.

[51] O'Rourke 2017; Poznansky and Perkoski 2018; Carnegie and Carson 2019.

[52] Jervis 1976; Goddard 2018.

[53] Lake 2010.

[54] Carr 1946; Ikenberry 2000; Haas 2005; Bukovansky 2009; Gunitsky 2017; Goddard 2018.

[55] Milner and Tingley 2015.

commitment to liberalism has waxed and waned over the years, which in turn affects its willingness to uphold certain parts of global order.[56]

An order's *strategic benefits* are the incentives for cooperation generated by the interaction among the actors within a given subsystem. These are the incentives actors have to regularize their interactions in a particular way, regardless of the political superstructure that prevails at any given moment. For instance, if two former colonies mutually want structured cooperation even after an empire collapses, it likely indicates that strategic benefits are strong.

Strategic benefits have three basic sources: economic, geostrategic, and communitarian. Economic incentives are probably the most common: they stem from mutual gains from trade, integration, and specialization. Complex economic interaction generates the need to cooperate or develop some form of order.[57] A second form of strategic benefits is geostrategic. For example, an actor might have an interest in controlling a territory, waterway, or capability associated with another actor in ways that create mutual benefits. The Strait of Hormuz is a geostrategic choke point, so actors want order around it, even when other political superstructures like the British Empire fall away. Third, actors with shared communities often want to interact across borders. These communities might stem from a common religion, diaspora, or even a deep-seated ideology.[58] For instance, a transnational diaspora could create a desire for recurring type of interaction, like the US-Israeli partnership. As these examples indicate, strategic benefits can be either material or ideational.

The sources of strategic benefits are partly exogenous and beyond the control of states or firms. The benefits of mitigating climate change, for example, derive in part from nature itself. Likewise, the gains from international trade stem from specialization and learning. Admittedly, political actors can also offer positive inducements to influence the availability of strategic benefits.[59] Also, sometimes actors seek to capture relative benefits, compared to some excluded rival(s).[60] Yet, ultimately, strategic benefits are born out of people's underlying incentives and values, aggregated across many people. That makes strategic benefits different from punishments, which powerful actors generate by conscious choice at a particular moment.

---

[56] Ikenberry 2020.

[57] Keohane and Nye 1977. Mutual gains stem from trade or interaction itself; strategic benefits indicate the incentives to regulate that interaction. For example, even enemies can generate mutual gains by trading commodities, without much cooperation or order between them (Barbieri and Levy 1999). In more complex interactions, however, people and firms need to work together to guard shipments, set product standards, manage supply chains, access credit markets, etc. The complexity generates strategic benefits to order.

[58] See Salehyan 2009 on rebel diasporas..

[59] Baldwin 1971; Drezner 2007; Carnegie 2015.

[60] Lascurettes 2020.

The Raj in India illustrates how the British maintained an order through a combination of punishments and strategic benefits. The Amritsar massacre of 1919 is an example of punishments. In that case, hundreds of Indians rebelled against British troops, who slaughtered them. An example of strategic benefits is the Indians who profited from their economic and cultural association with Britain, such as those educated at Cambridge and Oxford. Both compliance and strategic benefits are important for imperial stability.

Strategic benefits and punishments for noncompliance represent a contractual and coercive approach, respectively, to sustaining international order.[61] Actors maintain order using force, coercion, bargaining, and persuasion. Loosely speaking, force and coercion are associated with punishments for noncompliance; bargaining and persuasion are associated with strategic benefits.

Legitimacy and ideas play a vital role in shaping both strategic benefits and punishments for noncompliance. Powerful actors can rarely sustain an international order through bullying alone.[62] The legitimacy of an order, as perceived by its participants, affects both its benefits and its punishments. As such, changes in ideas and perceived legitimacy change can lead to change in the international order in a given subsystem. Indeed, major ideational changes can lead, over time, to disruptions across multiple subsystems. These ideational shifts take multiple forms, including altering perceptions of legitimacy, shifting the cost-effectiveness of various forms of coercion, and mapping out new potential governing arrangements.[63]

Origins of Change

These concepts shed light on when international order changes. The likelihood of change of a meaningful international order depends on the strength of the punishments for noncompliance and the relative strategic benefits within a given subsystem.[64] Figure 2.1 illustrates the relationship. When an international order generates positive strategic benefits, and actors face strong punishments for defecting from the order, change is unlikely. Key actors are satisfied most of the time, and punishments are meted out for those who do not comply. (It can be important *to whom* strategic benefits accrue.[65]) The top-left box describes that situation. The top-right box describes a situation where an order generates positive

[61] Coercive and contractual approaches have parallels in Tilly's (1992) notions of coercion and capital as the basis for state authority.
[62] Hurd 1999; Coleman 2007; Bukovansky 2009; Avant et al. 2010; Kang 2010; Lake 2011.
[63] On the role of ideas in IR, see Goldstein and Keohane 1993; Blyth 2002; Matthias 2020.
[64] Recall that I use "meaningful" international order to mean what Downs et al. (1996) call "deep cooperation," that is, it affects actors' behaviors relative to the counterfactual.
[65] See discussion of Figure 2.2 and later in this chapter.

Punishments for Noncompliance

		Strong	Weak
Net Strategic Benefits	Positive	Very stable	Often stable
	Negative	Stability requires sustained threat of imposed costs	Very unstable

Figure 2.1 The role of punishments and strategic benefits in international order

strategic benefits relative to other potential orders, meaning that it is able to persist even without a hegemon or other actor ready to impose punishments for noncompliance.[66] When an order generates fewer strategic benefits than some potential alternative, however, it creates negative relative benefits. The bottom row describes that situation when an international order is susceptible to change. The order is likely to persist only if there is at least one powerful actor continuously willing to impose discipline (bottom-left box). In that case, an order can be held together through the fear of punishment, but when change comes, it is likely to take the form of revolution or rupture.

When either the punishments or strategic benefits in a subsystem decline, it creates a threat to stability of the subsystem's order unless the other one increases. Changes in punishments are particularly important because historically they tend to occur across an entire international system. For example, a new technology or a new set of ideas can change the prospect of punishment across multiple substantive domains (like security, trade, or energy) at more or less the same time. Sometimes these shifts are gradual, sometimes rapid. When the strength of punishments declines, the continuity of the old order depends greatly on its strategic benefits.[67]

The logic can be crudely described in game-theoretic terms. First, some event weakens the punishments for noncompliance, possibly generating new actors (like newly independent states) or a new relationship between old actors. Each actor then faces a choice: does it want to preserve or change the old order within

---

[66] Keohane 1984.

[67] Similarly, when strategic benefits decline, the continuity of an order depends greatly on the strength of its enforcement, that is, its punishments.

a given subsystem? The actor's best strategy depends on the benefits it expects to receive, relative to alternative arrangements and rules. Each actor chooses to accept the status quo or challenge the order by "defecting." If an actor chooses to start defecting from the order, any other actor wishing to punish it for noncompliance responds accordingly. After all actors have settled on a course of action, a new order emerges if key actors have persisted in defecting from the old one and have set up alternative governing arrangements.

An example illustrates the theoretical logic. Ideas of self-determination and racial equality in the twentieth century transformed many colonies into newly sovereign states. That weakened the coercive authority that European metropoles had over those territories. In theory, decolonization could have led to any type of international order or disorder in the years that followed. States could have kept the old governance relationship between themselves; totally reversed it; made pacts of voluntary cooperation; or allowed complete disorder, with no regular pattern of behavior. In practice, different sets of states did most of these things. In some cases, decolonization changed only superficially between metropole and former colony, as in the UK-Brunei or France-Gabon relationships. In other cases, decolonization rapidly eroded the relationships, as in most of the former British Empire in Africa (e.g., Kenya, Tanzania, etc.). Even within a given bilateral relationship, some things changed while others stayed the same, though the amount of change varied a lot from relationship to relationship. Subsystems theory can account for this variation.

The fact that actors are constantly imagining other potential governing arrangements, and assessing the strategic benefits and punishments of the current order against those ideas, is significant. It means that actors' perceptions, imagination, culture, and causal beliefs play a role in an order's stability.[68] It also makes order historically contingent.[69] That is, yesterday's order within each subsystem profoundly affects today's order because actors assess strategic benefits and punishments in relation to that history.[70]

Figure 2.1 tells us something about *when* and *under what circumstances* order changes. *How* it changes often involves considerable experimentation, informality, coalition building, bottom-up entrepreneurialism, rival collective images, and challenges to authority, a process others have studied extensively.[71] My approach assumes that it is possible to step back from the ever-changing day-to-day practices of actors and institutions to analyze the big picture of those

---

[68] Swidler (1986) shows how culture offers a toolkit of ideas and strategies, which could inspire and shape an actor's sense of alterative governing arrangements.

[69] Cox and Sinclair 1996.

[70] On historical institutionalism see, among others, Mahoney 2000; Lawson 2006; Meunier and McNamara 2007; Farrell and Newman 2010; Fioretos 2011; Morrison 2012; Buzan and Little 2015.

[71] Cox and Sinclair 1996; Avant et al. 2010; Fligstein and McAdam 2012; Nance and Cottrell 2014; De Búrca et al. 2014; Sending 2015; Sending et al. 2015; Grabel 2017; Bueger 2018.

practices over time. Only then do we see when governing arrangements change, or not.

An order often disproportionately benefits its most powerful members. In turn, that affects punishments. Often there is a hegemon (or set of powerful actors) that is willing to impose punishments on the weaker actors in the subsystem. A hegemon itself might not face any punishment because there is no one to impose it. For instance, when President Trump threatened to break up the North American Free Trade Agreement (NAFTA), there was little that Canada or Mexico could do to punish the United States, other than to point out the significant economic benefits that NAFTA provided to sizeable parts of the US economy, and try to negotiate a new agreement that preserved most of what was valuable.[72] Still, a hegemon is often wise to maintain an order even when it faces no punishment for noncompliance because setting up a new, alternative order is costly. Consequently, hegemons often play a key role in maintaining an international order's stability.

Partial Hegemony and Instruments of Coercion

I have developed two of my three theoretical ideas: subsystems and the variables that explain change (strategic benefits and punishments). My core hypothesis, recall, is that those benefits and punishments are specific to a given subsystem— even after a major system-wide shock that affects many subsystems.

Changes to strategic benefits or punishments can happen for lots of reasons. Sometimes a new problem like climate change emerges in the world, which changes the goals that actors have. More commonly, the goals remain roughly the same but the ability to capture mutual gains or impose punishments changes. One particular source of those changes cries out for special attention: hegemonic decline.

How do changes in strategic benefits and punishments for noncompliance relate to hegemony? To answer that question, I offer my third and final theoretical idea: instruments of coercion. Those instruments are the source of punishments for noncompliance, and they also sometimes shape strategic benefits. Hegemons and other powerful actors have various instruments of coercion that they can use. Their cost-effectiveness can change over time as a result of world events or technological changes (affecting all actors), or internal shifts within an actor (affecting just one actor, initially). Changes in actors' ability to use their instruments of coercion can lead to change in governing arrangements—depending on the

---

[72] Those efforts yielded the US-Mexico-Canada Agreement that entered into force in 2020.

subsystem. Different instruments of coercion will be more or less relevant for different types of governance questions.

Multiple instruments of coercion exist,[73] but three are particularly prevalent: military coercion, economic coercion, and leadership selection. Military coercion stems from the threat, and occasional use, of military force to achieve a particular goal. For instance, the United States has regularly demanded that actors in the Middle East refrain from conquest or revision of territorial borders and it has threatened military force against those who would try. Sometimes, as in the war against Iraq in 1990–1991, the United States makes good on that threat.

A second instrument of coercion is economic, which stems from the ability to open or restrict access to capital, goods, resources, or other economic flows. States can use controls of their own borders to exercise this type of coercion on others who seek access to their domestic markets, but they can also exert coercive power internationally.[74] Sanctions, embargoes, and boycotts are examples. Banks and credit markets can also coerce struggling borrowers into repaying by threatening access to future credit.[75]

Finally, the third instrument of coercion is leadership selection. It involves an actor's ability to appoint or remove a political executive in a foreign polity, whether by overt means (e.g., imperial appointment of a colonial governor) or covert means (e.g., assassination of a foreign leader or coup d'état). Whereas military coercion confronts a state's armed forces, leadership selection is directed against a handful of individuals (e.g., the ruling executive and his guard). Empires could select leaders of subordinate polities directly, as the British did in Iraq, Egypt, and elsewhere; or they could appoint powerful "advisors," as they did in Iran. The United States and the Soviet Union did not want to appear imperial but often behaved that way, such as when the United States supported Batista in Cuba or put Pinochet in power in Chile. That behavior is not limited to the distant past—witness US support for leadership change in Venezuela in the twenty-first century—but it has grown more politically costly and hence rarer. In sum, the availability of three instruments of coercion changes over time and across subsystems.

The leading actor of a subsystem is not necessarily a hegemon. Saudi Arabia is the leading actor in the global oil-production subsystem at present, but it is not hegemonic. Hegemony—pure or partial—is defined in terms of actors' instruments of coercion, not subsystems. It is a status that exists across subsystems. Still, a partial hegemon tends to play a leading role in many

---

[73] Such as soft power (Nye 2004) and other forms of power (Baldwin 1989).
[74] Farrell and Newman 2019.
[75] Tomz 2007; Wellhausen 2015.

subsystems because of its size and capabilities. If an actor is a partial hegemon in one subsystem, it is necessarily a partial hegemon in the other subsystems of that time and region. Currently, the United States is partially hegemonic.

A partial hegemon can find that some of its instruments of coercion are in decline while others remain strong or get stronger. Over time, a state's power inevitably changes relative to others. This was the situation that the United States found itself in during the 1970s, with huge consequences for oil. Change in an actor's ability to use one of its instruments of coercion will affect the punishments it can impose, or the benefits it can offer, in some subsystems but not others. For instance, the United States' ability to appoint or remove a leader in Iraq might be relevant for oil production (because Iraq and its neighbors have huge proven oil reserves), but rather less relevant for decisions about how to contain global pandemics (because Iraq has no special role in disease prevention).

Consequently, the effect of hegemonic decline on international order can sometimes be like squeezing a balloon: its form shifts but stays intact. A partial hegemon, experiencing a shift in its capabilities, tends to reach for new or underused instruments of coercion to achieve whichever of its goals still seem feasible.[76] The extent to which it can preserve old governing arrangements depends on how its available instruments of coercion generate benefits and punishments in a particular subsystem (as in Figure 2.1). The perceived legitimacy of the governing arrangements will affect its ability to punish or reward. In subsystems where the partial hegemon cannot sustain old arrangements, it might use the arrangements in other subsystems to compensate, or at least achieve some of its goals.

Even if hegemonic decline does not mean the collapse of all governing arrangements, it often brings unpleasant surprises for the hegemon. Great powers tend to overestimate the strategic benefits that an international order offers other actors. There is no rational reason that hegemons must misrecognize other actors' benefits from an order, but they often do misread them anyway. Psychological biases[77] and sociological factors[78] suggest that actors who benefit disproportionately from a situation are unlikely to fully reckon the level of their privilege. For example, European imperial metropoles deluded themselves about how much their empires benefited the colonized, and sometimes they were surprised when newly independent states rejected parts of the economic or social order after decolonization. Thus, in various African

---

[76] More generally, all actors (not just a hegemon) will reach for new or underused policy instruments when the systemic conditions of world politics change in ways that threaten existing governing arrangements.

[77] Jervis 1976; McDermott 2004; Kertzer and Rathbun 2015.

[78] Fligstein and McAdam 2012: 11.

countries, newly sovereign states expropriated or threw out British-owned mining businesses, much to the shock and dismay of the British owners.[79] Their surprise indicates that the British were misperceiving the benefits of empire, not just tactically overstating them. Sometimes hegemons probably also overstate the benefits in an effort to bolster their legitimacy. Yet genuine misperception appears common. Thus, an order often rests more heavily on coercion than a powerful state realizes.

Implications of Subsystems Theory

Major power wars are not the only way order changes in a given subsystem. That implication of my argument contravenes a great deal of existing scholarship about international order.[80] It is true that major wars disrupt international systems and create change. I view those changes as primarily altering the benefits and punishments that various actors can mete out. World War II, for example, dismembered the German and Japanese empires, leaving them unable to impose the punishments on their neighbors, or offer the benefits, that they previously could. At the same time, the war increased the reach of the United States and USSR. But wars are not the only causes—change can and does happen in peacetime, quite commonly. That should give us hope when it comes to addressing peacetime challenges like climate change without recourse to war.

A second implication involves international institutions, both formal and informal.[81] Institutions play a double role in international order. On one hand, they are often manifestations or indicators of an order, and thus change simultaneously with it. For example, the elimination of the WTO would be a major change in the order for international trade. On the other hand, states and other actors can sometimes use institutions, especially new institutions, to change an international order.[82] For example, states that were dissatisfied with the International Energy Agency (IEA) created the International Renewable Energy Agency (IRENA) as a way to shift practices of global energy governance.[83] In this sense, change in some institutions can occur before the central governing

---

[79] Stockwell 2000.

[80] Giplin 1981; Ikenberry 2000; Lascurettes 2020.

[81] On informal institutions, see Stone 2011; Kleine 2013; Vabulas and Snidal 2013; Colgan and Van de Graaf 2015.

[82] Morse and Keohane 2014.

[83] Van de Graaf 2013. Similarly, actors dissatisfied with the World Health Organization created UN AIDS and the Global Vaccine Alliance (see Morse and Keohane 2014).

arrangements of an international order change. Whether institutions change prior to the shift in central governing arrangements, or simultaneously with it, some sort of innovation occurs.

So subsystems theory implies that *when the international order in a subsystem is upended or modified, it is associated with institutional innovation.*[84] This corollary modifies existing scholarship, which shows *why* states create and maintain international institutions as a way of minimizing transaction and information costs.[85] The corollary here focuses instead on *when* international institutions are created or changed.

The third major implication is that *while international relations are a complex, adaptive system, changes in international order follow a common underlying logic.*[86] Subsystems theory is consistent with the idea of complexity because it views governing arrangements as changing over time. They are durable but not permanent. The chief problem for those emphasizing the complexity and adaptivity of international relations, however, is that their line of argument tends to destroy the whole basis for social science, namely, that we can learn from the past. If we simply say that everything is complex and in flux, then we learn nothing. Instead, we should think about politics on three levels: behavior, scope conditions, and incentive-response.

Behavior changes frequently; scope conditions (like governing arrangements) change less frequently but they still change. Response to incentives, however, is permanent. Scholars worrying about complexity emphasize how much of our political knowledge is bounded within scope conditions that change, but they tend to overlook the permanence of incentive-response. Response to incentives is a basic characteristic of human (and animal) behavior, rooted in basic needs like food and shelter. The specific incentives—that is, benefits and punishments— change over time, but the fact that humans respond to them does not. That permanence creates the basis for a common logic for how governing arrangements change over time.

---

[84] This is a descriptive rather than causal claim, because institutions and order are mutually constitutive. When the order in a subsystem does not change, or it is eliminated completely, we can expect no institutional innovation.

[85] Keohane 1984; see also Lipscy 2017.

[86] Scholars commonly treat international relations as deterministic and Newtonian, which enables the search for generalizable patterns of political behavior. The goal is to find empirical regularities of the form "If X, then Y." However, a growing and intellectualy diverse chorus of scholars decries that view, instead arguing that international relations are complex and adaptive: see Jervis 1997; Gunitsky 2013; Katzenstein and Seybert 2018; Oatley 2019. Their basic insight is that generalizable patterns of behavior are recurring but not permanent. They point out, correctly, the limitations of searching for generalizable behavioral patterns when those patterns are specific to underlying conditions, and those conditions change. For instance, social scientists might theorize and test for a particular type of behavior, treating the governing arrangements that shape that behavior as fixed. Their findings about the behavior are limited in scope to the time and space when the governing arrangements hold constant. Sometimes scholars recognize that scope condition explicitly (to their credit); sometimes they do not.

Using the Theory: Oil Politics

To this point, this chapter has moved from a particular question (how to understand oil politics) to the abstract (theory of international order). Now we can return to the particulars of oil politics, armed with theory modified by my three core ideas.

I begin by considering how decolonization in the mid-twentieth century reduced the degree to which powerful actors could impose punishments for noncompliance. Decolonization means the dismantling of an empire.[87] One of the most remarkable transitions in all of human history occurred in the twentieth century.[88] In the year 1900, empires were the world's dominant form of political organization; by 2000, they were almost extinct. One can quibble about precisely when decolonization happened, and acknowledge that it happened at different times for different empires. The peak of decolonization, however, was between 1945 and 1970 when imperial powers granted independence to over seventy colonies, a rate far exceeding any previous or subsequent period.[89] The period between 1947 and 1960 was particularly intense.

Decolonization made it harder for great power states to use coercion against (formerly) colonial peoples.[90] That increase in the cost of coercion applied not just to imperial metropoles but also even to other great powers like the United States because it changed ideas worldwide about self-determination and racial equality.[91] Those ideational changes had consequences even for countries that were not formal empires, as the United States discovered in Vietnam. In my theoretical terms, decolonization reduced the cost-effectiveness of some instruments of coercion, especially leader selection.[92] After decolonization, it was rarer and more costly, though sometimes still possible, for great powers to choose who

---

[87] Different people use the term *empire* in vastly different ways (Nexon and Wright 2007; Barkey and Hagen 1997; Dawisha and Parrott 1997; Lutz 2009; Burbank and Cooper 2010; Jamal 2012; Morefield 2014; Nicolaidis et al. 2015). I define empire as a system of interaction between two political entities, one of which exerts political control over the internal and external policy of the other. That definition follows Michael Doyle's (Doyle 1986: 12, 19) renowned work on the subject, except that my conception is politically formal and direct. I do not include "informal" empires (Gallagher and Robinson 1953; Doyle 1986). Latin America in the nineteenth century, for example, was not part of the British Empire, even if the British did have influence there. Legal formality is unnecessary for empire, but direct political control of internal and external policy is required.

[88] Getachew 2019

[89] Philpott 2001: 155. Various forms of imperial contraction and decolonization had occurred prior to the twentieth century, including a wave in the late eighteenth/early nineteenth century (Abernethy 2002). What makes the twentieth century special is that formal empires had never before retreated from the globe so completely as they did by the year 2000.

[90] Decolonization and an increase in the costliness of coercion occurred together, and the causal arrow probably points in both directions.

[91] Philpott 2001; Crawford 2002; Morefield 2014; Getachew 2019.

[92] Decolonization also seems to have affected the incentives of postcolonial states to fight their near neighbors (Henderson 2009) and civil wars (Henderson and Singer 2000). Those incentives, however, are separate from my focus on great powers' instruments of coercion.

would run the government of distant subordinate nations. In turn, that had a profound effect on the global oil system.

Oil Subsystems

Subsystems theory relies on identifying key governing questions, by empirical induction.[93] For oil, there are two: production and security. The first question is, How much oil will be produced in each territory? The answer to that question shapes the global supply of oil, and hence its price. In the 1950s and 1960s, the so-called Seven Sisters[94] governed oil production as a cartel or oligopoly, in which each member had global oil production. They coordinated effectively, keeping oil prices steady and relatively low. In the 1970s, OPEC displaced the Seven Sisters as the key governing arrangement over oil production. OPEC wrought great changes in the 1970s but thereafter was unable to function as a cartel, as the next two chapters show. Given the importance of oil prices, many observers have treated this subsystem as *the* central governing question for oil.

However, there is also a second crucial governance question, which has to do with jurisdiction or sovereignty over oil (see chapter 5). The international distribution of oil fields matters partly because jurisdiction tends to imply ownership, or at least a share of the profits. Less obvious, but even more important, the distribution of oil fields generates market power. If a single state controls much of the world's oil, it can act as a monopolist, thereby exerting influence on the world's oil price. It might also limit access to oil supplies for certain buyers. Perpetually worried about energy security, countries that import oil have strong incentives to prevent that type of monopoly, and might use military force to do so.[95] Hence the key question for oil's second subsystem is, What portion of the world's oil reserves is under the jurisdiction of each state? Distinguishing this second subsystem (oil security) from the first (oil production) is vital because historically they changed at markedly different rates and in different directions. Savvy policymaking requires this understanding.

The central dynamics of global oil are structured by just these two subsystems. Admittedly, there are other questions of interest, such as about prices, the risk of embargoes, or the relationship between firms and states in producing territories. As significant as these are, however, closer inspection shows them to

---

[93] An analyst must identify subsystems by empirical inference. I illustrate how to do this: see chapter 3 and especially chapter 5. In chapter 6, I provide a more generalized, conceptual description of how analysts can identify subsystems.

[94] Recall from chapter 1 this nickname for the major Anglo-American oil companies, now known as ExxonMobil, Shell, BP, and Chevron.

[95] Kelanic 2020.

be second-order concerns at the global level. For example, while prices fluctuate for lots of reasons, in the medium term they are heavily influenced by the fundamentals of supply—which is the topic of the first oil subsystem (production).[96] Likewise, an oil embargo can be quite damaging, but embargoes are difficult to make effective in a global market with lots of oil exporters, which brings us back to the significance of the second oil subsystem (distribution of sovereignty over oil fields).[97] Finally, the relationship between firms and states can be significant for national political dynamics and corruption,[98] but at the global level their effect on oil markets is modest because the amount of "government take" from a state's oil industry depends only marginally on which arrangements it uses to extract it: taxes, royalties, production sharing, service agreements, etc.[99]

Perhaps the strongest candidate for a third subsystem in oil politics would revolve around the question, Under what conditions can oil be bought and sold internationally? The question is important because the United States uses sanctions in the oil market to apply political pressure.[100] At various times, it has restricted North Korea's access to import oil, and Iraq or Iran's ability to export it. Yet, there is little about these sanctions that make them uniquely a part of *oil* politics. The real dispute is usually about nuclear weapons or some other matter; oil is simply a convenient tool of coercion. Moreover, these sanctions generally affect small fractions of the world's total oil market at any given time.[101] Instead, they can be understood adequately within the broader category of economic sanctions that might apply to any commodity or economic good, about which much has been written.[102] Consequently, the two subsystems of production and security rise above all others in importance for understanding the dynamics of global oil.

Understanding Change in Oil Politics

Subsystems theory suggests that changes in the independent variables (strategic benefits and punishments for noncompliance) should cause change in international order, the dependent variable. Using the theory requires a way to assess changes in the variables at the subsystem level.

Assessing the variables is best done with comparisons rather than trying to calculate an absolute value. For instance, it is easier to say that strategic benefits

---

[96] Long-run prices are also affected by world demand. Demand is mostly an exogenous factor, driven by economics and technology.

[97] Gholz and Press 2010.

[98] Luong and Weinthal 2010; Ross 2012; Victor et al. 2012.

[99] Kyle 2014.

[100] On the United States' ability to use the "oil weapon," see Hughes and Long 2014.

[101] Gholz and Press 2010.

[102] Martin 1993; Drezner 1999; Farrell and Newman 2019.

increased or declined over time than it is to quantify them. In addition, changes in these variables are often linked to a change in an instrument of coercion.

Four types of indicators are useful to assess the variables. First, observable institutional changes can point to changes in the variables. When subordinate actors gain institutional capacities, for example, it can weaken powerful actors' ability to punish them. Such institutional changes, like the legal ability to nationalize an oil sector of a newly sovereign government, are directly observable. Second, structural changes can point to changes in the variables. An order's strategic benefits often depend on structural changes, such as in market conditions or technology.[103] Third, certain events can indirectly reveal the variables' values. For example, when a state calls for external military assistance because it fears for its survival, it reveals the strategic benefits of an order that allows for such a call to be made.[104] Fourth, evidence of actors' *perceptions* of the benefits and expected punishments is important for assessing the strength of those benefits and punishments.[105]

Table 2.1 maps the theory's variables in two time periods for each subsystem, generating four broad case-sets.[106] (Each "case-set" involves dozens of observations of different countries at various time periods.) Decolonization plays a key role: it weakened the powerful actors' (US and UK) ability to use leadership selection and economic coercion. By contrast, military coercion was still feasible, and perhaps even easier over time. In turn, those shifts in instruments of coercion proved crucial for the oil production subsystem (which changed dramatically), but not very important for the oil security subsystem.

Consider "Subsystem A," focused on oil production, in the first two rows of the table. In chapter 3 I show how the pre-OPEC order was held in place by punishments (e.g., economic coercion and quasi-imperial leadership selection) and strategic benefits (e.g., producers had incentives to work with

---

[103] As Keohane and Milner (1996) showed, an exogenous easing of international trade can increase the benefits of international cooperation, and thus affect order.

[104] Such demonstrative events might occur only rarely but they tend to be a long-lasting indicator of the order's value. Those events can also indicate a variable's value not only for the actors directly involved (e.g., the state that calls for help) but also for similar actors in similar circumstances. However, measurement based on demonstrative events is tricky. It depends on the analyst making informed judgments about whether the conditions that existed when the event occurred apply to other actors or other times.

[105] Actors' perceptions matter in part because they assist us in gauging the underlying material and social conditions. Perceptions also matter for behavior, even if those perceptions are wrong or slow to adjust. For example, weak actors in a system will hesitate to defect from an order if they believe the risk of punishment is high, even if the system's powerful actors have privately decided that they will no longer impose punishments for noncompliance. Measuring perceptions is also tricky: one cannot directly observe mental beliefs, and what actors say and write can be deceptive. Again, the analyst must make informed judgments.

[106] Compared to other economic goods, states have strong incentives to protect oil supplies and access from predation. So non-petrostates get fewer benefits to security relationships with powerful actors.

Table 2.1 Independent and Dependent Variables

	Time Period	IV: Punishment	IV: Strategic Benefits	Order (DV = chg. in order)	Institutions	Consequences
Oil Production (chapter 3–4) aka Subsystem A	Pre-1970	*Strong* (but weaker after 1950s)	*High:* Market incentives for petrostates to sell oil to international firms	Seven Sisters dominate market	Companies dominant, fledgling OPEC	Low, steady prices; rents accrue to Seven Sisters
	Post-1970	*Weak*	*Low:* Market conditions favor sales to traders by petrostates	*Order upended:* OPEC and nationalization	*High innovation:* OPEC, plus later IEA, OFID	Higher prices; rents accrue to petrostates
Oil Security (chapter 5) aka Subsystem B	Pre-1970	*Strong* (but weaker after 1950s)	*High:* Oil needs protection; other goods mostly don't	Patron protection	Imperial ties	Late decolonization for petrostates
	Post-1970	*Mixed:* Oil-for-security becomes optional for petrostates, but great powers can still defend them	*High:* Oil still needs protection	*Order largely preserved:* Patron protection	*Low innovation:* oil-for-security deals replace empire	US presence in Gulf

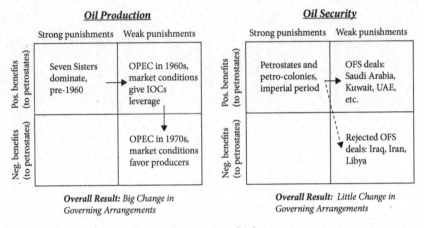

Figure 2.2 Change in order over time in two oil subsystems

the Anglo-American companies to get sales to customers worldwide). The petrostates then created OPEC in 1960, but could not yet overturn the Seven Sisters' order. In the 1970s, as market conditions changed, OPEC seized the opportunity to transform the order. Then, circa 1980, it sought to act as a cartel that limited world oil supply. Chapter 4 shows why OPEC proved thoroughly ineffective in that later effort.

While order in Subsystem A changed dramatically, it remained relatively constant in Subsystem B, focused on the military-sovereignty aspect of oil. Whereas Britain had previously protected various territories as part of its empire, decolonization meant that oil-for-security deals emerged as a more explicit feature of postcolonial Middle East politics. Britain and the United States offered protection to various petrostates in exchange for their cooperation associated with oil. The strategic benefit that was fundamental to this behavior was the fact that weakly defended, oil-rich territories made inviting targets of conquest, motivating powerful oil consumers to provide military protection. That held true even after decolonization. Thus, many petrostates continued to receive Anglo-American protection even as formal imperial authority dissolved. Some states rejected these deals over time, but others maintained them with little need for institutional innovation.[107] Only the identity of the external protector changed, in some cases, from Britain to the United States.

Figure 2.2 sketches how international order in the two subsystems changed over time. In Subsystem A, change came after the second of two shifts. First,

---

[107] The Gulf Cooperation Council, created in 1981, is only a superficial form of cooperation. The oil-for-security deals predated it and were little affected by it.

decolonization weakened the Anglo-American ability to select or remove leaders. The Seven Sisters' control and decision-making authority over production, however, was still in place (i.e., the old order). That situation demonstrates how crucial non-state actors—commercial firms, in this case—can be for international order. Then, when market conditions changed after about 1970, OPEC members responded by upending the order. The transformation in Subsystem A involved considerable institutional innovation: in OPEC (which innovated continuously in the 1960s and 1970s), and the creation of the International Energy Agency (IEA), the OPEC Fund for International Development (OFID), and others. In Subsystem B, much less change occurred over time. The two diverging arrows indicate that many petrostates maintained their oil-for-security deals after the decolonization period, while a few rejected them. Overall, the order in Subsystem B remained more stable than in Subsystem A.

Whom strategic benefits accrue to can be important. Figure 2.1 abstracted away from this question because in principle every actors' benefits matter. When explaining oil politics, however, it is necessary to be more precise. Figure 2.2 focuses specifically on the *petrostates'* strategic benefits of the pre-1960 order. That order also generated strategic benefits to the United States and Britain, of course. Those benefits were positive throughout this history, so I set them aside as a constant background. What matters is the variation in the petrostates' incentives.

Conclusion

Being able to see, and then properly explain, both change and continuity in international order is crucial for IR theory. I have argued that a new approach can help us understand global oil politics—or any area of IR. Three key modifications improve existing theories of international order: subsystems; two explanatory factors of change (benefits and punishments); and instruments of coercion. Together, these ideas reveal that international order is not monolithic. Instead, it exists within subsystems, which are anchored by a single question of governance or decision-making.

Moreover, subsystems theory provides us with expectations about when change occurs in international order. A partial hegemon losing some of its instruments of coercion will not simply fade, as some hegemonic theories might suggest. In fact, a declining hegemon might be able to prop up some governing arrangements that help compensate for the loss of others.

This new way of understanding international order in oil will generate some surprises for theorists of international relations. Contrary to some realist theories, for example, international order allows for a certain amount of functional differentiation between states, meaning that they specialize at different things.[108] Oil-for-security deals allowed some states to function as oil suppliers, protected by their patrons, even after formal imperial bonds disappeared. That meant that some petrostates (those that accepted the oil-for-security deals) did not devote themselves to militarily protecting their borders, even though they faced external threats. Instead, they chose to accept an international order in which another state supplied their military defense. This arrangement was most visibly demonstrated in Kuwait and Saudi Arabia in 1990–1991. In the context of the international system as a whole, the petrostates' function was *not* just self-help; instead, petrostates served as reliable oil suppliers to other states.[109]

The key surprise for most theorists, however, is in the relationship between the hegemon and international order. International order is not something that a hegemon simply forges after a major power war and does its best to sustain thereafter. Instead, the changing nature of partial hegemony over time leads to significant changes in international order outside of major power wars. Those changes occur in subsystems. At any given point in time, some subsystems are changing while others are relatively constant.

The next few chapters show how these ideas apply in oil politics. I postpone some broader questions—how does the aggregate theme(s) of international order emerge from individual subsystems? And under what conditions do ordering themes change?—until chapter 6. For now, my analytic focus is on the movements between the boxes in Figure 2.2, which helps make sense of the history of oil. A great story awaits.

---

[108] Waltz (1979) argues that anarchy implies functional differentiation is impossible because each state must focus on defending itself from the others. Subsystems theory shows that functional differentiation cannot be dismissed.

[109] Structural realists might object, responding that their theory applies only to great powers, not to the behavior of smaller players like most petrostates. Yet, this response only gets us back to their assumption that international order can be understood by looking at great powers only, which is deeply flawed.

3

The Rise of OPEC

"It is even probable that the supremacy of nations may be determined by the possession of available petroleum and its products."[1]
—President Calvin Coolidge, 1926

In global oil politics, it is not just kings and presidents who shape the flows of wealth and power. There are also people like Juan Pablo Pérez Alfonzo of Venezuela and Abdullah Tariki of Saudi Arabia, the founders of OPEC. Pérez Alfonzo and Tariki knew that their countries did not control their most valuable natural resource. What they wanted was nothing short of an economic sequel to decolonization.

Juan Pablo Pérez Alfonzo was an idealist. Born in Caracas in 1903, he saw earlier than most that oil politics would shape his country's political trajectory, for better and for worse.[2] An ascetic vegetarian and a strict ecologist, Pérez Alfonzo wanted to see his country's oil resources used wisely to benefit his country's people. Initially a medical student, he switched to law and eventually obtained a PhD in political and social sciences at the Central University of Venezuela. He was an outspoken political activist, founded the political party Acción Democrática, and served in Venezuela's first, short-lived democratic government from 1945 to 1948. Later imprisoned and exiled, he returned to Venezuela in the late 1950s with a vision to reshape the oil industry.

Abdullah Tariki was born in 1919 in Najd before it was integrated into Saudi Arabia. Tariki's father was a camel driver who organized caravans between Najd and the British colony of Kuwait. From these humble beginnings, he earned a chemistry degree from Cairo University and a master's degree in engineering from the University of Texas in 1947. After working briefly for Texaco, Tariki returned to his homeland to represent Saudi Arabia at the meetings of the Arab League's Oil Experts, which met in Cairo. He swiftly became a Nasserite and an Arab Nationalist, putting him at odds with the Saudi regime when he returned to Riyadh. He predicted to the *New York Times* in 1958, "we will soon have a

---

[1] Quoted in Auzanneau 2018: 108.
[2] Karl 1997: 23.

constitution; this country will shortly become a constitutional monarchy."[3] Despite his political views, the Saudi royals appointed him in 1960 as their first minister of petroleum and natural resources. He was an intriguing and complicated man who was destined to become a friend and admirer of Pérez Alfonzo.

In this chapter and the next I deal with one of the central questions of the global oil industry: How much oil will be produced in each territory? This question sits at the heart of what I call Subsystem A in oil politics. The history can be divided into three periods. The Seven Sisters oil companies dominated the first period, prior to the creation of OPEC in 1960.[4] They provided capital and technical expertise to produce, refine, and sell the oil. In exchange, the companies paid petrostate governments some combination of fixed concession fees (for access to oil fields, regardless of production amounts), taxes (on profits from production), and royalties (per barrel produced, regardless of profit). Petrostates that made trouble were punished. The second period, roughly from 1960 to 1974, was marked by the rise of OPEC as a serious organization. The period ended as OPEC overthrew the Seven Sisters' oligopoly, in part by nationalizing their oil. The third period began in the late 1970s and continues through today. Quite different political and market behavior characterizes each period.

This chapter explores three specific issues. First, what was the pre-OPEC economic order for oil, and how was it sustained? The oil companies, with the support of Great Britain and the United States, imposed real punishments on those who tried to defect from the order. They had strong instruments of coercion, including forcible change of a state or colony's political leader. It was not all bad for the petrostates: they reaped strategic benefits in the form of financial rewards. As long as the global oil market was loose (i.e., there was abundant supply), the Anglo-American oil companies had the upper hand and could prevent nationalization.

Second, how and why did the order change in the early 1970s? In the 1960s, decolonization meant the risk of punishment had declined. Britain and the United States were losing their instruments of coercion over petrostates: the difficulty of selecting or removing leaders, especially, rose. Perceptions of change were gradual, however, because petrostates were understandably uncertain about how much the risk of punishment had actually declined. Loose oil market conditions also meant that the existing order still offered the petrostates positive strategic benefits, relative to the risks of trying to operate outside of the Seven Sisters' system. But in the early 1970s, market conditions changed rapidly. In effect, those conditions raised the attractiveness of potential alternative governing arrangements to petrostates, thus lowering the relative benefits of the

---

[3] Quoted in Skeet 1988: 7.
[4] Sampson 2009; Painter 1986.

existing system. OPEC led the effort to develop those alternative arrangements, supported by a transnational group of anticolonial elites with new ideas. In this period, OPEC operated as a kind of collective bargaining unit working to alter the petrostates' relationship with the Seven Sisters. In that role, it ultimately proved highly successful.

Third, what were the consequences of those changes in the global energy order, especially in terms of who ultimately received the economic benefits of oil? The ripple effects were huge. Foreign aid, political influence, and even transnational terrorism took on new patterns. This chapter and the next trace some of those consequences.

The Seven Sisters in the Pre-OPEC Period

The modern age of oil in the Middle East began in 1908 with the discovery of commercial quantities of oil in what was then Persia, now Iran. The Anglo-Persian Oil Company that made the 1908 discovery eventually became British Petroleum, and by the 1930s the Seven Sisters dominated the oil scene. A French company called Compagnie française des pétroles (CFP), known today as Total, was also a player. Still, the global market was largely Anglo-American. Together, the Seven Sisters owned the exploration and production rights to almost all of the oil in the territories that are now known as Iran, Iraq, Saudi Arabia, and the smaller Gulf monarchies.

To operate successfully as an oligopoly, the Seven Sisters needed to solve two cooperation problems. The first was internal: they had to make sure that they could trust each other to stick to their agreements. They largely solved this problem by legally tying their hands together. Gradually, they developed a system of interlocking ownership over the big oil concessions around the world, especially in Iraq, Saudi Arabia, and later Iran. For example, Exxon, Mobil, Shell, the Anglo-Iranian Oil Company (the forerunner of BP), and the French company CFP jointly owned the Iraq Petroleum Company, which controlled the rights to produce essentially all of Iraq's oil.

Already by the 1920s, it was starting to become clear that vast amounts of oil were available in the Middle East—too much oil, in fact, to suit the oil companies. Oil prices were already volatile and sometimes too low for profitability. The companies wanted to control the speed at which oil fields were developed so they could restrict supply. In 1928, the major companies started to collude internationally. First, they signed the "Red Line Agreement," in which they agreed not to produce oil in the Middle East unless they all acted in partnership with each other. Drawn on a map, the "Red Line" enclosed the entire area from Turkey to Yemen, including Iraq, Saudi Arabia, and Qatar (though not Kuwait or Iran). Later that same year, Exxon, BP, and Royal Dutch-Shell also signed the Achnacarry (or "As Is") Agreement, in which they divided the market and promised not to engage in price competition. Although both the Red Line and Achnacarry agreements were dissolved by the late 1940s, their legacy continued to shape the oil industry for the next several decades, even after the deals were formally abandoned, by establishing a system of posted prices and by tying the companies together through joint ownership of various oil fields. OPEC would eventually rebel against that system of control.

Fatefully, the Red Line Agreement included Saudi Arabia, which in 1928 was only just integrating as a single country. Chevron and Texaco, two companies that had not signed the Red Line Agreement, discovered oil in Saudi Arabia in 1938. A few years later, they created the Arabian American Oil Company, known as Aramco. The massive Saudi oil fields threatened to undermine the supply management scheme in the emerging subsystem for oil production. It was that threat that led Exxon and Mobil (separate companies at the time) to abandon the Red Line Agreement in 1948 and purchase part of Aramco. Abandoning the Red Line Agreement created diplomatic complications, necessitating help from the US State Department to win acquiescence from the British and French. Even so, the Aramco deal was a victory for the oligopoly. Once under the joint control of four of the seven majors, Aramco's production was kept within strict limits.[5]

The Seven Sisters knowingly acted as an oligopoly to shut in vast amounts of potential oil supplies, thereby propping up prices. In Saudi Arabia, for instance, Aramco executives later privately admitted to the US government that it "would be perfectly feasible for our reserves to sustain a production of 20 [million barrels per day]," a figure publicly confirmed by the Saudi government in 1973.[6] Yet as late as 1970, Saudi production was only about 3.8 million barrels per day. An Exxon vice president explained why to US Senate investigators in 1974: "If we had used any one [producer country] to capacity, then we would have to shut the other back. There was no place to go with [the oil]. You can't dump it in the sea."[7] Excess oil production would have cratered the price, which the Seven Sisters had no intention of allowing. By 1970, Saudi production costs were estimated at only 12 or 13 cents per barrel, while sale prices ("posted prices") were roughly USD 2 per barrel.[8] Oligopolistic cooperation thus generated vast profits for the Seven Sisters.

In short, the oil companies used interlocking ownership to collude together. Those ownership arrangements were sufficient, because the benefits of

---

[5] This paragraph borrows from McFarland and Colgan 2018.

[6] Aramco visitor brief materials included with letter from CEO Frank Jungers to Joe Johnston, July 24, 1973; see US Senate 1975 ("the Church Report"): 519. (See also McFarland and Colgan 2018.)

[7] US Senate 1975, quoted in McFarland and Colgan 2018.

[8] US Senate 1975: 2, quoted in McFarland and Colgan 2018.

cooperation dwarfed any incentive for the companies to cheat on one another. Although they did bicker with each other, they were far more preoccupied with maintaining their favorable market position against the competition: the so-called independents, like Conoco, Philips, and Atlantic Richfield in the United States. The Seven Sisters had access to the low-cost oil fields around the world, and the market power that came with that access provided large strategic benefits to working together.

The second problem the Seven Sisters faced was external: they needed cooperation from the oil-producing governments like Iran or Kuwait. The companies not only wanted to retain their exclusive legal rights over the oil fields, known as concessions, but also wanted to minimize the costs associated with producing in those territories. Those costs included taxes and royalties paid to host governments.

Prior to World War II, the companies were able to obtain this cooperation relatively easily because of imperialism. The Seven Sisters benefited greatly from the Anglo-American political control and influence in the Middle East. For instance, when the Iraqi oil concession was "negotiated" in 1925, the British threatened to cleave oil-rich Mosul from the rest of the country and thereby "compelled the Iraqi negotiator to be lenient with the oil companies," according to Nadim Pachachi, an OPEC secretary general.[9] The British Empire had a strong presence in the Middle East, with one exception: Saudi Arabia. The Saudi king preferred to have American partners, who were more distant than the British, and thus, he hoped, less intrusive.

The Anglo-American oil companies extracted most of the profits from the production and sale of oil during this period, in the Middle East and elsewhere. The petrostates and the international oil companies (IOCs) bargained continuously over taxes and royalties, as the governments constantly sought, and gradually obtained, a larger portion of the oil profits. The IOCs gave ground as slowly as they could, responding to government demands with the threat of reducing production. For instance, from 1938 to 1946, Venezuela's tax rate rose too quickly for the companies' tastes, meaning that the share of government income coming from oil tax revenue increased from 35 to 65 percent. In response, the oil companies ramped up production in the Middle East while growing it more slowly in Venezuela. As Venezuela's Pérez Alfonzo later said, "Middle East petroleum had become a constant pressure factor and has been brandished against us as a threat by the oil companies."[10]

In 1945, a coup d'état put a new Venezuelan government in power with Romulo Betancourt as president. He asked Pérez Alfonzo, who had been the

---

[9] Quoted in Dietrich 2017: 95.
[10] Quoted in Terzian 1985: 5.

leading critic of the Petroleum Law of 1943, to serve as minister of development. This was Pérez Alfonzo's first real experience in the practical politics of dealing with the IOCs. Pérez Alfonzo argued that the 1943 law gave the companies an unfair 60/40 split of the profits, and he insisted on revisions to the tax laws. That created what became known as a 50/50 deal, which split the profits between the host governments and the IOCs equally. The companies were upset with Venezuela and retaliated by threatening to move their operations to the Middle East. In response, Pérez Alfonzo encouraged Saudi Arabia, Kuwait, Iraq, and other countries to adopt agreements on the same 50/50 principle, which they did over the next decade.[11] That principle became the global norm until 1970. Still, Venezuela and other petrostate governments had little say in how much oil the companies actually produced each year, which determined the size of their payments. Leaders in petrostates resented this arrangement, and none more than Pérez Alfonzo.[12]

The situation made nationalization an attractive option for petrostates. Governments around the world, even in developed countries, found that there were limits to how much of the oil industry profits they could extract from international oil companies by way of taxes, royalties, or concession fees. If a government demanded a payment rate that was too high, companies could always respond by slowing exploration and production in one country and expanding elsewhere.[13] Nationalization offered a potential solution to that problem—*if* the nationalized company could operate as efficiently and profitably as a private company. Most petrostates wanted to try.[14]

Oil-producing countries faced three major obstacles to gaining full authority over the oil production in their own territory. First, and perhaps foremost, was a legal-political problem, not for Venezuela, but for other future OPEC members like Kuwait, Libya, and Nigeria. In the immediate postwar period they were still colonies, so they had no legal right to independently nationalize their oil industries. Technically, there was no "nation" to do the nationalizing. Policies needed the tacit or explicit permission of their imperial metropoles, usually Britain, and the metropoles were utterly opposed to nationalization. The arrangements of the Seven Sisters brought profits to Western capitalists and the promise of energy security in times of war.

In addition to the legal constraint for colonies, there was a political one for many ex-colonies. During the process of decolonization, European governments often installed a compliant head of state that was partially beholden to the metropole (see chapter 5). King Faisal in Iraq and Mohammad Reza Shah in Iran were

---

[11] Karl 1997: 96.
[12] Dietrich 2017.
[13] Klapp 1987: 128; Hughes 2014.
[14] Victor et al. 2012; Mahdavi 2020; also see Luong and Weinthal 2010.

prime examples. To the extent possible, imperial metropoles selected individuals who were unlikely to nationalize. Thus, imperial instruments of coercion had consequences that lasted even somewhat after formal decolonization occurred.

Second, even those countries that were independent throughout the twentieth century, like Venezuela and Saudi Arabia, faced significant obstacles to nationalization. As relatively poor countries (Saudi Arabia more so than Venezuela, at the time), they needed access to foreign investment capital and technical expertise.[15] They also needed access to retail markets in North America and Europe. These were strategic benefits from the international order, in the terms of subsystems theory. Those benefits might easily disappear if they defected from the order.

Loss of benefits was exactly the experience of the one major oil producer that had managed to effectively nationalize its oil industry prior to the 1970s: Mexico.[16] President Lázaro Cárdenas had declared on March 18, 1938, that all oil reserves belonged to the Mexican nation, consistent with the Constitution of 1917.[17] The government expropriated all oil reserves and assets, and forbade foreign companies from operating. In retaliation, Standard Oil of New Jersey and Royal Dutch Shell began a boycott against Mexico.[18] Markets and investment dried up. In the years that followed, the consequences became clear. In the 1920s, Mexico had been the world's top oil exporter, a far larger producer than Venezuela. By 1960, Venezuela's oil production was about ten times as large as Mexico's. Although nationalization does not alone account for Mexico's decline, it was the dominant factor.

The third obstacle oil-producing governments faced was the fear that Western governments and firms would punish any state that nationalized their oil sector. In theoretical terms, these were punishments for noncompliance from the international order. Nowhere was this more dramatically illustrated than in Iran from 1951 to 1953, as I describe in chapter 5. Briefly, the new prime minister of Iran in 1951, Dr. Mohammad Mossadegh, nationalized the country's oil sector, seizing assets from the British. The Seven Sisters responded by punishing Iran with an economic boycott that crippled its oil industry. In 1953, the Seven Sisters' home

---

[15] Klapp 1987.

[16] Other countries had tried to nationalize. Mostly these occurred in minor oil producers (see Mahdavi 2020: 33 for a list), or they occurred in major oil producers like Iran and Iraq but were ineffectual. Iran's attempt in 1951 was overturned relatively quickly. Iraq's nationalization policy in 1961 applied to 95 percent of the country, but crucially, it did not apply to the territory that was actually producing oil.

[17] It did so in the context of a violent history that could be interpreted as punishments for noncompliance. In 1914, the United States invaded Veracruz and occupied the city for seven months, largely to protect American oil interests. Although the invasion was successful in securing US corporate oil access in the short term, it created a legacy of anti-Americanism and inspired the authors of the 1917 Mexican Constitution to forbid foreign ownership of Mexican oil (Cline 2013).

[18] Meyer 2014. In theoretical terms, the companies' boycott is probably best considered a punishment for noncompliance (i.e., removal of sales) as well as a loss of benefits (e.g., forgone investment capital).

governments used covert action to impose a further punishment. Operation Ajax, as the covert mission was known, removed Mossadegh and returned political power to the Shah, who was friendlier to British and Western oil interests. Other petrostates could not have failed to notice Iran's experience, and thought twice about nationalization. Iraq's similar experience in 1941 (see chapter 5) added to their caution.

Oil-producing governments were fully aware of the risks of punishment. Mahmood Maghribi of Libya saw nationalization, and oil negotiations more generally, as dangerous and fraught with peril in the 1960s. He would later become prime minister of Libya, and decide to brave those risks. In 1966, however, he wrote in his doctoral thesis (at George Washington University) that it would be "unwise" for any one country "to embark upon such a step alone." In particular, Iran's disastrous experience under Mossadegh had set a precedent that was "still too clear to be ignored."[19] Similarly, leaders in Iraq, Kuwait, and elsewhere perceived the threat of punishments by the Seven Sisters.[20] Table 3.1 summarizes the barriers to oil nationalization faced by each of the original five founding members of OPEC.

Although the obstacles to oil nationalization initially preserved the patterns of authority in the industry, resource nationalism continued to rise in the 1950s and 1960s. People living in petrostates felt that the oil belonged to them, and they resented the relatively small share of the revenues they received. The oil companies' racism and poor treatment of local workers did not help.[21] Slowly, the pressure for change built. Decolonization in Libya, Algeria, Nigeria, Kuwait, and eventually the other Gulf monarchies created the necessary legal opening. Anglo-American instruments of coercion weakened. Changing political tides, like the overthrow of Iraq's monarchy in 1958, also contributed. Even the Seven Sisters realized that they could not hold their concessions forever.[22]

Arab perceptions of the Anglo-American order were shifting. The Imam of Oman averred in 1960, for instance, that "the British fear Arab nationalism and they fight it by creating dissension among Arab leaders. They can only see their economic interest. They put interest above right, and this is ungodly."[23] At the time, the British had just increased their subsidy to the Sultan of Muscat to GBP 600,000 per year, in exchange for oil exploration rights.[24] They were also offering financial rewards to locals to break up the Omani resistance, to help

---

[19] Quoted in Dietrich 2017: 4.
[20] Dietrich 2017: 95, 113.
[21] Vitalis 2007.
[22] Marcel 2006.
[23] Private Papers of William E. Mulligan, archived at Georgetown University ["Mulligan Papers," hereafter]: Box 2, Folder 64, "Interview with the Imam of Oman," memo by Elie Salem, 7 January 1960.
[24] Mulligan Papers: Box 2, Folder 64, letter by Robert Headley, 31 January 1960.

Table 3.1 Pre-OPEC Conditions

	Kuwait	Iran	Iraq	Saudi Arabia	Venezuela
Colonial status	UK colony until 1961	UK protectorate until 1946; UK-US influence until 1979	UK colony until 1932; UK influence until 1958	Sovereign, created 1930	Sovereign since 1830
Major oil producer	Kuwait Oil Company (US-UK owned)	BP (originally Anglo-Iranian Oil Company)	Iraq Petroleum Company (US-UK owned)	Aramco (US-owned)	Creole Petroleum (division of Exxon)
Primary obstacles to nationalization (i.e., mechanisms for punishment)	Not legally sovereign until 1961, so needed UK permission	Shah beholden to UK; fear of angering UK/US; need for access to export markets; low capital and expertise	Beholden to UK until 1958; fear of angering UK/US; need for access to export markets; low capital and expertise	Fear of angering US; need for access to export markets; low capital and expertise	Fear of angering US; need for access to export markets; low capital and expertise

secure the Sultan's power. Outside of Oman, British troops stationed in the Persian Gulf at that time were managing various crises in the region. The need for higher payments (benefits) and greater displays of military power (implied punishments) was worrisome to some. US Consul General Walter Schwinn told an Aramco official that "the British seemed to be losing their ability to get things done by 'advising.' [Schwinn] feared they had no leverage other than force."[25] Schwinn's observations neatly illustrate what it means for a former regional hegemon to gradually lose its instruments of coercion.

Despite the shifting political conditions, the conditions for nationalization were not yet fully ripe. In the 1950s and 1960s, the world markets were awash with oil supply. It was a buyer's market. Those conditions meant that the petrostates were competing with each other for market share. If one petrostate tried to nationalize, it faced a double risk: loss of the strategic benefits it received, and the risk that it would be punished for noncompliance with the Anglo-American

[25] Mulligan Papers: Box 2, Folder 64, Memo by William Mulligan, 18 January 1960.

order. The latter risk was smaller after decolonization than it was in the days of formal imperialism but not gone completely. If the situation were going to change, the petrostates would need to learn to cooperate among themselves.

A transnational group of anticolonial elites played a key role in generating that cooperation.[26] These elites were a group of men (rarely women) from all over the developing world who were sufficiently wealthy or connected to obtain post-graduate education, often in the West. In the 1950s and 1960s, they generated and debated ideas in development economics and international law that could be used to promote, in their eyes, "distributive justice"—a shift toward better terms of trade and economic exchange for the developing world. They included Raúl Prebisch (Argentina), Juan Pablo Pérez Alfonzo and Francisco Parra (Venezuela), Fuad Rouhani (Iran), Kifle Wodajo (Ethiopia), Abdullah Tariki (Saudi Arabia), Mahmood Maghribi (Libya), Samir Amin (Egypt), Celso Furtado (Brazil), Julius Nyerere (Tanzania), and Eric Williams (Trinidad and Tobago). They were lawyers, diplomats, authors, and economists. Geographically, racially, and professionally diverse, they nonetheless occupied a common political and intellectual terrain. Their origins in the global periphery rooted their professional agendas.

Anticolonial elites were a systemic factor—that is, derived from the global system rather than any particular country—that might easily get missed by analysts focusing on the history of individual national cases or even a comparative analysis of them.[27] Members of this class, like Tariki, Pérez Alfonzo, Rouhani, and Parra, were instrumental in shaping the political and intellectual agenda that led to the change in the global oil industry. Their work found expression in events like the 1962 UN Resolution on the Permanent Sovereignty over Natural Resources. That resolution declared that "the right of peoples and nations to permanent sovereignty over their natural wealth and resources must be exercised in the interest of their national development and of the well-being of the people of the State concerned."[28] It defended nationalization or expropriation, with compensation to foreign businesses, as a legitimate state action.

The tight-knit global network of anticolonial elites helped generate a certain level of political solidarity among the newly independent developing countries. They also shared information, ideas, and tactical advice about how to advance their cause. Ideas diffused across borders.[29] Anticolonial elites created the political and intellectual preconditions for a major shift in the global oil industry. They viewed that shift as an "economic sequel to decolonization," even if it turned out to be somewhat less than that in practice.[30] To accomplish their goals,

---

[26] Dietrich 2017: 7–10; see also Getachew 2019.
[27] Oatley 2011.
[28] UN General Assembly Resolution 1803: Article 1.
[29] Finnemore 1993; Simmons et al. 2006.
[30] Dietrich 2017.

they needed an institutional platform specific to the oil industry. In 1960, they got one.

The Birth of OPEC

When Venezuela's government was overthrown in 1948, Pérez Alfonzo was jailed for nine months. Upon his release he traveled to the United States as a political refugee and spent his time learning about a relatively obscure organization called the Texas Railroad Commission. In the 1920s, Texas had been the most important oil-producing region in the world, and oil had traveled by rail. That gave the railroad commission leverage over the market. It set out to control the supply of oil in the hope of stabilizing and boosting oil prices. To a certain extent, it had worked. In the Texas Railroad Commission, Pérez Alfonzo saw a model for a new, international form of cooperation. US politicians would later rail against OPEC, but ironically, the founder of OPEC got his ideas from the United States.

Venezuela's military dictatorship fell in 1958. Pérez Alfonzo returned to his home country and became the minister of mines and hydrocarbons in 1959. The timing was fateful because that year saw the oil market moving against Venezuela and the Middle East. First, in February, the IOCs had unilaterally announced a drop in the posted price of oil, thereby lowering the petrostates' revenues. Then the Eisenhower administration imposed a quota system that limited foreign oil imports into the United States, which hurt not only Venezuela but other producers too.[31]

Pérez Alfonzo was ready. As minister, his first two initiatives were to pitch his project for an agreement between producing countries at the first Arab Oil Congress in Cairo, and then to invite the experts of the Texas Railroad Commission to Caracas. He asked the Texans to teach his ministry officials the techniques of controlling the oil market. When Shell announced a second drop in the price of Venezuelan oil just as the Arab Oil Congress began, Pérez Alfonzo angrily pointed out that the international price of crude had now fallen back to its 1953 level. The day of Shell's announcement, he argued: "We producers must try to find means of collaborating to avoid arbitrary fixing of prices."[32]

On the other side of the world, Abdullah Tariki had been preparing for this moment. An ardent Saudi nationalist, Tariki had watched his whole life as Anglo-American power shaped the oil industry in the Middle East.[33] He dreamed of changing all that. He was an early critic of Aramco, and wanted dramatic change

[31] Eisenhower 1959.
[32] Terzian 1985: 23; see also Ghanem 1986: 19.
[33] Skeet 1988.

in his country. He saw a kindred spirit in Pérez Alfonzo. Tariki said of him, "I was highly impressed with his strong personality, his dedication and loyalty, and his readiness to cooperate in our mutual interest . . . Since 1951 I had been looking forward to meeting him to gain from his experience."[34] Tariki hoped that, together, they could tackle the "history of petroleum colonization" that afflicted their countries.[35]

At the Arab Oil Congress, Pérez Alfonzo and Tariki put enormous pressure on their fellow negotiators to create an international oil organization. Iran was the most reluctant. As non-Arabs, Iran's delegation had come to Cairo only to observe the Congress, and wanted nothing to do with a formal agreement without explicit permission from the Shah. Pérez Alfonzo sidestepped the problem by proposing a gentlemen's agreement, later known as the Maadi Pact (or Mehdi Pact), to make recommendations to their respective governments. They signed a document confirming the pact at the meeting's conclusion. The head of the Iranian delegation later said, "Pérez Alfonzo almost twisted my arm to get me to sign."[36]

The IOCs underestimated the ideational and emotional impact that their international order had on those who were forced to accept it. Inadvertently, the Seven Sisters played a key role in bringing OPEC together. One analyst later wrote, "there is little doubt that the announcement of the reductions of posted price in Venezuela and the Middle East in February [1959] was instrumental in creating the necessary atmosphere and humiliation that led to the signature of the document."[37] In theoretical terms, the oil companies' actions had reduced the petrostates' strategic benefits from complying with the order—both the reality of those benefits and their perceptions of them.

The Maadi Pact was confidential but it leaked to journalists. In May, Tariki and Pérez Alfonzo went public, issuing a declaration calling for an international petroleum agreement.[38] The IOCs failed to take these signs seriously, however, and soon repeated their mistake on pricing. In August 1960, Exxon, BP, and the other companies announced another significant price decrease just days before producer governments were set to meet in Baghdad. Howard Page, Exxon's senior representative in the Middle East, later said, "I only regret one thing, my decision to cut oil prices in August 1960."[39]

---

[34] Quoted in Terzian 1985: 28.
[35] Dietrich 2017: 92.
[36] Quoted in Terzian 1985: 27.
[37] Skeet 1988: 16; see also Ghanem 1986: 18–23.
[38] Ghanem 1986: 22.
[39] Terzian 1985: 38. Francisco Parra (2004: 97) reports, however, that it was "Exxon's chairman of the board, Monroe (Jack) Rathbone, [who] decided . . . to reduce posted prices again, in spite of considerable opposition from some of his own directors, notably Howard Page. . . . Rathbone was jocularly dubbed 'Father of OPEC.'"

In September, Pérez Alfonzo, Tariki, and the others made good on the Maadi Pact. The outcome was far from certain when the Baghdad meeting opened. Iran was reluctant, especially about creating a permanent organization with its own secretariat. Then, on September 13, the Shah finally gave his delegate Rouhani the green light. Rouhani announced the next day, "Not only did he agree to the creation of a permanent organization, but he even proposed a name for it: the Organization of the Petroleum Exporting Countries."[40] Rouhani became the organization's first secretary general.

Venezuela, Saudi Arabia, Kuwait, Iraq, and Iran were the original signatories.[41] Almost all of the major oil-producing states of the Global South rapidly joined: Qatar (1961), Libya (1962), Indonesia (1962), UAE (1967), Algeria (1969), and Nigeria (1971). Even so, the meeting's success was a near miss. It had hinged upon the Maadi Pact of 1959, which in turn depended on the Arabs' sense of outrage. Afterwards, a member of the Venezuelan delegation admitted that it was the drop in prices announced by BP in 1959 that had driven "the producing countries to close ranks in a common reaction against BP's action. If BP had waited till the Congress was over, the Arabs would probably not have shown themselves so understanding of our viewpoint."[42]

The oil companies and even the US government largely underestimated OPEC's significance. President Eisenhower told his National Security Council that anyone could break up OPEC "by offering five cents more per barrel [to] one of the countries."[43] A few weeks later, at the Second Arab Petroleum Congress in October 1960, the oil companies haughtily dismissed Arab complaints. Tariki argued "that by manipulating prices the international oil companies have deprived the Arab states of vast sums of additional revenue."[44] The Aramco representative called Tariki's complaints "nothing but fantasies and fabricated allegations not related to reality."[45] At the same time, the companies threatened OPEC against upsetting existing arrangements: "There is no doubt Middle East crude will . . . lose its present outlets to North and South America."[46]

Too many officials at the oil companies believed that they could sustain the old order by playing OPEC members off against one another, as they had in the past. "Blinded by their power, believing everything was permitted to them in countries humiliated by decades of foreign domination, the oil companies proved incapable of adapting to changing circumstances," reflected Pierre Terzian, an

---

[40] Quoted in Terzian 1985: 42.
[41] Goldthau and Witte 2011.
[42] Quoted in Terzian 1985: 29.
[43] Quoted in Dietrich 2017: 87.
[44] Mulligan Papers: Box 4, Folder 14, "Report on the Arab Petroleum Congress, 1960," 12.
[45] Mulligan Papers: Box 3, Folder 3, "The Petroleum Question in the Light of Aramco's Accusations," editorial by Ahmad Tashkandi, Al-Nadwah, No.564, 21 November 1960.
[46] Quoted in Terzian 1985: 48.

analyst. "They were unable to envisage that the colonial style model of exploitation they had established over sixty years might be replaced by a formula more respectful of the producing countries' national aspirations."[47]

Not everyone at the oil companies was insensitive to their position, however. Aramco's internal documents reveal an awareness of the need to demonstrate the benefits the company offered. Privately, one wrote, "In the future Aramco should present more papers on industrial relations and on the various benefits and services which the company has brought to its employees and to Saudi Arabia. (It is felt that the Middle Eastern public does not appreciate the extent of these benefits)."[48] Another admitted that Tariki's accusations against the oil companies were "accepted by many in his Arab audience and the Arab public at large."[49] Thus, oil company officials were divided between those with disdain for OPEC, and those with a sense that their welcome in petrostates was wearing thin.

For Pérez Alfonzo and Tariki personally, the creation of OPEC was a short-lived triumph. When Pérez Alfonzo returned to Caracas from the Baghdad meeting in 1960, he was greeted at the airport by hundreds of enthusiastic demonstrators carrying banners that read, "Pérez Alfonzo, an anti-imperialist Minister worthy of the nation."[50] It soon became apparent, however, that the foundation of OPEC was the apex of their careers. Just three years later, a disillusioned Pérez Alfonzo resigned from his government. He criticized OPEC, saying, "Venezuela's association with producing countries of other regions is not producing any benefits for the country."[51] He retired from public office and devoted himself to writing about education and child health. Tariki, for his part, was fired in 1962 after falling out with the Saudi royal family. The underlying problem was his nationalist ideology, though other events triggered his dismissal. His nationalist vision for the oil sector had become embarrassing to the Saudis who sought to cement their relationship with the United States. OPEC failed to live up to the dreams of Pérez Alfonzo and Tariki. Their expectations were simply too high. By the time they left, OPEC was gathering steam.

OPEC Rising, 1960–1974

OPEC proved in the 1960s that it could facilitate international cooperation. It functioned as a semi-collective bargaining unit seeking higher oil revenues from

[47] Terzian 1985: 40.
[48] Mulligan Papers: Box 3, Folder 3, Memo from H. Alter to G. Mandis, 26 November 1960.
[49] Mulligan Papers: Box 4, Folder 14, "Report on the Arab Petroleum Congress, 1960," 12.
[50] Quoted in Terzian 1985: 44.
[51] Quoted in Terzian 1985: 82.

the IOCs. The broad outlines of the strategic environment, or "game," were as follows. The host governments allowed IOCs to produce oil in their territories, usually through intermediate companies called concessionaires. For instance, Aramco was the concessionaire operating in Saudi Arabia. National oil companies were initially nonexistent or weak (basically only collecting revenue, not producing oil). The IOCs were divided into two broad camps: the majors (the Seven Sisters) and the independents (smaller firms). The two groups of companies did not have the same interests. Still, the majors dominated the market in the early years, with independents initially producing just a small fraction of the oil outside the United States until the late 1960s. The 50/50 agreements nominally split the profits evenly between the host government and the producing company, but in practice the companies could use accounting tricks to their advantage.

A key part of this revenue-sharing game between oil companies and host governments had to do with the difference between "posted prices" and "market prices." Market prices were the revenues per barrel that the IOCs actually received by selling the crude oil to refineries in the downstream market. Posted prices, by contrast, were artificial accounting tools that formed the basis for tax and royalty payments to the oil-producing states. The companies initially set posted prices unilaterally. Consequently, there was no guarantee that posted prices would reflect the underlying value of the oil, which might allow oil companies to reduce their tax payments to host governments. Later, the host governments and the IOCs negotiated the prices—until the oil shock of 1973. After that time, posted prices gradually disappeared. Market prices replaced them as the basis for tax and royalty payments. The transition from posted prices to market prices reflected a victory for the OPEC governments over the IOCs.

In this strategic game, OPEC member states had some common interests, but they were also competing with each other. The IOCs were, in effect, an oligopsony: a small group of buyers dominating the market. These companies bought almost all of the oil produced in OPEC countries and sold it to customers in North America and Europe. If any individual state demanded too large a share of the oil revenues, the IOCs could respond by producing less oil in that state, and make up the difference by producing more oil in other states. That meant that as long as the OPEC states did not work together as a bloc, the IOCs were in a strong bargaining position to retain a large share of the available oil profits.

OPEC also faced the problem that individual member states might cheat or turn on one another. OPEC spent the 1960s experimenting with various forms of cooperation. It sought to mitigate risks for its individual member states. Some succeeded; others did not. OPEC facilitated cooperation in four important ways.

Technique #1: Tax Code Cooperation

First, OPEC encouraged and facilitated its member states in their efforts to reform their national tax codes for the oil sector, which they saw as unfair. The oil companies did not see a problem: they split their profits 50/50 with the governments, so why were the governments upset? The problem lay in the slippery definition of "profits," which opened the door to accounting tricks. For instance, the companies charged various expenses, like oil-marketing costs, before the 50/50 split was made, thereby lowering the tax revenue of the governments.[52]

Worse, many governments found themselves caught in a "race to the bottom," as they each competitively offered tax deductions or loopholes to attract investment in their oil sector. Those deductions also lowered the government take below 50 percent, making the loopholes costly. When one government offered a new tax holiday, it spurred other states to do the same, creating the race to the bottom.[53] Consequently, even when considered from a purely national perspective, each tax incentive was a mixed bag for the government: it might increase oil production but it would also certainly lower the per-barrel revenues. That made cooperation between OPEC members to limit tax deductions attractive. By offering higher taxes per barrel at relatively low risks, each state had only weak incentives to "cheat" by offering tax deductions in violation of the OPEC agreement.

OPEC's action on "royalty expensing" shows how cooperative tax reform worked to generate significant new government income. OPEC Resolution IV.33, passed in 1962, demanded that the IOCs cease the practice of royalty expensing—that is, deducting royalty payments from income tax due to producer governments.[54] The end of royalty expensing would raise OPEC members' revenues from the IOCs. Venezuela had already ended royalty expensing in 1962 but the other members wanted to as well. The OPEC states empowered their secretary general, Fuad Rouhani, to negotiate with the IOCs on their behalf.[55] OPEC members took risky actions to increase the pressure on the IOCs to accede to OPEC's demands. For instance, Iran imposed a "supplemental charge" on all tanker loadings equivalent to the financial effect of royalty expensing (11 cents per barrel, about 5 percent of the price).[56] Iran promised to remove the supplemental charge when the negotiations on royalty expensing concluded. This

---

[52] Ghadar 1977: 52.

[53] Tax incentives also needed to be fairly large to attract investment because tax rates were only one of many investment considerations. The IOCs also considered the geology, the infrastructure and logistics requirements, the state's political stability, and other factors.

[54] OPEC 1984.

[55] At least initially; later, some OPEC members sent their own national representatives. Skeet 1988: 30–33.

[56] Skeet 1988: 31.

action was risky for Iran, since it put Iran's oil at a relative competitive disadvantage, but the Shah of Iran requested and received assurance from Saudi Arabia and other OPEC members that they would support Iran's actions. Ultimately, OPEC reached an agreement with the IOCs in 1968 that the royalty expensing would be phased out by 1972.[57] The agreement represented additional revenue of several hundred million dollars for OPEC member countries.[58]

OPEC leaders could see the benefits of cooperating to reform the existing international order, and viewed the risks of intra-OPEC discord as manageable.[59] In 1966, for instance, a news service reported that "elimination of the 6.5 percent allowance would entail an increase of around 6–7 cents a barrel in the governments' receipts, which would work out at a total of about USD 160–170 million in additional income for Iran, Saudi Arabia, Libya and Qatar combined for 1967 alone."[60] These rewards had to be weighed against the risks because policymakers foresaw that "if, for example, one of the members were to show itself willing to settle for less than the others, the bargaining power of the Organization would be permanently crippled."[61] To mitigate the risks, OPEC countries agreed privately in advance on the measures they would take in the event of a showdown with the IOCs.

Even so, OPEC leaders could not be sure about the threat of punishment by the international order led by the Seven Sisters, even on relatively minor issues like tax treatment. The Shah felt this risk as much as anyone did. Mohammed Reza Pahlavi had seen his father deposed from office by the British. He had also seen how the IOCs treated Iran in 1952–1953 when Mossadegh tried to nationalize the oil industry. And the Shah knew that his own political position owed everything to the Western-led coup in 1953 that restored him to power. It was perhaps not surprising that he proved indecisive and tentative in these negotiations.[62] That meant that at first, OPEC achieved only relatively minor goals.

Technique #2: Policy Experimentation

OPEC's second technique was to foster experimentation with new models for the ownership and management of oil fields. Governments had many options for arranging their relationship with oil firms, including state-owned equity participation, joint production arrangements, or completely private ownership.[63] Each

[57] Skeet 1988: 37.
[58] Parra 2004: 107.
[59] Chalabi 2010.
[60] *Middle East Economic Survey* 1966 (October 15): 1.
[61] *Middle East Economic Survey* 1964 (January 3).
[62] Skeet 1988: 31–33.
[63] Klapp 1987: 68–76; Kyle 2014; Mahdavi 2020.

of these could be combined with various forms of government "take": taxes, royalties, and concession fees. The various permutations generated a huge variety of options. OPEC members experimented extensively during the 1960s with these options, and then used OPEC as a clearinghouse to share information about what worked well or not so well from the governments' point of view. For instance, the OPEC meeting in October 1966 called for an exchange of technical data and key personnel between OPEC members.[64] This helped increase the competence of the national oil agencies (nascent national oil companies), which was a crucial precondition for nationalization.

These policy experiments were risky. If they went badly, they could cost a government in lost revenue or bureaucratic efficiency. Many of these governments had low technical capacity and few people in their country with substantial knowledge of the oil industry.[65] The IOCs had much more expertise than the governments, as well as experience drawn from all over the world. As Tariki later admitted, "We were amateurs."[66] OPEC mitigated the governments' risk by sharing information among its members.[67] Fortunately, the policy experiments could be undertaken on a project-by-project basis, so any failed experiment would not prove too costly. And by sharing information, OPEC created an incentive for each of its member states to want to be a part of the organization—a club good, in economics jargon. Generating this mutual benefit helped reinforce the incentives for cooperation in OPEC's other activities.

Technique #3: Price Collaboration

Third, OPEC acted semi-collaboratively to ratchet up the posted prices of oil when the opportunity arose in the tighter oil market conditions from 1970 to 1973. A tight market meant that supply was scarce and demand was high. It was a dramatic shift: for years, oil companies had had access to more than enough oil reserves to satisfy their customers, but now demand was changing. It shifted for multiple reasons but principally because of skyrocketing car ownership. Figure 3.1 illustrates the pattern of car ownership in postwar Western Europe. With reviving economies and a growing middle class, car ownership became widespread in Europe for the first time.[68] The number of vehicles in North America and elsewhere also rose. Globally, increased car ownership drove demand for oil to new heights.

---

[64] Ghadar 1977: 52–53.
[65] Skeet 1988: 24; Cowhey 1985: 124.
[66] Terzian 1985: 56.
[67] Cowhey 1985: 129; Skeet 1988: 38; *Middle East Economic Survey* 1965 (April 2): 6.
[68] The Americanization of the European economy, facilitated by the Marshall Plan, contributed to this shift. See chapter 5.

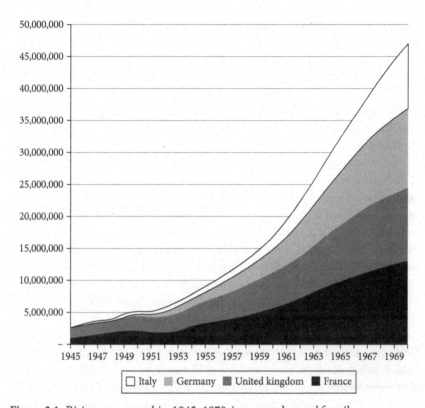

Figure 3.1 Rising car ownership, 1945–1970, increases demand for oil

Data source: Comin and Hobijn 2009. Missing data for France 1946–1949 are interpolated; missing data for Germany 1945–1948 and Italy 1945 are assumed close to zero.

OPEC, led by Libya, took advantage of this shift in market conditions. The 50/50 agreements were still in place until, in 1970, Libya negotiated with Occidental (an independent IOC) on the first deal to break that mold. That deal gave 58 percent of the profits to Libya and increased the posted price of Libyan oil.[69] All of the other IOCs operating in Libya soon acquiesced to similar terms. The oil companies then sought to preempt new demands from other OPEC countries by volunteering to accept a 55 percent tax rate and a small increase in the posted price.[70] The individual states initially accepted this agreement, but at Iran's urging, OPEC soon resolved that all members should receive the same posted price that Libya received.[71] They did. Libya then insisted on a further price

---

[69] Cowhey 1985: 155.
[70] Skeet 1988; Parra 2004.
[71] OPEC Resolution XXI.120 (December 1970).

increase for its oil exports, which were superior on technical grounds to other OPEC members' oil. This set the stage for further increases for OPEC as a whole. In each case, Libya's individual action paved the way for the rest of OPEC to insist on more. I call this behavior semi-collaborative, with Libya's departures from the OPEC standard working to the advantage of all OPEC parties.

The semi-collaborative OPEC actions combined with fractiousness among the oil companies to drive the price up in the early 1970s. Even though market conditions gave OPEC greater bargaining leverage, the oil companies still had more than enough oil at the time to meet world demand, in the aggregate. Had they been unified, the companies could have called any individual OPEC country's bluff (e.g., Libya) and refused to pay higher prices. If, for example, each oil company knew that it could purchase oil from its peers at a guaranteed price even if Libya shut it out, each company would have had incentive to take a hard line in price discussions. But the IOCs were divided between the majors and the independents, which had different interests. They failed to cooperate between themselves, fracturing their bargaining position. It was thus the combination of OPEC's negotiating tactics and the lack of solidarity among IOCs that led to higher prices.[72]

In a feedback process, the incremental nature of the price increases in 1970–1973 also reinforced OPEC by providing demonstrations of mutual solidarity. As Peter Cowhey notes, "at each step until 1972, members were hesitant and uncertain about seizing their new advantages. Each agreement [facilitated by OPEC] fostered a 'virtuous circle' of mutually reinforcing expectations, and a new shared vision of the future of the oil industry emerged."[73] In some ways, this is exactly the kind of repeated play that facilitates cooperation in international relations.[74] Still, OPEC faced the daunting task of challenging an Anglo-American international order—with the risk that they might provoke the companies to punish them economically or ask their governments to respond with force. They also faced the risk of internal discord: some OPEC member or members might offer a price discount to the IOCs in exchange for more oil production. This is why market conditions were so crucial: in the tight oil market of the early 1970s, all countries expected their production to increase. Consequently, OPEC members saw little upside in turning their backs on the group.

The issue of nationalization lurked behind these negotiations, and was part of what gave OPEC members so much bargaining leverage over the IOCs. The IOCs were afraid (justifiably, it turned out) that if they did not give the OPEC countries a sufficient share of the oil revenues, the governments would simply

---

[72] Cowhey 1985: 151–172.
[73] Cowhey 1985: 159. This is not to say there were not occasional setbacks and spats between members, however. Iraq in particular was disenchanted with OPEC in the 1960s. See Skeet 1988: 39.
[74] Axelrod 2006.

nationalize their oil assets. In terms of theory, the companies were trying to take as much of the order's strategic benefits as possible for themselves, giving rather little to the petrostates. Nationalization represented an alternative set of governing arrangements that might offer the petrostates higher strategic benefits. Nationalization was risky, however, as Iran, Iraq, and Mexico had discovered in previous decades—each was punished for attempting the transition. OPEC countries in the early 1970s were understandably wary.[75]

Technique #4: Supporting Nationalization

The fourth and final major way that OPEC facilitated cooperation among its members was to encourage and support nationalization.[76] The tight oil market conditions of 1970–1973 created the right opportunity, just as it had with price ratcheting. Prior to nationalizing, member states shared information within OPEC about potential tactics for nationalization. At its July 1971 meeting, for instance, OPEC created a special ministerial committee to study ways to nationalize that would "avoid erosion of prices on the international market."[77] And once countries began to actually nationalize, OPEC encouraged a position of solidarity to minimize the risks involved for the first movers. OPEC visibly demonstrated its solidarity when Saddam Hussein nationalized Iraq's oil sector. In June 1972, OPEC adopted a new policy: "member countries shall not allow oil companies to replace the crude oil exported by Iraq Petroleum Company at the level of 1970, by oil produced in their territories and/or to substitute that oil in its traditional markets."[78]

By supporting nationalization, OPEC members were denying themselves a short-term market opportunity. If the IOCs tried to boycott Iraq oil, they would want to buy more from the rest of OPEC, bringing those governments more revenue. OPEC members decided, however, that it was more important to make the nationalization experiment in Iraq (and Algeria and Libya, around the same time) successful, thereby paving the way to nationalization in their own countries. If nationalization was successful in Iraq, the IOCs would have a weaker hand in negotiations with others, like Kuwait, Venezuela, and Saudi Arabia. This is precisely what happened, though there was considerable variation in the degree of enthusiasm for nationalization. Some countries, including Saudi Arabia, were reluctant to nationalize, in part because they did not want to jeopardize

---

[75] Mahdavi 2020.
[76] Marcel 2006; Victor et al. 2012.
[77] OPEC Resolution XXIV.135; Ghadar 1977: 53.
[78] OPEC Resolution XXVIII.146.

Table 3.2 Reform Techniques Coordinated by OPEC, 1960–1974

Technique	Desired Benefit	Risk to an OPEC Government	OPEC Mitigated Risk by ...
Reforming domestic tax code (1960s)	Increase government share of oil profits	Any state that ended tax deductions might lose production to other states	... encouraging gradual harmonization across all of its member states
Experimenting with new management models (1960s)	Increase revenue and control of oil decisions	OPEC states initially had low technical knowledge, might create poor design	... facilitating club information sharing; creating incentive to cooperate within OPEC
Semi-collaborative ratcheting up posted prices (1970–1973)	Increase revenue and share of revenue	Any state insisting on a higher posted price might lose production to other states	... insisting, whenever one state gained a higher price from the IOCs, that all others got the same
Supporting nationalization (1970 onward)	Increase revenue and control of oil decisions	Any state that nationalized might be locked out of global oil markets or punished like Iran in 1951–1953	... committing not to allow IOCs to produce more oil in their fields while locking out an OPEC state

their relationship with the United States. In the end, however, Aramco, an American-owned company, became Saudi Aramco, owned by the Saudis.

Again, policymakers anticipated the possibility of punishment for noncompliance with the Anglo-American order.[79] For example, when asked about the potential for oil companies to boycott a country that nationalized its oil industry, Ahmad al-Sayyid Omar, director of the General Oil Affairs Department in Kuwait, replied: "This would be impossible. We in OPEC are bound by the principle that no member state should gain any advantage at the expense of another member state. There is solidarity among the producing countries."[80] While Omar exaggerated the group's solidarity, it was real nonetheless. Similarly, Libyan oil official Mahmood Maghribi had a keen sense of nationalization's risks for any individual state but he came to see OPEC cooperation as a way to make progress.[81]

Table 3.2 summarizes the four reform techniques that OPEC coordinated. They were interrelated and supported one another. For instance, OPEC fostered

[79] Chalabi 2010.
[80] *Middle East Economic Survey* 1965(April 9): 2.
[81] Dietrich 2017: 191–227.

imitation of innovations during the wave of nationalizations in the 1970s (technique #4), an outgrowth of the experimentation and information sharing during the 1960s (technique #2). As a second example, the OPEC action in the early 1970s to ratchet up oil prices (technique #3) was possible only because of prior strategic learning about negotiations in the 1960s (technique #1).[82]

Not all of OPEC's techniques succeeded. OPEC's strength was clearly on the rise from 1960 to 1973, but its most audacious effort failed completely. In 1965, it tried to adopt production prorationing—the practice of limiting the production of each member of the group to an agreed quota. If successful, this would have allowed OPEC to operate as a cartel. Pérez Alfonzo and Tariki had dreamed of forming a cartel, following the model of the Texas Railroad Commission. However, OPEC's members bickered among themselves, and they abandoned the experiment by June 1967. The central problem was that OPEC members could not find a way to allocate quotas without a high risk of cheating. It was a bad sign for future efforts.

Policymakers could already see the risks of a cartel attempt. For instance, Ahmad Yamani, Tariki's successor as Saudi oil minister, publicly stated: "I was worried from the very beginning that some member countries were not serious about the production program."[83] In the same interview, he issued a sharp warning against the dangers of an oil production race, clearly sensing that the risks of failure were too high for his government. A senior Exxon official, Howard Page, fanned the flames of these fears. He knew that the Shah had agreed to join OPEC only at the very last minute, and hoped to convince the Shah to change his mind. Page "confidentially" told the Shah that Exxon's subsidiary in Venezuela, the Creole Petroleum Company, was holding enormous reserves of crude oil and that the Venezuelan leaders' aim in getting OPEC to proration production was to strip the Gulf producers of their American and European markets. In Venezuela, however, Exxon's message was quite different—it accused the government of sacrificing Venezuela on the altar of OPEC.[84] In these ways, the IOCs sought to undermine OPEC.

Overall, however, OPEC was quite successful in this period. It built a strong working relationship and a certain amount of solidarity among its members. It showed that cooperation among them could work. Despite these successes, OPEC's leaders were disappointed with their progress. Francisco Parra, its secretary general in 1968, later wrote, "The trouble was, it didn't *feel* good. The protracted negotiation and the tiny concessions, tea spooned out by the companies, cent by cent, did not smack of victory to the member countries. No one at this

---

[82] Cowhey 1985: 17–18.
[83] *Middle East Economic Survey* 1966 (November 18).
[84] Terzian 1985: 51.

point was proud of OPEC."[85] Its members were hungry for something far greater. Though they scarcely realized it, they had laid the foundations for getting it.

The 1973 Oil Shock

The pinnacle of OPEC's success came in 1973. In the 1960s, OPEC had improved various aspects of their oil contracts, but one thing stayed the same. For the entire decade, the posted price of oil was USD 1.80.[86] OPEC wanted higher prices. In 1970, changing market conditions finally allowed it to start ratcheting up prices, gradually negotiating up to USD 2.18 per barrel in February 1971 and USD 2.59 at the start of 1973. Then OPEC sensed the full strength of its market position and pushed for major price increases: to USD 3.07 in August and USD 5.12 in October. Finally, at a meeting in Tehran in December, OPEC dropped all pretense of negotiating with the IOCs, and unilaterally moved the price to USD 11.65—more than four times what it had been a year earlier. Those price increases brought billions of dollars of new revenue to OPEC.

It was the Shah who drove the final, momentous decision in December. He had persuaded himself that oil was a "noble" fuel to be used only for purposes for which there was no alternative.[87] In practice, that primarily meant transportation and petrochemicals, not heating or electricity generation which, after all, could be fueled by coal or nuclear energy. The Shah's vision created an economic rationale for a higher price, considerably more than the Saudis preferred, but the rest of OPEC readily agreed. That left Yamani in a difficult spot. Having been given orders not to do anything that might destroy OPEC, he reluctantly accepted the Shah's proposal. Flush with victory, the Shah held a press conference to announce the deal even before the meeting had concluded, much to the annoyance of the other OPEC states.

Perhaps just as important as the quadrupling in prices was the change in the authority structure of the oil industry as the wave of nationalizations swept the globe. That wave included Libya (1970–1972), Algeria (1971–1974), Iraq (1972), Venezuela (1974–1976), Nigeria (1971–1979), Kuwait (1975–1977), Saudi Arabia (1973–1980), and Iran (effectively renationalized 1978–1980).[88] Collectively, these producers accounted for the majority of the world's oil reserves. OPEC's 1972 "participation agreement" with the IOCs was a significant

---

[85] Parra 2004: 107.

[86] Dollar figures quoted in this paragraph come from Yergin 2008: 607; Cowhey 1985: 161.

[87] Skeet 1988: 101–102.

[88] See Klapp 1987: 11; and Mahdavi 2020. As indicated earlier, Iraq's previous nationalization policy (in 1961) did not have much effect on the oil industry. Also note that the Shah negotiated in the 1970s, even before the revolution, to have the National Iranian Oil Company become the operator of the oil business, but this change did not take hold.

step in that process. The agreement gave the petrostates a 25 percent participation (equity) share in the private oil companies, which rose to 51 percent in 1983.[89] But even that deal was insufficient for many OPEC members, and it was soon overtaken by events. Most states wanted full nationalization and eventually got it. Nationalization meant that authority over production decisions changed decisively away from the IOCs, and put control in the hands of national governments and their agents.

While the events of 1973 delighted the oil-producing states, policymakers elsewhere were somewhat less pleased. "No crisis of the second half of the twentieth century fell on a world less prepared for it than the one triggered by the quadrupling of oil prices in the fall of 1973," wrote Henry Kissinger, who had served as US secretary of state at the time. That was not all. The Yom Kippur War of October 1973 also prompted the Arab oil embargo against the United States and other countries. Although not itself important for subsystems theory, that war was intimately tied to oil politics and oil money; indeed, Egyptian president Anwar Sadat was willing to launch the war only once King Faisal of Saudi Arabia had promised him a massive loan.[90]

Once the Yom Kippur War was underway, political pressure built for an oil embargo on Israel's military supporters. Rather than OPEC, it was the Organization of Arab Petroleum Exporting Countries (OAPEC) that froze sales to the United States and the Netherlands in 1973, though many of OPEC's members participated in the embargo (e.g., Kuwait, Saudi Arabia) or supported it rhetorically (Iraq). In practice, the embargo itself had a rather limited effect on the world oil market: the supply disruption was both temporary (a few months at most) and relatively small (about 2 to 4 percent of total world output).[91] Still, the embargo had a huge psychological effect (prompting worldwide fears of oil scarcity) and triggered a self-defeating policy response in the United States. The Nixon administration's response involved domestic price controls, which had the effect of creating fuel shortages and long lines at gasoline stations.[92] Whatever the underlying economics, OPEC was now a household name all over the world. Its image as an oil cartel was born.[93]

The wave of oil nationalizations in the 1970s shifted patterns of authority in the international energy order, but that did not mean that petrostates had a completely free hand. They still wanted market access to consumers in North America and Europe, and that meant cooperating with the IOCs. Most petrostates faced sufficient business challenges just nationalizing the production

---

[89] Yergin 2008: 566.
[90] Brown 1999; Bronson 2006; Chalabi 2010; Colgan 2013d.
[91] Colgan 2014.
[92] Frech and Lee 1987.
[93] Krasner 1974.

side of the business; they were not ready to also take on the refining, marketing, and retail challenges. They therefore wanted to sell their crude oil to Western oil companies that would refine it into products (e.g., gasoline, diesel) and sell it in retail markets.

Nationalization was accomplished by negotiation rather than government fiat. The governments agreed to compensate the companies for their assets. The hard question was how much each government had to pay. On the low end was the "book value" of the production assets—the drilling rigs, buildings, pipelines, etc.—which reflected how much they cost to purchase and install, updated for inflation and depreciation. On the high end, the assets' net present value reflected the expected revenue stream that could be generated from them. Very different valuations could be produced depending on the accounting formula chosen. For instance, the Kuwait Oil Company could have been valued at anywhere between sixty million and one billion dollars.[94] In the end, the companies received more than the book value of the assets (so they could still easily claim a profit for their investors) but far less than their net present value based on their future earnings potential. In that sense, the oil companies were "fully compensated" for their investments but very sorry to lose them nonetheless.[95]

The fact that petrostates generally needed or wanted the IOCs' technical and management expertise gave the companies additional bargaining leverage. In some cases, the transition was so smooth that the employees hardly noticed a difference. In Venezuela, for instance, many employees went to work at an American-owned private oil company one day, and worked at Petróleos de Venezuela (PDVSA, the nationalized oil company) the next day—in the same building with the same co-workers.[96] Similarly, Saudi Aramco continued to employ most of the people who had worked for Aramco prior to nationalization.

There was a second oil price shock in 1979–1980, caused by the twin upheavals of Iran's Revolution and the Iraqi invasion of Iran, but it was short-lived, and by the end of 1985 oil prices returned to 1978 levels. That second shock followed the historical pattern in the oil business as a boom-and-bust industry, but the first shock in 1973 was different. Unlike other oil booms, it permanently shifted the long-term average price of oil upward. Prior to 1973, the price of oil was low and steady for decades. Ever since, the price has been substantially higher, even adjusting for inflation (except for brief moments like April 2020). Moreover, the distribution of oil profits permanently changed, tilting more money toward the host governments and away from the oil companies.

[94] Yergin 2008: 566.
[95] Krasner 1978; Maurer 2013.
[96] Hults in Victor et al. 2012: 426.

On the whole, 1973 was a spectacular year for OPEC. The Shah was jubilant. In 1971, he had held an opulent celebration of Iran's 2,500th anniversary, as founded by Cyrus the Great. The Shah invited so many kings, presidents, world leaders, and celebrities that 250 Mercedes-Benz limousines were needed to shuttle them from the airport to the party. The goal of the event was to show off Iran as a rising power, returned to the global stage. The celebration was enormously costly, however, and an exiled cleric named Ruhollah Khomeini chastised it as the "Devil's Festival." The ayatollah's criticisms of the hubris and waste in the Shah's court would take its toll by the end of the 1970s, but that was not how things looked in 1973. As the year ended, the Shah believed he had at last laid the financial foundations for Iran's greatness.

Consequences of the 1973 Oil Shock

Decolonization had paved the way for changes in the global politics of oil, and the reverberations of those changes did not stop with nationalization and OPEC control.[97] The jump in world oil prices shocked the major oil-consuming nations in North America and Europe into responding with their own forms of political innovation.[98] Their immediate concern was how to respond to oil embargoes. They had reacted to the 1973 crisis in an uncoordinated and competitive manner.[99] Some pressured their oil companies into giving them preferential treatment. Others imposed restrictions on the export of petroleum. Companies in larger countries bid up oil prices on the spot market. Some European countries sought to distance themselves from the Dutch to appease the Arabs.

Faced with this challenge, the United States organized a new institution in 1974: the International Energy Agency (IEA). Initially Kissinger intended to set it up as an explicitly anti-OPEC organization, designed to smash the cartel. "We have to find a way to break the cartel," he told newly elected president Gerald Ford. "It is intolerable that countries of 40 million can blackmail 800 million people in the industrial world."[100] Europe and Japan, however, were more vulnerable to oil supply interruptions than the United States, and resisted Kissinger's proposal. It was economically infeasible in any case. By November 1974, they instead agreed on a program to establish the sixteen-member IEA as an autonomous agency of the OECD. The IEA's secretariat was housed in Paris, but

[97] Hughes and Lipscy 2013; Aklin and Urpelainen 2013; Baccini et al. 2013; Bazilian et al. 2014; Hancock and Vivoda 2014; Van de Graaf and Colgan 2016.

[98] Colgan et al. 2012.

[99] Ikenberry 1988.

[100] Kissinger 2000: 669.

ironically France did not join the IEA because it preferred to maintain good relations with the Arab countries. (France finally joined in 1992.)

The IEA has two principal functions. The first is to operate systems for coping with oil supply disruptions. Since its inception, the IEA has required its member countries to maintain a petroleum reserve equivalent to its consumption of net oil imports for a certain period of time, currently ninety days. In case of an international disruption to oil supply, the IEA is empowered to respond in a variety of ways. The organization also requires major oil companies to share information, including proprietary and classified data. The IEA's second key function is to help develop policy, information sharing, and technology transfer. During the long periods of non-crisis oil markets, this second function has been the organization's principal activity. While it never achieved the kind of influence to which Kissinger had aspired, the IEA does have a role in shaping energy policy.[101]

The turbulent 1970s also spawned another new institution, the Group of Seven (G7). Alarmed by the international monetary and energy crises of the early 1970s, the leaders of six major industrialized countries started to convene regularly. They first met as the G6 in 1975, then as the G7 with the addition of Canada in 1976, and then as the G8 after the addition of Russia in 1997 (until 2014). Energy concerns were on the agenda from the outset. The G7 later concentrated primarily on macroeconomic issues. Its attention to energy politics has waxed and waned, largely tracking oil price fluctuations.[102]

The developed countries were not the only ones innovating. The influx of oil money in the 1970s allowed the petrostates to expand their reach and influence in global affairs. Saudi Arabia pursued an even closer friendship with the United States. In June 1974, only three months after the official end of the Arab oil embargo, Prince Fahd and other senior Saudi officials arrived in Washington to sign a multipronged agreement of economic and security cooperation. The agreement started a massive program of "petrodollar recycling." The goal was to ensure that the vast sums of money that the United States now spent on OPEC oil returned to the United States in the form of weapons purchases and financial investments. For Kissinger, the real objective was to make sure that Saudi Arabia was a stakeholder in America's economic success so that the kingdom would never again have an incentive to embargo its oil sales.[103] This is exactly what happened: by 1976, Saudi Arabia had invested a cumulative USD 60 billion in the United States at a time when its annual GDP was just USD 64 billion.[104]

Some of OPEC's new wealth directly funded armed violence. Perhaps most famously, the Saudis spent billions of dollars in the 1980s to support the *mujahedin*

[101] Van de Graaf and Lesage 2009; Colgan and van de Graaf 2015.
[102] Colgan et al. 2012.
[103] Kissinger 2000: 677.
[104] Bronson 2006: 122–127.

in Afghanistan, who were fighting a resistance war against the Soviet occupation there. Saudi financing for insurgents extended far beyond Afghanistan, however. It included support for groups in Angola, Sudan, Nicaragua, Ethiopia, Yemen, and elsewhere—wherever there was an active battle against communists. The United States actively encouraged the Saudis to fund these groups.

Saudi Arabia was not alone in funding violence, though other petrostates took it in a rather different direction.[105] Under Muammar Qaddafi's rule, for instance, Libya supported approximately thirty revolutionary groups and foreign insurgencies around the world, from the Palestinian Liberation Organization to the Irish Republican Army (IRA) and the Black Panthers.[106] Libya also sponsored three major acts of international terrorism in the late 1980s, most famously the explosion of Pan Am Flight 103 over Lockerbie, Scotland, killing all 259 people aboard as well as 11 on the ground. To the extent that there was a theme in Libya's interventions, it was the struggle against what Qaddafi viewed as colonialism and neo-imperialism.[107] Iran also funded various violent groups.[108] It played an integral role in the creation and operation of Hezbollah in Lebanon; has significant connections with Hamas in Palestine, various armed groups in Iraq, and foreign insurgents in other countries; and has an elite division of the Islamic Revolutionary Guard, known as the Qods force, that is tasked with exporting the Islamic revolution. The Qods forces are suspected of having carried out lethal operations in multiple countries, including bombings in Germany and Argentina.

OPEC's success in shifting the distribution of global oil wealth gave the petrostates' newfound political influence in the developing world. OPEC's efforts to control oil had always been couched in the language and ethos of anticolonialism and "economic emancipation."[109] Its triumph in 1973 was roundly applauded by other developing countries. In 1974, the UN General Assembly passed a resolution in favor of a New International Economic Order (NIEO). The NIEO was an attempt to further transfer wealth from the Global North to the Global South, in areas beyond oil. Although it largely failed economically,[110] the NIEO positioned OPEC states in the political vanguard of developing countries.

At the same time, the increase in world oil prices in 1973 created economic hardship in much of the developing world. Most of those countries were net importers of oil, so the higher prices hurt their economies. Escalating oil bills began to bite in the mid-1970s. OPEC states feared that hardship would generate

---

[105] Lee 2016.
[106] Vandewalle 2006: 132; see also Colgan 2013d.
[107] Vandewalle 2006.
[108] Colgan 2013d.
[109] Dietrich 2017.
[110] Krasner 1985.

Figure 3.2 Oil wealth reverberates through foreign aid donations

Note: Foreign aid commitments in US dollars. Data source: PLAID Database (now part of aiddata. org).

political resentment against them, threatening to divide the G77 bloc of developing countries at the United Nations and elsewhere.

Thus, in 1976, OPEC created its Fund for International Development (OFID). By disbursing some of their new wealth in the form of foreign aid, member states "reaffirmed the natural solidarity which unites OPEC countries with other developing countries in their struggle to overcome underdevelopment."[111] By 2018, OFID's total approved commitments (including grants and contributions to other institutions) stood at USD 23 billion, benefiting 134 countries worldwide.[112] This was an astonishing amount. All told, Arab foreign aid in the early years after the oil boom was proportionally far higher, as a fraction of their GDP, than the aid from rich countries in the OECD.[113]

Figure 3.2 demonstrates the impact of the 1973 shift in the structure of the global oil industry on the foreign aid patterns by petrostates. The graph includes data on donations made by the five largest donors associated with petrostates: OFID, the Arab Fund for Economic and Social Development, and the bilateral donations made by three individual petrostates: Saudi Arabia, Kuwait, and UAE. As the figure shows, petrostates provided almost no foreign aid before 1973, but rapidly became significant donors afterward. This foreign aid largesse created a certain amount of political goodwill and influence for the petrostates.[114] Countries that were Islamic, voted similarly to Saudi Arabia in the

[111] Algiers Conference Solemn Declaration, 1975. Quoted in http://www.ofid.org/ABOUT-US (Accessed July 13, 2017).

[112] OFID 2018. See http://www.ofid.org/Portals/0/Publications/Profiles/ProfileOctober2018.pdf (accessed November 3, 2018).

[113] Neumayer 2003.

[114] Villanger 2007.

UN General Assembly, and did not have diplomatic relations with Israel were more likely to receive such foreign aid.[115]

Not all the money was spent on aid. Saudi Arabia, for instance, funded Islamic organizations such as the World Muslim League and the Organization of the Islamic Conference. In the 1970s, King Faisal hoped that these organizations would help Saudi Arabia craft a pan-Islamic leadership role for itself on the basis of its Islamic heritage and its holy sites in Mecca and Medina. This pan-Islamic vision was an attractive alternative to Nasser's pan-Arabism because it offered a popular ideology that was compatible with the existing nation-states of the Middle East. It was therefore nonthreatening to the Saudi regime. Pan-Islamism also widened the scope of the Middle East political dialogue to include states like Iran and Pakistan, which Saudi Arabia sought to use to dilute the influence of then-preeminent Egypt. Over time, however, pan-Islamism took a rather more anti-Western turn as jihadists used it to justify transnational terrorism.[116] The Saudis themselves supported a strict interpretation of Islam in the mosques that they funded overseas.[117] Jihadists have been able to build upon that version of Islam to recruit terrorists. It is no coincidence that fifteen of the nineteen terrorists who committed the 9/11 attacks in 2001 were Saudi citizens.

The oil shock reverberated in bilateral relationships, too. Venezuela, for instance, has used its oil revenues since 1974 as a tool for purchasing foreign influence. It is not as rich as Saudi Arabia, so its foreign largesse has waxed and waned with the price of oil. During the 1970s boom, Venezuela pursued an ambitious agenda. It cofounded the Latin American Economic System (Sistema Económico Latinoamericano y del Caribe, or SELA) and committed funds to the World Bank, the IMF, the Inter-American Development Bank, and several regional institutions.[118] For a while, its official development assistance to foreign countries amounted to an astonishing 3 percent of GDP (by comparison, US development assistance is roughly 0.2 percent of its GDP).[119] The oil income also allowed the government to significantly boost its military spending.[120] When the oil price crashed in the 1980s, however, Venezuela was forced to retrench. Only when oil prices rose in the 2000s did Venezuela return to its big-spending ways.

Under President Hugo Chávez, who took office in 1999, Venezuela pushed for the creation of four new regional oil initiatives: in the Caribbean (Petrocaribe), the Andean region (Petroandino), South America (Petrosur), and Latin America (PetroAmérica). These initiatives offered assistance for oil developments,

[115] Neumayer 2003.
[116] Hegghammer 2010.
[117] Yetiv 2011; Lee 2016.
[118] Martz, "Venezuelan Foreign Policy toward Latin America," chapter in Bond 1977: 158–169.
[119] Bond 1977: 228.
[120] Colgan 2011.

investments in refining capacity, and preferential oil pricing. In international trade, Venezuela joined Mercosur and created a new organization called the Latin American Bolivarian Alternative, known by its Spanish acronym, ALBA. At its peak, ALBA had eleven member states. In 2007, Venezuela left the World Bank to create Banco del Sur, an alternative development bank for South America (which exists only on paper). According to one Venezuelan NGO, Chávez offered more than USD 37 billion in aid to other countries in the period between 2002 and 2007, though the actual amount disbursed was probably considerably lower than the amount promised.[121] Still, Chávez used foreign aid, along with the prospect of cheap oil supplies, as a carrot to attract diplomatic partners and participation in his initiatives. For instance, Venezuela offered oil to Cuba and other members of Petrocaribe at preferential rates. In exchange, Venezuela received the services of Cuban medical doctors, security advisors, and a certain degree of diplomatic deference.[122] Venezuela also launched a number of new media operations including Telesur, an international cable television station.[123] Yet when the oil boom turned to bust in 2014, Venezuela's largesse dried up again, and its own economy crashed.

The oil shock shaped Muslim petrostates' bilateral relationships, too. Unlike Venezuela, however, the Muslim states sought to use their new economic clout and political influence to isolate Israel. For example, in the 1970s Libya sought to convert a number of state governments against Israel. By 1973, twenty-seven African states had broken diplomatic ties with Israel, in part as a result of lobbying and pressure from the Libyan government.[124] Libya also played host to several radical Palestinian groups: the Abu Nidal group, the Popular Front for the Liberation of Palestine, and the Palestinian Islamic Jihad all moved their operational base to Libya in the 1970s. Iran also used its influence against Israel. The Qods force smuggled weapons and materials to Hezbollah during its 2006 war with Israel, for example. Still, the nature of the oil-wealth reverberations for Israel depended greatly on the disposition of the petrostate's leadership.[125] King Abdullah of Saudi Arabia, for example, tried to work with Israel on a major Palestinian peace initiative in 2002. In 2020, UAE and Bahrain normalized their relations with Israel.

In short, the petrodollars that flowed in the years after 1973 generated multiple movements that continue to shape the world's economy and politics in the twenty-first century. Oil wealth led to institutions like the IEA, the G7, and OFID; it funded military adventurism and "freedom fighters" in various parts

---

[121] Fundación de Justicia y Democracia 2008, quoted in Colgan 2013d.
[122] Colgan 2013d.
[123] Jones 2008: 429.
[124] US Government 1989.
[125] Colgan 2013d.

of the world; it purchased political leverage both within petrostates and across the Global South; and it funded various forms of Islamism, some of which had deadly consequences in the decades to come.

Returning to the Logic of International Order

This chapter's overview of OPEC's early days gives only the essence of the story, setting aside many twists and turns described elsewhere.[126] Subsystems theory helps to understand these events, and interpret them as a shift in international order.

Table 3.3 lays out the three historical periods and their analytical characteristics. The key outcome is the governing arrangements over oil production: how were the decisions over production and price made in each period? The background condition was imperialism, with decolonization representing the big break. Decolonization symbolized the declining instruments of coercion that European states had available to enforce their preferred international order. By the time OPEC was created in 1960, the punishments for noncompliance were declining.

Yet it took over a decade before OPEC really had much effect on the global oil industry. Why the delay? Much of the explanation rests with the strategic benefits that the international order generated for its key participants. In the 1960s, the Seven Sisters still provided significant benefits to OPEC states. The companies were, after all, not just producers but also the gateways to retail customers in the United States and Europe. The IOCs also provided the capital to develop oil fields and a steady stream of payments to governments with budgets that had become dependent upon them.

Crucially, though, the benefits to petrostates varied according to market conditions. For decades, the global oil market had been loose, allowing the IOCs to prevent nationalization. Around the year 1970, however, the global oil market tightened quite suddenly: demand was rising faster than supply. The tight market created favorable conditions for the petrostates. Fortified by the previous decade's worth of cooperation and relationship-building at OPEC, the petrostates were ready to wrest control from the companies. They did so by unilaterally setting the posted price of oil and, in most cases, by nationalizing the oil sector.

The theory also helps explain one of the consistent themes of the negotiations between states and companies: compensation for nationalized assets. At first it might be surprising that petrostates would pay compensation at all. After all, the 1970s were a time when resource nationalism was popular in the developing

---

[126] Blair 1976; Skeet 1988; Parra 2004; Marcel 2006; Dietrich 2017.

Table 3.3 The OPEC Shift in International Order

Period	International Context	Strength of Punishments (IV)	Strategic Benefits: Market Conditions (IV)	Governing Arrangement (DV)	Effects
Pre-1960	Gradual decolonization	High	High: Abundant oil supply relative to demand favors IOCs	IOCs decide production	Most profits go to IOCs
1960–1973	Independent oil states	Low but uncertain	High: Oil supply abundant, but only until market tightens in early 1970s	IOCs decide production until 1970s; petrostates cooperate with each other on tax and other matters	Most profits go to IOCs until 1970s, then shift toward petrostates
1974–present	Independent oil states	Low	Low (in 1970s), then varies (after 1980)	Petrostates nationalize, have full authority on production	Petrostates gain profits; use some for foreign aid, Islamic support; oil consumers create IEA

world and Western oil companies were not.[127] There were populist groups across the Middle East who wanted to drive the Americans out of their home, violently if need be. Yet in almost all cases, from friendly Saudi Arabia to hostile Iraq, petrostate governments did decide, in the end, to pay the IOCs for their assets.[128] That consistent pattern of behavior can be explained by an invariant systemic factor: the desire of petrostates to have access to valuable markets in the Global North. These markets include not just the retail markets where consumers buy oil products but also credit and investment markets (for developing their economies), markets for technical expertise (to manage the upstream oil production business), and foreign equity markets (where wealthy petrostates could invest their excess oil earnings after the sustained price hike in 1973).

On the whole, petrostates profited massively from the change in the oil structure in the 1970s. They used their oil wealth for a variety of projects, including domestic economic development, foreign aid, and military adventurism.[129] Some have proved more economically successful than others, to say the least.[130] One thing cannot be denied, however: the shift in oil wealth had profound and unanticipated consequences for world politics.

OPEC's founders, Tariki and Pérez Alfonzo, differed in their final judgments about their creation. Although often critical of OPEC, in 1980 Tariki said with a certain pride, "OPEC is the only organization made up of Third World countries which has remained strong for twenty years and which has succeeded in defending its members' interests."[131] For Pérez Alfonzo, however, oil and OPEC were huge disappointments for his beloved Venezuela. In 1976, he said, "I call petroleum the devil's excrement. It brings trouble . . . Look at this *locura*—waste, corruption, consumption, our public services falling apart. And debt, debt we shall have for years."[132] His words proved prophetic.

---

[127] Dietrich 2017: 6.
[128] Maurer 2013.
[129] Colgan 2013d.
[130] Ross 2012; Colgan 2015.
[131] Quoted in Terzian 1985: 95.
[132] Quoted in *The Economist*, "The Devil's Excrement," May 22, 2003.

4

The Stagnation of OPEC

"We were amateurs."[1]

—Abdullah Tariki, co-founder of OPEC

OPEC triumphed in the 1970s. It had reshaped the world oil market with the 1973 oil crisis and seized control of production decisions from the Anglo-American oil companies. The members of OPEC soon discovered, however, that vanquishing the Seven Sisters oligopoly had a downside for them, too. Now that they were in charge, they faced some of the same challenges that the oil companies had before them. Above all, they needed to avoid flooding the global market with overproduction, thereby driving prices back down and reversing all of OPEC's hard-won gains. At first, the member governments worked together informally to limit production. Starting in 1982, however, OPEC started to act as a formal cartel. The members began to set quantitative production quotas for themselves, and adjusted them at periodic meetings. Could it work?

The conventional wisdom—among journalists, policymakers, and even scholars—is that OPEC pulls it off, albeit imperfectly. It sustains an image as an organization that manipulates the price of oil by coordinating and restricting supply. Economic studies investigating OPEC impact, however, have had difficulty finding conclusive evidence of its market impact. Those studies generate two questions. First, does OPEC actually operate as a cartel? Admittedly, people sometimes use the word "cartel" loosely to simply indicate a group of producers (as in "Mexican drug cartels"), but many people believe a second meaning also applies to OPEC: a group that significantly restricts its members' production in order to affect prices.[2] OPEC is obviously a group of producers, so the question is whether it actually restricts production. Second, if OPEC is not really a cartel in that sense, why do so many people believe that it is?

To answer the first question, this chapter conducts four empirical tests in search of OPEC's effect on oil production. I find that OPEC membership is not significantly correlated with lower oil production, after controlling for other

---

[1] Terzian 1985: 56.
[2] More formally, I use a technical definition from Mankiw (2011: 351)—more on that later.

relevant factors. At a minimum, there is no good evidence to believe that OPEC is a cartel, and some evidence to believe the opposite. This is due, in part, to endemic cheating by OPEC members (i.e., oil production in excess of their quotas). A cartel needs to set tough goals and meet them; OPEC sets easy goals and fails to meet even those.

This counterintuitive finding becomes clearer if we define precisely the concepts of cartel, economic influence, and price influence. A cartel is an organization that reduces its members' production levels from what they would have been, counterfactually. By doing so, a cartel can have economic influence, meaning that it affects average prices or production amounts over the long run, relative to the counterfactual in which it never existed. OPEC neither is a cartel nor has economic influence. It does, however, have influence on market prices in the short term. It does so mostly because oil prices are affected by market psychology in addition to fundamentals like production levels, and OPEC's statements can affect market psychology. OPEC also affects prices by acting like a spokesperson, revealing information about key market actors, particularly Saudi Arabia. Yet the causal role of OPEC as an institution on prices is really very thin: the institution in Vienna could be replaced by a spokesperson in Riyadh, and it would make almost no difference.

Subsystems theory can help explain why OPEC has largely failed to control the market since the 1970s. Unfortunately for OPEC, it has no real enforcement mechanism, and thus cannot impose punishments for noncompliance. Consequently, it has no way of punishing member states that cheat on their quotas. Without enforcement, the order, such as it is, depends solely on offering its members strategic benefits for acting in compliance with OPEC's dictates. This chapter shows why the benefits of doing so are too small for most OPEC members, and the costs are large.

This chapter thus continues the analysis of what I call Subsystem A, which relates to the economics of oil production. At the heart of Subsystem A lies the question, How much oil will get produced in each territory? While the Seven Sisters oligopoly offered a relatively effective set of governing arrangements to answer this question prior to 1973, OPEC as an institution has not been able to exert much authority over the question since then. Instead, OPEC's member states make production decisions based on their own self-interest. While it is true that OPEC tends to cut production when oil prices go down, and increase it when prices go up, that is hardly evidence of a cartel. After all, so do non-OPEC producers, too.

If OPEC does not operate as a cartel, why do so many people believe that it does? The idea of OPEC as a cartel is a "rational myth" that supports the organization's true principal function, which is to generate political benefits for its members. Scholars have found that various organizations adopt rational myths[3] and OPEC would not be the first international institution to outlive its original mandate.[4] OPEC's current role is obscured in part by the complexity of the world oil market, in part by the fact that one of its members, Saudi Arabia, probably does have some market power on its own (distinct from the organization to which it belongs), and in part by misdirection by OPEC itself. OPEC's perceived market power is a useful fiction that generates political benefits for its members with domestic and international audiences.

Again, subsystems theory can help us understand this behavior. As early as 1985, Saudi Arabia grew frustrated by the endemic cheating of its fellow OPEC members. To support OPEC goals, it had cut oil production from more than 10 million barrels per day in 1981 to just 2.5 million barrels per day in June 1985—at a huge cost in revenue.[5] Yet, other OPEC members continued to produce in excess of their production allocations. So Saudi Arabia decided, in 1985, to increase oil production to recapture the market share that it had lost while trying to make OPEC function effectively as a cartel. From that point onward, the more thoughtful policymakers in Saudi Arabia and elsewhere knew that OPEC was part of an international order that was, for them, undesirable: it had no real supranational governance.[6] The consolation prize for OPEC was the prestige and status that came with being perceived as an influential actor, even if the underlying reality was quite different. Thus, the rational myth emerged.

Statistical evidence supports this interpretation. As this chapter describes, OPEC membership is positively associated with increased ambassadorial representation from other countries, a measure of status and prestige. Consequently, policymakers within OPEC have no incentive to undermine the idea that OPEC influences the world oil market. This does not necessarily mean that they are actively lying, but rather that they have an incentive to behave in ways that are consistent with the cartel idea so long as that behavior is not too costly. Other knowledgeable actors outside of OPEC fail to dispel the myth for various reasons. In sum, the story of OPEC is mostly about politics, not economics.

---

[3] McNamara 2002; Boiral 2007; Meyer and Rowan 1977.

[4] Barnett and Finnemore 1999; Gray 2018; Duffield 1994; Wallander 2000.

[5] Claes 2018: 146.

[6] In November 2014, for instance, Saudi Arabian oil minister Ali al-Naimi explained his government's decision not to cut oil production in an effort to boost prices by saying, "The experience of the first half of the 1980s was still in our minds. At the time, we cut production several times. Some OPEC members followed our lead, and the aim was to reach a specific price that we thought was achievable. It didn't work. In the end, we lost our customers and the price. . . . We are not willing to make the same mistake again." (quoted in Claes 2018: 152).

Existing Ideas about OPEC

To understand the myth of OPEC, let us analyze step by step. Start with the basics. In 2021, OPEC had thirteen member states: Algeria, Angola, Congo, Equatorial Guinea, Gabon, Iran, Iraq, Kuwait, Libya, Nigeria, Saudi Arabia, the UAE, and Venezuela. Previously, Indonesia, Qatar, and Ecuador were members. Collectively, OPEC produced 43 percent of the world total in 2017, though individually even its largest producer has a relatively small market share (Saudi Arabia, 13 percent).[7] The organization meets regularly and makes decisions by consensus, which effectively gives each state a veto.[8] If OPEC were able to cooperate flawlessly, it could exert significant market influence.

The significant oil price increases of the 1970s convinced many observers that OPEC had become the cartel that its founders envisioned.[9] Political scientist Stephen Krasner even argued in a 1974 article entitled "Oil Is the Exception" that the characteristics of oil made it especially susceptible to an international cartel compared to other commodities.[10] Yet over time many studies have cast significant doubt on the idea that OPEC is a cartel.[11] Some scholars suggested a "dominant producer" model, namely, that Saudi Arabia alone exerted market power, because it seems to be the only state with sizeable surplus production capacity.[12] More recently, scholars have noted a series of limitations on OPEC's effectiveness.[13]

International relations research shows that states typically design international rules to avoid requirements for costly adjustments to their behavior.[14] That means that even when states appear to be cooperating, they are often behaving just as they would have done, even without the rules. Thus, OPEC quotas, even if strictly obeyed, might not actually require states to deviate significantly from their counterfactual behavior.

---

[7] BP *Statistical Review of World Energy* 2018 (reporting 2017 data).

[8] OPEC can set or change its members' quotas for oil production at any of its regular meetings, or it can do so in an "extraordinary session." Each member state appoints a delegate to represent it at OPEC meetings, typically the minister of oil or its equivalent.

[9] Osborne 1976; Seymour 1980; Doran 1980; Adelman 1982. See also internal US government reactions during the 1970s in Qaimmaqami and Keefer 2011.

[10] Krasner 1974.

[11] Griffin 1985; Dahl and Yucel 1991; Alhajji and Huettner 2000; Barsky and Kilian 2004; Reynolds and Pippenger 2010.

[12] Moran 1982. Adelman suggests that OPEC wobbles between acting as a dominant firm and as part of a cartel depending on market conditions. Adelman 1982.

[13] Gülen 1996; Kohl 2002; Kaufmann et al. 2008; Smith 2005; Hyndman 2008; Victor 2008; Goldthau and Witte 2011; Bremond et al. 2012: 125; Doran 1977 (chapter 6). On global energy governance more broadly, see Rudra and Jensen 2011; Colgan et al. 2012; Baccini et al. 2013; Hancock and Vivoda 2014; Claes 2018.

[14] Downs, Rocke, and Barsoom 1996.

Yet, even as scholars cast doubts on its effectiveness, there is sufficient ambiguity to sustain OPEC's image as a cartel. Multiple studies since 2004 argued that OPEC does matter for oil prices and production controls.[15] This ambiguity leads many scholars to continue to believe that OPEC is a cartel, albeit imperfect. Hyndman, for instance, asserts, "OPEC is obviously a cartel that restricts output in order to obtain super-competitive profits," an assertion shared by other economists[16] and political scientists.[17]

Consequently, we need to have a fresh look at the evidence. Existing studies tend not to provide direct evidence that OPEC members produce less oil than they would in the counterfactual world in which OPEC did not exist.[18] Moreover, many models do not incorporate relevant political variables, such as a country's regime type and level of investment risk, creating the potential for flawed conclusions.

Testing OPEC's Effect on the Market

I conduct four major tests of OPEC's market impact. I focus on the period since 1982, when OPEC first began to assign quotas (what it calls "market allocations") to its members. The tests focus exclusively on OPEC's impact on oil production, rather than oil prices, for two reasons. The first is practical: the relationship between OPEC quotas and world oil prices is fraught with potential endogeneity.[19] For example, low oil prices might cause OPEC to lower its production quotas, but if OPEC actually has market power, lower OPEC quotas would cause high oil prices. Thus, on its own the (lack of) correlation between OPEC quotas and oil prices does not give us enough information to make valid inferences about its status as a cartel.[20] Some sophisticated statistical techniques might be used to try to get around this problem, but they are not satisfying.[21] The second reason is

---

[15] Smith 2005, 2009; Demirer and Kutan 2006; Bentzen 2007; Kaufmann et al. 2008; Fattouh and Mahadeva 2013; Golombek et al. 2018. Others, like Bremond et al. 2012, point to OPEC's limitations, but still conclude that "OPEC influence has evolved through time," rather than rejecting it as a cartel.

[16] Hyndman 2008, 812; Smith 2005, 2009; Simpson 2008.

[17] Ikenberry 1988; Lieber 1992; Blaydes 2004; Shaffer 2009; Sovacool 2011.

[18] They typically focus instead on measuring the degree to which production changes in one OPEC member are correlated with production changes in the rest of OPEC, a correlation that could be explained in a variety of other ways, such as common reactions to market conditions. See Griffin 1985; Kaufmann et al. 2008; Bremond et al. 2012.

[19] See discussion later in this chapter.

[20] A simple bivariate OLS regression between world oil prices and OPEC's aggregate production target from 1982 through 2009 yields an R^2 value of just 0.15—that is, nothing to suggest price control by OPEC.

[21] To date, no one has identified a plausible instrumental variable or natural experiment. Other approaches exist but have not produced a consensus. See Dahl and Yucel 1991; Gülen 1996; Alhajji and Huettner 2000; Reynolds and Pippenger 2010; Bremond et al. 2012.

perhaps even more important: production constraints are a necessary element of cartel behavior. If OPEC is not constraining its members' production, then it is not a cartel, by definition.[22] Focusing on production allows us to directly investigate the extent of collusion between OPEC members, rather than looking at its indirect effect on prices.

What evidence should we expect if OPEC is a cartel? Mankiw defines a cartel as a group of producers that creates agreements about quantities to produce or prices to charge, and further that it "must not only agree on the total level of production but also on the amount produced by each member."[23] This definition implies that a gap between market price and marginal cost of production is not by itself evidence of a cartel.[24] Instead, we should see signs that the organization is cooperating to restrict production (to drive prices up). Specifically, we should see the following kinds of evidence: new members of the cartel have a decreasing or decelerating production rate (test #1); members should generally produce quantities at or below their assigned quota (test #2); changes in quotas should lead to changes in production, creating a correlation (test #3); and members of the cartel should generally produce lower quantities (i.e., deplete their oil at a lower rate) on average than non-members of the cartel (test #4). Failure to observe any of these phenomena would cast doubt about OPEC's status as a cartel, though none is totally determinative. The fourth test is perhaps the strongest because it is difficult to imagine how an organization that does not restrict output compared to non-members could be called a cartel—how else could it increase average prices?[25] To preview the results, OPEC fails all four of the tests.

First Test: Does Joining OPEC Affect Oil Production?

The first test of OPEC as a cartel is the impact that the organization has on the oil production rates of new members. I adopt a before-and-after methodology,

---

[22] Mankiw 2011: 351.

[23] Mankiw 2011: 351.

[24] Producers who stop producing before marginal costs equal market price (like some OPEC producers, possibly) are not behaving as one expects under perfect competition, but that does not necessarily imply cartelization.

[25] One of OPEC's stated goals is to stabilize prices. It is possible that an organization could seek to stabilize prices without affecting the long-run average price or production levels of its members. Yet such an organization could not be considered a classic cartel because it would not be profit-maximizing. It seems unlikely that OPEC is simply trying to stabilize prices without increasing their own profits.

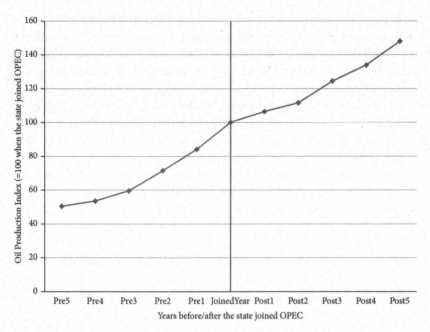

Figure 4.1. Impact of joining OPEC on oil production

following the event history approach used by economist Andrew Rose in his evaluation of the WTO.[26] If OPEC is having a constraining influence on oil production, states that join OPEC should have a decreasing or decelerating oil production rate. Conversely, states that leave OPEC should have an increasing oil production rate.

There is very little evidence that OPEC is having such an effect. Figure 4.1 shows the average oil production rate of all states in the five years before they join OPEC and the five years after they join OPEC.[27] Each state's oil production is standardized to a value of 100 in the year that it joined OPEC so that the relative increase or decrease can be compared. As the graph shows, the average production rate increases at a similar rate before and after the state joins OPEC. The rate of increase is somewhat lower after a state becomes an OPEC member, but not by a huge amount—thereby providing rather weak evidence, if any, that OPEC constrains oil production.

---

[26] Rose 2004; see also Goldstein, Rivers, and Tomz 2007.

[27] Figure 4.1 includes only OPEC members that joined prior to 2014, when the analysis was conducted.

Table 4.1. Relationship between OPEC Quotas and Production, 1982–2009

OPEC Member	% Months Production Exceeds Quota	Correlation between Production and Quota*		
		beta coeff.	p-value	R-sqr
Algeria	100%	0.105	0.035	0.014
Iran	72%	0.002	0.981	0.000
Iraq**	82%	0.065	0.819	0.000
Kuwait	90%	0.106	0.450	0.002
Libya	83%	0.183	0.038	0.014
Nigeria	88%	0.138	0.383	0.002
Qatar	90%	0.118	0.245	0.004
Saudi Arabia	82%	0.138	0.130	0.007
UAE	96%	−0.140	0.170	0.006
Venezuela	77%	0.095	0.472	0.002
OPEC-9 (excl. Iraq)	96%	0.153	0.017	0.018

* Values displayed are from bivariate OLS regression of first-differences, where DV = changes in production.

** Up to March 1998 only. Iraq was not assigned an OPEC quota after March 1998.

Two Tests on the Impact of OPEC Quotas

The second test focuses on cheating: production by states in excess of their assigned allocation. A strong cartel would have little cheating. Over the period 1982–2009, OPEC as a whole overproduced its own production allocation a staggering 96 percent of the time. I use monthly production data, drawing on data from the US Energy Information Agency.[28] Table 4.1 shows the variation among OPEC members (second column). Most members overproduced more than 80 percent of the time. Moreover, some OPEC countries managed to avoid having quotas for significant periods of time, further weakening the organization's effort to act as a cartel.[29] The magnitude of overproduction varies

[28] EIA estimates can differ from OPEC's reported production data. OPEC's data are not fully credible because they are self-reported by member countries that have an incentive to dissimulate when they are overproducing.

[29] Iraq did not have a quota between 1998 and 2017. Iran, Angola, and Ecuador have also had periods without a quota. OPEC production allocations available at http://www.opec.org/opec_web/static_files_project/media/downloads/data_graphs/ProductionLevels.pdf. Accessed 10 November 2013.

over time and across states, but it is not trivial: on average, the nine principal members of OPEC produced 10 percent more oil than their quotas allowed.[30] This is equivalent to 1.8 million barrels per day, on average, which is more than many individual countries produce in total. Even on the relatively rare occasions when member countries are not overproducing, the root cause is often involuntary production constraints such as a strike or accident, rather than a conscious decision by the government to obey its OPEC quota.

One might wonder how much this level of cheating actually undermines the cartel's operation. One possibility is that OPEC anticipates a certain amount of cheating and sets the quotas accordingly. If so, the real questions are whether OPEC production rates are affected by quotas, and whether they are lower than the counterfactual in which no quotas were set. The remaining tests investigate those questions.

The third test reveals that OPEC quotas do a poor job of accounting for variation in production levels. Returning to Table 4.1, it shows the R-squared value of a linear bivariate time-series regression between changes in an OPEC member's production and changes in its quota (last column).[31] For all but two of the states (Libya and Algeria), changes in the OPEC quota are not correlated with production at standard thresholds of statistical significance. The R-squared for the nine major OPEC producers as a group was just 0.018, meaning (roughly) that at most 1.8 percent of the variation in the month-to-month changes in this group's oil production can be explained by changes in their OPEC quotas. In other words, roughly 98 percent of the variation is explained by factors other than OPEC.

Even in the face of this negative evidence, one might still argue that OPEC acts as a cartel in one of two ways. First, one could argue that anticipation by various actors in the oil market obscure OPEC's constraining effect. For instance, perhaps OPEC members change production levels between OPEC meetings because they anticipate forthcoming changes in the quotas.[32] Second, some have argued that even if OPEC's quota system is entirely meaningless, OPEC still affects oil production over the long term because it encourages the adoption of a slow depletion policy and underinvestment in production capacity.[33] Both of these propositions have a clear empirical implication: the oil production or

---

[30] The nine members were: Algeria, Iran, Kuwait, Libya, Nigeria, Qatar, Saudi Arabia, UAE, and Venezuela. Calculated using data from the US Energy Information Agency for actual production, and from OPEC for market allocations, 1982—2009. Note that Smith (2008) estimates that overproduction averages just 4 percent, using ostensibly the same data (though for a different time period).

[31] Formally, the dependent variable is the first difference in oil production, and the independent variable is the first difference in oil quota. The observations are monthly averages, although the values are measured in barrels per day.

[32] Parra 2004: 321–322.

[33] Smith 2009.

depletion rate of OPEC member states ought to be significantly less than the pro-duction or depletion rate of comparable non-OPEC members. This leads to my fourth test.

Final Test: Do OPEC Members Have Slow Depletion Rates?

Depletion rates vary widely around the world. (A country's depletion rate is equal to its oil production divided by its proven oil reserves.) Broadly speaking, deple-tion rates will vary according to three supply-side factors (in addition to global demand for oil): the business climate of the producing country (e.g., companies' technical skills, investment climate, the incidence of war or sanctions, etc.); the "lift costs" of oil production (costs of getting oil to the ground, including explo-ration); and the government's depletion policy. OPEC membership could affect depletion policy, but so could other factors, such as the state's fiscal needs, the incentives generated by its position in the global market (e.g., as a "dominant firm"), and the time horizons of the political leadership.

I investigate the cross-national variation in depletion rates over a thirty-year period, 1980–2010.[34] The analysis includes all forty-two oil-producing states for which data are available.[35] The analysis includes the variable *OPEC*, a binary measure indicating whether the state is a member of OPEC in a given year. It also includes several other explanatory variables, like *fiscal strength*, measured by the natural log of oil reserves per capita; the state's *investment risk* (which affects the ease with which international businesses can operate); and *world economic growth*, a proxy for global demand for oil. Variables for international events like wars and sanctions are also included.[36] Details of the analysis and robustness checks are described elsewhere.[37]

Table 4.2 presents the results of the regression analyses. Model 1 shows a simple bivariate model that indicates that OPEC membership is statistically associated with low depletion rates, as expected by the conventional "OPEC-as-cartel" hy-pothesis. Crucially, however, the statistical significance of OPEC membership disappears when other variables are added in the subsequent models. Model 2 shows a baseline model, without taking into account the potential impact of

---

[34] BP *Statistical Review of World Energy* provides data on proven reserves starting in 1980. It provides data on forty-seven oil-producing countries, but Brunei, Chad, Equatorial Guinea, Turkmenistan, and Uzbekistan are not included due to data unavailability for other variables.
[35] BP *Statistical Review of World Energy*.
[36] Sanctions data from Hufbauer, Schott, and Elliott 2007.
[37] Colgan 2014.

Table 4.2. Regression analysis on states' oil depletion rates, 1980–2009

	(1)	(2)	(3)	(4)	(5)	(6)
OPEC Member—All	−3.9569 (−4.08)***		−0.733 (−0.76)			−0.81 (−0.84)
Saudi Arabia				−1.625 (−1.59)	−1.734 (−1.26)	
OPEC Member, Non-Saudi				−0.683 (−0.71)		
OPEC Core Member					−0.911 (−0.6)	
OPEC Non-Core Member					−0.627 (−0.62)	
Polity Score		0.039 (0.73)	0.034 (0.68)	0.03 (0.59)	0.028 (0.5)	0.052 (0.91)
World Economic Growth		0.051 (0.76)	0.044 (0.67)	0.045 (0.68)	0.046 (0.68)	0.047 (0.71)
Fiscal Strength		−0.992 (−4.42)***	−0.91 (−3.18)***	−0.905 (−3.15)***	−0.892 (−2.68)**	−0.905 (−3.16)***
Investment Risk		−0.084 (−2.59)**	−0.079 (−2.33)**	−0.08 (−2.36)**	−0.081 (−2.4)**	−0.079 (−2.37)**
International War		1.097 (0.80)	1.155 (0.86)	1.112 (0.83)	1.043 (0.69)	1.104 (0.86)
International Sanctions		−0.649 (−1.0)	−0.61 (−0.98)	−0.654 (−1.05)	−0.677 (−1.1)	−0.57 (−0.92)
Lift Cost						−0.17 (−1.09)
Observations	1286	993	993	993	993	993
R-squared	0.181	0.373	0.376	0.377	0.377	0.379

t-scores in parentheses (based on robust standard errors clustered by state).
* significant at 10%; ** significant at 5%; *** significant at 1%.

OPEC. Model 3 reveals the key finding, by reintroducing the OPEC variable into the regression.

In Model 3, OPEC membership is *not* statistically significant. Moreover, it does nothing to improve the explanatory power of the model (the R-squared moves from 0.373 to 0.376). The data fail to show evidence that OPEC membership reduces a state's depletion rate.

Thus, OPEC members produce oil at more or less exactly the same rates that they could be expected to produce in the absence of OPEC. The findings imply that, to the extent that OPEC members underproduce compared to non-OPEC members, they do so because of other factors in the model (e.g., fiscal strength, investment risk) that have nothing to do with their OPEC membership. Some OPEC members might restrict their depletion rate as a conscious act of policy, but they appear to do so out of their own self-interest, without institutional support from OPEC. For instance, Saudi Arabia appears to maintain spare production capacity that it uses strategically to alter the oil supply.[38]

Some OPEC members tend to produce oil at rates as fast or faster than comparable non-OPEC members. For instance, Indonesia and Ecuador often had depletion rates higher than the global average despite being members of a "cartel" with the nominal goal of restricting oil production. Other OPEC members, like Saudi Arabia and the other Gulf monarchies, produced more slowly, but this seems adequately explained by their market position, high oil revenues per capita, and business inefficiencies.[39] Note that several countries outside of the OPEC "cartel," such as Azerbaijan, Mexico, and Kazakhstan, had depletion rates that were as low or lower than most OPEC members, again probably due to the poor business and investment climates in those countries.

What about the "dominant producer" hypothesis? Model 4 and 5 in Table 4.2 suggest that it is plausible that Saudi Arabia has a significantly lower depletion rate than one would otherwise expect, implying that its policymakers could be consciously choosing a slow depletion rate to affect the world oil market. Moreover, Saudi Arabia varies its depletion rate considerably over time. Its motives for the changes seem to vary from case to case because Saudi Arabia sometimes seeks higher oil prices (e.g., 1982–1985), greater market share (e.g., 1985–1986),[40] or to provide emergency oil supply (e.g., in the wake of Iraq's invasion of Kuwait in 1990, or the US invasion of Iraq in 2003). To assess the dominant producer idea, Model 4 is applied. It is the same as Model 3 except that it divides the OPEC variable in two: an indicator variable for Saudi Arabia, and one for all other OPEC states. The coefficient for Saudi Arabia is more than double

---

[38] Yergin 2008; Parra 2004.
[39] Saudi Arabia and the other Gulf monarchies fall into this category. In countries like Iran and Iraq, low depletion rates are also strongly influenced by the poor business climate in those states, which in turn are affected by factors like managerial incompetence, wars, corruption, and political risk for investments.
[40] Yergin 2008; Parra 2004.

the size of the coefficient for the other OPEC states, and while it is still not sta-tistically significant at standard thresholds, it is close (t-score = 1.59, p < 0.12). Some scholars have argued that OPEC is divided between a "core" and "non-core" set of member states, in which the core oil-rich states deplete their oil more slowly.[41] Model 5 tests this possibility by further dividing the OPEC variable into three categories: Saudi Arabia, other OPEC core states (defined as Kuwait, UAE, Qatar, and Libya), and the "non-core" OPEC countries. In Model 5, the coeffi-cient for Saudi Arabia is again the strongest and most negative, followed by the other "core" OPEC countries. However, none of the variables is statistically sig-nificant, and only Saudi Arabia's is even close (t-score = 1.26). Finally, Model 6 controls for *lift costs*; the findings are consistent with Model 3.[42] In sum, these models provide little to no evidence that OPEC has any systematic causal effect on depletion rates, and there is some (weak) evidence of Saudi Arabia as a dom-inant producer.

As in all statistical models, it is impossible to affirm the null hypothesis (i.e., to *prove* that OPEC has no impact), but there is no evidence that OPEC is having a causal impact. One might wonder whether the statistical tests here are too imprecise to identify the effect OPEC is having on its members' deple-tion rate. To test this idea, let's suppose that the difference between an OPEC member (except Saudi Arabia) and its baseline predicted oil production (from Model 2) is really caused by a difference in depletion policy, not simply sta-tistical noise. On average, OPEC countries (except Saudi Arabia) produce 6.6 percent less oil than predicted.[43] In recent years, 6.6 percent of non-Saudi OPEC oil was equal to roughly 2.0 percent of the world oil market. While two percent of world oil matters a lot in terms of short-term disruptions, it is diffi-cult to believe that such an amount is having a major impact on world oil prices over the medium or long term, even assuming (1) that it is a conscious policy of the OPEC states and (2) that it induces no supply substitution from non-OPEC oil sources.

One might wonder whether selection bias is a threat to the analysis here. OPEC membership is not random. Only states with relatively large oil re-serves are likely to join OPEC. We might expect such states to have relatively low depletion rates because states with large oil reserves could meet their

[41] Blaydes 2004. See also Teece 1982; Alhajji and Huettner 2000.

[42] Unfortunately, there is a lack of publicly released, cross-national time-series data for meas-uring lift costs. As a proxy, the lift cost data for different countries can be estimated using data from a Goldman Sachs report on the largest 125 upstream development projects under development. Waghorn et al. 2006. The issue of data quality is considered further in the discussion of robustness checks.

[43] Calculated by subtracting actual depletion rate minus the post-estimation predicted rate from Model 2.

fiscal needs even without maximizing oil production. Yet if OPEC "selects for" the states with low depletion rates, that should make it even easier to observe that OPEC states systematically underproduce compared to non-OPEC states. There is no such evidence. The only way that a selection effect could mask OPEC's impact as a cartel is if the states that join OPEC are systematically likely to have higher depletion rates than non-OPEC members. There is no reason to believe that is true.

One other striking feature of the market for oil is its remarkable resilience to the impact of international events such as wars and economic sanctions. Although there can be little doubt that wars do have impact in some circumstances (e.g., Kuwait in 1990), the evidence suggests that those disruptions occur only in the face of truly catastrophic violence and even then are quite short-lived. International sanctions also have a mixed record. Some sanctions, such as those placed on Angola, Libya, Syria, and Sudan, appear to have had very little impact on oil output. However, the sanctions on Iran in recent years and some of those on Iraq in the 1990s seem to have had more effect. Additional work is needed to evaluate the true effectiveness of sanctions on oil-exporting states.

The statistical models were subjected to a battery of robustness checks, the full description of which is available elsewhere.[44] For instance, I tested the possibility that OPEC has an effect on its members' production in only certain time periods or under tight market conditions. Again, I found no evidence of OPEC's impact.

In sum, I used four tests to try to identify the market impact of OPEC, and each test returns the same basic result: there is no evidence that OPEC is restricting its members' oil production rate as a cartel would. It is national governments and oil firms, not a supranational body, that hold the real authority in the modern international order for oil production.

Subsystems theory highlights the importance of punishments for noncompliance. Like most international organizations, OPEC relies on states to enforce its decisions. Some international organizations can make this work. The WTO, for instance, facilitates states holding each other accountable for violations of the trade commitments, by providing a quasi-judicial process and stipulating how states can impose reciprocal trade tariffs on the noncomplying country. OPEC has no such option for enforcement. Its member states do not actually trade much with each other; their major export goes to non-OPEC countries. So if one OPEC country agrees to a production quota but then cheats on it, there is precious little the other member states can do (short of invading it

---

[44] Colgan 2014.

militarily—typically an unattractive and infeasible option). In short, OPEC has no mechanism for punishing for noncompliance.

In principle, an international order could be maintained through strategic benefits alone, even without punishments for noncompliance. In the case of Subsystem A, the strategic benefits would take the form of increased oil revenue that resulted from a state's compliance with an OPEC quota. Yet to achieve an increase in oil revenue, the increase in price would have to outweigh the loss of production for the state complying with OPEC's quota. That is highly unlikely for most states, each having a small share of the total world market. For instance, consider a state producing 2 million barrels of oil per day (mbd), roughly what Nigeria produced in 2017. Suppose it cut its production by 20 percent, equal to 0.4 mbd. That amount is large for Nigeria but small for the world, equal to roughly 0.4 percent of the total world market. For Nigeria to break even, the 0.4 percent reduction in supply would need to increase the price by 25 percent—a highly unlikely market response! Consequently, for typical OPEC members like Nigeria, complying with an OPEC quota simply does not make economic sense. It costs them money. Only a very large oil producer like Saudi Arabia has a hope of profitably manipulating the price of oil. Thus OPEC offers weak strategic benefits for most of its members. Not surprisingly, OPEC has struggled to sustain the international order it wanted.

Understanding OPEC's Persistence

If OPEC is not a cartel, why does it live on and what exactly is it doing? The short answer is that OPEC can be understood as a political club that generates diplomatic and other political benefits for its members, and its cartel reputation is an integral source of political strength for the organization. It therefore sustains a "rational myth." A rational myth is an idea that is illusory or false but persists in part because some actors have incentives to sustain it.[45] Some non-OPEC actors realize that its image is incorrect, but few of them have strong incentives to contradict it. Most people simply do not know enough about the details of OPEC, and quite rationally rely on others' judgment. Given that almost no one directly and forcefully contradicts the idea that OPEC is a cartel, the myth persists.

The 1973 oil crisis established OPEC's perceived power to influence oil markets. Its member governments proved in that year that they were capable of cooperation and joint decision-making about production (or at least some of

---

[45] McNamara 2002.

them, because not all of them participated in the oil embargo).[46] Even though the magnitude of the supply disruption was both temporary and relatively small, it sent a powerful signal that OPEC governments could and would cooperate in setting their production levels. At the time, all the evidence seemed to suggest that OPEC was an effective cartel: oil prices rose; OPEC members coordinated a cut in oil exports and enforced an embargo on some of their customers; and OPEC members were actively and openly colluding.[47] Scholars, journalists, oil companies, and policymakers agreed.[48] The diplomatic cables of US State Department officials around the time of the 1973 oil crisis provide ample evidence that policymakers viewed OPEC as a cartel.[49]

Much has changed since 1973. Some of the actions that OPEC took in 1973 cannot be repeated: posted prices no longer exist, and oil nationalization has already happened in most major producers. Only the third action taken by OPEC members, an embargo, could happen in today's oil market. Yet in terms of affecting oil prices, the embargo was probably been the least important of the three major OPEC actions. Moreover, oil-consuming countries have put in place, since 1973, a number of safeguards to mitigate the effect of such an embargo.[50] Without insisting that it is impossible, OPEC is unlikely to ever again influence the oil market as it did in 1973.

Still, popular beliefs have been slow to change since the 1970s. Part of the problem is that analysts and journalists tend to interpret any OPEC production cuts or growth as evidence of cartel activity.[51] This is misleading. Just because OPEC often cuts production when oil prices are falling, that does not mean that it is a cartel. Even in perfectly competitive markets, supply tends to shrink when prices are low and grow when prices are high. Both OPEC and non-OPEC producers tend to follow this pattern, but the media pays outsized attention to OPEC.

The forces perpetuating OPEC's image as a market manipulator go deeper than that, however. Some actors have incentives to perpetuate the myth.

---

[46] Only Saudi Arabia, Iran, Iraq, Abu Dhabi, Kuwait, and Qatar announced production cuts and unilateral increases in posted prices on October 16, 1973. Even among this group, not all of them followed through.

[47] Claes 2001; Parra 2004; Yergin 2008.

[48] Krasner 1974; Osborne 1976; Seymour 1980; Doran 1980.

[49] Qaimmaqami and Keefer 2011: 165, 167, 285, 366, 432, 489, 1019.

[50] Gholz and Press 2010. In addition, long-term contracts mostly have been replaced, making the market more flexible. The effect of an embargo, while not zero, would be mitigated by these innovations. Perhaps not surprisingly, there has not been an international embargo by producers since 1973 (compared to three in the period 1956—1973).

[51] As just one of many examples, see: https://www.cnbc.com/2016/11/30/opec-reportedly-reaches-agreement-to-cut-oil-production.html.

OPEC's Incentives to Continue as a
Political Club

The belief that OPEC states are members of a cartel generates significant political benefits for them, both at home and abroad. So long as OPEC is viewed as powerful, its leaders can claim credit at home for their "economic stewardship" of the global economy. Leaders of OPEC member states have sought to take credit for their rising economic fortunes in exactly this way. For example, Venezuelan president Hugo Chávez, who was elected in 1998 as oil prices were plunging, later publicly argued that he revitalized OPEC and thus caused world oil prices to rise.[52] This narrative gave Chávez a significant political asset in Venezuelan domestic politics. Similarly, Iranian leaders lucky enough to be in power during periods of rising oil prices have sought to use OPEC to take credit in the eyes of the Iranian public.[53] OPEC thus serves as a useful tool for state leaders when communicating with their domestic constituency.

In addition, the perceived power of OPEC allows its members to reap political rewards in terms of diplomatic influence and attention paid to them. Perceived power brings prestige, and prestige is the currency of international diplomacy. One empirical implication of this hypothesis is that OPEC members ought to have greater diplomatic recognition by other countries than comparable non-OPEC countries, all else equal.

The evidence supports this hypothesis. It suggests that OPEC helps its member states receive more diplomatic recognition than they otherwise would. For instance, Ecuador is noteworthy because it joined OPEC, left, and then rejoined and left again. That variation makes it unlike most other OPEC members. Ecuador joined OPEC in 1973, and by 1975 eleven countries had newly sent diplomatic representatives (an ambassador, chargé d'affaires, or other representative) to Ecuador, whereas only one had withdrawn its representative (Ethiopia).[54] The eleven countries with new representatives—Canada, Haiti, Luxembourg, East Germany, Poland, Hungary, Bulgaria, Romania, Russia, South Korea, and India—represented a broad cross-section of the world, geographically, economically, and politically. By contrast, when Ecuador suspended its OPEC membership in 1992, it sustained a net *loss* in diplomatic representation. When Ecuador rejoined OPEC in 2007, it again enjoyed a net gain in diplomatic representation,

---

[52] For more details, see Colgan 2014.

[53] See Krauss 2011; UPI.com 2011. For more details, see Colgan 2014.

[54] Diplomatic representation is measured only once every five years in the COW data set, so I describe changes in diplomatic representation in the five-year window within which the state joined or left OPEC.

this time consisting of eighteen new embassies or consulates over the next five years. Similarly, when Gabon joined OPEC in 1975, it gained diplomatic representation from nineteen new countries and lost representation from four; when Gabon left OPEC in 1992, it gained representation from only one country and lost it from four others.

These examples are illustrative of a wider pattern. Statistical tests confirm that OPEC generates diplomatic benefits for its members, even after controlling for many other potentially confounding variables.[55] For instance, the models controlled for the following variables: each state's military capabilities; each state's status as a nuclear power; the political regime type of each state; the geographic distance between a pair of states; whether the pair contains an alliance and/or a political rivalry; and whether the state is an oil producer (regardless of OPEC membership). In short, OPEC membership is strongly and positively correlated with levels of diplomatic recognition, indicating that OPEC members are more likely to be diplomatically recognized (and reciprocally, to recognize other states) than comparable non-OPEC members. This finding is true for all OPEC members, not just of Saudi Arabia.

One striking result is the size of the impact that OPEC has on diplomatic representation. The results suggest that OPEC membership has roughly the same impact on diplomatic representation as having nuclear weapons. This is remarkable, because nuclear weapons are often seen as the ultimate status symbol.[56] On average, OPEC membership is correlated with an increase in diplomatic representation from nine additional states, compared to an equivalent (oil-producing) country that is not an OPEC member.

The value of increased diplomatic representation is hard to gauge, but it is not trivial. For instance, many of the new diplomatic connections were with relatively rich countries, which therefore represented opportunities for increased trade, investment, and tourism. Specifically, about 40 percent of the countries that sent diplomatic representatives to a new member of OPEC had income (GDP per capita) higher than the world average. Moreover, during the Cold War, the new diplomatic connections spanned the divide between East and West. Many OPEC members were otherwise rather marginal to global geopolitics, so diplomatic connections to both sides of the Cold War could bring valuable information, political leverage, and perhaps foreign aid.[57] Diplomatic recognition also brings a certain amount of status

[55] Colgan 2014.
[56] Sagan 1997.
[57] Bueno de Mesquita and Smith 2016.

and prestige that is hard to measure objectively, but states pursue status for its own sake.[58]

Given the political benefits OPEC generates for its members, they have no incentive to expose OPEC as an ineffective cartel. To the extent that the members are aware, they are willing to go along with the rituals of acting as a cartel. There is also the potential for cognitive dissonance, in which policymakers inside OPEC do not reconcile their understanding of the oil market with their desire to believe in OPEC as a cartel.[59]

Note that in recent years, the staff of OPEC has sought to avoid use of the word "cartel," because of various legal challenges (or potential challenges) they face in the EU and the United States. Even so, they publicly say OPEC aims to "coordinate and unify the petroleum policies of its Member Countries and ensure the stabilization of oil markets,"[60] and it does so by attempting to proration supply—which is exactly what a cartel aims to do.

Non-OPEC Members' Incentives and Beliefs

Why hasn't the rest of the world seen through the "rational myth" of OPEC as a cartel? Informed oil market participants outside of OPEC such as commodity traders and oil companies have the analytical skills and data to assess OPEC's behavior and impact. They might be able to see that OPEC is not a functioning cartel. But market participants and commercial analysts are not necessarily interested in the question of whether it is a cartel.

Instead, they want to know: Does at least one of the members of OPEC have some market influence, at least some of the time? The answer to that question is probably yes. Saudi Arabia appears to have market power: it claims to have significant spare capacity, which is plausible; it depletes its oil quite slowly and probably far below its marginal cost of production; and it makes major, observable changes to its oil production levels that correlate (imperfectly) with its statements about its desire to loosen or tighten global oil supply. Other states like UAE and Kuwait might also have a modest amount of market power, though the evidence here is less clear. The question of whether at least one member of OPEC has market power is important to non-OPEC market participants because it means that the

---

[58] Wohlforth 2009; Paul et al. 2014; Renshon 2017; Zarakol 2017.

[59] For instance, a former secretary general of OPEC insists that OPEC shapes world oil prices: "The control was, and remains, long-distance, erratic, imprecise, and unpredictable—but in the end, very real . . . The system is slow, clumsy, partly dependent on necessarily inaccurate demand forecasts, and bedeviled by indiscipline within OPEC's ranks. But, by and large, it works" (Parra, 2004, 321–322).

[60] OPEC website, https://www.opec.org/opec_web/en/about_us/23.htm.

behavior of OPEC (as a group, not as an organization) can affect market prices and production, and thus the strategies of oil market participants.

Consequently, some expert market participants understand, to varying degrees, that OPEC is not a cartel. Yet, mostly, they do not care. They still pay attention to OPEC for signals about present and future Saudi behavior. This is comparable to the way observers pay attention to the White House press secretary for clues about the president's thinking, even though the press secretary has no real power of his or her own. Thus, OPEC's announcements could affect market perceptions, which matter in the short term for commodity traders.[61] It is rational for market participants to observe OPEC even if they believe that the organization itself does not alter market fundamentals. Instead, they are principally interested in OPEC as shorthand for "the members of OPEC," just as other market analysts are interested in the BRICs as shorthand for "Brazil, Russia, India, and China" without implying that these countries are in some way colluding.

What about other informed analysts, such as academic scholars? Scholars have difficulty reaching a unanimous or even dominant view on questions that involve complex causality and where experimental testing in laboratory conditions is infeasible. Indeed, scholars face professional incentives to generate debate by providing novel arguments and contrarian empirical findings. The topic of OPEC as a cartel is causally complex. Not surprisingly, consensus has been difficult to achieve, as the research reviewed earlier indicates. Given the ongoing debate among scholars, and the fact that academics often find it difficult to sway public opinion even on matters where there is considerable scholarly agreement, it is not surprising that they have failed to persuade non-academics to change their view about OPEC. The problem is made worse by the incentives facing journalists. Certain journalists might have the knowledge necessary to question the cartel myth, but they seem to find it useful to treat OPEC as a cartel: it provides a simple, convenient narrative to explain increases and decreases in the price of oil.

Government analysts are also well informed, and their failure to realize that OPEC does not operate as a cartel, and/or to forcefully articulate that point to their political bosses, is more surprising and puzzling. It is not entirely clear whether the problem is one of knowledge or of communication. Government analysts are presumably capable of conducting the same analysis this chapter describes, but to date either that analysis has not been done or it has not been widely disseminated. My personal discussions with various officials in the US government suggest that there is a wide range of beliefs about OPEC in the bureaucracy, and some analysts are indeed quite skeptical of OPEC's ability to

---

[61] Hyndman 2008.

behave as a cartel. Even so, the modal belief of government analysts seems to be that OPEC is a semi-functional cartel.[62]

The mistake by government analysts should be understood in light of the topic's analytic complexity. For instance, in the first half of 2008, oil prices rose over $140 per barrel in July, before plunging below $40 per barrel in January 2009. OPEC's oil production rose significantly as prices increased, and fell when prices were falling. This looked to many like evidence of OPEC's cartel behavior. Yet, OPEC's behavior might be simply a profit-maximizing response to price changes. Notably, non-OPEC behaved almost exactly the same way. Moreover, only one OPEC country (Saudi Arabia) made an especially large production cut, which is hardly evidence of cartel coordination. There is no evidence that cuts made by other OPEC members were larger than a perfectly competitive market response.[63]

For everyone who is not a specialist in oil—that is, politicians, senior officials, the public, and most scholars and journalists—the question of whether OPEC is a cartel is not something that much matters. Quite rationally, they choose not to devote time and effort into investigating this question because they have other jobs and concerns.

Presidents, legislators, and other senior government officials appear to fall into this group. We cannot directly observe leaders' beliefs but clues can be obtained from their memoirs. For instance, in one of the few mentions of OPEC in former president Bill Clinton's autobiography, he writes, "Energy was a huge issue [in 1980] because of OPEC's steep increase in the price of oil, which raised prices for everything else, too."[64] Elsewhere he writes, "[In 2000] I wanted to see the price stabilize at between $20 and $22 a barrel and hoped OPEC could increase production enough to do that."[65] Those statements seem to indicate that Clinton viewed OPEC as an effective cartel. Bill Richardson, Clinton's secretary of energy, also states in his memoirs, "What we faced was a combination of OPEC power in the marketplace, our dependence on imported oil, and demand pressures."[66] He also recalls making many trips to various OPEC countries "to jawbone for hikes in output that would moderate the increase in prices."[67]

Does the myth about OPEC really matter? Yes, though the consequences are not huge. I discussed one of those consequences earlier: domestic audiences in oil-producing countries tend to give credit to OPEC leaders like Hugo Chávez for raising the price of oil, even though there is no real evidence that he actually

---

[62] For details, see Colgan 2014.
[63] See also Claes 2001 (chapter 7) on this point.
[64] Clinton 2005: 268.
[65] Clinton 2005: 900. He adds on the same page, "I spoke with King Fahd of Saudi Arabia about the possibility of OPEC increasing its production."
[66] Richardson 2005: 266.
[67] Richardson 2005: 269.

caused such a change. A second example is that many people outside of oil-producing countries are psychologically disposed to pay more attention to OPEC members like Iran or Venezuela when prices are high or rising. This could mean a tendency for diplomats to defer to OPEC members and offer favors in exchange for promises of increased or decreased OPEC oil production.[68] Some studies suggest that, regardless of whether policymakers actually should let oil politics affect their policies, they do in fact behave that way.[69] For instance, policymakers are willing to incur considerable material costs in order to increase oil imports from one country (e.g., a friendly neighbor) or lower them from another (e.g., a potential risky supplier), despite the tendency of a fungible world market to re-adjust the flow of oil to reach equilibrium.[70]

A third example of the negative consequences of misunderstanding OPEC comes from legislative politics. Politicians in the United States and other oil-importing states blame OPEC for manipulating world oil markets, especially during times of high oil and gasoline prices. For instance, the No Oil Producing and Exporting Cartels (NOPEC) Act of 2021 introduced in the US House of Representatives served as a rallying point for those who sought to blame OPEC. Other NOPEC bills have been introduced at least fifteen times since 1999, though to date none have become law.[71] The continued introduction of these bills distracts Congress and the public, thereby imposing an opportunity cost on the political system.

Understanding OPEC as a political club also helps answer certain puzzles. One such issue is the variation in OPEC's membership. In the 1970s, OPEC enjoyed a certain level of prestige when developing countries saw it as an orga-nization that "took on" the rich countries and won (by raising oil prices). Several oil-exporting developing countries that were not already members wanted into the club: Ecuador and Gabon joined the organization in 1973 and 1975 respec-tively, only to leave the organization as its prestige fell in the 1990s. Then in the 2000s, with oil prices on the rise, OPEC membership became fashionable again: Ecuador rejoined (before leaving again in 2020), Angola was accepted as a new member in 2007, and Sudan sought membership, though it was not accepted.[72] This variation in OPEC membership is counterintuitive behavior if OPEC is a cartel because membership in the organization would be most costly

[68] Richardson 2005: 266–274.

[69] Clayton and Levi 2012.

[70] Arguably there might be wartime benefits to manipulating oil imports in this way, but scholars are skeptical of those benefits (see Gholz and Press 2010).

[71] Verrastro et al. 2011.

[72] Gabon, Equatorial Guinea, and the Republic of Congo also joined OPEC in the period 2016–2018, as OPEC's status rose by joining forces with Russia to form "OPEC+." Indonesia's departed in 2008; that might have had less to do with prestige and more to do with its new status as a net importer of oil. Puzzlingly, it rejoined OPEC in 2016. Still, that lasted only for a few months.

at times when oil prices are high (in terms of forgone oil sales, to the extent that such exist). The fluctuations in OPEC's membership, which seem to correlate with oil prices, make more sense when viewed from the perspective of the perceived political clout and prestige of the organization.

Member states perceive OPEC membership as a signal of status and prestige. For instance, when Angola joined the organization in 2007, it took out full-page advertisements in *The Economist* to announce that it had joined OPEC and should be seen as a country of rising importance. Implicitly, the advertisements tied these two claims together: Angola was rising in importance, in part, *because* it had joined OPEC.

In sum, the story of OPEC's continued existence is primarily a political one. It is based largely on the perpetuation of a rational myth. Still, OPEC is not necessarily useless. The organization probably facilitates information sharing and lowers transaction costs between states, like many other international regimes.[73] As chapter 3 described, OPEC has long served as a forum for sharing strategies for dealing with international oil companies, best practices for writing contracts, and approaches to tax policy. OPEC members also share predictions about the oil market, which are important for investment decisions. Overall, though, OPEC's chief purpose appears to be political.

Conclusion

This chapter showed that OPEC quotas are irregularly applied, frequently ignored by its members, and have little if any effect on actual production. Still, many scholars and policymakers continue to believe that OPEC has great power over oil markets. One might say that OPEC probably has market power because it includes Saudi Arabia, but only in that sense; the evidence undermines the idea that the OPEC as an organization manipulates the world oil supply.

OPEC's failure as a cartel makes sense in light of subsystems theory. OPEC has no way to punish its own members for their noncompliance with production quotas. After all, if a member state overproduces, what can the other members do about it? Without enforcement, the modern international order for oil production, such as it is, does little to regulate prices or boost their average levels. From the perspective of net oil importer countries, like the United States and much of Western Europe, OPEC's inability to control prices is a mixed blessing. Net importers benefit, on the whole, from lower oil prices, but they suffer somewhat from the volatility in the prices that comes hand-in-hand with the lack of an effective mechanism for regulating global supply.

[73] Keohane 1984.

By 2012, the organization was openly struggling with its identity and purpose. It had stopped even trying to assign individual production quotas to its members, instead only identifying a (pointless) production target for the group as a whole. Moreover, OPEC members faced new challenges in an era of climate change and declining per-capita oil revenues. Some analysts see OPEC caught in a "perfect storm."[74] It is squeezed between decelerating global demand, in part due to climate change and alternative energy technologies, and rising global supply, in part due to fracking and unconventional oil supply in the United States and elsewhere.[75] These challenges only intensified in the Covid-19 pandemic.

Yet, the favorable geology in OPEC countries means that their oil will likely remain competitive in a low-cost environment, even if it does not generate the massive profits it once did. Moreover, starting in November 2016, OPEC began a comeback bid by forming a partnership with Russia. In 2017, it reinstituted production allocation targets (i.e., quotas). Noncompliance with those targets continued to be an issue for OPEC. The larger problem, however, was the questionable extent to which the organization was really altering its members' behavior from what they would have done anyway. It is unclear just how much the Russia-OPEC agreements actually affect behavior, and how durable they will be, but it is possible that this new form of cooperation will prove more than skin deep.

The leaders of OPEC often seem to enjoy the lack of clarity in the global oil market, and their ability to reveal information when it suits them. In September 2020, for instance, Saudi energy minister Prince Abdulaziz bin Salman said, "Anyone who thinks they will get a word from me on what we will do next is absolutely living in La La Land."[76] Whatever its future role in the economics of oil, OPEC has a place in the political narrative.

My findings have implications for both theory and practice. For scholars, the fact that a widespread belief about the world's most important commodity market appears to be wrong should alter how we study international political economy. One implication is that scholars should be careful about how the bargaining dynamics within OPEC are studied and conceptualized because they do not occur within the context of a classic economic cartel.[77] Second, OPEC appears to be an important case within the category of international regimes that have outlived their original mandates.[78] A third implication of these findings is to reinforce the research demonstrating that actors' knowledge of causation is imperfect, especially in economic policy.[79] Finally, the case of OPEC undermines

[74] Van de Graaf 2017.
[75] Van de Graaf and Verbruggen 2015; Colgan and Van de Graaf 2017.
[76] Raval 2020.
[77] Blaydes 2004.
[78] Barnett and Finnemore 1999; Gray 2018; Duffield 1994; Wallander 2000.
[79] Darden 2009; Blyth 2002; Morrison 2012.

the idea of international organizations as a product of rational design.[80] OPEC was designed long before its eventual function was fully understood.

In the realm of practical politics, journalists and pundits should stop assuming that OPEC's actions are the key drivers of world energy markets. They are not. Most of the credit or blame for shifting oil prices in recent years rests with the changing energy demands of Asian customers, not diabolic moves by OPEC. Moreover, policymakers in oil-importing countries should stop being so fearful and resentful of OPEC. Legislation such as the various "NOPEC" bills in the US Congress may be useful for scoring political points, but they have little bearing on the reality of the global oil markets. With the world price of oil set by market forces almost entirely outside of its control, OPEC is along for the ride like everyone else.

---

[80] Koremenos, Lipson, and Snidal 2001.

5

Oil and Security

"If Iraq wins, no small state is safe. They won't stop here. They see a chance to take a major share of oil. It's got to be stopped."
—Prime Minister Margaret Thatcher to President George H. W. Bush, 1990

When Winston Churchill became First Lord of the Admiralty in 1911, he soon faced one of modern history's most consequential decisions. Churchill was not then the man known to posterity now. Just thirty-six years old, he was an unproven, cocky, self-promoting man most famous for his daring escape as a prisoner of war during the Second Boer War in South Africa. First elected to Parliament as a Conservative in 1900, he switched to the Liberal Party in 1904 and swiftly became a cabinet member, first as an undersecretary and then in a senior post. In 1911, Britain was building powerful battleships as part of a naval arms race with the Germans. The American and German navies already had new oil-powered ships. Britain's battleships, to that point, only had coal-fired steam engines.[1] Oil, when properly refined, could fuel faster and deadlier ships. The catch was that Britain had all the coal supplies it needed in its home isles, but precious little oil.[2] The Admiralty wanted to know: did the new First Lord want to switch to oil or stick with coal?

Churchill made the momentous set of decisions in 1912–1913 to switch the British fleet from coal to oil. He later called it a "fateful plunge."[3] In doing so, he gave British military power a boost, but at the price of creating a new worry. Britain, like most of Europe, would have to get most of its oil from overseas. It could import from the United States, but Churchill wanted the British Empire to have its own supplies. Fortunately, Britain had a head start. In 1908, a new outfit called the Anglo-Persian Oil Company had discovered commercial quantities of oil in territory that is now called Iran. Later, that company became British

---

[1] The Royal Navy also had some oil-powered destroyers and submarines, but much of the fleet, including all of its battleships, still ran on coal. Auzanneau 2018: 85.

[2] Offshore oil fields in the North Sea, shared by the United Kingdom and Norway, were unknown at the time, and not commercially viable until the 1970s.

[3] Churchill 1923: 130–136.

Petroleum, and then simply BP. Britain's growing thirst for oil during World War I meant it was soon looking for more. It became clear that security of oil supply meant controlling the Persian Gulf and the path to it.

The British Empire was not alone in its desire to lock up oil. France, Russia, and other empires found that some of the territories they controlled had valuable oil deposits, and they struggled mightily to keep them. Even more dramatically, imperial Japan invaded Southeast Asia in 1941 in search of petroleum, after being cut off from American oil. The United States, while not formally an empire, practiced *de facto* imperialism,[4] in part to develop and exploit its nascent oil industry. Yet the tide was turning against imperialism. The twentieth century eventually saw the greatest wave of decolonization in human history. What were the great powers to do?

This chapter traces the big developments of the twentieth century in the context of subsystems theory. In the first half of the century, oil played a key role in imperial expansion and war. Britain's thirst for oil was a driving force of its last surge of imperial growth in the Middle East, where it was the regional hegemon. For oil companies, the British Empire had just the kind of instruments of coercion that they needed to obtain political cooperation from various locals in exchange for a trickle of financial benefits. After World War II, oil shaped decolonization and the Cold War. Oil created an incentive to delay decolonization, with the result that petro-colonies were often among the last to get independence. Even after legal decolonization, Anglo-American oil companies and their governments had ways, temporarily, of maintaining control and punishing those in the Middle East who sought true independence. Eventually, such forms of coercion became too costly, and what remained were arrangements based on mutual benefit to the petrostate and its protector. The key actors—oil firms, Western governments, and petrostates—interacted with each other as a pair of evolving subsystems emerged from the ashes of European imperialism.

One of these subsystems, which I call Subsystem B, focused on the issue of state sovereignty and military security. On the surface, the shift away from formal imperialism toward the sovereignty of independent states seemed like a huge one. It was, in certain ways, but on the crucial matter of military security, the shift was often far more superficial than it appeared. Many of the new or decolonized petrostates eventually followed in the footsteps of Saudi Arabia, by accepting a semi-formalized security guarantee from an external power. Initially both the United Kingdom and the United States played the role of external protector. By the 1970s, Britain had withdrawn.

The Iraqi invasion of Kuwait in 1990 vividly demonstrated the significance of the oil security subsystem. In the weeks following the invasion, US president

---

[4] Vitalis 2007; Yergin 2008; Cline 2013; Morefield 2014; Pepinsky 2015.

George H. W. Bush discussed the situation with British prime minister Margaret Thatcher on multiple occasions. Going to war against Iraq was not a foregone conclusion. Yet Bush and Thatcher had inherited an international order that maintained a steady flow of oil from the Persian Gulf to Western economies and their allies, and there were powerful incentives to preserve it. The order in that subsystem was underpinned by oil-for-security deals.[5] Britain and the United States forged them with a variety of petrostates, including Saudi Arabia and Kuwait.[6] Initially that list included other petrostates like Iraq and Iran, but eventually they rejected those deals.

Analytically, this chapter shows the origins and nature of oil-for-security (OFS) deals as the backbone of a second subsystem for oil, distinct from the oil production subsystem highlighted in chapters 3 and 4. The next two sections of the chapter are mainly descriptive, to provide historical context. The remainder of the chapter offers evidence that OFS deals exist and represented governing arrangements. It also describes the conditions under which the OFS deals broke down on three occasions: in Iraq, in 1958; in Libya, in 1969; and in Iran, in 1979. The OFS deals—both those that collapsed and those that continued—continue to shape the politics of the Middle East in the twenty-first century.

The Last Burst of Imperial Expansion

World War I was, in a sense, the first oil war.[7] It was not a fight *over* oil, but it was a fight using technologies based on oil. Coal-fired naval ships became obsolete, unable to match the new battleships. Churchill also saw the potential of a new military technology: the tank. As a cabinet member, he used Admiralty funds to support research to create them. In the late stages of the war, only tanks could cut through the mud and barbed wire of modern trench warfare. They played a small but pivotal role in that war, and a much larger one in the next world war. Additionally, oil-fueled military technologies proved instrumental not only on land and sea, but also in the air: World War I witnessed the deployment of military aircraft for the first time. Again, Churchill was a supporter. As the war became increasingly mechanized, the Allies' superior access to oil and gasoline gave them a decisive advantage in the late stages of the war. Lord George Curzon, soon to become the British foreign minister, declared in 1918, "We might almost say that the allied cause had floated to victory upon a wave of oil."[8] Notwithstanding his insights on military technology, however, World War I spelled political

---

[5] Painter 1986; Bronson 2006; Duffield 2007; Yetiv 2011; Bapat 2019.
[6] Mitchell 2002; Yergin 2008; Kim 2019.
[7] Winegard 2016.
[8] Quoted in Auzanneau 2018: 92.

disaster for Churchill. He masterminded the failed Dardanelles campaign that led to a slaughter of allied forces at Gallipoli (mostly from Australia and New Zealand). Forced to resign from Cabinet, Churchill would have to work for years to restore his tarnished reputation.

After World War I, oil was more than just a military commodity. It became the economic lifeblood of advanced economies, starting in North America and gradually the rest of the world. The United States was the key producer and exporter of oil, supplying close to 70 percent of the world's oil supply in the first half of the twentieth century. Much of the rest of the oil was produced in the Americas, notably Canada, Mexico, and Venezuela. John D. Rockefeller's Standard Oil dominated the industry in the Americas until it was broken up by an anti-trust lawsuit in 1911. Three of the successor companies—Standard Oil of New Jersey (later Exxon), Standard Oil of New York (later Mobil), and Standard Oil of California (now Chevron)—eventually became members of the Seven Sisters.

In the 1920s, European empires wanted to control their own destiny in oil, and imperial expansion was still very much an option. Britain had the largest empire in the world, even if it could no longer match the industrial might of the United States. France, Holland, Belgium, and Portugal also governed far-flung colonial holdings. While these empires began to release their grip on some territories, they grabbed up others. That process was driven partly by the desire for oil, especially in the Middle East.

For Britain, Iraq and Iran were the principal prizes. In the closing days of World War I—actually *after* the armistice ending the war—the British military extended its Mesopotamian Campaign in modern-day Iraq to seize the oil fields near Mosul.[9] A Royal Navy memorandum informed the prime minister that those fields represented "the largest undeveloped resources [of oil] at present known to the world."[10] The British created Iraq out of three provinces from the disintegrating Ottoman Empire, and formalized their control with the Anglo-Iraq treaty of 1920. In Iran, they exerted power and influence. Reza Pahlavi became Iranian prime minister in 1923. His then four-year-old son, Mohammad Reza Pahlavi, grew up watching his father and the Iranian government try to maintain just the right amount of independence from the British, a tricky balancing game that he himself would play later in life.

Oil was later discovered in other British territories. The small gulf monarchies of Kuwait, Bahrain, Qatar, and the United Arab Emirates (UAE) might not even exist as independent countries today, if not for their oil. They came under British control well before oil was discovered there, but as oil grew in importance after 1945, it suited both the local elites and their British overlords for the territories

---

[9] Kelanic 2016: 145; Winegard 2016.
[10] Quoted in Barr 2012: 66.

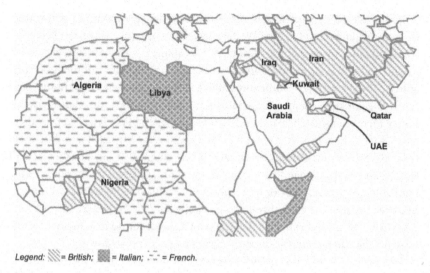

Legend: ▨ = British; ▩ = Italian; ▧ = French.

Figure 5.1   Imperialism in the Middle East and North Africa, ca. 1930
Note: Country names indicate future OPEC members.

to remain colonies. The British navy managed for the most part to keep the peace in the Persian Gulf, allowing trade routes to flourish and local rulers to prosper.[11] Not everyone was pleased, however. Many in Iraq believed that Kuwait ought to be a province of their country. When the British granted Iraq its independence in 1932, they installed King Faisal I on the throne, who accepted borders that did not include Kuwait. Iraq's claim over Kuwait would surface again in later decades.

Colonialism was the common heritage of much of today's global oil system. France controlled Algeria as a colony until the 1950s. Libya was an Italian colony, then an Allied protectorate, and did not gain its independence until 1951. Kuwait, UAE, Qatar, Iraq, and Iran were or had been under the British. Thus, seven of the eight future OPEC members in the Middle East and North African region were European colonies or quasi-colonies; only Saudi Arabia was not. In Africa, Nigeria, Gabon, and Angola were also colonies and future OPEC members. Colonialism varied considerably from place to place, of course. In some territories, oil was often not discovered until very late in the colonial period, and in a few cases, like Libya, commercial development did not begin until after independence. Still, colonial institutions tended to leave a mark, particularly with regard to control over oil production. Figure 5.1 shows the scope of European imperial control in the Middle East and North Africa, ca. 1930.

[11]   Crystal 1990.

By the late 1930s, a pattern of international order was emerging. It involved three principal types of actors: Western governments, international oil companies, and elites in oil-rich territories. At this stage, the two subsystems (of oil production and security) overlapped so closely that they did not function separately. The Western governments established the political and legal framework for their companies to operate globally. The companies took the oil in exchange for payments to local elites in the oil-rich territories (initially Iran and Iraq; then Saudi Arabia; later the others, as oil fields were developed). The local elites used these payments to shore up their own political support. If the elites "defected" from this order by demanding too much, the companies and the empires would punish them economically or militarily. Actual punishments were uncommon, however, because the mere threat was generally enough. So long as imperialism was strong, all parties expected that the punishments for noncompliance would be high. That changed as the imperial system began to break down.

One of the seeds of this order's eventual demise was its own racism. The oil companies set up enclaves within petrostates, often physically separate from the local population. Conservative Islamic governments like the Saudis encouraged this arrangement, to minimize Western cultural influence. Yet a clear racial hierarchy developed that placed local, darker-skinned employees in subordination to white, Western managers.[12] That hierarchy created social frictions and grievances.[13]

World War II and Its Aftermath

Adolf Hitler launched World War II by ordering the German armies to invade Poland on September 1, 1939. The Polish army was thoroughly outmatched. Ten percent of its units were mounted cavalry, a technology whose day had passed. The German Panzer divisions of armored tanks rolled across the country so quickly that they conquered Poland completely by early October (with help from the Soviets). The battle for Poland demonstrated a simple lesson, one that would be repeated over and over throughout World War II. Modern warfare ran on engines, and engines ran on fuel. No fuel, no victory.

Some of the most decisive battles in the whole war came down to this simple truth. It did when the Germans invaded North Africa and sought to drive the British out of Egypt. If the Germans had succeeded, they could have closed the Suez Canal, cutting off the British Isles from the Middle East, from which much of

---

[12] Vitalis 2007.

[13] Decades later, al Qaeda and other terrorist groups would twist some of those same grievances, multiplied by other concerns, to attract recruits. (El-Gamal and Jaffe 2010: 66).

their oil came. Erwin Rommel, one of Germany's best generals, was sent to Libya to conduct the campaign. Initially, his army had considerable success. In May 1942, his forces advanced three hundred miles in a single week as the British fell back. Rommel's forces gathered strength as they went along: at one point, 85 percent of his transport was provided by captured British and American vehicles.[14] By late June, he was less than sixty miles from Alexandria, with the Suez not far beyond. He stopped at a railway junction called El Alamein. Intoxicated by the prospect of victory, Italian prime minister Mussolini flew over to North Africa, and brought with him a white horse, on which he planned to make a triumphant entry into Cairo. But Rommel's forces were hamstrung by a shortage of fuel. He was forced to fall back. His army surged forward a second time, but again, fuel shortages crippled them. At the Second Battle of El Alamein, the British routed the Germans. The Suez Canal was safe, and with it, Britain's lifeline to the Middle East and India.

Crude oil can be refined into various fuels like gasoline, diesel, and jet fuel, and in warfare, the particularities of fuel matter a lot. Arguably the most decisive battle in the whole war turned on this point. Hitler could see that Germany needed more oil for its war machine, so he ordered his armies to invade Soviet Russia on June 22, 1941, in violation of the Molotov-Ribbentrop Pact. He had multiple goals, but chief among them was to seize the oil fields in and near modern-day Azerbaijan. On June 1, 1941, Hitler had predicted, "If I do not get the oil of Maïkop and Grozny, then I must end the war."[15] The Soviets mounted a ferocious defense, throwing millions of men in the way of Germany's advance. At first the German forces made great progress. They captured Russian fuel supplies as they went along, just as they had done in France in 1940. This time, however, they found that Russian tanks ran on diesel, which was useless to them. German Panzers ran on gasoline. That difference helped save the Russians. Before reaching the rich oil fields near Baku, fuel shortages forced the Germans to turn back.[16] In August 1942, the two armies met at Stalingrad, and then waged a bitter campaign against each other for five months. Close to two million were killed, wounded, or captured during the battle. Finally, the German armies were exhausted. They had run out of supplies, none more crucial than gasoline. Without fuel, their famed Panzer divisions could not maneuver. Stuck in one place, the tanks became immobile gun turrets. The Soviets encircled the Germans and ultimately shattered the Sixth Army. It was the turning point of the battle for the Eastern Front, which in turn cost Germany the war.

[14] Yergin 2008: 323.
[15] Gorlaski and Freeburg 1987: 174.
[16] Yergin 2008: 320.

Fuel type also proved crucial for the Battle of Britain. In July 1940, Hitler sent his air force, the Luftwaffe, against Britain. He sought to bomb Britain into submission. Britain responded with Spitfires, the speedy single-pilot fighter aircraft sent to shoot down the German bombers. In turn, the Nazis sent a fleet of Messerschmitt fighters to defend their bombers and counterattack the Spitfires. Crucially, though, the Spitfires used 100-octane jet fuel, while their German foes mainly used 87-octane. The better fuel helped the Spitfires to accelerate more quickly and outmaneuver the Messerschmitts, allowing them to inflict heavy losses.[17] The difference meant that fewer German bombers were available for the rest of the Battle of Britain. In the end, the British people were left unbroken.

The Allies' superior oil resources were crucial in the late stages of the European war, too. Petroleum was no less than half the total tonnage sent from the United States across the Atlantic and the Pacific, including the vehicles, weapons, ammunition, and food.[18] Meanwhile, the Germans were in dire straits. In June 1944, just after the Allied invasion of Normandy, German field marshal Gerd von Rundstedt ordered his troops: "Move your equipment with men and horses; don't use gasoline except in battle."[19] The Allies preyed upon the German fuel shortages, exacerbating the problem. Over a million tons of explosives, a tenth of all bombs dropped on the Reich in 1944 and 1945, were aimed at fuel facilities.[20]

In the Pacific, oil again played a central role in the war. Japan had no oil fields of its own, nor had it managed to conquer any in northern China in the early part of the war. On August 1, 1941, the United States imposed a complete oil and gasoline embargo on Japan, cutting off essentially all of its supplies. So in 1941, Japan invaded the Dutch East Indies (today known as Indonesia), in search of oil and other natural resources. For months, they established a long-distance supply chain, shipping the oil back to Japan's home islands. As the war progressed, however, the US Navy arrived in ever-greater numbers and began to sink the Japanese shipping fleet. Less and less oil got to Tokyo, creating crucial shortages as the war went on.

On October 23–26, 1944, the two sides fought the Battle of Leyte Gulf. By tonnage, it was the largest naval battle in history, in the waters just offshore of the Philippines. The stakes were high. General MacArthur was positioning an invasion force to retake the Philippines, en route to Tokyo. The Imperial Japanese Navy mobilized nearly all of its remaining warships to try to repel the Allied invasion. So desperate were they to win the Battle of Leyte Gulf, the Japanese

---

[17] Converting to 100 octane gave the Spitfires' engines 30 percent more horsepower than when using 87 octane, according to Gorlaski and Freeburg 1987: 275–277. But also see Baily 2008 and Hough and Richards 1989: 387, Appendix XII.

[18] Auzanneau 2018: 168.

[19] Gorlaski and Freeburg 1987: 254.

[20] Auzanneau 2018: 167.

used for the first time a new style of attack: *kamikaze* planes that rammed suicidally into Allies naval forces. On October 25, Admiral Kurita, commander of the Japanese Second Fleet, got into position to enter Leyte Gulf and destroy General MacArthur's lightly defended invasion fleet. It would have been an easy victory. Yet, just forty miles away, Kurita abruptly pulled off and sailed away. Asked why, he later said, because "of shortage of fuel."[21] Having failed to achieve its objective, the Japanese navy suffered heavy losses, and never again sailed to battle in comparable force. The majority of its surviving heavy ships, deprived of fuel, remained in their bases for the rest of the Pacific War. Once again: no fuel, no victory.

World War II proved that oil was an indispensable military resource.[22] The postwar reconstruction made it an essential asset for the civilian economy, too. Prior to the war, private vehicles were mostly located in North America. After the war, car ownership in Western Europe skyrocketed, as described in chapter 3. The spread of private and commercial vehicles helped transform European economies, enabling more rapid delivery of everything from foodstuffs to passengers.

In 1947, while at Harvard University, Secretary of State George Marshall announced a plan to help reconstruct the economy of the Western European allies. The Marshall Plan became famous as one of the most important disbursements of foreign aid of all time. Less well known, however, is that US policymakers intentionally set out to manipulate European economies and increase their oil consumption. Washington explicitly encouraged vehicles and road construction, and discouraged the European preference for railways. The main reason was simple: US companies provided the oil, and the vehicles that consumed it. They wanted a new market. Consequently, petroleum made up fully 10 percent of the US taxpayers' funds spent under the Marshall Plan, more than $1.2 billion dollars in 1948–1951. Another 10 percent was spent on machines and vehicles, of which 98 percent were supplied from US companies.[23] From the companies' perspective, the project was a success. Until then, coal had been the dominant energy source, but the Marshall Plan helped oil triple its share of European energy consumption, from 10 percent in 1947 to 32.3 percent in 1960.[24]

In effect, the oil component of the Marshall Plan offered strategic benefits to each of the actors involved. Europe received vital aid. American oil companies got new markets. Governments in the Middle East, where the Anglo-American oil companies increased their production, received more royalties and tax revenue. And the US government achieved two strategic priorities. First, Europe's

[21] Quoted in Yergin 2008: 343.
[22] Kelanic 2016.
[23] Painter 2009: 165.
[24] Painter 2009: 164.

increasing consumption of Middle Eastern oil reduced the drain on petroleum reserves in the Western Hemisphere, long a concern in Washington.[25] Second, the Marshall Plan created a tool to steer European development in directions that were friendly to US businesses. For instance, when the Europeans wanted to develop their refining capacity, Washington feared that this would hurt US companies, possibly even endanger their Middle East oil concessions. Consequently, Washington refused to finance any projects that threatened to compete with US companies, including most European refineries.[26] Thus, historian David Painter concludes, "the true significance of the Marshall Plan lay not in the quantity of aid it supplied to Western Europe, but rather its contribution to the construction of a new European and a new international order."[27]

Punishments played a role in the Marshall Plan, too. Positioning oil as Europe's primary transportation fuel (rather than coal used in railways) provided the United States with a useful source of leverage over its allies. If they got out of line, Washington could threaten to cut off their oil. For instance, the United States could foster German economic recovery without having to worry about the recurrence of German military aggression—a serious concern in the immediate postwar period. If need be, the United States could always strangle Germany's fuel supply, because American companies in the Middle East provided it. As it turned out, Washington did take this type of action, but not against Germany. Instead, the target was the United Kingdom and France in the 1956 Suez Crisis. When Britain and France assisted Israel's invasion of the Sinai Peninsula against the US government's wishes, the Eisenhower administration threatened to cut off its European allies from their oil imports. The two allies quickly backed down.

Petro-colonies against the Tide of Decolonization

A global wave of decolonization followed in the decades after the war. The wave had many causes. A shift in ideas was perhaps most important: ideas about racial equality; about self-determination and territorial sovereignty; about legitimacy; and about the economic returns of colonies to their imperial metropoles.[28] Imperial legitimacy had already suffered after World War I when metropoles

---

[25] Previously, much of Western Europe's oil came from the United States, Canada, or Venezuela. US policymakers wanted to preserve oil reserves in the Americas, in case the United States should have need of them in the future.

[26] This type of foreign aid donor behavior continues today: see Milner and Tingley 2015; Bermeo 2018.

[27] Painter 2009: 159.

[28] Frieden 1994; Cooper and Stoler 1997; Philpott 2001; Crawford 2002; Abernethy 2002; Gartzke and Rohner 2011; Morefield 2014; Colgan 2016; Getachew 2019.

had broken their promises for increased colonial autonomy after the war, most notably in India. More broken promises after the second war did not help. Pro-independence movements that had grown in the interwar period now had momentum.[29] The financial strain of the war itself also undermined imperial cohesion.

British prime minister Winston Churchill stood staunchly opposed to decolonization. He regarded India as the jewel of the empire. He foresaw the loss of power and influence that would accompany the breakup of the British Empire. To make matters worse, he was racist, like most of his contemporaries. He looked down on non-whites, and saw the British Empire as a civilizing presence.[30] "I hate Indians. They are a beastly people with a beastly religion," he told Leo Amery, his secretary of state for India and Burma.[31] He had described Gandhi as "posing as a [half-naked] fakir."[32] Yet with the war ending, the British public had tired of Churchill. In the election of July 1945, he lost his post as prime minister, and did not regain it until October 1951. With Churchill out of office, the British Empire suffered what turned out to be a mortal wound. On August 15, 1947, India became an independent nation.

World War II did not finish European imperialism, however. The war had proven costly, but policymakers saw the colonies as a tool of their economic rebirth. In the late 1940s and early 1950s, Britain and others invested in their colonies, hoping that colonial growth would generate new prosperity for the metropoles. This led to a resurgence of colonialism in the early 1950s, though short-lived. In Britain, it was not until Harold Macmillan became prime minister that London decided it had to let go of its colonies, starting in the late 1950s. France was even more reluctant, leading to terrible wars in Algeria and Vietnam (then French Indochina).[33] Belgium, Holland, Portugal, and others all had to come to terms, in their own way, with losing an empire.[34] There was variation how the metropoles did this, but just as important, there was variation across colonies within each empire. Some colonies gained sovereign independence early, some much later.

Oil was a big part of the reason why. Colonies where oil reserves had been discovered or were strongly suspected ("petro-colonies") gained sovereignty late for two reasons.[35] First, empires were reluctant to grant independence to their

[29] Wimmer 2013.

[30] Roberts 2018 (see chapter 17). On the Bengal famine as evidence of Churchill's racism, however, there is some debate: see Mukerjee 2011; Mukherjee 2015: 6; and Roberts 2018.

[31] Quoted in Varadarajan 2018.

[32] https://www.mkgandhi.org/students/thiswasbapu/144halfnakedfakir.htm.

[33] Kahler 1984; Cooper 1996.

[34] Spruyt 2005.

[35] For instance, the British saw in 1952 that "The unexploited oil areas of politically backward Muscat (Oman) and Abu Dhabi are considered highly promising." CAB-129-57-50, "Saudi Arabian Frontier Dispute: Memorandum by the Secretary of State for Foreign Affairs," December 19, 1952. Yet, at that time, the oil companies did not want to exploit Oman's oil reserves because they already

petro-colonies. For a while, the benefits of maintaining political control of oil-rich territories were too valuable to ignore, even in the dying days of European imperialism. Direct colonialism, mandates from international organizations, and other forms of political control reduced the risk that local governments would expropriate European assets or the oil supply would be interrupted.[36] And second, some of the petro-colonies themselves, especially the small ones, were unenthusiastic about independence: they needed the military protection that imperialism offered them. Consequently, the petro-colonies were among the last to be decolonized.

Kuwait's experience is illustrative. Its rulers were so loath to give up imperial protection that they negotiated security guarantees from Britain even after its independence. Historian and oil analyst Pierre Tierzan explains why:

> Coveted both by Iraq and Saudi Arabia, this little country of 17,000 sq km with a population of a few hundred thousand, relied on the mutually neutralizing ambitions of its neighbours and on British protection for its continued existence. The latter was obviously not provided without strings attached. . . . London had in fact imposed a whole series of agreements on its Gulf protégés. . . . These agreements stipulated that the states concerned must have the consent of the British government to grant, sell, rent, concede or allocate for any purpose any part of their territory to a foreign government or its subjects. London was thus appropriating and jealously guarding the oil interests of a whole area of the Gulf.[37]

Ultimately, though, even the oil fields were not sufficient to justify formal imperialism. British officials observed privately in 1960 that the costs of protecting British interests militarily would be too high to justify, despite the value of the oil.[38] Moreover, rising industrial capacity made it more cost-effective to simply buy the oil and energy supplies rather than militarily seizing them.[39] If Kuwait wanted the oil, the British government was not going to use force to hold it. In theoretical terms, the British had decided by 1960 not to impose military punishments for noncompliance—though actors in the Persian Gulf remained uncertain about British intentions. It was not until 1968 that these trends, along

---

had too much supply and did not want to undermine prices. One Exxon official said, "I might put some money in [Oman] if I was sure we weren't going to get some oil" (Howard Page, quoted in US Senate Subcommittee on Multinational Corporation 1974, Part 7, 309).

[36] Frieden 1994.
[37] Terzian 1985: 9–10.
[38] CAB 129/100, C(60)35 "Future Policy Study, 1960–1970: Cabinet Memorandum, Report of Officials' Committee," 24 Feb 1960, reprinted in Hyam and Louis 2000: 99. Also see PREM 11/4679, ff56–59, "Aden, the Yemen, and Middle East Policy: Minute by J. O. Wright," 8 Apr 1964, reprinted in Hyam and Louis 2000: 640.
[39] Colgan 2016; Congressional Research Service 1975.

Table 5.1 Petro-colonies and the Timing of Decolonization[*]

	New States, 1901–2002	
	Avg. Date of Independence	n (# of countries)
Oil-rich colonies	1972	18
Non-oil colonies	1960	126
Difference	12 years	
p-score	0.04	
	New States, 1901–1990 (e.g., no ex-USSR)	
	Avg. Date of Independence	n (# of countries)
Oil-rich colonies	1964	13
Non-oil colonies	1955	110
Difference	8.3 years	
p-score	0.09	

[*]Colonies classified as oil-rich if producing oil at the time of decolonization. Excludes Malaysia and Republic of Congo due to uncertainty about knowledge of oil at time of independence. Data sources: BP Statistical Review of Energy 2017; Goldsmith and He 2008.

with ongoing fiscal strain, culminated in the British withdrawal from territories "east of Suez."

As soon as one thinks to pay attention to petroleum, it might seem obvious that a metropole would be reluctant to let go of petro-colonies. Oil is valuable, after all. Yet, on deeper reflection, the nature and consequences of these relationships is not at all obvious. Other valuable commodities, ranging from copper and gold to coffee and cotton, might have had a similar effect on decolonization. What made oil special, however, was not merely the profits from exploiting the resource, but also the metropoles' intense desire to have security of supply. Interruptions in the gold or coffee markets might be inconvenient, but in a modern economy, an interruption of a state's oil supply could be economically or militarily catastrophic. Oil shortages in Japan and Germany during World War II illustrated how crippling they could be.

Thus, as Table 5.1 shows, oil meant that petro-colonies achieved national independence later than non-petro-colonies. It compares the date of independence of all new states in the twentieth century.[40] Petro-colonies were slower on

[40] For analytical consistency, the data include all new state formations, regardless of whether those new states were previously called colonies, mandates, provinces, or Soviet republics. The general pattern remains the same, however, even when the breakup of the Soviet Union is excluded (as discussed later in this chapter).

average by twelve years to break away. This pattern gets little attention by most studies of decolonization, which emphasize system-wide changes like the rise of nationalism and changes in the norm of territorial sovereignty.[41] Those theories do not explain why some colonies achieved independence quickly while others did so decades later.[42]

While Table 5.1 indicates the trend, a more robust statistical analysis is needed to confirm that oil actually helps cause the delay. After all, other factors matter too, like the pace of decolonization around the world, the pace within a particular geographic region, and the strength of the nationalist challenge, as indicated by the existence of national political organization (e.g., Congress in India). Fortunately, sociologists Andreas Wimmer and Yuval Feinstein have analyzed these and other factors in a statistical model.[43] When a measure of oil reserves is added to their analysis, it confirms what Table 5.1 indicates: oil is strongly associated with a slower process of decolonization, even after accounting for other factors. Table 5.2 shows the analysis results.[44]

British history illustrates the importance of oil in decolonization. Britain fought to retain its political influence over the Middle East countries for as long as possible, and the Foreign Office reminded Cabinet that British interests were "above all the security of oil supplies."[45] Numerous primary documents in British archives reveal that their principal interest in the Middle East was oil.[46] The small and oil-rich British protectorates were among the last to be granted independence: Bahrain, Qatar, and UAE in 1971, and Brunei not until 1984. Of course, not every oil-rich protectorate was slow to leave the Empire's grasp: Iraq gained independence in 1932, Kuwait in 1961. In the main, however, Britain was still

[41] Philpott 2001; Crawford 2002.

[42] Other theories of decolonization emphasize the variation between metropoles in the process of decolonization, such as the British vs. French experience (Spruyt 2005; Kahler 1984), but not the variation among the colonies.

[43] Wimmer and Feinstein 2010. They use a logit model to estimate the probabilistic effects of various potential explanatory variables, where the unit of analysis is the territory-year, and the dependent variable is new state creation. I use their models to identify potential omitted variables. I then add a (dichotomous) measure of oil reserves.

[44] The analysis controls for other potential correlates of decolonization. First, the global diffusion of decolonization, measured by: the total of nation-states in the world, the number of new states born from a given empire in the previous five years, and the number of neighboring new states in the previous five years. Second, the strength of the nationalist challenge, as indicated by the existence of national political organization (e.g., Congress in India). Third, other features of the colony/territory, such as its degree of modernization as indicated by literacy rates. In every regression, six regional control variables and a temporal cubic spline are included but not shown in the table.

[45] Goldsworthy 1994, xxxiii.

[46] For instance, CAB 129/78, CP(55)152, "Middle East Oil: Cabinet Note by Mr. Macmillan," 14 Oct 1955, reprinted in Goldsworthy 1994: 135; FO 371/170165, no 17, "Review of Middle East Policy, Objectives and Strategy: Memorandum by Sir R. Stevens to Sir H. Caccia," 19 July 1963, reprinted in Hyam and Louis 2000: 269–274; CAB 134/1315, PR(56)40, "Overseas Investment Policy: Memorandum by Treasury for Cabinet Policy Review Committee," 30 July 1956, reprinted in Goldsworthy 1994: 120–121.

Table 5.2 Statistical Analysis of the Timing of Decolonization

	(1)	(2)	(3)	(4)	(5)
Oil reserves	−0.818 (0.307)***	−0.973 (0.348)***	−0.497 (0.231)**	−0.509 (0.227)**	−0.513 (0.249)**
Num of Nation States, World		−0.040 (0.011)***	−0.054 (0.013)***	−0.055 (0.013)***	−0.051 (0.014)***
Empire's New States, Previous 5yrs		0.161 (0.035)***	0.161 (0.044)***	0.163 (0.045)***	0.133 (0.044)***
Neighboring New States, 5yrs		0.907 (0.137)***	0.88 (0.156)***	0.882 (0.159)***	0.84 (0.185)***
Metropole's IGO memberships		0.016 (0.005)***	0.01 (0.007)	0.009 (0.007)	0.007 (0.008)
Extent of direct colonial rule			−0.174 (0.098)*	−0.141 (0.104)	−0.234 (0.117)**
Colonial national org			2.007 (0.727)***	2.043 (0.735)***	1.905 (0.704)***
Years of colonial national org			−2.231 (4.369)	0.198 (5.172)	0.04 (4.688)
Literacy rate, %				−0.008 (0.007)	0.004 (0.008)
Wars in empire					0.363 (0.071)***
Wars in that territory					0.474 (0.276)
Regional indicators	[yes]	[yes]	[yes]	[yes]	[yes]
Cubic spline for time	[yes]	[yes]	[yes]	[yes]	[yes]
Observations	7,161	7,161	4,141	4,141	4,141
Log pseudolikelihood	−567.066	−513.542	−377.643	−377.151	−356.859

robust standard errors clustered by state

* significant at 10%; ** significant at 5%; *** significant at 1%

struggling to keep its control and influence in petro-colonies even after it was decolonizing in India and Africa.

Oil played a crucial role in the behavior of other metropoles, too. Unlike the British, other empires mostly tried to tighten their grip and hang on, which only generated violent resistance. It led to some of the world's bloodiest decolonization conflicts: in Algeria for the French, in Indonesia for the Dutch, and in Angola for Portugal. Each of these had oil. One reason the fighting in Algeria, for instance, continued for so long was the insistence by French policymakers on retaining partial oil rights in Algeria in the long negotiations of the 1962 Evian Accords.[47] Demand for oil thus incentivized states to try to maintain their imperial control, even at high costs.

Powerful oil-consuming states were not only choosy about when they decolonized their colonies; they were also particular about how they did so. The British, for the most part, were able to select the first post-independence leader and the nature of the new state's regime.[48] In the Middle East, monarchy was Britain's post-colonial regime type of choice. Egypt, Libya, Iraq, Jordan, Kuwait, the UAE, Qatar, and Bahrain were all monarchies at the time of their independence—as were Oman, Iran, and Saudi Arabia, though they were not formally colonized. British support for monarchies set the stage for post-colonial relations.

The Origins of Oil-for-Security Deals

Decolonization represented one major trend in the Middle East after World War II. A second trend was the region's increasing oil exports. In 1945, the United States was still a net exporter, producing 53 percent of the world's oil.[49] Soon, the United States became a net importer. Middle East oil production was relatively small but grew rapidly as demand soared in North America, Europe, and elsewhere. This had a profound effect on geopolitics. Advanced economies and militaries are highly sensitive to interruptions in their supply of oil, and by 1945 policymakers knew it. While substitutes like coal and natural gas exist for electricity production, petroleum had no commercially viable substitute in the transportation sector and as a feedstock for petrochemicals. The question was, How could the powerful countries of the North Atlantic secure the oil supply they needed, even as their empires were dissolving?

A third trend made this question urgent: the emerging Cold War. While the United States imported only a little oil from the Middle East, the region was a major oil supplier to American allies. If the Soviet Union gained control of the region, it could strangle the flow of oil. Each side of the Cold War therefore had incentives to try to exert political and military control over the Middle East.

---

[47] Cooley and Spruyt 2009: 58–61.

[48] British Cabinet documents reveal this type of influence. An example: "We should endeavor, by all practicable means of persuasion, to ensure that the Kuwaitis introduce suitable civil and criminal codes, penal reform and courts of law, and that our relinquishment of jurisdiction proceeds only *pari passu* with such reforms." CAB-129-99-24, "Jurisdiction in Kuwait: Memorandum by the Secretary of State for Foreign Affairs," November 24, 1959 (British National Archives).

[49] Bialos 1989: 241; Keohane 1984: 197.

Together, these trends shaped a crucial subsystem in world politics: the provision of military security for oil. For centuries, European imperialism had provided the overarching political structure for the relations between Europe and the developing world. That umbrella structure covered a whole range of subsystems in international trade, finance, diplomacy, and law. Military guarantees for the local rulers of colonial oil fields had been an integral part of empire. Now, that subsystem was breaking away.

The United States government was interested in change in that subsystem only insofar as it entrenched American companies. The Departments of State, Defense, and Interior jointly wrote in 1953 that it was "vastly important that the operations of the great oil fields of the world remain as far as possible in the hands of American-owned companies."[50] The government report noted that the oil was a vital energy source for Western Europe and "the principal source of wealth and income in the Middle Eastern countries in which the deposits exist." For many of those countries, the oil companies were "the principal contact of the local inhabitants with American enterprise. What such people think of the oil companies, they think of American enterprise and the American system." US-owned international oil companies were, in effect, extensions of the United States itself.

Without anyone explicitly designing it, the international subsystem for oil security took on its new shape in the 1950s and 1960s. Gradually, country by country, the United States and Great Britain began to extend oil-for-security deals to petrostates.[51] As patron state(s), they would protect and support the petrostate's regime, in exchange for economic benefits and a certain degree of policy cooperation. Consequently, while the subsystem superficially appeared to change dramatically during decolonization, these international bargains provided considerable continuity in the basic behaviors of oil-providing territories and their external protectors.

Decolonization reduced external influence in oil-producing territories, but did not eliminate it. British influence and instruments of coercion over post-independence regimes and leaders facilitated the shift to oil-for-security deals. They had helped install King Faisal in Iraq, the Pahlavis in Iran, and overtly or tacitly supported royal families elsewhere. A monarchical regime gave Britain and the United States a single individual with whom they could work (or coerce). Some of these monarchies were later overthrown. At least initially, however, monarchies paved the way for oil-for-security bargains.

Decolonization and Cold War rivalry led to Western great powers to offer OFS deals to *all* major oil-producing states in the Middle East and North Africa, not

---

[50] *FRUS 1952–1954*, vol. IX, Part 1, Doc. 279 (Report by the Departments of State, Defense, and the Interior, January 6, 1953); quoted in McFarland and Colgan 2018.
[51] Painter 1986; Bronson 2006; Yetiv 2004, 2011; Duffield 2007; Kim 2019.

just some of them. Non-petrostates (Morocco, Tunisia, Syria, Jordan) were not ignored, but on average, they received less attention. Egypt was something of an exception. Though it did not produce much oil itself, it was strategically important to Western actors because of the Suez Canal, through which a vast amount of oil passed. Overall, the pattern suggests that oil was a determining factor of post-colonial relations.

The fact that there was an increasingly Anglo-American oil order in the Persian Gulf and North Africa does not imply that relations between the United States and Great Britain were entirely friendly and cooperative. On the contrary, there was considerable rivalry between the two.[52] British policymakers were particularly uncomfortable with the reality that they had to share control of a region that previously had been largely under their influence. The rivalry and friction between the two great powers did not prevent them, however, from cooperating on the general structure of the oil industry. Moreover, they acted in concert at some key moments, most vividly in Iran.

The preservation of an Anglo-American oil order, even as decolonization unfolded, was a national interest not only to Britain and the United States, but also for their allies in Western Europe. In 1953, for example, one French diplomat stressed "the great importance to both France and Western Europe of having sufficient supplies of Middle Eastern oil at a reasonable price."[53] The Seven Sisters were aware of these pressures, and understood that they had to cooperate with the governments, to preserve their special immunity to anti-trust prosecution under US law. An Exxon executive explained the decision to keep prices low for Western Europe: "Foregoing localized high returns would not be serious enough to interfere with satisfactory aggregate returns. *It would be an investment in future sound and satisfactory relationships*" (emphasis added).[54] Thus, the Anglo-American companies and governments worked together to maintain an order that benefited both.

The era of decolonization represented a major shift in the instruments of coercion and the punishments for noncompliance associated with the governing arrangements for oil. As chapter 3 described, nationalist leaders in petrostates began to see new possibilities for their oil industry, which did not comply with the old governing arrangements. Instead of the mere threat, the Western states need to actually implement punishments, as they did in Iraq (1941) and Iran (1951–1953), described later in this chapter. Even as the expectation of punishments began to fade, however, and even after the oil nationalizations of

---

[52] Barr 2018.
[53] *FRUS 1952–1954*, vol. IX, Part 1, Doc. 320; quoted in McFarland and Colgan 2018: 14.
[54] US Senate 1975: 83, quoted in McFarland and Colgan 2018: 14.

the 1970s and the price hikes of 1973, most of the OFS deals continued, based on continued benefits to both the protector and the protected state.

Anglo-American Defense of Oil

The oil-for-security bargains developed at different times in different places. The most important were Saudi Arabia, Kuwait, Iraq, and Iran.

In Saudi Arabia, the 1945 meeting between President Franklin D. Roosevelt and King Abd al-Aziz Al Saud aboard the USS *Quincy* made official an already nascent OFS deal. During World War II, the United States had provided aid to Saudi Arabia through the Lend Lease Act. The OFS deal developed in scope and depth over time. The 1951 "Mutual Defense Agreement" between the United States and Saudi Arabia helped solidify the arrangement.[55] The relationship was reaffirmed multiple times over the next two decades, for instance on the occasion of Crown Prince Faisal's 1962 visit to Washington, DC, to meet President John F. Kennedy.[56] Having promised military protection to the Saudis, the United States first delivered on this promise in the 1960s. During the Yemeni civil war, it defended Saudi Arabia from the threat of Egyptian attacks. Even more dramatically, it protected Saudi Arabia in 1990 from potential Iraqi invasion, first through Operation Desert Shield and then Desert Storm.

In exchange, Saudi Arabia has provided the United States with a number of economic benefits, and continues to provide them. Saudi Arabia prices oil in US dollars, for instance, which supports the dollar as the world's primary reserve currency.[57] It buys vast amounts of US military equipment.[58] It is a reliable oil supplier: even during the 1973 Arab oil embargo, Saudi Arabia secretly sold oil to the United States to ensure that US military needs would be fully met.[59] And it supports various American foreign policy operations. For instance, Saudi Arabia and the United States jointly financed and supported various anti-communist operations, most famously in Afghanistan during the Soviet occupation of the 1980s. In just the years 1987–1989, the Saudis gave the Afghan *mujahedin* at least

---

[55] "Saudi Arabia: Mutual Defense Agreement," published in *United States Treaties and Other International Agreements* (Washington DC: US Government Printing Office, 1951), Vol. 2, part 2, 1460.

[56] "Telegram from the Department of State to the Embassy in Saudi Arabia," Nov 2, 1962, *Foreign Relations of the United State, 1961–1963*, Vol. XVIII, Near East, 1962–1963, https://history.state.gov/historicaldocuments/frus1961-63v18/d88. President Lyndon B. Johnson reiterated in 1963 the US commitment to the security of Saudi Arabia, https://history.state.gov/historicaldocuments/frus1961-63v18/d389.

[57] Norrlof et al. 2020.

[58] Nitzan and Bichler 2002; Aarts and Nonneman 2006.

[59] Bronson 2006.

6.75 billion riyals (USD 1.8 billion).[60] The Saudis also quietly financed a number of other American projects, including the weapons provided by the CIA to the Nicaraguan Contras in the 1980s (part of the Iran-Contra deal).[61] It also seems likely, while difficult to prove, that Saudi Arabia has adjusted the amount of oil it produces according to American suggestions and requests.[62]

Prince Faisal's visit to Washington in October 1962 was a notable development in the OFS agreement for three reasons. First, in the lead-up to the meeting, the Saudis sacked their nationalist oil minister Abdallah Tariki, replacing him in March 1962 with Ahmed Yamani, an official with a pro-American attitude. The Western press had nicknamed Tariki the "red sheikh" because of his leadership in creating OPEC (see chapter 3) and his tough stance against Anglo-American oil companies, both of which the USSR favored. The royals had other reasons to fire Tariki, and the timing might have been a coincidence, but in any case it helped smooth US-Saudi relations. Second, following the meeting, President Kennedy released a letter in which the United States declared that it "would not stand passively by in the event of any act of aggression against Saudi Arabia," which was in open conflict with Egypt at the time.[63] Third, it was significant that Kennedy's letter does not mention King Saud, who was struggling with his brother Prince Faisal for power. That "omission" was interpreted in Saudi Arabia as a US preference for Faisal over Saud.[64] Less than two years later, the royal family deposed Saud, and Faisal ascended to the throne.

The OFS deal with Kuwait differed in the details, but had the same basic structure as the deal with Saudi Arabia. In Kuwait, there was already an imperial relationship in place prior to the discovery of oil. The sheikhdom of Kuwait became a British protectorate in 1899. British military protection was part of the arrangement, initially against the Ottomans, and for reasons other than oil. The discovery of Kuwaiti oil in 1938 radically increased the value of the territory for Britain. Oil production grew rapidly, and by 1952 Kuwait was the largest oil exporter in the region. The British resisted decolonization, seeking to retain its oil benefits for as long as possible. In Kuwait, furthermore, the sheikh was not so sure he wanted the reality of independence, but he was eager for its trappings.[65] In July 1958, he insisted, "the British Government must be prepared to allow to Kuwait the greatest possible appearance of independence." At the same time, he

[60] Hegghammer 2010.

[61] Jonathan Marshall, "Saudi Arabia and the Reagan Doctrine," *Middle Eastern Research and Information Project*, No. 115 (1988) http://www.merip.org/mer/mer155/saudi-arabia-reagan-doctrine.

[62] Yergin 2008.

[63] Pierre Terzian 1985: 57.

[64] Terzian 1985: 58.

[65] On the politics of state recognition generally, see Coggins 2014.

asked "whether the British Government could give him any further written undertaking that they would continue to protect him."[66]

Kuwait received its independence in 1961, but almost immediately Sheikh Abdullah Al-Salim Al-Sabah felt compelled to call for British protection, to deter Iraq from attacking. On June 25, 1961, Iraq's leader Abd al-Karim Qasim had announced that Iraq would incorporate Kuwait.[67] Section 4 of Kuwait's independence agreement stated that Kuwait could ask Britain for military support, which it did on June 30, 1961. Operation Vantage saw the deployment of British air, sea, and land forces in Kuwait. Britain's motivations were clear: its greatest concern was an interruption of the flow of oil to the United Kingdom.[68] The operation was a success. Iraq did not attack, and recognized Kuwaiti independence (again) in 1963. Britain continued to provide an explicit security guarantee for Kuwait until May 1971.[69]

As the British withdrew, Kuwait increasingly turned to the United States for protection. This relationship was based on mutual strategic interests, not coercion of Kuwait or an expectation of punishment by the United States. A 1968 briefing memo to President Johnson pointed out, for instance, "The 1968 UK announcement that it intends to withdraw militarily east of Suez by the end of 1971 . . . alarmed Kuwait."[70] An associated document reported, "With the exception of the Arab/Israel question, relations between Kuwait and the United States are close and cordial. US private industry has a substantial stake in the exploitation of Kuwait's huge oil reserves . . . and the continued availability of Kuwait oil is extremely important to our Western European allies and Japan. . . . On its side, the Kuwait Government recognizes that its prosperity and perhaps ultimately its sovereignty depend on close political and economic ties with the US and the West."[71] Kuwait's history thus served as context for the Anglo-American reaction to Iraq's invasion in 1990.

In Iraq, the British set the tone for its OFS deal right from the start, when it granted Iraq's independence in 1932. In 1925, the Iraqi government was compelled to grant an oil concession to the Iraq Petroleum Company, controlled by Western interests and designed to continue to the year 2000.[72] Despite a commitment in 1920 to

---

[66] British Cabinet CAB-129-95-28, "Kuwait: International Relations. Memorandum by the Secretary of State for Foreign Affairs," November 4, 1958 (British National Archives).

[67] Mobley 2001.

[68] Snell-Mendoza 1996.

[69] Mobley 2001.

[70] US Department of State, "Visit of His Highness Amir Sabah al-Salim al-Sabah of Kuwait, December 11–12, 1968: Background paper, Kuwait and the Persian Gulf." Lyndon B. Johnson Presidential Library, National Security File Box 149.

[71] US Department of State, "Visit of His Highness Amir Sabah al-Salim al-Sabah of Kuwait, December 11–12, 1968: Scope paper." Lyndon B. Johnson Presidential Library, National Security File Box 149.

[72] Auzanneau 2018: 117.

allocate 20 percent of future oil profits to the Iraqi government, the concession did not do so, instead giving the oil companies the vast majority of the revenues. At independence, Britain's former vassal King Faisal remained on the throne; the British military retained its bases and transit rights; and British oil companies continued to operate in Iraq. In essence, Britain insisted that Iraq would provide a secure oil supply, even if Iraq was an independent state in other ways. This was an OFS deal by coercion.

Britain showed its resolve to enforce its OFS deal with Iraq in 1941. On April 1, Rashid Ali led nationalist Iraqi forces in a coup d'état, installing a new government in Baghdad that intended to sell some of its oil to Germany. Within two months the British, with the help of local forces, overthrew Ali and re-installed the Hashemite dynasty, now under Faisal II and his Regent Abd al-Ilah. Even in wartime, the message was clear: Britain would not allow Iraq to choose its oil policies.

The British did, however, help Iraq avoid interstate conflicts with its neighbors, with assistance from the United States. In the 1940s and early 1950s, the Western powers facilitated diplomatic interactions and smoothed disputes between Iraq and its neighbors Iran, Jordan, Syria. For instance, prior to the dissolution of the OFS deal in 1958, there was not a single shot fired between Iran and Iraq over the issue of the Shatt al-Arab waterway, an issue that later produced dozens of military disputes between the two parties. Anglo-American diplomacy played an important role in keeping the peace. Moreover, in 1955, the United States facilitated the creation of the Baghdad Pact, later called Central Treaty Organization (CENTO). The treaty joined Iraq with Iran, Pakistan, Turkey, and the United Kingdom. Diplomatic pressure and promises of aid from the United States played an essential role in the creation of the organization. The period 1945–1958 was notable for its relative peacefulness for Iraq. Its government sought regional influence and leadership, but not through conquest or violence.

Iraq's revolution in 1958 not only eventually dissolved the OFS deal, but also was arguably the first visible evidence that punishments for noncompliance with the Anglo-American oil order were on the decline. Unlike some previous changes of government in the region, Britain and the United States did not try to reverse the revolution in Iraq. The British-installed Hashemite dynasty came to an end. The new regime had some radically different ideas about how its oil industry should operate. Though those ideas were not immediately implemented to any great effect,[73] the mere existence of an Arab regime that vocally opposed the Anglo-American oil arrangements was a departure from previous practice. The new Iraqi regime also wanted to go its own way in foreign policy, effectively

---

[73] Colgan 2013d.

ending the OFS deal with the Anglo-American powers. In hindsight, it was a portentous moment.

Dissatisfaction was growing in Iraq and elsewhere partly because the petrostates often perceived the US government and US private corporations as acting closely in each other's interests.[74] Declassified evidence now available in archives shows that they were correct. In Iraq, the US government took meetings to help the interests of US oil companies,[75] and the companies consulted with the US government about its negotiations with the Iraqis.[76] In turn, the Iraqi government asked the US government to press the oil companies to settle their negotiations with the Iraqi government.[77] In Kuwait, the Gulf Oil Corporation obtained a 50 percent interest in the Kuwait Oil Company through "the active support of the Department of State."[78] In Saudi Arabia, declassified documents show that representatives of the US-owned Aramco collected intelligence and relayed information to the US government.[79] The CIA even had a top-secret contingency plan, in the event of a Soviet invasion, that involved company employees sabotaging oil wells to keep them out of Soviet hands.[80]

Last but not least, there was the Anglo-American relationship with Iran. Britain had vied for power and influence in Iran prior to World War II with its longtime rival, Russia. In 1941, the two great powers jointly invaded Iran. They forced the ruling Reza Shah Pahlavi, whom they suspected of favoring Nazi Germany, to abdicate in favor of his son, Mohammad Reza Pahlavi. The new Shah signed a treaty with the Soviet Union and Britain in 1942 that committed the two Allies to leave Iran not more than six months after the end of the war. When the deadline arrived on March 2, 1946, the British began to withdraw, but the Soviets refused. Separatist elements among Azerbaijanis and Kurds in Iran gave the Soviets a pretext to remain. The ensuing Iran Crisis of 1946 was arguably the beginning of the Cold War, the first serious dispute between the Soviet Union and its former allies.

---

[74] On this general point, see Gendzier 2015; Graaff 2012.

[75] National Security Advisor Walt W. Rostow, Memorandum for the President, January 21, 1967. Lyndon B. Johnson Presidential Library, National Security File Box 138 [1 of 2], Iraq File.

[76] Multiple files in Lyndon B. Johnson Presidential Library, National Security File Box 138 [1 of 2], Iraq File; see, for example, Department of State Telegrams from Baghdad Embassy to Secretary of State on May 4, 1964, Oct 26 1964, and June 2 1965.

[77] Department of State, "Memorandum of Conversation: Secretary's Delegation to the Twenty-First Session of the United Nations General Assembly," October 5, 1966. Lyndon B. Johnson Presidential Library, National Security File Box 138 [1 of 2], Iraq File.

[78] US Department of State, "Visit of His Highness Amir Sabah al-Salim al-Sabah of Kuwait, December 11–12, 1968: Background paper, Kuwait Relations with US." Lyndon B. Johnson Presidential Library, National Security File Box 149.

[79] Aramco representatives relaying information to USG—1964 March 22. Lyndon B. Johnson Presidential Library, National Security File Box 155, File 2. Also, multiple files in the Private Papers of William E. Mulligan.

[80] Everly 2016.

The Iran crisis tested Britain, Russia, and the United States. The Soviets had multiple interests in Iran, including security concerns.[81] At or near the top of the list was their desire for a deal giving them control of northern Iran's oil, in the same way the British controlled the southern oil fields.[82] In March 1946, while still occupying the country, the Soviets coerced the Iranian government into signing an agreement that gave it 51 percent ownership of a company that would control the northern oil fields. In a sense, the Soviets were trying to get their own OFS deal, though it was unclear how much security they were offering Iran. They were offering Iran mostly punishments, not benefits. In response, the British and Americans worked to resist Soviet influence. When fighting broke out between the Iranian Army and the Soviet-backed insurgents, the United States and the United Kingdom supported Iran at the UN Security Council. The new council passed Resolutions 2, 3, and 5, which encouraged Iran and the Soviet Union to resolve their conflict.[83] Then, on September 11, 1947, US ambassador to Iran George V. Allen publicly decried the coercion used by "foreign governments" (i.e., the Soviets) to secure commercial concessions in Iran, and promised full US support for Iran to decide the fate of its own natural resources.[84] A month later, the Iranian *majlis* voted 102–2 against ratifying the Soviet-Iranian oil agreement. Even now, it remains unclear how much it was Anglo-American pressure that caused the Soviet Union's decisions, but the results were unambiguous: the Soviets withdrew.[85] The Anglo-American hold on Iran's oil was secure—temporarily.

Iran, Mossadegh, and Operation Ajax

In the 1950s, as European empires were weakening but not dead, it was not obvious what state sovereignty really meant for oil politics in the Middle East. Many politicians, elites, and military officers in the petrostates were keen to throw off the vestiges of Western control. Could they do so without being punished? Iran

---

[81] The Soviets saw a threat on their southern flank, chiefly due to the growing US military and political presence in the Middle East (e.g., its agreement with Saudi Arabia in 1945 to build a major new air base at Dhahran). The United States was principally competing with Britain for influence in the area, but that did not eliminate Soviet concerns. Arguably, this created a security dilemma that prompted the Soviets to beef up their own presence. See Lawson 1989; Barr 2018.

[82] Yegorova 1996.

[83] Remarkably, the Soviet Union allowed these resolutions to pass despite its veto power.

[84] Lenczowski 1990: 12.

[85] Many American historians attribute the Soviet withdrawal to US diplomatic pressure, but it is not obvious why words alone would have that effect. President Truman later said he made military threats privately (Lenczowski 1990: 13), which might have been enough. Alternatively, some speculate that the Soviets left because they believed they had obtained their goal, an oil deal with Iran. If so, they were premature: Iran refused to ratify the agreement in 1947. See Yegorova 1996; Lawson 1989.

served as a test case for how far the West was willing to let them go. The answer was not very far at all.

In 1951, Iran wanted control over its oil industry. The Shah knew he could not afford to anger the British, but he was weak politically, dependent on an elected prime minister and *majlis* (parliament). Moreover, Iran's people were angry. Not only did the British own most of the industry and receive most of the profits, but there was also a clear social hierarchy within the oil sector, with white British managers on top and Iranian workers at the bottom. On March 15, the *majlis* voted to nationalize the oil sector, seizing assets from the British-owned Anglo-Iranian Oil Company. A week later, oil workers called for a paralyzing general strike against the company, which had refused to meet their financial and social demands. These developments spelled the end for Iran's moderate prime minister, Hussein Ala, and he was replaced by a far more strident nationalist: Dr. Mohammad Mossadegh. The new prime minister immediately created the National Iranian Oil Company.

The British were furious. Cabinet officials regarded the events as a "stunning blow to British prestige."[86] They filed a legal case against Iran at the International Court of Justice in The Hague. On July 5, 1951, the Court issued an interim ruling in favor of Britain.[87] Britain also called upon the UN Security Council to intervene. Neither international organization could sway Mossadegh's resolve to nationalize. So London's next move was to organize an international boycott of Iran's oil. Using the Court's judgment, they persuaded Europe and Japan to close their ports to Iranian oil. By portraying Mossadegh's government as "red" (i.e., communist-leaning), Britain swiftly convinced the United States to support the move.

With the boycott, Western countries imposed immense costs upon Iran for trying to defect from the Anglo-American order. In 1950, Iran had produced 665,000 barrels per day, but that dropped by 96 percent to just 27,000 barrels per day in 1952 and 1953, almost entirely for domestic consumption. Meanwhile, the Anglo-American oil companies ramped up oil production in their subsidiaries in Iraq, Kuwait, and Saudi Arabia to make up for the lost Iranian supply. After the boycott was over in 1954, Iran's oil production swiftly recovered, even as production fell in Iraq, Kuwait, and Saudi Arabia in 1956 and 1957.[88] The boycott demonstrated plainly to all observers that the Seven

---

[86] British Cabinet CAB-129-57-50, "Saudi Arabian Frontier Dispute: Memorandum by the Secretary of State for Foreign Affairs," December 19, 1952 (British National Archives).

[87] The interim ruling was later reversed, but not until July 1952, after the UK-led boycott was in place. See: https://www.icj-cij.org/en/case/16.

[88] Terzian 1985: 14.

Sister companies could, and would, decide which countries would produce and sell oil on the world market—and which ones would not. The ability to punish was evident.

Yet such was Mossadegh's political resolve that even the boycott was not enough to change his mind. The economic costs of the boycott took hold in 1952–1953, threatening his political popularity at home. Still, he rallied his constituents by blaming Western imperialism for the country's economic problems, much as Fidel Castro would do a few years later, half a world away. While Iran's economy did suffer, the boycott was not bringing about political change quickly enough for the oil companies or their supporters in the British and American governments. In November 1952, Foreign Minister Anthony Eden met with Secretary of State Dean Acheson, who crafted a joint plan to overthrow Mossadegh's government.[89] The US Central Intelligence Agency (CIA) and the British Secret Intelligence Service (known as MI6) would lead it.

Mossadegh's decision to dissolve Parliament, giving himself and his cabinet complete power to rule, served as the pretext of the coup. That decision effectively stripped the Shah of all political power. Up to that point, the Shah had opposed the coup plans and supported the oil nationalization. Even on August 3, just days before events unfolded, the Shah told the CIA that he was "not an adventurer" and did not want to topple Mossadegh.[90] After Mossadegh's power grab, though, the Shah signed royal decrees dismissing Mossadegh and appointing General Fazlollah Zahedi as the new prime minister.

CIA and MI6 operatives carried out Operation Ajax, as the plan was known, on August 15–19, 1953. Kermit Roosevelt Jr., grandson of President Theodore Roosevelt, led the American side of the operation. It was the first time the United States conducted covert action to overthrow a foreign government during peacetime. The American and British agents hired mobsters in Tehran, among others, to stage pro-Shah riots and take over the streets. Roughly 300 people were killed.[91] The Shah's military court arrested and convicted Mossadegh of treason. He spent the rest of his life under house arrest, and many of his supporters were imprisoned or killed.

The Shah had fled the country during the tumultuous four days of the coup. Returning afterwards, he felt compelled to explain his absence publicly. He released a statement that once he realized that "his orders were not

---

[89] Oil was a major factor, but not the only one, behind the decision to intervene covertly. See Brew 2019.

[90] Milani 2011: 179.

[91] Ward 2014.

being followed, he left the country to prevent further bloodshed and further damage."[92] Although initially worried about how his departure would look, the British and American governments soon warmed to his return. Winston Churchill sent a message congratulating the Shah on his safe return. "May I express the sincere hope that success will now attend your efforts to guide Persia toward those better things which you have always so ardently desired for her."[93] Churchill tactfully chose not to mention oil.

The coup was carried out in the Shah's name, and greatly strengthened his political position. He ruled a *de facto* military dictatorship until 1979, with the *majlis* mostly toothless after 1953. The Shah proved friendlier to British and Western oil interests. He might have been friendlier out of gratitude, but in truth he had little choice in the matter. Iran's national oil company, created by Mossadegh, continued to exist but it was subservient to the Western oil companies that operated there. Iran's experience neatly illustrates the West's desire to retain influence in petrostates even after the end of a period of formal political control.

The deal that formalized that renewed influence was signed in 1954. As the price for its cooperation with Britain in Operation Ajax, the United States demanded that a consortium of eight oil companies replace the old Anglo-Iranian Oil Company—the same eight companies that had enacted the oil boycott of 1951–1953. A new company, British Petroleum, took control of 40 percent of the old company, while five American companies (Exxon, Mobil, Chevron, Gulf, and Texaco) received another 40 percent. Royal Dutch-Shell received 14 percent and the French company CFP got 6 percent.[94] The consortium's tight control of Iran's oil industry was a bitter pill to swallow even for the Shah's new government, which owed everything to Britain and the United States. When news of the arrangement broke, Iranian oil workers protested with a huge strike. The government arrested nearly 600 people. The oil companies refused to release their boycott until the Iranian government submitted. It signed the deal on September 19, 1954.

For Iranian nationalists, 1953 contained no small dose of bitter irony. Earlier that same year (in April), Winston Churchill was knighted. The man who had done so much to put Iranian oil under British control was remembered for victory in World War II and showered with honors. The man who tried to remove that control, Mossadegh, was put in prison.

---

[92] Quoted in Milani 2011: 188.
[93] Quoted in Milani 2011: 192.
[94] Ghanem 1986: 9–10.

Departures from Oil-for-Security Deals

By the 1950s, nine OFS deals were in place or developing in the Middle East: Saudi Arabia, Kuwait, Qatar, UAE, Iraq, Iran, Libya, Bahrain, and Oman.[95] The only petrostate in the region to refuse an OFS deal even initially was Algeria, and even there, France had (unsuccessfully) offered one.[96]

In 1958, however, revolutionaries came to power in Iraq and radically revised its relationship with the West. Qasim, its new ruler, abolished Iraq's treaty of mutual security with the United Kingdom, withdrew from its military agreements with the United States, and established friendly relations with the Soviet Union. In 1969, Muammar Qaddafi led a coup against King Idris in Libya. Qaddafi, too, rejected his country's relationship with the West. In the 1950s, the British and Americans had built up a military presence there, making Libya the single biggest per-capita recipient of US foreign aid in the world.[97] Qaddafi asked the Americans and British to leave, and Libyan relations with the West rapidly deteriorated.[98] Finally, in 1978–1979, the Iranian Revolution deposed the Shah. Ayatollah Khomeini and the other revolutionaries swiftly rejected Iran's previously close relationship with the United States. Thus, the nine OFS deals became only six after 1980.

Historically, every state that has rejected an OFS deal has done so by way of a domestic revolution. While technically it seems possible that a petrostate might calmly decide to end an OFS deal without overturning its regime, in practice this has never occurred. The correlation between revolutions and ending OFS deals is significant because in previous research, I found that revolutionary petrostates are highly likely to engage in international conflict.[99] I attributed that finding to the domestic dynamics of revolutions: they install leaders who tend to have revisionist preferences and high risk tolerance, which makes them conflict-prone. The political interactions between oil and revolutions makes petro-revolutionary states especially conflict-prone, even more than revolutionary non-petrostates. This book's focus on subsystems, however, suggests an additional explanation: the revolutionary petrostates were also breaking their OFS deals. In so doing, they were taking a counter-hegemonic position against the Anglo-American powers, which probably contributed to their subsequent conflicts with other states.

---

[95] Three were firmly in place: Saudi Arabia, Iraq, and Iran. The Anglo-American oil industry was active in four additional territories, which subsequently became sovereign states: Kuwait, Bahrain, the UAE, and Qatar. In Oman and Libya, OFS deals grew incrementally. Oil production did not begin until the 1960s, but oil deposits were known. (See also note 35 on why oil companies delayed production.)

[96] Cooley and Spruyt 2009: 58–61.

[97] Vandewalle 2006: 45.

[98] Colgan 2013d.

[99] Colgan 2013d.

	OFS accepted	OFS rejected
High oil per capita	Saudi Arabia Kuwait UAE Oman Bahrain Qatar	Libya (1969)
Moderate oil per capita		Iraq (1958) Iran (1979) Algeria (1962)

Figure 5.2 Oil-for-security (OFS) deals accepted and rejected in the Middle East

Why did some states and not others reject their OFS deal? The answer seems to depend a great deal on domestic politics and choices made by individual leaders. Still, one striking pattern is the correlation between such rejections and the size of the petrostate's per-capita resource endowment. In many resource-rich states, leaders provide goods to citizens in exchange for political quiescence, a core part of the resource curse.[100] Yet, the limits to that exchange depend on the government's wealth. Petrostates with high oil revenue per capita can spend a lot of money in exchange for political quiescence and a relatively free hand in arranging its foreign relations. This seems to make OFS deals feasible even with unpopular and culturally distant foreign patron states. In petrostates with only a moderate amount of oil per capita, however, the regime can expect less political quiescence and more objections to OFS deals with unpopular foreign powers. The historical pattern supports this view, albeit with only a few cases. Figure 5.2 identifies all major petrostates in the Middle East and North Africa region. Three can be considered as having moderate oil income per capita, while the others can be considered as having high income per capita.[101] The three moderate cases were Iraq and Iran, which both initially accepted but later rejected an OFS deal, and Algeria, which never really had an OFS deal because it rejected it in the process of gaining its independence from France. By 1979, none of the petrostates with moderate oil income per capita had an OFS deal anymore. By contrast, among the seven petrostates with high oil income per capita, six kept the OFS deal and

[100] Ross 2012; Bellin 2004; Mitchell 2011; Hancock and Vivoda 2014; Wenar 2015; Barma et al. 2011; Le Billon 2012; Liou and Musgrave 2013; Rudra and Jensen 2011; Hertog 2010; Colgan 2015.

[101] Bahrain is a complicated case. In the twenty-first century, Bahrain's oil fields are mostly exhausted. I consider it a petrostate, however, because of its ongoing role in Saudi Arabia's oil industry (for which it receives huge Saudi payments) and its rentier political economy.

continue to do so. Only Libya rejected its OFS deal. Libya's anomalous outcome might be attributed to two factors. First, its oil rents had only started to flow for a few years before Qaddafi's 1969 coup, meaning that rentier politics did not yet fully shape its social contract. Second, Libya's next-door neighbor Egypt, which was then led by the revolutionary Gamal Abdel Nasser, powerfully influenced Libya's politics.

No other variable seems capable of explaining the pattern of OFS acceptance and rejection. Not their regime type: all nine OFS petrostates[102] were monarchies before Iraq, Libya, and Iran had revolutions and simultaneously rejected the OFS deals. Not their location: all were in what contemporaries called the Near East. Not religion: all states in Figure 5.2 are majority Muslim. Admittedly, the rulers in all six OFS states are Sunni, but there is no evidence that Sunni-led states are especially peaceful (witness Libya, Pakistan, or Iraq under Hussein). It might be their size, as the OFS-accepting states tend to be smaller on average than OFS-rejecters, but their pattern is not very consistent: Saudi Arabia (28 million people) has a population more than four times that of tiny Libya (6 million people), and Oman is larger geographically than Lebanon, Syria, or Azerbaijan. In short, there is no reason to believe that the states that continue to accept the OFS deals are systematically different from those that rejected them, other than by levels of resource endowment.

Even with the departure of Iraq, Libya, and eventually Iran from the Anglo-American orbit, OFS deals continue to shape the region's politics. The United States offers military protection to guarantee the commercial flow of oil and avoid the one thing that it cannot abide: an independent foreign power with dominance over the Persian Gulf's oil riches.

From British to American Power in the Middle East

As Operation Ajax unfolded in Iran in 1953, a young man named George H. W. Bush, thousands of miles away, was learning the ropes of the oil market. Born in 1924, he had deferred his college education after the Japanese attacked Pearl Harbor so that he could enlist, on his eighteenth birthday, in the US Navy. He became the Navy's youngest aviator. After World War II, he and his wife had their first son, George W. Bush. After graduating from Yale in 1948, the new father moved his family to Texas, where he ventured into the oil business. Five years later, Bush cofounded the Zapata Petroleum Company in Texas, while half a

---

[102] Excluding Algeria.

world away the CIA was busy in Iran. Perhaps fittingly, two decades later Bush would lead the CIA as the Director of Central Intelligence, before becoming US vice president in 1981 and finally president in 1989. But back in the 1950s, he made his fortune with Zapata Petroleum. By age forty, he was a millionaire, a rarity in 1964. In those years, Bush and his fellow Texan executives rightly saw themselves as the center of an industry that was not merely American, but increasingly global.

By the time George Bush was making his name in the oil industry, the international order for oil was changing. Operation Ajax showed that international oil companies could still expect their governments to back their commercial aims with armed force and coercion even into the 1950s. Yet that mode of government behavior, leadership selection, was increasingly illegitimate. The political cost of imposing punishments like Operation Ajax was rising. That favored an order more heavily based on strategic benefits.

Anglo-American policymakers knew the situation was shifting. One example of many from British Cabinet documents in the late 1950s: "It is likely to become politically impossible for us to resist indefinitely the [Kuwaiti] Ruler's demand for a reduction of our jurisdiction. To do so would sour our relations with the Ruling Family to a point where our oil interests . . . might be affected. It would also give cause, locally, for popular agitation against us in Kuwait and in the Arab-Asian world."[103]

This shift also meant that over time, the subsystem for military security became analytically distinct from the one governing the economics of production. The retreat of imperialism boosted the sovereignty of petrostates. Some of them obtained legal independence (i.e., former colonies), and some of them gained more autonomy because of reduced quasi-imperial presence (e.g., Iran). Their rising sovereignty meant different things for different subsystems. Petrostates' ability to influence the legal-economic decisions over production, while still less than they would have liked, was considerably larger than their military power in most cases. Militarily, many petrostates were weak. In fact, some were too weak to guarantee their own borders (or their regimes) against serious threats. The distribution of oil fields was now a separate matter from the economics of oil production, to be resolved within the geopolitical games of the modern territorial state system. Thus, the imperial curtain swept back, revealing two main oil subsystems where before they had looked like just one.

Even in this twilight stage of imperialism, Britain could still exert influence over leader selection, one of its tried-and-true instruments of coercion in the region. In 1966, the British carried out a bloodless coup to install Sheikh Zayed bin Sultan Al

---

[103] British Cabinet CAB-129-99-24, "Jurisdiction in Kuwait: Memorandum by the Secretary of State for Foreign Affairs," November 24, 1959 (British National Archives).

Nahyan as ruler of Abu Dhabi, the youngest of four brothers in the royal family. They did so at the request of Abu Dhabi's elite, who sought to replace Shakhbut, Zayed's eldest brother. Shakhbut was xenophobic and averse to spending the territory's oil revenues. The British chose to install Sheikh Zayed, who went on to lead the new United Arab Emirates at its founding in 1971. That choice laid the groundwork for the UAE's post-imperial partnership with the Anglo-American powers, anchored by oil sales.

The British Empire held out for as long as it could in the Middle East. In January 1968, a few weeks after a major devaluation of the pound, Prime Minister Harold Wilson announced that Britain was withdrawing all of its troops from military bases "east of Aden" (a port in what is now Yemen) in 1971. In effect, Britain recognized that it could no longer offer substantial military protection to its territories or former territories east of the Suez Canal. The fiscal strain of maintaining its far-flung military was the proximate cause of Britain's withdrawal, but long-term trends were more fundamental. Rising industrial capacity suggested to Western policymakers that it was more cost-effective to simply buy the oil rather than to control it directly.[104] Indeed, it was with some reluctance that Bahrain, Qatar, and the (newly united) UAE gained their independence.

British withdrawal left the United States as the dominant external provider of military security in the Persian Gulf. Archival evidence reveals that the US government was aware that the Persian Gulf's littoral countries were anxious for reassurance and security guarantees.[105] By this time, the United States already had a network of bases and relationships with states in the region. Still, it was reluctant to be drawn into an even larger role. In a 1968 memo, Secretary of State Dean Rusk advised President Johnson, in preparation for a meeting with the prime minister of Iran, to "indicate pleasure concerning the Shah's recent visits to Saudi Arabia and Kuwait and confidence that the security of the Persian Gulf area following the British departure in 1971 will be assured by

---

[104] Colgan 2016.

[105] Based on the author's review of dozens of documents at the Lyndon B. Johnson Presidential Library, especially the National Security File, Boxes 138, 149, and 155. For instance, on April 29, 1968, Walt Rostow wrote to President Johnson, "He [the Shah of Iran] knows the British are pulling out. He fears even more that our policy since last June indicates diminished US interest in the Mid-East" (Rostow, 1968. "Memorandum for the President," National Security File Box 138 [1 of 2], Iran Folder 4). Similarly, a briefing book to the President on Kuwait says, "Since the announcement in January, 1968, that the British would withdraw from the Persian Gulf by the end of 1971, Kuwait has displayed more interest in its ties with the US . . . we do believe that the Kuwaitis will be increasingly interested in our maintaining an effective role in Gulf affairs behind the scenes" ("Visit of His Highness Amir Sabah al-Salim al-Sabah of Kuwait, December 11–12, 1968: Background paper, Kuwait Relations with U.S.," National Security File Box 149).

cooperation among the littoral countries."[106] In other words: the Persian Gulf should take care of itself.

The United States faced other problems besides the British withdrawal. Iraq left the American orbit in 1958, as did Libya in 1969 and Iran in 1979. These political departures, and the tumult in the oil markets of the 1970s, created the concern that the United States was losing its grip on the Middle East. Then, one additional event struck real fear in the hearts of Washington policymakers—and ensured the continuation of the American military presence in the region.

In 1979, the Soviets invaded Afghanistan. Some Americans, like National Security Advisor Zbigniew Brzezinski, saw the Soviet invasion as a mistake. Still, to many others, it raised the troubling possibility that the Soviets would extend their reach into the vital Persian Gulf region. President Jimmy Carter responded forcefully, with what became known as the Carter Doctrine. He declared that the United States would use military force if necessary to repel any "outside force" from gaining control of the Persian Gulf.[107] Carter then established a military task force for this purpose, now known as Central Command. That force has been active ever since, notably in the wars in Iraq in 1991 and 2003. In a twist of fate, Central Command was responsible for the United States' own invasion of Afghanistan in 2001, failing to learn from the Soviet disastrous experience there.

The United States' rivalry with the Soviet Union caused it to entrench in the Middle East in the 1980s, but the longer historical evidence shows that Western powers' commitment to petrostates goes much deeper. It is rooted in their energy interests. The history of decolonization and its aftermath demonstrates that oil was, and is, the driver of the modern relationships between petrostates and their patrons. That fact remained central to post–Cold War politics.

The Gulf War, 1990–1991

Iraq invaded Kuwait on August 2, 1990, and swiftly occupied the tiny country.[108] US president George H. W. Bush had to decide how to react. The Cold War had ended with the fall of the Berlin Wall in 1989. By late summer 1990, the Soviet Union was on its last legs, and Bush faced considerable geopolitical uncertainty.

[106] Secretary of State Dean Rusk, "Memorandum for the President," December 2, 1968. Lyndon B. Johnson Presidential Library, National Security File Box 138 [2 of 2], Folder "Visit of PM Hoveyda of Iran."

[107] Jimmy Carter, "State of the Union Address," January 23, 1980, *The American Presidency Project*, http://www.presidency.ucsb.edu/ws/?pid=33079.

[108] The invasion's date can be confusing. It began at 2:00 A.M. local time, which meant that it occurred on what was still August 1 in Washington DC.

British prime minister Margaret Thatcher sought to influence his thinking through multiple conversations.

Like Bush, Thatcher was a right-wing conservative who favored business interests. She climbed up in a man's world to become the longest-serving British prime minister of the twentieth century. Born Margaret Roberts in 1925, she graduated from Oxford with a degree in chemistry in 1947 before becoming a barrister. She defeated Edward Heath in 1975 for the leadership of the Conservative Party, and was elected prime minister in 1979. Her popularity soon flagged, and she faced a growing revolt in her own party until the 1982 Falklands War. Thatcher insisted on an uncompromising response to Argentina's attempt to seize the Falkland Islands, a British colony. Military victory in that war brought Thatcher a wave of public approval. Her grit, strength, and determination earned her the nickname the "Iron Lady." When Saddam Hussein ordered Iraq's armies to invade Kuwait in 1990, she had no doubt about the proper Anglo-American response.

While still unwilling to commit to war, President Bush announced, on August 5, "This will not stand. This will not stand, this aggression against Kuwait."[109] Having inherited an international order underpinned by oil-for-security deals, Bush and Thatcher decided that they must impose punishments on Iraq for its noncompliance with the subsystem's basic rules. Perhaps the United States and Britain could overlook violations of territorial sovereignty in less strategically important regions, as they did when various African armies crossed over borders in the 1990s. But in the Persian Gulf, home to two-thirds of the world's oil reserves, they did not want noncompliance from an international order that benefited them. Brent Scowcroft, Bush's national security advisor, put it bluntly in an emergency meeting of the national security council on August 3: "My personal judgment is that the stakes in this for the United States are such that to accommodate Iraq should not be a policy option. There is too much at stake. . . . They would dominate OPEC politics."[110] Others, including Defense Secretary Dick Cheney and Deputy Secretary of State Lawrence Eagleburger, agreed.[111]

From the outset, the president and other US policymakers saw Iraq's invasion of Kuwait through the lens of oil. Declassified White House documents make that clear, despite some public justification of the US-led counter-invasion being about world order and defending the norm of territorial sovereignty.[112] Perhaps not coincidentally, Bush personally had long-standing oil business ties to Kuwait.

---

[109] Remarks and Exchange with Reporters, August 5, 1990, *Public Papers of the Presidents: George Bush.*

[110] Quoted in Kreps 2011: 56.

[111] Brands 2004: 116–118.

[112] Many of those documents illustrate that Bush was primarily interested in US oil assets in the region. See Kreps 2011: 62; also Brands 2004; Alfonsi 2006; Colgan 2013b.

At a White House dinner a few weeks later, he revealed that Zapata Offshore, the firm that he had founded and owned, built Kuwait's first offshore oil well.[113]

If OFS deals worked perfectly, Iraq should never have invaded Kuwait in 1990. After all, the United States had an implicit OFS deal with Kuwait, which should have deterred Iraq (though a formal US-Kuwait defense treaty did not exist until *after* the war). Yet, the role of deterrence is observable even in the breach. Saddam Hussein feared that the United States would militarily respond. In a fateful meeting between Hussein and US ambassador April Glaspie on July 25, 1990, Hussein asked about the US position on the dispute between Iraq and Kuwait. According to a transcript of the meeting, Glaspie said, "we have no opinion on Arab-Arab conflicts like your border disagreement with Kuwait."[114] The significance of that conversation is the matter of some dispute. Hussein might have misinterpreted that conversation as a green light signal for military action against Kuwait. More likely, however, Hussein had already made the decision to go to war by that point.[115] Had Hussein anticipated that the United States would respond militarily to an Iraqi invasion of Kuwait as it did, it is hard to believe that he would have gone ahead. One possibility, however, is that Hussein expected Saudi Arabia to refuse US troops, thereby preventing an American counterattack in Kuwait.

One telling indicator of the difficulty that actors within subsystems have in assessing strategic benefits and the likelihood of punishments for non-compliance can be found in a crucial conversation between President Bush and King Fahd of Saudi Arabia on August 5, 1990. Bush feared the possibility of an Iraqi invasion of Saudi Arabia, and wanted Fahd's permission to land American troops in his territory. Fahd said he appreciated the offer, but did not immediately accept it. He doubted American resolve, though he could not say so directly. He remembered how, in the 1980s, the Americans had landed in Lebanon but withdrew swiftly after an attack on their base killed 200 American marines. He did not want to be left in a similar situation with a vengeful Saddam Hussein on his doorstep in possession of a far larger army than his own. When Bush realized this was the crux of the matter, he recommitted to the oil-for-security deal:

> Another point I want to make here involves a word of honor. The security of Saudi Arabia is vital—basically fundamental—to US interests and really to the interests of the Western world. And I am determined that Saddam will not get

[113] Phillips 1991.
[114] Simons 2016: 349.
[115] Brands and Palkki 2012: 625–659.

away with all this infamy. When we work out a plan, once we are there we will stay until we are asked to leave. You have my solemn word on this.[116]

Persuaded, Fahd soon gave his permission, and US troops began to land in Saudi Arabia on August 8.

In the event, the United States not only defended Saudi Arabia (Operation *Desert Shield*), but also led a counterattack against Iraq (Operation *Desert Storm*). Wisely, President Bush and Prime Minister Thatcher worked hard over several months to build a broad multilateral coalition of states that would endorse the military action and participate in it, albeit only nominally in many cases.[117] The actual fighting was over remarkably quickly. The air war that began on January 16, 1991, lasted forty-two days, and the ground war was over in 100 hours. Despite having been prepared for a major confrontation, with thousands of allied casualties, the US military found what General Norman Schwarzkopf later called an "easy fight."[118] Iraqi forces fled from Kuwait, and the US-led coalition did not pursue them into Iraqi territory.

The outcome left Saddam Hussein in power in Iraq. It set up another decade of relatively low-level military and economic conflict between Iraq and US-led forces.[119] The United Nations authorized a set of sanctions on Iraq, and swiftly became embroiled in the worst corruption scandal in its history, associated with the Oil-for-Food program. Simultaneously, the United States enforced a "no-fly zone" on parts of Iraq, with mixed results. By the end of the decade, it was clear that these efforts had done little if anything to weaken Hussein's hold on power.

The Persian Gulf Area since 1991

The 1990–1991 Persian Gulf War was perhaps the clearest demonstration of the oil-for-security deals that underpin what I call Subsystem B, the set of actors and understandings that protect a non-monopolistic pattern of sovereignty over oil fields. The United States and its allies spent the rest of the 1990s trying to sanction and contain Iraq, keep a lid on other political tensions, and swat away terrorist groups. The al Qaeda attack on September 11, 2001, changed all that. It led to the disastrous decision to invade Iraq in 2003. The post-invasion fiasco in Iraq, a flawed intervention in Libya in 2011, various terrorist groups that seemed to feed off the Western military presence, and ongoing hostility with Iran contributed to tension and violence in the region.

[116] Bush and Scowcroft 1998: 330.
[117] Kreps 2011; Henke 2019.
[118] Quoted in Kreps 2011: 60.
[119] Colgan 2013d: 112–122.

Structural changes in the twenty-first century have motivated both the United States and the petrostates to reconsider the OFS deals. One way that these relationships have changed since the mid-twentieth century is that the United States is now by far the most important external patron in the Middle East. Britain's withdrawal from the Persian Gulf in 1971 was the most important milestone in this transition (though in 2017, it announced a small-scale return to the Gulf).[120] The preeminence of the United States takes on particular significance when combined with a transition in America's energy security since 2010: the rise of fracking and the tight oil industry. New technologies meant that the United States was temporarily a net exporter of oil in 2019–2020.[121] Some nonstructural considerations, like Saudi Arabia's erratic and bellicose foreign policy under Crown Prince Mohammed bin Salman, add to the doubts in Washington about OFS deals.

On the other side, some of the petrostates find their partnership with the United States increasingly difficult to sustain. The United States' actions in the Middle East renders it broadly unpopular among Arabs and Muslims. The Saudis especially have struggled with their ties to America. The United States occasionally expects the Saudis to make costly interventions in the global oil market. Over time, the Saudis are less able to afford those interventions, as their population rapidly increases and oil rents are stretched thin to support a bloated welfare state. The Saudis have also repeatedly expressed frustration with US policy toward Israel and the lack of a viable peace plan for Palestine. Growing tensions between the United States and Saudi Arabia since the late 1990s, well documented elsewhere,[122] might suggest that the oil-for-security partnership is weakening. Saudi Arabia's conflict with Yemen since 2015 added strain to the OFS deal.

Yet, it is far too early to declare the demise of OFS arrangements. The Trump administration, if anything, reinforced US ties to Saudi Arabia and other petrostates, as evidenced by its hard-line position on Iran and arms sales to the Saudis.[123] Moreover, the United States continues to seek cooperation from Saudi Arabia and others on the global oil market. While increased US oil production changed the psychology and rhetoric of American "energy security," the underlying economic fundamentals have not much changed. The United States continues to participate in a world market for oil, meaning that it is significantly

---

[120] "With silver and lead, Britain woos new allies in the Gulf," *The Economist*, February 18, 2017, http://www.economist.com/news/britain/21716953-post-brexit-search-strategic-partners-arrives-middle-east-silver-and-lead.

[121] On some of the geopolitical implications, see O'Sullivan 2014, 2017.

[122] Bronson 2006.

[123] For an analysis on the possible consequences in the Strait of Hormuz of Iranian hostility, see Talmadge 2008.

affected by world prices and the politics of oil-producing countries.[124] Further, consistent with its OFS deal, the United States still appears to be an imperfect but important constraint on Saudi foreign policy aggression.

A diplomatic fracas between Saudi Arabia and Qatar in 2017 illustrated the ongoing role of OFS deals. Saudi Arabia appeared to have gained tacit permission from President Trump before lashing out against Qatar over some longstanding irritants in their relationship. In the crisis, Saudi Arabia and the UAE placed a *de facto* embargo on Qatar. Saudi Arabia appears to have planned a fullfledged invasion of Qatar, in part to seize its rich oil and gas fields.[125] Only a diplomatic intervention by Secretary of State Rex Tillerson and Defense Secretary James Mattis appears to have stopped Saudi Arabia from invading.[126] The incident highlights the significance of US protection for Qatar, and its ability to restrain Saudi Arabia at least some of the time. Both suggest the persistence of OFS deals.

Another change in the twenty-first century is the increasing importance of Asian customers for Middle East oil, especially China.[127] This development raises the question of whether China might offer oil-for-security deals, thereby displacing the United States. Yet China does not yet have sufficient military prowess to offer real protection to Middle East states. At least for the immediate future, the United States has no peer in terms of projecting military power.

Assessing the Evidence of an Oil-for-Security Subsystem

This book claims that subsystems theory provides a lens to understand the history of oil politics we have just reviewed. To assess that claim, two tasks remain: delineating the subsystems to show how they operate on different logics, and highlighting the role of instruments of coercion as mechanisms to maintain international order. First, delineating the oil subsystems. Chapter 2 asserted that there were two such subsystems, and chapters 3 and 4 provide ample evidence that one exists for the economics of production. What about the military-sovereignty subsystem? What evidence do we have that oil-for-security arrangements characterized this subsystem, before, during, and after the gradual withdrawal of the British Empire from the Persian Gulf?

---

[124] Colgan and Van de Graaf 2017.
[125] McFarlane et al. 2019.
[126] Emmons 2018; Reuters 2018 (January 30).
[127] Kemp 2010; Lind and Press 2018.

First, if an oil security subsystem exists and provides OFS deals, we should see evidence that powerful external states offer military protection to petrostates at pivotal moments. We see evidence of this behavior on multiple occasions. It takes two different forms: active defense deployments and deterrence efforts. In terms of defense deployments, this was most evident in the US defense of Saudi Arabia and Kuwait in 1990–1991. Yet even prior to the 1970s, we see evidence. Britain defended its claim to oil in Iraq in 1941, primarily against internal (Iraqi) enemies. It did so again in Iran in 1946, and again in Kuwait in 1961, both times against external enemies (the Soviet Union and Iraq, respectively). The United States, for its part, actively deterred Egypt from attacking Saudi Arabia in the 1960s. Both the United Kingdom (before 1970) and the United States (increasingly over time) had military bases throughout the region, which served as deterrents to would-be attackers. Some of these were very substantial: Wheelus Air Base in Libya was, at one point in the 1960s, the largest US military facility outside the United States. Last but not least, the 1980 Carter Doctrine is striking evidence of US commitment to defend certain petrostates. The Carter Doctrine can be interpreted as an explicit statement of the OFS deals then in place, designed in part to reassure the Gulf monarchies in the wake of the British withdrawal from the region in 1971.

A second empirical indicator of an oil security subsystem is petrostates offering some kind of oil benefits to their protectors. Until the 1970s, before most petrostates nationalized their oil industries, the chief economic benefit for the protectors came in the form of profits to the Anglo-American oil companies.[128] The Seven Sisters benefited enormously from the political relationships between their home countries and the petrostates. After nationalization occurred in the 1970s, the benefits provided by petrostates to their protectors changed and shrank. Still, they continued to exist. Petrostates' willingness to price oil in US dollars, for instance, has the effect of supporting the dollar as the world's primary reserve currency, which generates significant economic benefits for the United States.[129] Also, petrostates offer reliable access to supply with a minimum amount of politically induced price volatility. Tangibly, this means avoiding policies that would disrupt supply and cooperating with their patrons to secure oil transit routes and infrastructure. They have done so, quite consistently, for decades. The 1973 Arab oil embargo is the apparent exception to the rule, but there have been no embargoes since 1973. Even on that one occasion, as chapter 3 explained, the

---

[128] British Cabinet CAB 129/100, C(60)35 "Future Policy Study, 1960–1970: Cabinet Memorandum, Report of Officials' Committee," 24 Feb 1960, reprinted in Hyam and Louis 2000: 99. Also see PREM 11/4679, ff56–59, "Aden, the Yemen, and Middle East policy: Minute by J. O. Wright," 8 Apr 1964, reprinted in Hyam and Louis 2000: 640.

[129] Norrlof et al. 2020.

"oil shortages" in the United States were a product of the Nixon administration's price control policies, rather than petrostates' policies.[130] Overall, the OFS states provide consistent and reliable oil access to their patrons—access that their external protectors prize greatly.[131]

Privileged access to oil is not the only key benefit OFS deals offer to the patron. The "petrodollar recycling" program from Saudi Arabia to the United States, beginning in 1974, is another example (see chapter 3). After the oil shock, US officials wanted money spent on oil returned to the US economy in the form of profits to American companies, investments in the United States, and purchases of American goods. The petrostates' massive weapons purchases from their patrons became a sizeable part of that benefit. One American military officer commented, "I do not know of anything that is nonnuclear that we would not give the Saudis."[132] Those purchases proved crucial for US defense companies: their profits increased from about 4 percent of the total profits of Fortune 500 companies in the late 1960s to about 10 percent by the late 1980s, making arms exports one of the leading sectors of the US economy.[133] Collectively, Saudi Arabia, the UAE, and Kuwait were the United States' biggest customer for arms exports during 1990–2015 (Saudi Arabia was the second largest on its own).[134] Saudi arms purchases, made possible by its oil income, are widely seen as part of a strategy to cement the Kingdom's international relationships.[135]

Third, if OFS deals existed as part of empires, decolonization should have been different for petrostates—generally occurring later, and with greater reluctance on the part of the colonizer or colony or both, than in non-petrostates. As shown earlier, this is exactly the pattern we observe. An underlying bond between the colony and the metropole was not easily severed. In light of the other historical evidence, it is reasonable to interpret the decolonization pattern as further indication of an oil-for-security deal that was at one time integral to the imperial relationship, and after decolonization had to be reconstituted as a formal or informal pact between sovereign states.

In short, there is considerable evidence that OFS deals exist, forming the backbone of a second subsystem. That does not mean, however, that all OFS deals were destined to last. In three cases—Iraq, Libya, and Iran—the petrostate turned away from its relationship with the Anglo-American powers. It is certainly possible that other petrostates might do the same in the future, or that the United States might turn its back on them.

---

[130] Frech and Lee 1987; Colgan 2014.
[131] Kelanic 2020.
[132] Quoted in De Onis 1974.
[133] Nitzan and Bichler 2002: 211–216.
[134] "Importer/Exporter TIV Tables," *Stockholm International Peace Research Institute*, http://armstrade.sipri.org/armstrade/page/values.php, accessed May 30, 2017.
[135] Aarts and Nonneman 2006.

The final task is to show evidence that order within the subsystem depends significantly on punishments for noncompliance. The strength and probability of those punishments varied over time. In the final stages of imperialism, punishments were still strong. Britain and the United States used two instruments of coercion in particular: leadership selection and economic coercion. The British intervention in Iraq in 1941 overthrew the regime, making it clear to all that Britain would not tolerate Iraq's efforts to export oil to British enemies. The removal of Mossadegh's government in Iran, along with the boycott of Iranian oil during 1951–1953, similarly demonstrated that the United States and the United Kingdom would not tolerate nationalization of their oil assets, which violated the implicit rules of oil at the time.

After Operation Ajax, however, the Anglo-American powers did not impose any more leadership punishments. That created a period of uncertainty through the 1960s about exactly what the petrostates could do without fear of punishment. Eventually, Libya and Iran severed their relationships with the United States, as Iraq did in 1958. Most of the oil-for-security deals, however, persisted based on mutual interests (strategic benefits) rather than coercion. When those deals were threatened, both parties tended to cooperate to repair the damage. The US-Saudi arrangements created immediately after the 1973 oil crisis, and the formalization of the US-Kuwaiti alliance after 1991, are cases in point. Thus, the period since the 1970s illustrates that OFS deals are able to persist largely on the basis of strategic benefits alone.

Conclusion

For over a century, oil has been a central feature in battles over power, wealth, and national sovereignty. In the world's most important oil patch, the Persian Gulf, Britain and the United States have been the dominant external actors. They have offered protection to their local allies and partners, while doling out severe economic, political, and military punishments to those who have sought to undermine their control. In contrast to the principally economic issues of the oil production subsystem covered in chapters 3 and 4, this second subsystem is infused with military power and force.

When it comes to the crucial issue of demarcating and enforcing national boundaries (subsystem B), decolonization represented a relatively superficial change (unlike in subsystem A). Saudi Arabia's early oil-for-security deal with the United States became the blueprint for many new petrostates. Those deals vary significantly in their timing and details, but the basic structure is remarkably consistent: the patron state(s) protect and support the petrostate's regime, in exchange for economic benefits and policy cooperation from the petrostate in global oil markets. As these deals took shape, mostly one state at a time, the distinct subsystem for oil security took form in the second half of the twentieth century. It continues today.

In the twenty-first century, prominent scholars and thinkers are calling for the United States to pull back or even abandon the Middle East altogether.[136] Decades of military involvement in the region with little visible success, changes in global energy markets that reduce US dependence on oil imports,[137] and a certain degree of moral repugnance for Saudi Arabia's leadership after 2015 have spurred an active debate about the extent to which the United States and others should continue to engage in the region. The reaction is understandable, and there is little question that US policy could be improved. Yet advocates for change have found the US policy remarkably resistant to change. One reason, often unacknowledged, is that OFS deals provide benefits to both sides, not just costs.

An incident in 2019 illustrated the continuing relevance of OFS deals. The most important oil facility in the world, Saudi Aramco's Abqaiq, was attacked on September 14, 2019. It initially crippled the facility, which handles roughly half of Saudi Arabia's oil production on a daily basis. Although Yemeni rebels claimed credit for the attack, others alleged that Iran was behind it. Oil prices spiked upward. Within a week, the United States announced its intention to send troops to Saudi Arabia to defend the territory.[138] By the end of that year, thousands more troops were forward-deployed in the Persian Gulf area. Oil-for-security deals, it would seem, are alive and well.

---

[136] Layne 2007; Gholz and Press 2010a, 2010b; Posen 2014; Glaser and Kelanic 2016; Thrall and Friedman 2018. See also Mearsheimer and Walt 2016. For a very different take, see Brooks and Wohlforth 2016; Rovner and Talmadge 2014.

[137] O'Sullivan 2014.

[138] Myers 2019. Available at: https://www.militarytimes.com/news/your-military/2019/09/20/following-attacks-pentagon-prepping-to-send-troops-to-saudi-arabias-aid/.

PART II

BEYOND OIL

6

Using Subsystems beyond Oil

"Because they deal with systems that are highly complex, adaptive, and not rigorously rule-bound, the social sciences are among the most difficult of disciplines, both methodologically and intellectually."[1]

—Editorial Board of *Nature*

The question of change in international order extends far beyond oil politics. Identifying changes of international order is not easy, let alone diagnosing their causes and effects, but it is vital nonetheless. International order shapes our world. Easy to take for granted, it is often only at times of crisis or disruption that we perceive or appreciate international order. Many scholars consider the problem of order—how it emerges, breaks down, and reemerges—the central problem of international relations.[2]

My job in this chapter is to show how subsystems theory can be applied to issue areas beyond oil. That job is linked to four broad questions I postponed in chapter 2. First, what guidelines should someone follow to develop a subsystems analysis? Second, how can we tell if one analysis improves upon another (or is it just a matter of taste)? Third, what empirical examples illustrate the range of subsystems, in terms of the strength of the strategic benefits and punishments for noncompliance? And finally, how do changes at the subsystem level aggregate up to affect an ordering theme at the systemic or global level (e.g., the liberal order)? I address each question in turn.

The first is perhaps the most important. In addition to offering guidelines, I will illustrate how to apply a subsystems approach using two new topic areas: nuclear politics and peacekeeping operations. Subsystems theory encourages analysts to do various things they might otherwise not do. One is to define analytically the main behavior in the issue area associated with functional tasks. Specifying that behavior often identifies a wide constellation of actors as relevant to that behavior. This descriptive step is necessary to counter the tendency in political

---

[1] *Nature* 2012.
[2] Ikenberry 2000: 22; see also Carr 1946 [1964]; Bull 1977; Goh 2013; Phillips and Sharman 2015.

science to jump too quickly into causal inference, seeking to explain either the cause or effect of international institutions (or their non-effects). A focus on governance and decision-making, rather than on particular institutions, is essential for understanding change and continuity.

It might seem obvious that analysts ought to do these things, but intelligent scholars working across different issue areas show a common proclivity to jump straight into causal inference, rather than seeking to describe and understand context.[3] This tendency leads to certain blind spots about actors who affect an international order. The value of my argument in this chapter is thus mainly heuristic. Its premises are not theoretically original or controversial. However, the approach I describe leads to new analysis and conclusions.

Subsystems Theory as a Method

Subsystems theory can help scholars analyze whether, when, and why international order changes in various issue areas. As I will describe, a subsystems approach is compatible with a wide range of ontological and epistemological positions, including positions that are often at odds with each other, such as neopositivism and historicism.[4] Analysts should use four steps to start applying subsystems theory to their area of interest. They should: observe empirical patterns; identify key questions of governance; relate the theory's conceptual elements to the empirics; and investigate a subsystem's political dynamics.

The first step is to start with the political behavior of interest, and situate it within the patterns and the context of that behavior. This is intuitive. Most researchers start by looking out into the world and wondering about it. The point of taking this step consciously and systematically is to secure two benefits. First, we want to pin down those behaviors as anchors for the rest of the analysis. In the process of spending months or years on a project, researchers sometimes lose their way or go down rabbit holes. Identifying the primary empirical pattern (or lack of pattern) helps guide the research project in times of need. The researcher can always revise their primary interest, of course, but doing so should be a conscious process of lifting anchor rather than just drifting about.

The other benefit to taking this first step is that it broadens the landscape in which the research takes place. For example, suppose one began with an interest in the politics of Iran's nuclear program. Some researchers might focus solely on Iran's experience. Most political scientists, however, would see the

---

[3] Oatley 2011; Gerring 2012; King 2012; Chaudoin et al. 2015; Bauerle Danzman 2017; Winecoff 2017.
[4] King et al 1994; Cox and Sinclair 1996; Hobson and Lawson 2008.

country's behavior as a case of potential nuclear proliferation, and thus relate it to other experiences in the Middle East: Iraq and Libya failed to acquire nuclear weapons but Israel obtained them. Seeing this immediate pattern is good but still incomplete. Broadening the analytical lens further, the researcher might see the history of nuclear proliferation as a whole: a slow trickle of states gradually acquiring nuclear weapons since 1945. That slow trickle stands in contrast with the extraordinary growth in the destructive power of the nuclear-armed states, chiefly the United States and USSR. The Cold War superpowers generated some attempts at limiting the development and deployment of nuclear weapons, with varying degrees of success. Observing these broader patterns, and the governing arrangements that they generated, helps with the subsequent steps in the analysis—without losing sight of the original motivation concerning Iran's nuclear program.

The second step is to identify the key question(s) of governance that represent the central core of the subsystem(s). Identifying those questions requires description and descriptive inference.[5] It is as much art as science; the process cannot be specified precisely. Yet what should be clear from my analysis of oil politics in previous chapters is that subsystems and their governance questions are identified from a bottom-up process of empirical induction, rather than top-down deductive reasoning.[6] Subsystems are not self-specified by the actors in the real world, but neither are they entirely a matter of analytical choice.[7] They fall in a kind of middle ground: firmly rooted in the empirics, and based on the behaviors that have greatest significance. The analyst must make their own judgments about what those are.

As guidance, four criteria might help in identifying governance questions, even if no precise recipe exists. First, governance questions cover the most *significant* decisions in the issue area. Significance cannot be defined objectively, of course, but it can be inferred empirically from the breadth and depth of behavioral consequences. If a potential question of governance can affect more people (breadth) and has a greater impact (depth) than another potential question of governance, then it is more significant than the narrower potential question.

Second, governance questions are distinct from one another. If some subsystems, as defined by the analyst, have nearly identical actors and describe similar behavior, a better specification probably exists that would yield fewer subsystems in the issue area. That would be simpler and clearer. Governance

---

[5] While the process is heavily descriptive and relies primarily on descriptive inference, it can also involve a certain amount of tentative causal inference about basic relationships between the relevant actors.

[6] Indeed, it can involve both induction ("generalizing from a sample of events") and abduction ("positing underlying structures that account for those events"). Wendt 1999: 87.

[7] My argument here parallels Adler 2019: 147; Kratochwil and Ruggie 1986: 763–764.

questions are well specified when the fewest number of them exist to adequately describe the issue area's most significant behavior.

Third, questions of governance focus on decisions and behavior, not on actors or institutions. They generally ask *what* things are done, overall—not *who* does them, *how*, or *where*. The issue of *who* makes decisions *for whom* is, of course, crucial for understanding politics,[8] but in general it can be misleading as a starting point for analysis. It can lead analysts to zero in on the actors and institutions that make the most headlines or appear superficially most important. It is better to start instead by understanding *what* underlying behavior and kinds of decisions really matter, first—and only later work to see who really makes those decisions and how.

Fourth, well-specified questions of governance can be phrased concisely. As a rule of thumb, a governance question can be specified in fifteen words or less. Longer formulations tend to lead to conceptual wooliness. Taken together, these four pieces of advice offer some guidance for identifying the governance questions within an issue area.

The third major step of the subsystems method is to relate the general conceptual elements of subsystems theory to the empirical particulars of the issue area, such as actors with proper names or particular behaviors. Five conceptual elements are especially important: the subsystem's constituent actors; the punishments used to enforce order in the subsystem; the relevant instruments of coercion; the strategic benefits that motivate continuation of the existing order; and the potential strategic benefits under plausible alternative arrangements. For example, once a question of governance is identified, an analyst should identify all of the actors that can significantly affect the answer to that question.

Often this step highlights actors that otherwise might receive little or no attention. Actors at all levels of analysis could be relevant: not just international organizations and major states, but also firms, informal networks, and other non-state actors. The analyst should devote attention to actors roughly in proportion to the degree that they can affect the answer to the governance question. Major actors should receive major attention; marginal actors receive less. Depending on the subsystem, capabilities and instruments of coercion can come in different forms: money, troops, regulatory power, expertise, etc.

This third step is important as a heuristic tool to put descriptive inference ahead of causal inference. As I indicated earlier, I believe that a subsystems approach is largely compatible with neopositivist[9] and historicist[10] positions. At

---

[8] Avant et al. 2010; Shilliam 2010; Towns 2010; Sjoberg 2013; Henderson 2013; Acharya and Buzan 2010.

[9] King et al. 1994.

[10] Kratochwil and Ruggie 1986; Cox and Sinclair 1996; Hobson and Lawson 2008; Bukovansky 2009; McNamara 2010; King 2012.

least in principle, both positions recognize the importance of description in social scientific analysis. In practice, however, neopositivists often prioritize causal
inference over description.[11] That tendency encourages them to swiftly zero in
on a particular actor, or type of strategic interaction, and then spend most of
their analytic effort identifying its cause or effect (or non-effect).[12] For example,
neopositivists seeking to understand globalization have extensively studied bilateral investment treaties (BITs). A meta-analysis of seventy-four research articles finds that the impact of BITs "is so small as to be considered zero," suggesting
that the massive research effort behind those seventy-four articles focused on a
small piece of the picture.[13] The problem here is not with the initial research on
BITs—a few studies evaluating their causal impact was valuable—but the continuing, outsized prioritization of causal analysis even when the underlying subject
matter is a marginal aspect of the overall subject.

By contrast, subsystems theory encourages analysts to focus on something
logically prior to causal analysis: describing and identifying the most important
behaviors, and then the actors, involved in each of the key governance questions.
As a method, that helps the analyst carefully nail down the *what* and *who* before
diving into the *why*. For example, analysts of globalization should identify and
study the actors and governing arrangements shaping large economic flows, not
just the actors and arrangements most amenable to causal analysis (like BITs).[14]
Of course, determining "the most important" behaviors is an iterative process,
and causal analysis helps refine our judgment about what is important. In general, however, careful descriptive inference goes a long way in guiding the analyst to see the bigger picture.

The logic of neopositivism nominally prohibits analysts from skipping over
description and descriptive inference. Indeed, the central neopositivist text on
research design, *Designing Social Inquiry*, spends an entire chapter on descriptive inference and provides much valuable advice about how to do it carefully.[15]
That advice reminds us that: careful description is vital for analysis; description involves culturally and historically sensitive interpretation; and a detail-
intensive, relatively unstructured process of familiarization known as "soaking
and poking" can be extremely helpful. The text also points to the value of "thick"
description but notes that even in the thickest description, simplification is necessary for knowledge.

---

[11] Gerring 2012; King 2012.
[12] Lake and Powell 1999: 4–5.
[13] Brada et al. 2020.
[14] Subsystems theory is helpful but not necessary to adopt this research approach—for example,
see Mosley 2003; Copelovitch 2010; Pelc 2010; Blyth 2013; Chaudoin 2014; Peters 2017; Carnegie and
Gaikwad 2017; Bauerle Danzman 2019.
[15] King et al. 1994: chapter 2.

Assessing strategic benefits and punishments for noncompliance requires interpretation and historical sensitivity. Not all interpretations are equally valid.[16] In one context, a change of a few cents in the price of a barrel of oil might be rather meaningless, even if it leads some actors to rhetorically condemn it; but in another, it could mean a substantial decrease in the strategic benefits of a subsystem, provoking genuine outrage among participants. The difference is akin to Clifford Geertz's description of a wink versus an eye twitch: an analyst observing the same physical actions will badly misinterpret them unless she or he understands the context in which those actions are taken.[17] Subsystems analysis frequently requires this type of interpretation. For instance, did the Saudi King Faisal's decision to impose an oil embargo on the United States in 1973 represent a major breach in the relationship or, instead, an action taken reluctantly to appease a domestic audience? As neopositivists acknowledge, a good-quality answer to that question requires interpretation informed by historical knowledge.

Even so, historicists often highlight something in their descriptive method typically missing from neopositivist accounts: a dialectical sensitivity to social contradictions or opposing forces.[18] For example, Robert Cox usefully distinguishes between two kinds of ideas: "intersubjective meanings, which tend to cut across social divisions; and rival collective images of social order, which are *specific to competing social forces*."[19] These rival collective images are significant. Neopositivists' approach to descriptive inference encourages the analyst to "distinguish the systematic from the nonsystematic."[20] That advice suggests that there is typically a kind of central pattern or essence to be discovered and highlighted within any observed phenomenon. Cox, on the other hand, reminds us that there are nearly always competing social forces at play that render any central pattern contested and temporary.[21]

That insight leads to the fourth and final key step for subsystems analysis: investigating the dynamics and political contestation within and across subsystems. Social contradictions and tensions are important to subsystems theory for two main reasons. First, rival collective images of social order often contain within them potential alternative governing arrangements that serve as the seeds of change.[22] Specifically, perceptions of strategic benefits depend on such ideas. As I have emphasized in previous chapters, the strategic benefits of

---

[16] Both positivists and interpretivists share this view; see Wendt 1999: 85.
[17] King et al. 1994: 38–39.
[18] Philpott 2001; Bukovansky 2009; Phillips 2010; and see Young 1982 for an exception among neopositivists, which also identified inner contradictions as a source of regime transformation.
[19] Cox and Sinclair 1996: 10 (emphasis added).
[20] King et al. 1994: 55–63.
[21] To be clear, these two positions are not logically incompatible with each other, but rather differ in their emphasis.
[22] Finnemore and Jurkovich 2020.

any given international order must be understood in a relative sense: that is, they are the benefits that actors receive under one set of governing arrangements relative to the benefits they would receive under an imagined alternative set of arrangements.[23]

Second, social contradictions, tensions, and rival images generate noncompliance, which in turn generates potential punishments. Some actors might refuse to comply with a set of governing arrangements because they are following one collective image, like national autonomy; actors who choose to punish them follow another, like a certain economic ideology. In oil politics, the transnational group of anticolonial elites I described in chapter 3, who set out to undermine the Seven Sisters' economic control, is a good example of actors with rival collective images manifesting social contradictions and tensions. In turn, those tensions affect both perceived strategic benefits and noncompliance.

Analysts exploring the political dynamics of subsystems should explore the incumbent/challenger distinction used in social movement theory and sociology.[24] Incumbents are actors who "wield disproportionate influence within a field [i.e., subsystem] and whose interests and views tend to be heavily reflected in the dominant organization of the strategic action field."[25] Incumbents' interests typically shape a subsystem's governing arrangements. Challengers occupy subordinate roles and niches within a subsystem and typically struggle to wield influence over its governing arrangements. Nonetheless, they can often articulate an alternative vision for the subsystem. On rare occasions, challengers are able to upend a subsystem and transform its governing arrangements—as OPEC did in 1973.

These four analytic steps collectively imply that a great deal of descriptive work is required for good subsystems analysis. Identifying the central question(s) of governance in an issue area, especially, requires the kind of interpretation and judgment that depends on a firm grasp of an issue area's empirical history. Without it, an analyst might subdivide the issue area too much or not enough for the purposes of their analysis, leading to confusion or flawed conclusions.

Examples of the Subsystems Method in Action

To make my method here more concrete, I illustrate it for two new topic areas: nuclear politics and peacekeeping operations. I carry out only the first stages of this method, to give a sense of how it might proceed. This is by necessity: it took the

---

[23] An actor's culture offers a toolkit of ideas and strategies, which inspire and shape potential governing arrangements (Swidler 1986).

[24] Gamson 1975.

[25] Fligstein and McAdam 2012: 13; see also "co-adaptation" in Gunitsky 2013.

first five chapters of this book to describe my analysis of the oil subsystems, and I have neither the space nor the expertise to carry out a full analysis of these topics. Still, I can show how one would get started, and why it would be worth doing so.

Subsystems in Nuclear Politics

Our first step is to observe the political behavior and patterns of interest. For nuclear politics, we might begin with the two patterns I indicated earlier: the slow trickle of states that have become nuclear weapons states since 1945, and their extraordinary growth in destructive power. On reflection, we might broaden our gaze slightly further, and think about the track record of the civilian nuclear industry. While there have been three spectacular failures—at Three Mile Island, Chernobyl, and Fukushima—nuclear power's overall track record is remarkably safe compared to other forms of power like coal.[26] These and possibly other patterns we observe can help us think about the main behaviors in this issue area.

The method's second step is to identify the key questions of governance. There are at least three. One subsystem centers upon the question, What nuclear technology can be acquired or blocked internationally? A second revolves around the question, Once acquired, in what ways can nuclear weapons be used for deterrence, compellence, or force? A third asks, How can nuclear technology be used safely for civilian purposes? These can be labeled the "proliferation," "weapons management," and "safety" subsystems. The analyst might not identify all of these subsystems right away, and might need to add or revise them after deeper analysis. Still, it is a good start.

Each of these subsystems has generated a body of academic research. Many scholars have examined the issue of proliferation.[27] Others have studied the second subsystem, examining the nuclear taboo, efforts to limit arms races, the positioning of nuclear weapons in allied territories, nuclear compellence, and other topics.[28] The politics of civilian nuclear safety, and its possible relationship to weapons, generates a third body of research.[29]

As with oil politics, there is no reason to believe that the subsystems of nuclear politics always change at the same time in the same direction. The rates and directions of change might even diverge considerably. Consequently, viewing the international nuclear order as a monolithic issue area might cloud analysts' eyes

---

[26] McKenna 2011.
[27] Miller 2014; Coe and Vaynman 2015; Gavin 2015; Braut-Hegghammer 2016; Mehta and Whitlark 2017; Bell 2017; Carnegie and Carson 2019; Colgan and Miller 2019; Gheorghe 2019.
[28] Jervis 1989; Solingen 2009; Tannenwald 2007; Lieber and Press 2020; Green 2020.
[29] Nelkin 1981; Sagan 1995; Miller 2017.

to variation within that order. During the Trump administration, for example, various arms control agreements between Russia and the United States that sought to manage the use of those weapons collapsed or weakened. At the same time, the United States pressured North Korea and Iran for their alleged nuclear proliferation efforts. That pressure appears to continue a long-standing pattern of US behavior vis-à-vis those countries, albeit with different rhetoric and tactics. Rather than collapsing, anti-proliferation efforts continued. Thus, the subsystem for weapons management and the one for nonproliferation appear to be changing in different ways and at different speeds.

The third and fourth steps of the method follow from this setup. I will not pursue them in depth here, but only point a way forward. Focusing on the nonproliferation subsystem, for instance, we can immediately identify some of the key actors, which would include the United States, the other nuclear powers, the International Atomic Energy Agency (IAEA), and the non-nuclear states. The benefits to governing arrangements like the Nuclear Nonproliferation Treaty (NPT) and the Nuclear Suppliers Group exist for all states, but flow disproportionately to the nuclear states, which benefit from the asymmetrical balance of power. The ongoing political contestation and rival collective images are worth noting, as they are manifested in aspirational agreements like the 2017 Treaty on the Prohibition of Nuclear Weapons. Those agreements are not real governing arrangements (because the nuclear states, the only actors whose behavior they would constrain, don't participate) but they still represent rival images and potential governing arrangements. As we saw with OPEC in the 1970s, sometimes potential arrangements replace the dominant ones.

A subsystems approach to nuclear politics offers three advantages. First, punishments for noncompliance play a key role in nuclear politics, in exactly the way subsystems theory expects. Dominant states cooperate to develop new rules or mechanisms for punishing weaker states.[30] That motivation was crucial in the creation of the IAEA and subsequent nuclear safeguards.[31] Sometimes those punishments are overlooked as an explanation for the nonproliferation regime.[32] Of course, some states—notably, India, Pakistan, Israel, and North Korea—have managed to avoid or withstand these punishments and develop nuclear weapons despite the nonproliferation regime. Still, many other states that might have developed nuclear weapons decided against it, a pattern sometimes described as a "secret success" of the nonproliferation regime.[33] And in one case, South Africa, a state was actually compelled to give up nuclear weapons after it had developed them.

---

[30] Coe and Vaynman 2015.
[31] Colgan and Miller 2019.
[32] Martin 1992: 779; Brown 2015.
[33] Miller 2014; Gavin 2015; Narang 2017.

Second, the subsystems approach highlights the fact that a lot of what gets lumped together as "nuclear arms control" is actually addressing different questions, namely weapons management versus proliferation. The Intermediate-range Nuclear Treaty and the NPT are both forms of arms control, but one was focused squarely on Russia and the United States' use of those weapons, whereas the other aims to avoid proliferation by weaker states. Noticing these differences helps analysts see that changes have occurred at different rates and in different ways in the two subsystems. It also suggests explanatory factors, like power asymmetries. Major power asymmetries exist between the actors in the proliferation subsystem (i.e., the United States is much stronger than other non-nuclear states), whereas the power asymmetries are smaller, more uncertain, and more variable over time in the "weapons management" subsystem (in which the United States, USSR/Russia, and China try to restrain each other). If we lump "nuclear arms control" together as a single issue area, we fail to see the differences between these subsystems. In other words, nuclear politics is another example of where analysts ought to notice change in the midst of continuity, and continuity in the midst of change.

Third, the subsystems approach helps surface the full constellation of actors that matter in a particular subsystem. For example, in the proliferation sub-system, it is not just the IAEA and the great powers that matter but also the una-ligned and subordinate states. My research with Nicholas Miller found that those unaligned states were not merely acted on; they acted in their own right, and thereby steered the system.[34] That approach leads to new findings, in comparison to previous work that focused largely on the great powers.[35] Our work shows how rival hierarchies (led by the United States and USSR, respectively) actually *provoked* each other to share nuclear technology through competitive shaming[36] and outbidding,[37] as they competed to attract the unaligned states to their side. The unaligned states responded by playing the superpowers off against each other and extracting more favorable terms of exchange. In the language of subsystems theory, the strategic benefits that each superpower offered other states in its orbit was crucial for the behavior of the overall subsystem. Specifically, rival collec-tive images of social order helped change the subsystem's behavior. In this case, the United States and USSR promoted those rival images, unlike in oil politics,

---

[34] Colgan and Miller 2019.

[35] Fuhrmann 2012; Brown 2015.

[36] Competitive shaming resembles, but stands apart from, "naming and shaming" in other policy areas, such as international human rights (Hafner-Burton 2008; Murdie and Davis 2012; Hendrix and Wong 2013). In that case, the nominal goal of the shaming state is to compel the target state into changing its behavior. Competitive shaming works differently: the shaming state aims not so much to compel different behavior as to make the target state look bad in front of world audiences.

[37] Bueno de Mesquita and Smith 2016 find outbidding operative among foreign aid donors. On outbidding between sub-state actors, see Crenshaw 1981; Snyder 1991; Kydd and Walter 2006; Toft 2007.

where anticolonial actors in developing countries challenged a relatively unified Anglo-American order.

Naturally, a subsystems approach offers more value to some research questions than others. If one is interested in only the bureaucratic fights inside the Iranian regime over nuclear questions, a subsystems approach might not be worth the effort. For many questions, however, a broader perspective could prove highly fertile.

Subsystems in Peacekeeping

Consider a second issue area: international peacekeeping. To benefit from a subsystems approach, again we might start by observing patterns of political behavior that interest us. Our initial motivation might be what we observe in a single country like Liberia, or perhaps across multiple countries in Africa. We notice certain patterns: peacekeeping troops typically come from poor countries like Bangladesh; rich countries tend to pay for them; and the troops have certain predictable behaviors when they are on mission, like engaging in prostitution. Other questions, like which conflicts the UN decides to deploy peacekeepers to, might not have patterns that are readily observable to the untrained eye.

The second step is to identify those key questions of governance. It would be tempting to start with questions that simply mirror the patterns we observe, such as, Who provides the peacekeepers? And who pays for them? However, in keeping with the advice offered earlier, it is generally useful to focus on the *what* questions before the *who*. In addition, the analyst should try to find a systematic way to cover the whole issue area, for example, by using the life cycle of peace-keeping missions. Thus, the four questions might be: "how are peacekeepers supplied?" "where do they get sent?" "what do they do during their mission?" and "in what ways do peacekeeping missions end?" These questions might be re-vised as the analysis proceeds, but they offer a systematic starting point.

Each of these questions anchors a subsystem. Scholars have studied each one. The supply of peacekeepers is a political process.[38] The choice of when and where to send peacekeepers is even more political, in the sense that it involves intense contestation and unpredictable outcomes.[39] Research also focuses on peacekeepers' behavior on mission, ranging from their official mandates to un-official troop behaviors.[40] Finally, the transition of peacekeeping to various post-conflict outcomes, from elections to policing, is a growing part of political science,

---

[38] Bove and Elia 2011; Haass and Ansorg 2018.
[39] Fortna 2008; Allen and Yuen 2014; Ruggeri et al. 2018.
[40] Autesserre 2014; Lake 2014; Beber et al. 2017; Karim and Beardsley 2017; Blair 2019; Howard 2019.

often using advanced methods of causal inference.[41] The patterns observed in each subsystem might be linked to particular governing arrangements that represent a kind of international order, and that evolves over time. Like other areas, it involves change amid continuity. For instance, peacekeeping mandates have become more ambitious and invasive over time, even as the institutions that draft those mandates, and the veto players within those institutions, have remained more or less the same.

As before, I will not dive into the third and fourth steps in any great detail. Even so, one can immediately see certain actors involved, like the United Nations, NATO, the countries that supply peacekeepers, and the conflict-torn countries potentially targeted for missions. Other actors, like certain NGOs, might also be relevant. Political contestation about the manner in which peacekeeping occurs is evident. For example, the International Criminal Court manifests one possible governing arrangement for troop conduct, but some actors hotly contest it.[42] Rival collective images are at work in that contest.

This subsystems approach to peacekeeping offers at least four potential advantages. First, it might spur the analyst to see new questions that would otherwise go ignored, especially where transnational governing arrangements are concerned. Suppose the initial research question was about the behavior of peacekeeping troops, and it was relevant that those troops came from poor countries. The exercise of mapping the subsystems might spur the researcher to wonder about why peacekeeping troops previously tended to come from rich countries like Canada. Why did the pattern of peacekeeper supply change over time, and what does it tell us about today's peacekeeping outcomes? Those questions lead the analyst to consider the governing arrangements by which peacekeepers are supplied (i.e., new dependent variables).

Second, this approach likely surfaces the linkages between the subsystems. For instance, peacekeepers' mandates and rules probably depend on who pays for them to be there. In turn, that could lead to richer, more accurate explanations of behavior (i.e., new independent variables). Third, it encourages analysts to see peacekeeping non-institutionally—placing NATO operations in the Balkans and Afghanistan alongside UN operations. That scope of study contrasts with analyses that do not take a subsystems approach and focus narrowly on a single institution like the United Nations.[43] Again, part of the value of a subsystems approach is heuristic.

Fourth, a subsystems approach can complement the strengths of a more micro-level causal inference study. Recently, researchers have deployed field

---

[41]   Zaum and Cheng 2011; Matanock 2017; Blair et al. 2019.
[42]   Chapman and Chaudoin 2013; Bosco 2013; Jo and Simmons 2016.
[43]   Doyle and Sambanis 2006.

experiments to study specific peacekeeping behaviors and related activities like policing.[44] Being pitched at a more macro-level, subsystems analysis will probably offer little to improve the internal validity of field experiments or similar studies focusing on those causal effects. What it can offer is a more sophisticated understanding about the *external validity* of those studies. For example, if researchers find a particular effect of peacekeeping in a certain country at a certain time, one still wants to know the conditions under which that effect holds true in other places and other times. If we understand such conditions as persistent (at best) rather than permanent,[45] our analytic gaze turns to the governing arrangements that help determine those conditions. Identifying changes in those governing arrangements is a big part of what subsystems theory is all about.

Reliability and Validity in Subsystems Analyses

How can we tell if a subsystem analysis really generates new understanding? After all, subsystems are defined by the analyst, and require an interpretation of history. They are not fully objective, even if they are also not fully subjective. Considering that two analysts, working independently on the same issue and history, might identify different subsystems with different governance questions, it is reasonable to wonder whether subsystems analyses are reliable or valid. A *reliable* method suggests that analysts should identify the same subsystems in a given issue area, anchored by the same questions of governance, more or less. A *valid* method accurately captures the phenomenon under study. Disinterested analysts ought to be able to distinguish between analyses with more or less validity.

The subsystems method I propose scores poorly on reliability, but much better on validity. Two analysts might identify the same subsystems within a given issue, especially if that issue had relatively clear boundaries and had been analyzed by previous scholars. Yet, there is no guarantee. In some issue areas—like climate change, where our grasp of the root problem is emerging and developing quickly—there is little reason to expect independent analysts to identify subsystems in exactly the same way. This lack of reliability, however, is hardly a fatal flaw. In fact, social science already contains many different ways to analyze social behavior, and there is no such thing as a general approach that leads all analysts to exactly the same conclusions.

The more fruitful question is whether there is some way to evaluate the validity of different analyses. To the extent that progress is possible in social science, it happens by developing better explanations than those that previously

---

[44] Karim and Beardsley 2017; Blair 2020.
[45] Oatley 2019.

existed.[46] To have a "better" explanation we need standards of quality. It is not always possible to determine "the best" analysis because quality is multidimensional. But without some standards, there is no difference between the scholar's analysis and the quackery of an armchair pundit.

I propose three criteria for evaluating competing subsystems analyses of the same subject matter: accuracy, parsimony, and breadth. The first, accuracy, relates to the degree to which a given analysis can explain the major events within the history of the issue area under examination. If there are major turning points or behaviors that do not match the expectations of the analysis, it is less accurate than an analysis where reality does match expectations.

The second criterion is parsimony. Simpler theories with fewer concepts and variables are more parsimonious than those with more concepts and variables.[47] Parsimony is a virtue because all humans have cognitive limits and make mistakes as things get more complicated. Simple theories—like Newton's laws of motion, which describe the basics of physics in three simple equations—are enormously valuable.[48] Of course, simplification creates the risk of inaccuracy, so there is some tension between the criteria of accuracy and parsimony.

The third criterion is breadth. A subsystems analysis that covers the full scope of behaviors, decisions, and institutions in a given issue area is better than one that covers only some of those behaviors, decisions, and institutions. Inevitably, that generates debates about where the boundaries of an issue area actually are. Those debates are not resolvable in a purely theoretical, *a priori* way. Instead, they depend on empirical knowledge and good judgment. Still, the basic point should be clear: a subsystems analysis that covers the full range of a subject under investigation is better than one that covers just part of it, all else equal.

These three criteria give scholars a basis for using subsystems analysis in an analytically productive way. One claim in this book, for instance, is that using two subsystems improves our understanding of global oil politics, rather than the vaguely defined issue area that was common to previous analyses. If someone can show, instead, that the same history of oil can be explained with just one subsystem, without any loss of accuracy or breadth, that would improve upon my analysis. Alternatively, someone might improve upon my analysis if they can show that three or more subsystems are needed to explain the same history of oil (assuming that the improvement in accuracy or breadth justifies the loss of parsimony).

---

[46] Kuhn 1970; Lakatos 1976.

[47] Waltz 1979.

[48] As Katzenstein and Seybert (2018) point out, social science is not Newtonian. Human behavior is not deterministic. Still, parsimonious theories of cause and effect can be enormously useful in explaining recurring patterns of politics (e.g. the security dilemma).

Evaluating the robustness of a subsystems analysis is easier to do when there is a large body of relevant historical data. There is, thus, a difference between a *retrospective* subsystem analysis (like in oil politics), where the quality of a subsystems analysis can be judged with some confidence, and a *prospective* subsystem analysis (like in climate change), where the quality of analysts' interpretations is still unknown. In prospective analysis, only tentative judgments are possible, and the quality of a subsystems analysis can be fully understood only after some years have passed.

Mapping a Range of Subsystems

Chapter 2 theorized the sources of change in subsystems across two explanatory variables: strategic benefits and punishments for noncompliance. Those variables suggest a way of categorizing subsystems in four different quadrants (Figure 2.1). I showed how the oil production and oil security subsystems moved across three of the four different quadrants (Figure 2.2). Now that my discussion is moving beyond oil, we can consider some empirical examples in all four categories. I categorize governing arrangements according to the extent that they generate durable "deep cooperation," in the sense of modifying actors' behavior relative to the counterfactual world in which those arrangements didn't exist.[49] Figure 6.1 shows examples to help illustrate the full range of analytic outcomes.

Starting in the top-left box, we see that some subsystems generate strong benefits for participants and are supported by strong prospects for enforcement. My theory expects these subsystems to generate deep cooperation. The Seven Sisters' oil oligopoly of the early postwar period was one example. A second example is the set of rules and governing arrangements that prohibit territorial conquest, as articulated in Article 1 of the UN Charter and elsewhere. States occasionally violate the rules, but powerful actors typically seek to enforce them, either by force (e.g., reversing Iraq's 1990 invasion of Kuwait) or by sanctions and diplomacy (e.g., punishing Russia for its invasion of Ukraine). Although they are not perfect, the basic rules have been steady for decades. And they generate results: the rate of territorial conquest is lower since the UN was founded than it was before.[50] The biggest violations to those rules come from the most powerful actor, the United States, because no other actor can punish it.

---

[49] The extent to which governing arrangements generate durable deep cooperation (Downs et al. 1996) is slightly different, though tightly connected, to change in international order—the main dependent variable in previous chapters. Also note that "cooperation" might be a slightly misleading term: as Adler 2019 points out, modifying actors' behavior might have as much to do with altering their identities and preferences through interconnectivity.

[50] Fazal 2007. Note that the question of whether there has been a decline in war itself is a matter of some debate (Fortna 2013; Braumoeller 2019), but distinct from the decline in territorial conquest.

Punishments for Noncompliance

		Strong	Weak
Net Strategic Benefits	Positive	- 1950s oligopoly for oil - Anti-conquest rules, *e.g.* UN Art 1	- OPEC in 1960s - Universal Postal Union
	Negative	- 1930s European imperialism - Nuclear nonproliferation - Pre-2008 rules against capital controls	- OPEC post-1980 - Nuclear Weapons Ban Treaty

Figure 6.1 Mapping subsystems according to strategic benefits and punishments

Subsystems in the top-right box generate strong benefits for participants, but have little in the way of punishments for noncompliance. OPEC operated this way in the 1960s, as chapter 3 illustrated. There are other international organizations and regimes that operate in a similar fashion, such as the Universal Postal Union. These organizations often solve coordination problems (e.g., standardizing procedures and technical issues, for which distributional costs are small and the gains are large) rather than true collaboration problems, which involve distributional winners and losers.[51]

The bottom-left box is the one that did not get much attention in previous chapters. Order in these subsystems is maintained only by the constant threat of punishment, because some actors (subordinate ones) are not getting positive net benefits from participating. Classic European imperialism of the sort that existed from roughly 1870 to the 1940s provides examples of this type of subsystem, depending on the relationship between the metropole and the subordinate (e.g., colony). As the wars and rebellions in Kenya, Algeria, Vietnam, Malaysia, and elsewhere suggest, imperialism was often maintained more by coercion and force than by voluntary association. European imperialism was not opposed always and everywhere, of course, but frequently it generated governing arrangements that fit in this bottom-left box. Similarly, in global finance prior to 2008, the International Monetary Fund (IMF) often punished developing countries for attempting to use capital controls. That seems to have changed after 2008.[52] Indeed, the IMF seems to have changed its position after some states

---

[51] Martin 1992.
[52] Gallagher 2015. The changes in the treatment of capital controls after 2008 amplified a trend that began after 1998.

insisted on using capital controls, against IMF wishes, which is another example of a rival collective image about politics.

The nuclear nonproliferation subsystem probably also fits in this bottom-left box. Actors who violate the prohibition on nuclear acquisition often do face punishments, as Iran, North Korea, Libya, and others can attest. Moreover, the strategic benefits of the subsystem are small or net negative for non-nuclear states. The benefits instead accrue disproportionately to its powerful members, especially those states that already have nuclear weapons. International order in this subsystem entrenches international hierarchy.[53] For that reason, many countries have historically opposed the nonproliferation constraints placed upon them.[54] After all, for non-nuclear states, the current subsystem offers only two strategic benefits, neither of which seems large. One is a symbolic and insubstantial promise that nuclear states will someday denuclearize—though there is zero evidence that those states are following through on their promise. The second is commercial access to non-military nuclear technology like power plants and medical isotopes—but it is access only because the non-nuclear states must pay full price for actually acquiring such items. Indeed, it seems plausible that the "benefit" of access would exist even in the counterfactual world in which there was no NPT.

Finally, the bottom-right box indicates subsystems where there is neither positive strategic benefits, nor much in the way of punishments for noncompliance. These subsystems are highly unlikely to generate meaningful cooperation between actors for very long. OPEC since the 1980s provides a clear example (see chapter 4). The Treaty on the Prohibition of Nuclear Weapons, passed in 2017 at the United Nations, seems destined for a similar fate. None of the states that have nuclear weapons sees any strategic benefits in the treaty so they choose not to participate. There is no actor capable of compelling them to do so. So while the treaty could offer benefits to the participating non-nuclear countries if they could get the nuclear states to participate, the nuclear states are unwilling. Without them, the treaty is merely symbolic, at best.

From Subsystems to Global Order

How does an aggregate theme of international order emerge from individual subsystems? And under what conditions do ordering themes change? While I have stressed the importance of understanding change at the subsystems level,

---

[53] Hecht 2006.
[54] Coe and Vaynman 2015; Colgan and Miller 2019.

the theory would not be complete without sketching the manner in which it translates into change in an ordering theme at the systemic or global level.

Identifying and diagnosing change in international order at the aggregate level is a recurring problem that scholars have struggled to address satisfactorily.[55] For example, two events of 2016—the Brexit referendum in the United Kingdom and the election of President Donald J. Trump—spurred a major debate about the fate of the liberal order.[56] Some analysts and scholars thought they saw evidence of a significant transformation that had been long in the making but was only then revealing itself.[57] Others were more skeptical, arguing that the liberal international order is resilient and had been repeatedly declared dead before, incorrectly.[58] Still others argued that the liberal order was always mythical and thus not capable of dying.[59] Thus, the question of change in international order regularly occupies the pages of publications like *Foreign Affairs*, *Financial Times*, and *The Economist*. Analysts need theory and concepts to help guide this debate.

Similarly, the financial crisis of 2008 generated significant debate over whether the international order had changed, and if so, what to do about it. Many scholars concluded that the status quo in the international financial order held firmly despite the crisis.[60] They viewed the post-crisis reforms as superficial and representing little real change. Others disagreed, arguing that the long-standing dominance of the IMF was starting to give way to a more fractured, incoherent global financial system.[61] The debate was more than academic. If the "system worked,"[62] then there was no need to push for fundamental reforms. But if it actually splintered in the process of working, policymakers needed to understand that change to prepare for subsequent crises.

Debates over the extent of change happen, in part, because different people locate international order at different levels. For instance, one can describe the IMF as part of the liberal international order, thereby treating order as a property of the system. The advantage of this viewpoint lies in highlighting the IMF's interconnections with other institutions like the World Bank and the WTO as part of an overall strategy by powerful states to facilitate a liberal world economy—one that is rules-based and relatively open. A disadvantage is that describing the order of an entire system as "liberal" often masks the various ways that it is not liberal at all, and obscures the heterogeneity of what liberal means in finance or trade or military security.

[55] One effort involves assemblage theory: see Sassen 2006; Acuto and Curtis 2014.
[56] Eilstrup-Sangiovanni and Hofmann 2020.
[57] Jentleson 2018; Friedman Lissner and Rapp-Hooper 2018; Rose 2019; Cooley and Nexon 2020.
[58] See, for instance, Chaudoin et al. 2017; Norrlof et al. 2020.
[59] Barma et al. 2013; Porter 2018.
[60] Helleiner 2014; Moschella and Tsingou 2014; Drezner 2014; Lipscy 2017.
[61] Grabel 2017; Gallagher 2015; Kring 2019.
[62] Drezner 2014.

My view is that scholars often look for international order in the wrong place. They usually conceive of it at the systemic level.[63] Order exists at that level only in the way that a digital image exists: as an emergent property of thousands of pixels. Instead, it is in the more specific governing arrangements that international order actually exists. At the systemic level, themes exist across these governing arrangements, like "liberal" (in the US-led order since 1945) or "monarchical" (in Europe after 1815). Focusing on changes in order at the subsystem level, and then thinking about how such changes aggregate up, can help avoid intractable debates about whether and how much the overall theme has changed.[64]

In fact, the political scientist and Nobel laureate Elinor Ostrom argued that for many governance challenges, we would not *want* a single international order. Instead, a more fragmented, "polycentric" form of governance has significant advantages.[65] It allows for governing arrangements to reflect the specific political power that actors have on a given problem. It also allows for greater policy experimentation, among other advantages.

As I noted in chapter 1, I see the themes of international order occuring because powerful actors, especially great power states, participate in many governing arrangements and have large influence over the ones in which they participate.[66] Order itself exists as governing arrangements. Those arrangements address particular substantive issues, like how to regulate trade or nuclear arms control. A theme exists when those governing arrangements share common underlying principles, like "economic openness" or "multilateralism." Great power states tend to generate themes across multiple governing arrangements to the extent that they have a coherent, consistent view about foreign policy. Studying those systemic themes can be useful.[67] To fully understand order and change, however, we also need to focus on governing arrangements.

The relationship between a theme and the governing arrangements of subsystems can be described visually. Figure 6.2's horizontal axis plots a subsystem's importance, while the vertical axis plots the consistency between the subsystem's governing arrangements and the system's theme. This immediately opens up some vexing questions: what is "importance"? How can we measure thematic "consistency"?, etc. Answering these questions precisely or objectively is impossible, which is why there will always be room for debate about

---

[63] See Ikenberry 2000; Kissinger 2015; Reus-Smit 2018: 197; Lascurettes 2020.

[64] An example of such debates was the fate of the liberal order after 2016. For examples of highly divergent views, compare Chaudoin et al. 2017 and Haass 2018; see also Cooley and Nexon 2020 and Norrlof et al. 2020.

[65] Ostrom 2010; see also chapter 7.

[66] Pratt (2018) shows that powerful states' influence is amplified by institutional deference within a regime complex.

[67] Jones et al. 2009; Barma et al. 2013; Wright 2017; Jentleson 2018; Friedman Lissner and Rapp-Hooper 2018; Rose 2019.

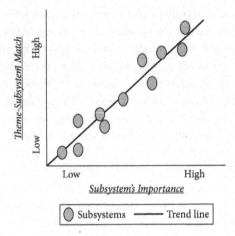

Figure 6.2 Relating subsystems to ordering themes

international order. Fortunately, practical considerations mark the boundaries of this debate's plausible realm. Ranking the importance of subsystems, for instance, would certainly generate debate, but it is easier at the extremes: the subsystem for international trade is more important than, say, the subsystem for international telephonic dialing codes. A breakdown in dialing codes would be temporarily inconvenient but a breakdown in trade would dramatically reduce prosperity and possibly cause starvation or medical harm. Similarly, not all interpretations of the consistency between a subsystem and an overall theme are equally valid. A subsystem with low barriers to economic integration, for instance, is more liberal than one with high barriers, all else equal. In principle, then, one can imagine plotting each subsystem on this graph.

Conceptually, *it is the character of the governing arrangements in important subsystems that gives an international order its theme.* Figure 6.2 indicates this proposed relationship between a theme and its subsystems. An order that was perfectly consistent in its theme would have all of its subsystems arranged in a straight, horizontal line near the top, indicating a high degree of match between the theme and the governing arrangements in every subsystem. In reality, of course, no international order looks like that. A more realistic alternative would be an order that had its subsystems arranged on a roughly forty-five-degree trend line, as pictured, indicating that high-importance subsystems contained governing arrangements with a high degree of consistency with the theme. In an international order with a strong theme, only relatively unimportant subsystems have governing arrangements that contradict the overall theme.

There is a risk here of reductionism: seeing the whole as only the sum of its parts. The central themes of an order are not just about what goes on inside the subsystems; they are also about the relations between subsystems. Still, the most important subsystems are a very good starting point for understanding the overall theme of an order. It is the character of these subsystems that shape the crucial behaviors of the system's actors. It is for precisely that reason that we identify some subsystems as more important than others.

Change in a global order's overall theme, then, occurs in two ways. First, change in individual subsystems that moves the trend line's intercept (e.g., its average point) upward indicates a higher degree of thematic consistency. In that case, in a liberal order, one could speak of the system getting "more liberal." Conversely, if the line's intercept moved downward, it would be "less liberal." Second, changes in the *slope* of the line also affect the overall theme. A positive slope is better than a negative slope, all else equal, for the consistency of the theme.

Change in either the theme or the governing arrangements can be consequential. For some questions, the theme of an order will be more important than the specifics of its governing arrangements; but for other questions, the reverse will be true. If we want to understand the degree to which the world is open to economic flows, an order's theme might be crucial. If, however, we want to understand the degree to which a financial crisis or a pandemic or an energy shortage indicates the need for reforms, we are better off studying the governing arrangements in the relevant subsystems.

Obsessing about the overall trajectory of an international change can be foolish. Consider for instance, a hypothetical scenario in which all states commit to greater respect for national sovereignty, and an increasingly rules-based international politics. To support that vision, the United States in this scenario posts a USD 2 trillion bond that it would legally sacrifice if it militarily violated another state's sovereignty without authorization by the UN Security Council. As an unintended consequence of this deeper commitment to sovereignty, however, warlords around the world felt emboldened to commit genocide and human rights abuses against their own people, safe in the knowledge that the international community was unlikely to intervene. To what extent has international order become more liberal in this scenario? There are offsetting effects: more rules-based politics seem more liberal, but more human rights abuses seem less liberal. On balance, one might argue that the international order has become a bit more liberal, or a bit less, or about the same. Yet substantively—in terms of human lives affected—the shift in the governing arrangements seems quite large. In this case, the change in governing arrangements seems more important than the change in the order's theme. Thus, while we should not ignore the theme of an international order, we should not be so fascinated by it that we forget the substance of the actual governing arrangements.

Conclusion

Subsystems theory lends itself to a method of analysis that emphasizes descriptive inference before leaping to causal analysis. Four key steps in that method are: observe empirical patterns; identify the key questions of governance in a given issue area; relate the general conceptual elements of the theory—such as actors, punishments, and strategic benefits—to the specifics of the issue area; and investigate political dynamics and contestation in subsystems. Analysts can take these steps only by obtaining a solid empirical understanding of an issue area, which necessarily involves significant description and descriptive inference. This method can be applied to a wide range of issues and topics, beyond the oil politics that has been my focus in this book.

The method developed here also makes use of some neglected concepts in social science, like Robert Cox's notion of "rival collective images." Rival images are part of the social contradictions and tensions that exist in all parts of politics, domestic or international. They are important because they often contain potential alternative governing arrangements, which serve as the seeds of change. Social contradictions and rival images generate noncompliance, which in turn threatens stability and generates the potential for innovation and change. Rival images are a recurring component of the politics of international order, as we see in oil politics (especially in chapter 3), global finance (e.g., states' decision to use capital controls, against IMF wishes),[68] and in nuclear politics (e.g., rival ideas about the IAEA).[69]

While offering enough to get started, this chapter leaves some theoretical questions for future work. One of those questions is how to analyze the overlap and connections between subsystems. Fortunately, sociologists have given this question a great deal of thought.[70] I make one additional distinction that might be helpful. Overlap between subsystems comes in two basic varieties: intrinsic and instrumental. Subsystems are intrinsically connected when action in one automatically influences action in the other, whether actors choose it or not. Instrumental linkages, by contrast, occur when actors choose to connect two subsystems. Recall, for instance, how in 1941 a new regime in Iraq threatened

---

[68] Gallagher 2015.
[69] On the IAEA, see Colgan and Miller 2019.
[70] Fligstein and McAdam 2012.

Britain's oil supply, and Britain used its military capabilities in Iraq to overthrow that regime and restore the monarchy (see chapter 5). In that case, Britain instrumentally used its power in one subsystem, the one for oil security, to create change in another subsystem, the one for oil production. In the next chapter, we look at an overlap between two quite different subsystems: climate change emissions and international trade.

7

Climate Change

"The good Earth—we could have saved it, but we were too damn cheap and lazy."[1]

—Kurt Vonnegut

"Not everything that is faced can be changed, but nothing can be changed until it is faced."

—James Baldwin

The previous chapter showed how to use subsystems theory as a method for understanding international order in issue areas beyond oil. This chapter has an even tougher task: using the theory to understand and prescribe an evolving, incomplete international order, namely, the one associated with climate change. While analytically challenging, that task is too important to ignore.

Climate change is the most important global challenge of the twenty-first century. I wish subsystems theory revealed a dynamic, rapidly strengthening international order on climate. Alas, there is not much yet in the way of meaningful climate governance, at least at the international level. Although there have been a series of conventions and agreements, starting with the United Nations Framework Convention on Climate Change (UNFCCC) in 1992 and more recently the Paris Agreement of 2015, they are largely toothless. They exert almost no authority, in the sense of requiring states and firms to restrict greenhouse gas (GHG) emissions. Indeed, scholars have characterized the intergovernmental negotiations as largely gridlocked.[2] Yet, there is hope for progress.

In this chapter I offer a subsystems analysis of climate politics. Although it is not as deep as the one developed for oil politics in chapters 2 through 5, the analysis illustrates how to break climate politics into distinct subsystems. I identify four such subsystems, associated with: reducing emissions; allocating

---

[1] Vonnegut 2005: 122.
[2] Victor 2011; Hale et al. 2013.

climate-related capital; developing negative-emissions technologies; and managing climate-related trade.

My principal task in this chapter, however, is prescriptive rather than explanatory. I use what we have learned about international order to identify what policymakers might do to address climate change. In oil politics, we learned that governing arrangements backed by enforcement (e.g., the Seven Sisters cartel) are much more effective than those that are not (e.g., OPEC since 1980). Meaningful enforcement has gone missing in global climate deals. This chapter lays out a path for supplying that type of enforcement. We also learned that linking policies (e.g., as OPEC did when supporting Iraqi nationalization) and policy experimentation (e.g., OPEC in the 1960s) are key tools for effective governance. Policymakers should apply those lessons to climate governance.

Addressing the climate crisis requires subsystems-level thinking because it is not an individual-level problem. For example, if an individual invests in energy-saving technology in her home, she might lower her emissions and save some money. Yet, if she puts those savings in a bank, which then uses her deposit to create loans to fossil fuel companies, it could undo the effort she made to lower her emissions.[3] Individual action is not enough. Seeing climate change as a set of interconnected subsystems helps frame the problem properly.

Specifically, I consider how an international network of trade measures, known as carbon tariffs or border adjustment taxes (BATs), can be used to support domestic pro-climate policy efforts. BATs and other measures could play a key role in generating the enforcement and punishments necessary to sustain a "climate club" of countries. Only a large climate club that includes Europe, the United States, and China makes sufficient decarbonization politically sustainable over time—and that carries implications for the non-climate parts of American and European foreign policy, particularly with regard to "decoupling" from China.

This chapter's epigraph includes a quote from Kurt Vonnegut. Although I share his frustration, I do not share his diagnosis. The world's failure on climate change to date is not primarily a matter of being cheap or lazy. True, humans are selfish, but also remarkably industrious, and capable of mobilizing huge amounts of money for certain projects. The heart of the problem lies instead with Adam Smith's "invisible hand," which fails on environmental matters. Spontaneous market action alone will not suffice. We need a *visible* hand: institutions and governance to guide our behavior to socially desirable outcomes. In short, on climate change, we desperately need a change in international order.

---

[3] Adapted from Hoffmann 2020.

Conceptualizing Order for Climate Change

The current international order for climate is weak. While international climate negotiations, like the UNFCCC's Conference of the Parties (COP) meetings, receive a lot of attention, much of the substantive politics lies at the domestic level, playing out in national and subnational arenas. The fight is principally between the relative winners and losers from climate change—or perhaps more accurately, the slight losers versus the severe losers. Much of that fight will depend on asset revaluations.[4] Climate change and climate policy are altering the value of assets, from real estate to power plants, which in turn generate contentious political battles over which assets will retain value. Consequently, rather than seeing climate change as a *static* collective action problem, we should instead see climate politics as distributional and *dynamic*—choices made in one time period affect the value of assets, and the choices made, in future time periods. In turn, assets tend to lock in stakeholders' policy preferences in future time periods.[5] Domestic politics will set the conditions under which a meaningful international order for decarbonization can occur.[6]

Even in the absence of a deep international order for climate, subsystems theory can offer insights about its past and future. To start, consider the blizzard of international organizations, nongovernmental organizations (NGOs), corporate firms, states, private individuals, and other actors involved in climate change governance in some way.[7] There is no single, universal governing body for climate change. Instead, hundreds of different actors are involved, and none of them has authority over all the others.[8] In this "regime complex," there is a nonhierarchical, overlapping network of organizations and institutions, each operating on a set of related issues.[9] Studying the regime complex for climate generates insights. For instance, a single, universal regime is unlikely to emerge and cohere to deal with the whole problem. Even if it did, it would likely be less efficient than a polycentric approach that involved different levels of action.[10]

Yet, if we treat climate governance simply as a cloud of interlocking networks and institutions, it is hard to analyze or assess its impact. As with other issue areas, a focus on institutions can make it harder to step back and see the key questions of governance. By contrast, subsystems theory suggests we identify the governance questions that characterize the issue area, from close empirical

---

[4] Colgan et al. 2021.
[5] Seto et al. 2016; Bernstein and Hoffman 2019; Mildenberger 2020; Stokes 2020.
[6] Harrison and Sundstrom 2007; Allan 2018; Colgan et al. 2021.
[7] VanDeveer and Dabelko 2001; Backstrand 2008; Newell 2008; Aldy and Stavins 2009; Andonova et al. 2009; Ostrom 2010; Jinnah 2014; Bulkeley et al. 2014; Hadden 2015.
[8] Bernstein et al. 2010; Andonova and Mitchell 2010; Axelrod and VanDeveer 2014.
[9] Thompson 2010; Keohane and Victor 2011; Bernstein and Cashore 2012.
[10] Ostrom 2010; Keohane and Victor 2011.

inspection. Each governance question anchors a subsystem. The key insight here is that there are *multiple subsystems at work* in climate governance. In each one, actors respond to strategic benefits and the prospective punishments, which in turn are underpinned by instruments of coercion.

Two of the three major instruments of coercion studied in this book are irrelevant for climate change. States are highly unlikely to invade one another over climate change, so military coercion is largely off the table, at least for now (though one can imagine future scenarios where one state uses military force to prevent another state's geo-engineering efforts). Likewise, states are unlikely to assassinate foreign leaders over the issue, or use other methods of leadership selection. That leaves economic coercion as the principal instrument of coercion available to states. States and non-state actors also use other forms of coercion, such as naming and shaming, but those are weaker. Consequently, any international order associated with climate change is likely to rest on the strategic benefits that it can offer its participants, and the economic coercion that actors are willing to use as punishments for noncompliance or nonparticipation.

Hegemonic stability theory does not get us very far in understanding international order in climate change. One might argue that the United States, to the extent that it is the world's hegemon, does not really want a binding international order that limits its GHG emissions, and thus, no such order exists. Yet, that argument is weak. At best, the United States is getting half of what it wants: no economic costs of reducing emissions, but also no solution to the climate problem, either. Most US voters, businesses, and even the military want a climate solution. Alternatively, one might argue that the global failure to cooperate on climate change is a reflection of the United States as a declining hegemon, powerless to enforce a climate order. That argument has some merit, but it faces two problems. First, it assumes there's no chance for a cooperative arrangement in the absence of a hegemon, an idea that contravenes considerable theory and evidence.[11] Second, it cannot account for the various ways that non-state actors, particularly in finance capital and among central banks, are starting to readjust practices in light of climate change. We need to go beyond hegemonic theory to understand what has happened, and what is likely to happen in the future.

Identifying the Subsystems

Four subsystems are central to climate politics.[12] The first centers on the following question: How much GHG emissions is each actor allowed to produce? The

---

[11] Keohane 1984; Martin and Simmons 1998.
[12] I thank Robert O. Keohane for sharpening my thinking on these subsystems.

primary arenas for decision-making in this subsystem are governments, primarily national and sub-national, plus one notable supranational organization: the European Union.[13] This subsystem's actors are legislators, regulators, and the many actors that influence them: corporate lobbyists, environmental NGOs, the media, student movements, individual leaders, etc. Courts play a growing role too, such as in the 2019 *Urgenda* case in the Netherlands.[14] In that case, the court ruled that the Dutch government was knowingly exposing its present and future citizens to danger, and mandated that it cut more of the country's emissions. Germany's constitutional court made a similar ruling in 2021. A Dutch court applied the same basic principle at a corporate level for the first time in 2021, commanding Royal Dutch Shell to more rapidly lower its GHG emissions.[15]

The emissions subsystem is central because the rate of GHG emissions drives the pace of climate change itself, which in turn affects all of the other associated subsystems. To date, international organizations have played a modest role, though that could change.[16] Again, domestic politics are essential to climate politics, and are likely to remain that way.

Many different policies belong in this subsystem, ranging from national carbon taxes to aviaition fuel standards set by the International Civil Aviation Organization, and from public-private partnerships to lower global methane emissions in the oil and gas industry to city-level decarbonization efforts. For policymakers, it might seem counterintuitive to lump so many different policy types in a single subsystem. For analysts of international order, however, the key point is that they all relate to a single (and measurable, in this case) functional task: limiting the amount of atmospheric GHG emissions. This single task, or governance question, anchors the subsystem and makes it possible to analyze the extent to which order in this subsystem is changing over time in the aggregate.

As one would expect, strategic benefits play a key role in this subsystem. For instance, China saw few strategic benefits to accepting emissions restrictions in the 1997 Kyoto Protocol, and thus refused to accept them. (China signed the protocol only after insisting that it was a developing country, and thus exempt from restrictions on emissions.)[17] By the 2015 Paris meeting, however, China was willing to participate as a full member. Given that China still wants to be

---

[13] On the EU, see Schreurs and Tiberghien 2007. Private actors are also relevant (Green 2013; Green and Colgan 2013) but unlikely to adequately restrict emissions on their own.

[14] The number of climate-related court cases is rising dramatically (Setzer and Byrnes 2019), in part due to equity concerns (Robinson and Carlson 2021). In addition to compelling states to adopt climate policies, courts also assign liability for climate damages in disputes between private or public actors (Byers et al. 2017). On the general role of courts in world politics, see Voeten 2010; Alter 2014; Kalyanpur and Newman 2019.

[15] Raval 2021

[16] On international climate finance, see Graham and Serdaru 2020.

[17] The lack of binding targets for China and other developing countries weakened the Kyoto Protocol's strategic benefits for the Global North.

considered a developing country in other contexts, this move is somewhat puzzling.[18] Why did its leaders change their mind?

Most of the answer lies with a happy accident: Chinese leaders wanted to clean up local air pollution in their cities for health reasons, and doing so tends to yield climate "co-benefits."[19] Closing dirty factories, for instance, not only reduces urban smog, but also cuts GHG emissions. Still, that does not tell the whole story. Some of the explanation for China's climate shift also seems to lie in the fact that it became a global leader in the production of wind, solar, and battery technology. Since 2001, for instance, China has gone from producing 1 percent to 66 percent of the world's solar panels.[20] It also produces roughly 70 percent of the world's lithium-ion batteries and a third of the world's wind turbines.[21] All of these industries stand to benefit significantly from a strong emissions-reduction regime. Thus, China saw strategic benefits from participating in the UNFCCC process.

Punishments for noncompliance—or the lack thereof—also play a key role. Lack of enforcement was one factor that undermined the Kyoto Protocol.[22] The agreement specified how much each state would reduce its GHG emissions by a specified date, compared to its emissions in a baseline year (1990). Wealthier states like Japan, the United States, and most of those in Western Europe agreed to reduce their emissions by 2008. However, when most of the key states broke their promise, the Kyoto Protocol had no real mechanism to punish them for it. The Kyoto Protocol's lack of punishments was a crucial weakness, as various countries broke their promises, pulled out, or simply refused to ratify the deal. The protocol also failed because it did not provide sufficient strategic benefits for developed countries. The United States, especially, objected to the lack of binding targets for China and other developing countries, which undermined the protocol's environmental goals.[23]

Within this first subsystem, governance is fragmented, a trend that seems likely to continue. Scholars have pointed out the difficulties of developing a single governing arrangement to reduce GHG emissions, and proposed a variety of different ways to use multiple governing arrangements.[24] It might be politically or economically advantageous to regulate the six major GHGs separately,

---

[18] China continues to seek loans from the World Bank to assist its efforts in reducing poverty. China also asserts its status as a developing country in trade and finance. See Kastner et al. 2018.

[19] Christensen 2015; Gallagher and Xuan 2019; Weiss and Wallace 2021.

[20] Helveston and Nahm 2019: 794.

[21] Helveston and Nahm 2019: 794.

[22] Opposition to the Kyoto Protocol in the United States had multiple sources: see Aklin and Mildenberger 2020.

[23] Victor 2001. The Senate passed the Byrd-Hagel resolution, which stated its refusal to ratify the Kyoto Protocol unless developing countries also got "specific scheduled commitments to limit or reduce greenhouse gas emissions."

[24] Andonova et al. 2009; Barrett 2011; Keohane and Victor 2011; Bernstein and Hoffmann 2019.

for instance, or to regulate different industries in different ways. Alternatively or in combination, a governance model that uses small- and medium-scale governance units (like cities) might increase actors' trust about whether others are doing their part to reduce climate change.[25] At the international level, states negotiating governing arrangements might use strategic benefits (such as offers of pro-climate policies that are contingent on what others do) and punishments for noncompliance (using trade measures).[26] Depending on whether and how governing arrangements emerge, it might become analytically helpful to divide this subsystem into multiple subsystems.[27] The pros and cons of doing so would depend on the analytical question being addressed.[28] At present, however, this subsystem can be considered as a single entity.

A second subsystem centers on the question, How are climate-related assets treated as capital, especially assets associated with fossil fuels? The relationship between assets and capital is not simple. Laws of property, collateral, bankruptcy, and other issues transform an asset (like a house) into capital (as collateral for a mortgage, for instance). Those laws reflect political decisions that are not universal or invariant.[29] In some communist societies, for instance, residents had housing assets that could not be privately owned or used as collateral for a loan. Even in capitalist societies, corporate assets are subject to a plethora of laws and regulations about how they are treated as capital, such as bank financial reserve ratios or accounting rules on depreciation. For instance, analysts in 2021 wondered whether it still made sense to have sixty-year depreciation allowances for coal plants that might not last nearly that long. Similarly, climate risks and policies will affect the value and usage of various assets. Conceivably, policymakers might ban coal or other fossil fuels, just as they have banned other products ranging from ozone-depleting chemicals to endangered species.[30]

Market actors play a central role in valuing assets like fossil fuel reserves still in the ground. That valuation is already being affected by the global energy

[25]　Ostrom 2010: 39.

[26]　Victor 2011; Rajamani 2016.

[27]　As I indicated in chapter 6, subsystems are not purely objective, in the sense that they exist independently of an analyst's judgments. Still, the analyst should balance the need for precision with the problem of analytical complexity: dividing subsystems can improve precision while worsening complexity.

[28]　For example, if the analyst sought to answer the question, How much have the governing arrangements over GHG emissions changed over time? and there was evidence of strong heterogeneity in the strength of those arrangements, then it would be wise to divide this subsystem further. On the other hand, if the question was, How did governing arrangements over the environment change in the twentieth century? then it would likely make more sense to treat the subsystem for GHG emissions as a whole, for the purpose of comparing it to subsystems over key questions of governance, like those relating to ozone depletion, fish stocks, biodiversity, etc. In answering the second question, one could reasonably characterize governance in the subsystem for GHG emissions as consistently weak to date.

[29]　Pistor 2019; De Soto 2000.

[30]　Mitchell and Carpenter 2019; Newell and Simms 2020.

transition toward renewable energy sources (discussed in chapter 8). Markets will also play a key role in the valuation of assets such as coastal real estate or agricultural land, since those also fall in the category of climate-related assets. A huge range of assets, from municipal bonds to energy utilities, is at risk of climate-related damages from storms, fires, and other effects.

Central banks could play a major role in this second subsystem. They are becoming increasingly concerned about various climate risks and the potentially destabilizing effects those risks might have on the global financial system. Regulators are currently considering corporate reporting requirements for climate risks, especially to ensure macroeconomic stability.[31] The European Central Bank (ECB) is also considering "green quantitative easing" into its monetary policy. One option for the ECB is to avoid environmentally unfriendly assets in its corporate bond purchase program.[32] Some scholars encourage them to do more.[33]

Insurers could also play a significant role in this subsystem.[34] Insurers are finding that they have not correctly priced climate risks, like flooding or fires.[35] The price and availability of insurance will significantly affect the value of land and other assets that are at risk for climate damages. In turn, insurance markets will affect patterns of climate adaptation, such as the construction of sea walls or other damage-reduction systems.[36]

There is overlap between subsystems: decisions made in the first climate subsystem—involving how much GHGs each actor can produce—will affect the second (how climate-related assets are considered as capital), and vice versa. For instance, a tax on GHG emissions might lower the value of fossil fuel reserves as capital. Yet, this second subsystem is distinct from the first, in three ways. First, it affects not only climate mitigation (e.g., reducing emissions) but also climate adaptation (e.g., building sea walls to protect valuable land). The emissions-reduction subsystem, by contrast, focuses entirely on climate mitigation. Second, it affects climate mitigation through a distinct, indirect pathway. At least theoretically, one can imagine significant decarbonization occurring entirely because of decisions in this subsystem (e.g., bans on fossil fuel assets, or raising the cost of investment capital), without any policies on emissions per se. Third, the climate-related capital subsystem directly affects the macroeconomic financial system, as central bankers' concerns indicate.

---

[31] Farid et al. 2016.
[32] FT Editorial Board 2019.
[33] Tooze 2019.
[34] Colgan 2018.
[35] Flavelle and Plumer 2019.
[36] Javeline et al. 2019.

As with the first subsystem, the second one involves both public and private actors, but the balance of influence is different. Markets and private economic actors play the central role in deciding how to value and use climate-related assets. Governments and central banks can affect those decisions through regulation and other means. State-owned enterprises and public utilities that own major climate-related assets occupy a middle ground between public and private spheres. NGOs, divestment campaigns, and other actors can also play a role in this subsystem by shaping norms or creating a moral stigma associated with particular assets.[37]

Actors deploy a variety of benefits and punishments to affect other actors in this subsystem, ranging from moral shaming to legal penalties associated with financial regulations. Activist shareholders, for instance, are finding ways to punish corporations that are not taking sufficient steps to address climate change, for instance by voting against appointments to such companies' board of directors.[38] Intriguingly, business actors are using some of the same tactics that governments used in Cold War nuclear geopolitics to achieve change, such as competitive shaming and outbidding.[39] As a second example of tactics used in this subsystem, many investors refused to bid for big petroleum opportunities offered by Saudi Arabia and Brazil in 2019, in part because of investors' desire to diversify away from the fossil fuel sector. Thus, even in the absence of a centralized authority, many smaller actors are finding some ways to generate incentives for pro-climate behavior.[40] Yet the interactions between strategic benefits and punishments in this subsystem are complex. For instance, research suggests that anti–fossil fuel normative campaigns work best when combined with appeals to an economic logic.[41]

A third subsystem centers on the question, How should negative-emission technologies be incentivized and developed? Most policy scenarios that limit global warming to a particular target, such as 2 degrees Celsius, assume that new technologies will be developed to remove GHGs, or existing technologies will be deployed at an unprecedented scale. Yet this type of technological innovation involves a constellation of actors distinct from those who dominate the previous two subsystems. Private entrepreneurs, and the venture capitalists who support them, will play an outsized role. Research by certain governments could also play a key role, but probably only the relatively wealthy ones that govern high-tech industries.[42] Their interactions are likely to have different political

---

[37] Hadden 2015; Blondeel et al. 2019.
[38] Hook and Tett 2019.
[39] On climate, see Tett 2019; on nuclear politics, see Colgan and Miller 2019.
[40] Green 2013.
[41] Blondeel et al. 2019.
[42] Barrett 2006.

dynamics than those characterizing the other climate subsystems. For example, the US National Academies of Sciences predict that negative-emissions technologies will have dramatic implications for land use, affecting food availability and biodiversity.[43]

Investment is rising in this third subsystem. Early-stage funding for climate technology companies rose from USD 418 million in 2013 to USD 16.1 billion in 2019.[44] In total, venture capitalist funds invested USD 60 billion into more than 1,200 climate tech start-ups over that same period. Of that amount, USD 29 billion flowed into US companies, USD 20 billion into Chinese, and only USD 7 billion in Europe—a pattern of leaders and laggards that is arguably the opposite of the one in the first subsystem (emissions mitigation). A *Financial Times* analyst writes, "Saving the planet from catastrophic climate change is humanity's biggest challenge. It may also represent the most spectacular investment opportunity of our lifetimes."[45]

Related to this third subsystem, some analysts propose a Green Lend Lease at the international level to accompany a Green New Deal at the domestic level (at least in the United States context).[46] In World War II, the United States used the Lend Lease program to transfer military materials and technologies to allied countries to achieve the common goal of winning the war. By analogy, a Green Lend Lease would see a transfer of negative-emission or clean-energy technology from the Global North to Africa, Asia, and Latin America. Such transfers might be an economically efficient way to reduce emissions.[47] Politically, however, it is a mixed bag. It would represent a transfer of wealth away from Global North countries, which voters might find unappealing. Some politicians might use such transfers as a way to rally opposition to pro-climate policies.

A well-functioning international order for intellectual property rights is the foundation for providing good incentives for research and development of negative-emissions technologies. However, across borders, intellectual property rights law is patchy. Some countries, most notably China, stand accused of widespread intellectual property theft and espionage. Punishments for this kind of noncompliance are difficult and rare. The considerable differences between democratic and autocratic countries in the legal rules and norms around intellectual property are therefore a serious challenge to meaningful governing arrangements in the negative-emissions subsystem. Possibly, like-minded democratic countries could set up an exclusive club arrangement to support and

---

[43] National Academies of Sciences and Engineering 2019.
[44] Thornhill 2020.
[45] Thornhill 2020.
[46] Mulder 2019.
[47] But see Dauvergne and Neville 2009.

share negative-emissions research among themselves. To date, however, very little in the way of international governing arrangements exist in this subsystem.

A fourth subsystem centers on the question, How should jurisdictions with different climate policies trade with each other? Various pro-climate policies—such as carbon taxes, cap-and-trade systems, regulation, or outright bans on certain practices—can be used to limit GHG emissions within a country's jurisdiction. All of them create the risk of "leakage," whereby GHG reductions in one jurisdiction inadvertently increase GHG emissions in another jurisdiction. One way that leakage can happen is by raising the cost of producing items that depend on fossil fuels in one jurisdiction but not others.[48] In a competitive world with international trade, that impact on production costs could be a problem for countries that want to avoid climate change.[49] Aluminum, glass, cement, iron, and steel manufacturing, for instance, depend heavily on energy. Aluminum manufacturers in states with pro-climate policies, all else equal, have higher costs than those in states without pro-climate policies, and might be tempted to move jurisdictions.

National governments manage the inherently political tradeoffs between trade competitiveness and other issues like environmental goals, making them the principal actors in this subsystem. The WTO, other trade bodies, labor unions, and private firms will also play a role. The latter two will lobby governments to make decisions that favor their interests.

To date, studies find little evidence of GHG leakage in practice.[50] However, that finding likely arises from the weakness of climate governance and emissions-reduction policies that those studies investigated. As environmental policies strengthen, leakage is set to become a greater problem. Already, international trade has a way of masking a country's moral responsibility for emissions. For example, one study finds that approximately 21 percent of China's carbon emissions are a result of goods produced for the US market.[51]

Trade and climate subsystems overlap intrinsically and, potentially, instrumentally. As we saw in chapter 6, subsystems can overlap in two ways: as an inevitable interconnection (intrinsically), or as a choice made by policymakers (instrumentally). Climate change will disrupt trade intrinsically by damaging ports, intensifying the storms that oceangoing ships must navigate, and causing other effects.[52] It might also facilitate trade in certain respects, such as by opening up shipping lanes through the Arctic. Of even greater interest for policymakers, however, is the possibility of instrumental links between climate and trade, such

---

[48] The second principal way it occurs is by changing global energy prices. I set aside this channel to simplify the discussion. For more details, see Frankel 2010; Barrett 2011.
[49] Bordoff and Shoyer 2008; Mathys and de Melo 2011; Morin and Jinnah 2018.
[50] Curtin 2019.
[51] Lin et al. 2014, quoted in Zhou 2017.
[52] Dellink et al. 2017.

as border adjustment taxes. The next three sections discuss that possibility in some detail.

One type of instrumental linkage between trade and climate is a certain kind of "green protectionism." Specifically, governments might find it politically convenient, or even necessary, to promise local economic benefits along with pro-climate policies like carbon taxes.[53] The proposed "Green New Deal" in the United States has this character.[54] Green protectionism can take the form of local content regulations and other incentives to induce local job creation, but these same regulations and incentives create frictions with the WTO or other international trade institutions, which seek to prohibit favoritism toward local producers. Amplifying the problem is that some countries want to become first movers in strategic industries, especially in manufacturing renewable energy technologies.[55]

The distinguishing feature of the fourth subsystem is its potential for punishments for noncompliance and nonparticipation. The trade system gives powerful actors like the United States, the EU, and China an instrument of coercion, should they choose to use it. This makes the fourth subsystem substantially different from the other three, where it is much harder to see how actors can be punished for excessive pollution. This potential for coercion and punishment suggests a way forward for climate governance.

Before exploring that potential way forward, it is worth noting that additional subsystems might become relevant for climate change. For example, the politics of climate adaptation and geo-engineering might result in significant subsystems of their own.[56] Development finance—involving wealthy countries providing loans or grants to poorer countries, especially for energy projects—is another topic with potential to become a significant climate subsystem in the future (though, to date, climate finance for development is dominated by insufficient or broken promises). Related topics—human migration, biodiversity, forestry, technical standards, etc.—could generate further interactions. Even if the main topics of governance remain within the four subsystems that I identify, other analysts might divide them up into subsystems in different ways.

We can evaluate competing interpretations of climate subsystems according to the criteria set out in chapter 6, namely: accuracy, parsimony, and breadth. Overall, subsystem analysis is meant to help make sense of the blizzard of events and trends related to climate politics. If another analyst can generate new insights

---

[53] See also chapter 8, on similar dynamics in the global energy transition.
[54] Aronoff et al. 2019.
[55] Lewis 2014.
[56] Javeline 2014; Jinnah et al. 2018; Hill and Martinez-Diaz 2020. Some forms of climate adaptation are already under way, but these exist mostly at the national and subnational level.

about climate politics, using a different set of subsystems that have even greater accuracy, parsimony, and breadth, so much the better.

Subsystems Theory's Added Value

Subsystems theory helps us interpret the politics of climate change in three key ways. First, it shifts the analytical focus from the various institutions and actors to the *de facto* governing arrangements on key questions of governance. That shift encourages analysts to evaluate the extent to which the flurry of climate-related political activity actually generates real impact. That shift in analytic focus is a key difference between subsystems analysis and observations of a regime complex.[57]

Second, the theory identifies a common logic of how meaningful governing arrangements endure, which facilitates learning from experience in other subsystems. As I indicated at the outset of this chapter, the history of oil politics offers three key lessons: the need for punishments and enforcement; the value of linking policies; and the utility of policy experimentation. OPEC's tax policy experiments in the 1960s, for instance, grew its members' expertise because they shared information with each other about what worked. National, subnational, and city governments should take the same approach with climate policies (and are, to some extent). Venture capitalists and researchers should be similarly supportive of experimentation when trying to support innovation in negative emissions technology.

Third, the theory highlights the importance of strategic benefits and punishments for noncompliance, especially punishments. The case of OPEC since the 1980s (chapter 4) is instructive: a subsystem is unlikely to be effective if it does not have an actor that can enforce compliance by imposing costs on actors who defect from it. That is exactly the problem that plagues OPEC: when its members decide to "cheat" on its production quotas, or simply set quotas that allow plenty of production, there is no actor that can enforce tighter discipline on the group. Thus, OPEC fails to manage global oil supply in a way that stabilizes oil prices, as the Seven Sisters did.

Several of the climate subsystems face a similar problem: there is no international enforcement mechanism for disciplining actors. The enforcement problem (and other factors) undermined the Kyoto Protocol, and international negotiators have shied away from binding emissions targets ever since. The 2015 Paris Agreement is weak on punishments, though it does provide oversight that imposes some reputational costs on climate laggards.[58] Still, the Paris Agreement

[57] Keohane and Victor 2011; Henning and Pratt 2020.
[58] Rajamani 2016.

is a *de facto* acknowledgment of the primacy of domestic politics because it principally facilitates a bottom-up process that permits states to set their own levels of ambition. While politically astute, the Paris Agreement has not done much to actually change behavior. As such, it is a very thin form of international order.

Deeper cooperation will likely require some form of punishments or incentives for climate laggards to change their ways. Strong climate governance should rely on more than just enforcement, of course: it should also seek to offer strategic benefits.[59] This might include incentives, technology transfers, and side payments of various kinds from the most pro-climate countries to the laggards. Still, history suggests that enforcement and punishments play a vital role.

The fourth climate subsystem, at the nexus of climate and trade, offers an intriguing way to address that problem. Some states are adopting pro-climate policies faster and more aggressively than others.[60] If we characterize the leading states' pro-climate policies as a kind of international order, the laggard states are noncompliant with it. But far from facing punishments for noncompliance, laggard states actually have an *incentive* to avoid pro-climate policies because avoidance offers their producers a competitive advantage in trade.

Border adjustment taxes (BATs) offer a way to reverse that incentive, and instead create punishments for noncompliance. BATs are taxes applied to only imported goods, not nationally made goods.[61] In principle, the amount of the BAT depends on the cost differential created by climate policies in the importing and the exporting states. BATs close that gap, thereby leveling the competitive playing field in trade. Nobel-winning economist William Nordhaus argues BATs are essential for sustaining pro-climate policies among a group of countries because they offset the competitive effects.[62] States with pro-climate policies will want BATs to raise the cost of products being made in countries that do not have equivalent pro-climate policies. (In the United States, BATs might be called "fees" because right-leaning politicians abhor taxes, but the choice of name makes no policy difference.) Some US industry lobby groups advocate adopting BATs in conjunction with pro-climate policies.[63] Certain trade agreements already have climate provisions.[64]

States could use other trade measures besides BATs to punish noncompliance or to encourage others into adopting pro-climate policies.[65] Specifically, some

[59] Victor 2011.

[60] Harrison and Sundstrom 2007; Victor 2011; Goldthau and Sitter 2015.

[61] Governments might also use export subsidies to affect exported goods, in addition to import tariffs, to try to level the international playing field. I focus on import tariffs only to simplify the discussion.

[62] Nordhaus 2015. Note that Cirone and Urpelainen 2013 show that BATs' effects are not unambiguously positive for environmental cooperation. Still, in practice the political advantages of BATs appear to swamp the disadvantages.

[63] Schwartz 2017.

[64] Morin and Jinnah 2018.

[65] Green and Colgan 2013; Farrell and Newman 2015, 2019.

scholars urge US policymakers to use its regulations as a tool for setting *de facto* global standards, such as automotive fuel economy requirements.[66] Although any single government cannot typically force others to adopt their standards, multinational businesses often find it efficient to adopt standards from large markets like California in their worldwide operations, and others follow suit.[67] As Daniel Nexon and Abraham Newman argue, "the power of US rules resides in the fact that companies themselves want access to American consumers, the US financial system, or other critical US markets."[68] Governments could also use "green sanctions" to target carbon-intensive sectors, thereby raising the financing costs of businesses with heavy GHG emissions. In many cases, governments already have the institutional apparatus to implement such sanctions, such as the US Treasury Department's Office of Foreign Assets Control. For simplicity, I focus on BATs in the rest of this chapter, but conceptually we could imagine replacing BATs with pro-climate regulations or other trade measures that have similar effects.

A "Climate Club" at the Climate-Trade Nexus

Economists have analyzed the potential interactions between climate and trade governance extensively.[69] Conventionally, they view climate change as a classic collective action problem that generates free-riding. Barrett and Dannenberg describe the free-riding problem concisely: "For every player [country], irrespective of how others choose, not contributing to the global public good yields a higher payoff than contributing [by reducing emissions], and yet all players are better off collectively when every player contributes."[70] Based on this assumption, they show that linking climate cooperation to trade measures like BATs might hurt international cooperation as much as it helps.[71]

Their conclusion, however, depends critically on the premise that the chief driver of a state's climate policy is its concerns about short-term strategic interactions with the other states in the world.[72] By assumption, in the standard game-theoretic model, no country wants to be first to reduce its GHG emissions. It is not clear that this assumption is accurate. While it's true that every state contains some individuals and firms who object to being a climate leader, such concerns are increasingly being swamped by a growing public awareness of the

[66] Nexon and Newman 2019; but see also Drezner 2019.
[67] Vogel 1997; Simmons et al. 2006.
[68] Nexon and Newman 2019.
[69] Brainard and Sorkin 2009; Aichele and Felbermayr 2015; Nordhaus 2015; Caron et al. 2015.
[70] Barrett and Dannenberg unpublished: 7–8.
[71] Barrett and Dannenberg unpublished; Cirone and Urpelainen 2013.
[72] For critique of this assumption, see Aklin and Mildenberger 2020; Colgan et al. 2021.

looming negative effects of climate change. On balance, that can generate demand for policy action. As of 2020, a total of forty-six countries had implemented or scheduled carbon-pricing schemes.[73] Many of these schemes are modest, meaning that they induce relatively small reductions in emissions. Still, such policies exist and look to grow stronger over time. States are adopting pro-climate policies despite the fact that, from the perspective of conventional economic theory, those policies are *irrational* because of the incentive to free-ride.

Those policies look irrational to social scientists, however, because of faulty assumptions. In particular, social scientists tend to incorrectly see climate politics as a static collective action problem, rather than a dynamic one in which each actor's actions influence others' preferences and behavior as part of a sequential process over time.[74] Pro-climate advocates argue that the wealthy, early-industrializing states of the OECD should reduce emissions even if other states are initially unwilling or unable to reciprocate.[75] Also, some first-mover industrial or commercial advantages likely exist for being a climate leader. In short, some states seek a certain amount of pro-climate policy *regardless* of what other states do in the short term. Decisions by the European Union, and some of its member states especially, illustrate this tendency.

The problem of climate change looks quite different if there are at least some states willing to pursue climate leadership—that is, willing to make costly reductions in GHG emissions even when other states don't reciprocate. In that case, the critical questions become, How much of the world's economy falls into this club of climate leaders? And, how much cost are they willing to bear? A higher answer to each question implies faster decarbonization. However, there is a tradeoff implicit in the two questions: a "climate club" of such countries can expand its membership if it makes it easy to join by reducing the amount of costly action required for membership, or, alternatively, the club can demand more costly action of its members, at the risk of losing members.[76] For instance, an EU-US climate club would cover roughly 50 percent of the world's GDP, but at least through 2020, the United States has not been willing to agree to climate policies that are as stringent, and thus costly, as some of the European members would like. Those European states have to weigh the pros and cons of pursuing more aggressive climate policies in the absence of reciprocation by the United States.

An international climate club could operate in the following way.[77] First, all member countries have minimum levels of domestic pro-climate policy, such

---

[73] Mountford 2019.
[74] Colgan et al. 2021.
[75] For example, see https://www.sunrisemovement.org/green-new-deal Accessed November 27, 2019.
[76] Victor 2015, 2017; Falkner 2016.
[77] Prakash and Potoski 2007; Falkner 2016; Hovi et al. 2016.

as carbon pricing (taxes or cap-and-trade) or equivalent regulatory measures.[78] Second, to offset the competitive disadvantages associated with those policies, all members of the club apply BATs on products coming from countries outside of the club. All concrete proposals for a climate club follow these two basic principles, though they vary in their details.[79] For instance, ideally a climate club would not only punish outsiders but also offer shared benefits to the insiders. Some scholars suggest that shared research findings, common standards, and other tools could generate those club benefits; others see a simpler model with no explicit benefits as more feasible. Other details, like whether to make tariffs product specific, or to create exceptions for green firms operating in non-green countries, also vary across proposals.

We should not, however, lose the forest for the trees. The essential features of the climate club are that (1) it encourages pro-climate policies inside the club; and (2) it creates an economic disincentive for states not to participate. A third desirable feature is a clear path for outsiders to join the club, perhaps through "climate accession deals" similar to the way states join the WTO.[80]

A climate club of some sort is possible in the future, though far from inevitable. Major emitters like the EU, China, and the United States might decide, either unilaterally or in coordination with each other, to enact a set of pro-climate policies within their own domestic economies. Bottom-up domestic political pressure is essential to make that occur. As of 2021, both the United States (under the Biden administration) and the European Union had promised to implement some form of BATs, though few details were pinned down. Given a desire to implement pro-climate policies in their own economies on the basis of domestic politics (still uncertain), it follows that such states would seek to offset the competitive disadvantage of those policies by creating BATs or other trade measures.

BATs should be designed to encourage states to adopt climate policies and discourage free-riding. In the language of subsystems theory, they should impose punishments for noncompliance—and nonparticipation in the climate club counts as noncompliance. BATs could be sector-specific or applied economy-wide to targeted states. Experts debate the best approach.[81] Either way, however, policymakers should take advantage of political support for BATs from disadvantaged industries inside the climate club.

A key question is how to set BATs in such a way that they encourage states outside the climate club to join it. High BATs are economically disruptive, but if

---

[78] Rosenbloom et al. (2020) point out that carbon pricing, while useful, is not sufficient to decarbonize an economy. Worse still, Green (2021) argues that carbon prices have very low effectiveness in terms of reducing emissions.

[79] Urpelainen 2013; Rossi 2014; Keohane et al. 2017; Green 2017; Nordhaus 2020.

[80] Victor 2011

[81] Victor et al. 2019 and Cullenward and Victor 2020 support a sector-specific approach; Nordhaus 2020 supports an economy-wide approach.

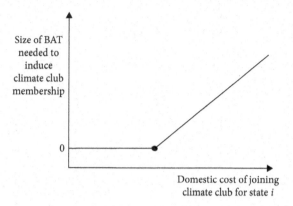

Figure 7.1 Politics of a climate club and border adjustment taxes (BATs)

the BATs are too low, outsider states—those that have not enacted pro-climate policies and are thus outside of the climate club—might decide to live with the export-reducing impact, and not change their policies at all. Outsider states are more likely to keep their old (climate-unfriendly) policies in proportion to the costliness, for their economy, of adopting pro-climate policies needed to join the climate club. For some countries, such as those with agricultural or mixed economies like India or Indonesia, the costs of joining the club might be relatively modest, and thus worth doing to avoid the BATs. For other economies, especially those heavily dependent on fossil fuels, adopting pro-climate policies might be so costly that they would prefer to remain outsiders.

Figure 7.1 represents the problem structure. The domestic costs of joining a climate club for each state are measured on the horizontal axis. These costs are not strictly economic—they are better understood as domestic political costs, albeit informed by the economic interests of domestic individuals and firms. On the left-hand side, there are climate leaders: states that support pro-climate policies purely on domestic political grounds. Consequently, the domestic cost to join the club, for them, is effectively zero. Moving to the right, states face increasing costs for joining the climate club because of domestic resistance. On the vertical axis, we can then plot the size of the BAT imposed by the climate club (assume all states inside the club impose the same BAT, for simplicity). The higher the BAT set by the climate club, the more outsider states have incentive to join the club.

The climate club's effectiveness depends on not only the BAT rate but also the economic size of the club. Figure 7.2 illustrates how three climate clubs of different sizes have different effects on outsiders. The smallest climate club (A), which has few members with sufficient domestic pressure to adopt pro-climate policies, will struggle to attract additional members. Because the club is small,

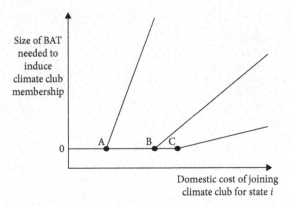

Figure 7.2 Politics of different-sized climate clubs

outsiders would lose only a small portion of the world market for their exports if they refused to comply with the required pro-climate policies. Consequently, a small climate club requires high BATs to attract even a few additional outsider states to join. As the initial climate club grows larger (B, then C), however, the value of access to the climate club's internal market grows. Being shut out of that market becomes more costly for outsiders, and so even a relatively modest BAT could incentivize them to adopt pro-climate policies.

Consequently, *building a political coalition for a large initial climate club* is vital for climate cooperation. The need to build a large club means that the costliness of the pro-climate policies cannot be too high, despite the environmental urgency of climate change. As much as environmental advocates want dramatic, immediate decarbonization, the advisability of that approach depends crucially on the political conditions that exist in the world's key economies, especially Europe, China, and the United States. The environmental need for rapid emissions reductions must be balanced against the incentive to include as much of the world's economy in the climate club.

In practice, there will be many additional details that will affect outsider states' decisions about whether to adopt pro-climate policies. For instance, the trade network position of certain states will matter. A state that trades mostly with one other, as Canada does with the United States, is more sensitive to that other's membership in a climate club than a state that has a diverse set of trading partners.[82] The dominant-partner trade situation could introduce nonlinearities in coalition building. For example, if European states can persuade the United

---

[82] Keohane and Nye 1977.

States to join a climate club, they are likely to get Canada too.[83] Moreover, the climate club might have heterogeneous BATs, which could be tailored to put additional pressure on outsiders.[84]

Ideally, the mere threat of BATs or other trade sanctions, rather than their use, would be sufficient to encourage most states to adopt pro-climate policies. That way, environmental policies get adopted without introducing economic inefficiencies in the trade system. Trade sanctions used to enforce previous environmental agreements have worked in this way.[85] There are some early signs, not yet clear, that the EU's proposed border adjustment mechanisms might have the effect of improving climate policies in Russia.[86] So the threat of BATs or other sanctions might prove quite useful. Yet, no policy tool is perfect.

Practical Challenges for Border Adjustment Taxes

While BATs help solve one enforcement problem, they create two other potential problems. The first is that states might abuse BATs, setting them high to protect their own industries from foreign competition.[87] In the worst case, climate change might serve as only a convenient excuse for states to offer advantages for producers in their own territory, thereby creating economic inefficiency that hurts overall prosperity ("green protectionism"). BATs are a type of tariff, after all, and tariffs inhibit international trade. The WTO was built for just the opposite purpose, namely, to reduce tariffs and promote trade. States need to balance two different policy goals: promoting efficient international trade while still allowing reasonable BATs or other trade measures to support pro-climate policies.

Fortunately, the world already has mechanisms in place to achieve a balance between trade and other goals. Trade dispute-resolution tribunals are those mechanisms. The WTO, for instance, lets each state set its own policies but allows

[83] This effect is enhanced by Canada's self-image as greener than the United States. Together, these effects make Canada's climate position conditional on the American one. Indeed, the Canadian prime minister reportedly instructed his negotiators at the Kyoto Protocol to commit to a bit more than whatever the United States agreed to (Hampson and Heinbecker 2010: 375).

[84] On firm-level complexities in climate preferences, see Kennard forthcoming.

[85] Jinnah 2011. Barrett (2011: 1881) argues that the "most effective international environmental agreements have relied on trade restrictions. But these agreements have been so effective that trade has not actually needed to be restricted." It might be possible for climate governance to emulate that pattern. But the comparison to other environmental agreements is not simple. The Montreal Protocol, for instance, included the threat of trade sanctions and is often seen as having "worked" to help ozone depletion. Arguably, however, the more important success factor was technical: the development of a cheap chemical alternative to ozone-depleting CFCs. The policy design features of the Montreal Protocol probably played a modest role.

[86] Astrasheuskaya and Khan 2021

[87] Furthermore, as Frankel (2010: 78) points out, "Just because a government measure is given an environmental label does not necessarily mean that it is motivated primarily—or even at all—by bona fide environmental objectives."

other countries to challenge those policies if they are perceived as breaking the agreed-upon rules.[88] So one way to accommodate BATs is to simply incorporate them under the existing WTO rules.[89]

Unfortunately, the WTO's current rules and judgments are hindering pro-climate policies rather than helping them. In particular, the main WTO environmental exemption only allows for provisions that are strictly "necessary," thereby minimizing the disruption to trade.[90] This legal standard implies that an environmental policy is not strictly necessary if one can imagine some other way to accomplish the same goal, regardless of the policy's political feasibility or lack thereof. In effect, the WTO rules prioritize trade over the environment.[91] This could cause states to hesitate to enact BATs, and, in turn, discourage pro-climate policies.

As the effects of climate change become dire, however, I hope political pressure will build to reverse the WTO's current prioritization. Instead, the WTO might put environmental goals above trade. For instance, the new principle might be that policies that minimize climate change have precedence. Trade provisions that conflict with climate goals are allowed only when they are strictly necessary to maintain a relatively open trade system. Alternatively, a different principle might balance trade and environmental goals, rather than giving strict priority to one before the other. Regardless, the world trade system should not be used an as excuse to avoid the BATs necessary to sustain pro-climate policies.

More controversially, I believe that international organizations should allow BATs that are higher than those needed to merely level the competitive playing field.[92] Climate-leading states should be allowed to charge a premium: a BAT rate that is higher than the level needed to make an outsider merely indifferent between paying the BAT or having its own state adopt the importer's pro-climate policy.[93] In the language of subsystems theory, that premium imposes a punishment on states that are not complying with a pro-climate order. Russia, Turkey, Brazil, and other climate-laggard states ought to face such penalties if they continue to pollute the climate. A BAT premium creates an incentive for exporters in laggard states like Russia or Turkey to lobby for pro-climate policy. Any international organization (like the WTO) passing judgment on the permissibility of BATs should allow a modest premium. Actors might even wish to quantify an appropriate range for the premium. Especially if it was done at a multilateral

---

[88]   Davis 2012.

[89]   Tucker and Meyer 2021.

[90]   GATT Article XX.

[91]   Tucker 2019.

[92]   See also Stiglitz 2006; Barrett 2011.

[93]   Trade bodies might not be able to strike down a BAT directly, but they have a history of encouraging compliance. See Davis 2012; Pelc 2010; Sattler et al. 2014.

setting, quantifying a premium would increase the legitimacy of such practices, and might preempt clashes with international trade law.[94]

BATs not only provide an incentive for states to adopt pro-climate policy; they also create a network of monitors. As Elinor Ostrom and others have shown, monitoring is a key problem in environmental governance, and having a poly-centric network of monitors can be helpful.[95] Import-competing industries in each country have an incentive to monitor exports from climate-laggard states so that they can lobby for higher BATs in their own markets. Of course, this creates administrative challenges and the need for technical standards about how to conduct monitoring, but diffuse subnational actors have already proven capable of such technical work.[96]

Additionally, BATs send a signal about how much of a laggard a state truly is, based on its own climate policies. A credible third-party actor could use this information to generate a global climate ranking. Researchers have found that other state rankings, like the World Bank's "Ease of Doing Business" index, have powerful effects on behavior.[97] This new climate signal would be hard for a na-tional government to manipulate politically—after all, *other* states' governments set the BATs. In a state that faces high BATs for its exports, politicians would have an incentive to favor lowering those BATs, which could in turn generate support for pro-climate policies.

In sum, subsystems theory offers ideas for crafting durable governing arrangements to mitigate climate change. It suggests the political likelihood of BATs as leading states balance their pro-climate policies with their desire for competitiveness in international trade . And it shows that BATs can be used to generate monitoring and information to render pro-climate policies politically sustainable.

The Risk of Retaliatory Tariffs

The use of BATs to create a climate club leads to a second potential problem: re-taliatory tariffs. If countries inside the climate club use BATs on imports from nonmembers, nonmembers might seek to retaliate with tariffs of their own against the climate club. Those retaliatory tariffs would reduce world trade and market efficiency. They also would weaken the political support for pro-climate

---

[94] Brainard and Sorkin 2010: 77.
[95] Ostrom 2010.
[96] New Climate Institute 2019; Green and Colgan 2013.
[97] Kelley and Simmons 2015; Cooley and Snyder 2015. For climate, an actor like the UN or a trusted NGO could tabulate the various bilateral BATs to generate a credible ranking of each state's performance on pro-climate policies. That ranking system would indicate to everyone how each state's climate policies measure up against other states.

policies inside the club. By hurting the economic competitiveness of exporters from inside the climate club, they would create or strengthen an internal constituency (i.e., the climate club's exporters) that opposes the policies that allow the climate club to function. For example, if club nonmembers imposed tariffs on German-made machine tools or American airplanes, those industries might want to weaken the climate club's pro-climate policies, or even obstruct them altogether, as a way to eliminate the tariffs.

Already, some countries are working to create a climate club, and face the risk of retaliatory tariffs. The EU has carbon pricing for European producers, which raises the costs of manufacturing in certain sectors. Understandably, such manufacturers want a level competitive playing field when facing imports from countries that do not have carbon taxes or other pro-climate policies. That gave rise, in 2020, to an EU plan to implement a BAT in the future, which would raise the cost of imports from non-green jurisdictions. Under the Trump administration, the United States immediately threatened retaliatory tariffs. At the time of writing, it is unclear how the Biden administration would react if the EU moves forward, given that the Biden administration seeks its own BATs.

Expanding a climate club beyond the EU to include the United States would be a leap forward in climate governance. On its own, the EU is not going to be able to solve the climate challenge. It accounted for just 10 percent of global emissions in 2019, ranking third behind China (more than 25 percent) and the United States (15 percent). The day could come, however, when the US Congress and White House will want to adopt carbon pricing. Admittedly, the Republican Party has proven reluctant to tackle climate change, but there are some signs of change. For instance, industry lobby groups like the Climate Leadership Council advocate a carbon tax in conjunction with BATs.[98] The right-leaning, libertarian Niskanen Center has made pro-climate policy one of its top priorities. Many Democrats are already keen. If and when serious decarbonization policies are on the table, some form of BAT is very likely to be part of the bargain, as it was in the 2009 Waxman-Markey bill that passed the US House of Representatives but failed in the Senate.

If US domestic politics do not allow for carbon pricing, BATs become less likely but not impossible. Most proposals for a climate club depend on domestic carbon pricing above some minimum threshold for all member states that are part of the club—and the absence of such carbon pricing in nonmember countries is what justifies the application of BATs. Conceivably, one could imagine states in the club deciding that a certain level of green industrial policy—that is, costly efforts to decarbonize an economy—is "equivalent" to a given level of

[98] Schwartz   2017;   https://www.clcouncil.org/media/2017/03/The-Conservative-Case-for-Carbon-Dividends.pdf.

carbon pricing. That would allow states to construct a carbon club even in the absence of carbon pricing in the United States or elsewhere. But the technical and political difficulties of creating policy "equivalences" between green industrial policy and carbon pricing are daunting. Whether and how to create such equivalences is an open question.

Ideally, China would volunteer to participate in an EU-US climate club. In 2020, China committed to net zero emissions by 2060, but its leaders stopped short of supporting a club approach. A climate club that includes the United States and the EU without China is infeasible, partly because of the environmental and political problems of allowing Chinese free-riding. Environmentally, proceeding without China would be insufficient because China is the world's largest GHG emitter. Politically, it would allow American and European critics of a climate club to cry foul. The US Senate, for instance, voted ninety-five to zero in favor of the 1997 Byrd-Hagel resolution, which opposed any climate treaty unless it "also mandates new specific scheduled commitments to limit or reduce greenhouse gas emissions for Developing Country Parties." That resolution passed even before China became the world's largest emitter. In other words, participation by China is probably a necessary condition for the political feasibility of US participation.

Even if that problem could be overcome, leaving China outside a climate club would create strong incentives for it to retaliate against the club's BATs. Imagine, for instance, what would happen if China threatened to target major US exports like soybeans, aircraft, and motor vehicles for tariffs, making clear that they were a response to climate-related BATs. That threat would put enormous pressure on many US politicians to oppose BATs, particularly if China could signal its intentions before the BATs were put in place. If domestic carbon pricing (or equivalent) and the associated BATs were able to pass into legislation in the United States at all, in this scenario, they would do so at a low level reflecting political compromise. Given the historical track record, it seems very unlikely that such policies would adequately address global warming.[99]

Consequently, the United States and Europe should work together to put China to a crucial decision on a climate club: China can either accept its share of the global task to mitigate climate change, or face the economic and political disadvantages of acting as the chief obstacle to a climate solution.[100] The political risks for being an obstacle are significant for China.[101] Assuming a credible EU-US proposal for a climate club exists, China risks shouldering the political blame for climate change among both global and domestic audiences. Environmental

99 Green 2021.
100 Colgan 2020b.
101 Kastner et al. 2018.

concerns rank high among China's own people.[102] Even with China's propaganda machine and ferocious censorship, it would be hard to avoid a global narrative painting China as the bad guy on climate change. That would undermine its legitimacy domestically and abroad. Reputational concerns have motivated China to change its policies in the past with respect to humanitarian interventions.[103] If, instead, American and European policymakers made an attractive path forward for China to join a climate club, its leaders would have to take that option seriously.

That said, a climate club that includes China can only exist in a relatively open world of global economic exchange, not a "decoupled" two-economy world, as I've argued in detail elsewhere.[104] Briefly, a conditional climate club proposal that threatens to exclude China from significant EU-US economic access cannot work if China is already excluded (because of decoupling for other reasons). Many politicians in the United States support trade decoupling from China on security or economic grounds, ignoring climate considerations. This is foolish. The key strength of a climate club is that it makes economic access to major markets conditional on environmental behavior.

Short of military action, economic access is often the strongest instrument of coercion that countries have in international relations. A decoupled global economy, carved into US-led and Chinese-led spheres of influence, takes that instrument off the table preemptively. In fact, a decoupled economy is an anti-strategic move.[105] Strategic moves are those that depend on another player's actions; a decoupled economy severs ties with China regardless of its climate policy. The United States and Europe simply cannot afford an anti-strategic approach on climate change.

Thus, the need for a climate club carries broader implications for American and European engagement with China. The policy debate about that engagement is largely framed in terms of the security benefits versus the economic costs of decoupling.[106] There are some security advantages to decoupling, but those security benefits have to be weighed against the very large economic costs.[107] Introducing the need for a climate club tips the balance even further. While the

---

[102] Christensen 2015; Weiss and Wallace 2021.

[103] Fung 2019.

[104] Colgan 2020b.

[105] Schelling 1966. (Ironically, Schelling's own views on climate change were deeply flawed; see Schelling 1997.)

[106] Decoupling is a matter of degrees, not absolutes. One can imagine a totally open, insecure global economy or a highly decoupled world of two completely distinct spheres of influence. Realistic alternatives are in the middle. One attractive possibility is a one-world open economy with a small number of carveouts for security reasons, such as on electronic equipment that can be exploited in cyber-warfare. Former Treasury secretary Henry Paulson (2019) described that option as building a "high fence around a small yard to protect our national security."

[107] Ratner et al. 2019; Farrell and Newman 2020; Gewirtz 2020; Rosenberg et al. 2020.

United States and Europe can and should protect a small number of economic sectors that are critical for national security and health emergencies, they should find ways to live with a competitive global interdependence that includes China for most economic activity.[108]

A Vision for a Climate Order

A big range of possible futures is open when it comes to climate politics. Some of the possibilities are bleak: futures in which international coordination fails completely and the global environment suffers catastrophically. Yet, there are also more positive possibilities.

I envision an evolving international order in which BATs and other trade measures are used to enforce *de facto* international standards for controlling GHG emissions in the world's major economies. That order would be based primarily upon national policies by climate-leader states, responding to grassroots domestic political pressures. Transnational advocacy networks like Fridays for Future could reinforce pro-climate political coalitions at the national and subnational levels.[109] Of course, their political opponents will use transnational networks in the reverse direction: to oppose pro-climate policies. It is unclear how much of a role international organizations like the United Nations will play.[110] International organizations are more likely to play a coordinating function than they are to serve as the primary arena of policymaking and authority, which will remain with national governments (and the EU).

The form of international order I envision puts domestic politics first, and places the international component (BATs and other measures) in a supporting position. Much greater attention, then, must be paid to the politics of building political support for pro-climate policies at the domestic level—a topic of a growing body of research.[111] Domestic policy sequencing is especially important, for two reasons.[112] First, it is essential for some countries, especially the United States, to demonstrate climate action in their own economies before demanding more of other countries.[113] Second, cross-national research shows that some early steps, like green industrial policy, play a key role in expanding the political coalition that supports subsequent measures, such as carbon pricing.[114]

---

[108] Colgan 2020b.
[109] Keck and Sikkink 1998; Hadden 2015.
[110] Conca et al. 2017.
[111] Harrison and Sundstrom 2007; Meckling 2011; Bernauer and Gampfer 2015; Stokes 2016; Ross et al. 2017; Mildenberger and Tingley 2017; Koubi et al. 2018; Blondeel et al. 2019; Bechtel et al. 2019; Tingley and Tomz 2019.
[112] Dimitrov 2016; Meckling et al. 2017; Aklin and Urpelainen 2018.
[113] Shaia and Colgan 2020.
[114] Meckling et al. 2015.

Carbon pricing has the political disadvantage of putting its costs to voters first in time, with the policy's benefits (for the climate) following much later in time; green industrial policy does the opposite, putting benefits first and costs (based on borrowing) later.

The primacy of domestic politics does not mean, however, that the design of an international climate order can be ignored until domestic policies are settled. International rules that allow for BATs and other economic measures could make the adoption of costly domestic policies more politically palatable because they would minimize free-riding and reassure actors against the risk of competitive disadvantage in global markets. Moreover, designing the international rules might prove easier than adopting costly domestic policies. For example, US leaders might accept new international rules that allow the EU to enact pro-climate BATs, even before the same US leaders are willing to pass pro-climate legislation in Congress. Still, Europe should work to bring both the United States and China into a climate club over time. For the reasons identified earlier, those negotiations might initially generate only relatively weak BATs. They could be ratcheted up later as domestic political conditions allow.

Conclusion

International order for climate is, at present, incomplete. It is too weak to sufficiently reduce GHG emissions and prevent damage to the earth's atmosphere. There is little point in blaming the United Nations for this failure. The nature of world politics means that international organizations have limited authority over their member states; they are mostly the servants of states, not the masters. Yet there are ways to shape international relations to support pro-climate policy.

A clear understanding of the problem is the precursor to effective policy. Analysts can use subsystems theory to break the problem into distinct questions of governance. In this chapter I've sketched out a preliminary analysis that identifies four key subsystems. One significant advantage of this approach is that it avoids a focus on the myriad organizations, NGOs, and other actors. That approach can prove superficial, especially if those actors aren't actually accomplishing much. Instead, subsystems analysis focuses on the deeper questions of governance that ultimately affect behavior.

Overlapping subsystems can be difficult to analyze. One way of overcoming these difficulties is to treat the overlap as a subsystem in its own right, as I have done here. What I call the fourth climate subsystem is really the intersection of two other subsystems: an emissions-reduction subsystem and a trade subsystem. Analyzing these interacting dynamics as its own subsystem brings to the surface the inevitable policy tradeoffs—and political tradeoffs—that actors face.

Meaningful international cooperation in support of pro-climate policy is possible. An international climate club supported by trade measures, such as BATs, appears to be the best hope for supporting domestic pro-climate policy efforts. It would help solve the enforcement and punishment problem that has bedeviled earlier attempts such as the Kyoto Protocol. I argued that states should modify WTO trade rules to allow BATs or other trade measures. Moreover, those measures should be allowed to do more than merely compensate for the potential competitive disadvantage of pro-climate policies; instead, they should punish actors that are not complying with pro-climate policies. Crucially, an effective climate club requires the participation of China, which in turn implies limits for US-China "decoupling."

8

Conclusion

"Most of all, consistent realism breaks down because it fails to provide any ground for purposive or meaningful action.... Such a conclusion is plainly repugnant.... Any sound political thought must be
based on elements of both utopia and reality."[1]

—E. H. Carr

In a world where large parts of global order seem to be in turmoil, we need robust
concepts and theory to guide our thinking. In this book I've sought to offer some
of those guiding concepts, based on an extended analysis of oil politics. I then
illustrated the breadth of those ideas by examining climate change, nuclear politics, peacekeeping, and other topics.

This last chapter briefly recaps the argument before considering two broader
topics. The best summary of my argument lies in chapter 1, and I will not rehash
it. Here, I step back from the particulars of the argument to assess how, compared
to more conventional theoretical approaches, subsystems theory adds value to
understanding issues like oil or climate.

I then turn to two final topics. The first is the global energy transition that is
currently underway—a shift from fossil fuels to increasing reliance on renewable
energy technology. The second topic is what subsystems tell us about the debate
over liberal international order as a whole. Many analysts see the current liberal
order in a crisis, which is the latest in a series of crises.[2] The idea of subsystems
prompts us to ask not *whether* to save the liberal order, but *which parts* we want
to save.

Sizing Up the Argument

This book is designed to generate some "aha!" moments stemming from a new
perspective on international order. Ideally, it would be like those Gestalt pictures

[1] Carr 1946 [1964]: 92–93.
[2] Ikenberry 2020.

where an image that is initially seen one way (e.g., as a candlestick holder) suddenly resolves in a different way (e.g., two faces). Depending on one's starting position, some might experience a similar shift upon the realization that what looked like a single international order can be understood differently: "the" international order is actually multiple orders, consisting of governing arrangements in subsystems. Change in those arrangements is quite distinct from, and substantively no less important than, change in the partially coherent themes that link them. Indeed, analysts probably worry too much about the adjectives, like liberal or mercantilist, that we use to describe international order.

For others, subsystems might put a specific issue area in a new and powerful light. Many saw the 1970s as a revolution in global oil politics, for instance. It certainly was a revolution for international political economy. Yet, in another way, the 1970s was notable for the *continuity* of a basic pattern of international politics, namely, the way in which an external state provided military protection to oil-rich territories in the Persian Gulf. These oil-for-security deals had existed for almost as long as oil was a militarily significant commodity, and continue even to the present day, though the United States has gradually replaced the UK as the key protector. Decolonization was far less consequential for oil security affairs than it was, eventually, for global oil production. Recognizing two subsystems of oil politics, rather than one monolithic issue area, makes it possible to see and appreciate the different rates of change within them.

An appreciation of multiple subsystems is not merely an academic exercise. It has practical implications. It helps explain, for example, why countries like Saudi Arabia can seem to be both hostile and friendly to the United States at the same time. The events of 1973–1974 put this tendency on display: Saudi Arabia publicly refused to sell oil to the United States while simultaneously working hard to maintain a close military relationship, going so far as to buy billions of dollars' worth of American weapons that it could barely use. Distinguishing the oil production subsystem from the oil security subsystem could also sharpen policymaking in the United States. They are linked, but the degree of separation between the two subsystems helps explain why the massive US military presence in the Persian Gulf offers little in the way of influence over the day-to-day behavior of the oil market.[3] Conversely, it might help people understand that the fracking revolution in the United States does not, on its own, greatly affect the question of whether the military should withdraw from the Persian Gulf. The idea of "energy independence" is profoundly misleading and often abused.

US policymakers should pay particular attention to the benefits of oil-for-security arrangements in the Persian Gulf region before too lightly abandoning them. Those deals have helped avoid wars. They also underpin nonproliferation

[3] Gause 2009: 8.

efforts in the region by extending US protection to weak states that would otherwise want nuclear weapons. Unfortunately, the same deals seem to have contributed various security problems (such as providing grievances that fuel terrorism), so they are not costless.[4] Possibly, they also contribute to excessive US support for various dictators and tyrants,[5] though wiser US leadership could curb that problem. Overall, there are some compelling reasons to change the US relationship with various petrostates in the Middle East, but those advocating for change should be mindful of the potential unintended consequences.[6]

I have also tried to show how strategic benefits and punishments for noncompliance drive the conditions under which international order changes. I encourage scholars to pay special attention to the second factor: punishments for noncompliance, backed by instruments of coercion. Liberal institutionalists sometimes overlook or discount the role of punishments; others mischaracterize them or treat them as derivative of the distribution of power and material capabilities. The reality is that punishments for noncompliance are typically essential for maintaining an order. Regardless of the direction in which we seek to improve the current order, we must reckon with the central importance of enforcement.

I drew lessons from the international order for oil and applied those lessons to other issues. Chapter 6 studied a variety of other issues, including nuclear politics and peacekeeping. It showed that certain debates about international order might be more fruitfully analyzed from a subsystems perspective.

Chapter 7 turned to climate change. I suggested that there are at least four major subsystems for climate politics: emissions reductions; climate-related capital; negative-emissions technologies; and the climate-trade nexus. I see the fourth one as especially important for generating punishments for noncompliance, to be applied to actors who refuse to adopt policies to reduce carbon emissions. Specifically, I expect states to develop border adjustment taxes (BATs) to offset the competitive disadvantages of pro-climate policies in international trade. The most promising route is a multilateral climate club, starting with the three major emitters China, the United States, and the EU.[7] Although this climate club creates some tensions with existing WTO rules, trade rules should be modified to allow pro-climate measures. BATs can and should be used to support a more pro-climate international order.

---

[4] Moran and Russell 2009; Colgan 2013b; Lee 2016.
[5] Wenar 2016.
[6] Layne 2007; Gholz and Press 2010a, 2010b; Glaser and Kelanic 2014; Posen 2014; Ashford 2018; Thrall and Friedman 2018. For a different take, see Brooks and Wohlforth 2016; Rovner and Talmadge 2014.
[7] Colgan 2020b.

Politics of the Global Energy Transition

A potentially monumental shift is gradually unfolding, namely, the global energy transition away from fossil fuels and toward renewable energy.[8] In fact, some analysts use the term "energy transitions" to indicate multiple related trends, which include more energy efficiency, more electricity, and more renewables.[9] Taken as a whole, the energy transition could have significant consequences for world politics.[10] What does a subsystems analysis tell us about how that shift might unfold?

As always, we must begin with description. Two principal factors underpin the energy transition: climate change, and the increasingly attractive economics of low-carbon technologies.[11] Climate change, and the anticipated policy shifts in responses to it, are causing inventors, energy producers, and investors to seek alternatives to fossil fuels.[12] Even within the fossil fuel sector, natural gas is displacing coal, with significant consequences.[13] Technological and commercial advances in battery and renewable energy technologies, especially wind and solar, are also reshaping the global energy market.[14] Per-unit electricity generation costs, for instance, are now typically lower for new wind turbines and solar generation plants than they are for new coal plants (and in some cases, even for existing coal plants). A growing awareness of how fossil fuels cause political problems, and a desire to shift away from them, adds to the motivation for this transition.[15]

The scale of the desired transition is massive. Many trillions of dollars of new investment are involved. For climate change mitigation, it is not enough for the current transition to follow the pattern of previous energy transitions. Those transitions tended to ramp up *all* forms of energy, the old and the new.[16] When coal usage took off in the nineteenth century, for example, it did not lead to a global decrease in wood and traditional biomass as fuels; instead, the total amount of energy consumed increased. Similarly, when oil took off in the twentieth century, it did not displace coal, but rather added to total consumption.

---

[8] Miller et al. (2015) define energy transitions as "shifts in the fuel source for energy production and the technologies used to exploit that fuel." See Sovacool 2016 for other definitions.

[9] IRENA 2019.

[10] O'Sullivan et al. 2017; Jaffe 2018; IRENA 2019; Goldthau and Westphal 2019; Bazilian et al. 2019; Van de Graaf et al. 2020.

[11] The International Renewable Energy Agency (2019) identifies six drivers: declining cost of renewables; environmental benefits (for air pollution and climate change); technological innovation; government adoption of renewable energy standards (RES); corporate and investor action; and shifts in public opinion. The two principal factors I identify here underpin all of these drivers.

[12] Mitchell and Carpenter 2019; Blondeel et al. 2019; Fox-Penner 2020.

[13] Kennard 2020; Vormedal et al. 2020.

[14] Stokes and Warshaw 2017; Aklin and Urpelainen 2018.

[15] Ross 2012; Colgan 2015; Wenar 2016.

[16] York and Bell 2019.

Worldwide, coal is consumed at a far higher rate in the twenty-first century than it was at any point in the nineteenth century. Thus, in each case, previous energy transitions tended to shift the *relative mix* of fuels consumed, without reducing the *absolute* amount of traditional fuels.[17] From a climate change perspective, this is a huge problem. The atmosphere does not care about the relative mix of fuel sources; only the total amount of greenhouse gas (GHG) emissions matters. To meet the UNFCCC's climate change mitigation goals, we need a *historically unprecedented* global energy transition.

Compounding this challenge is the slow time scale of the transition. It is slow for three reasons. First, the capital turnover cycle takes decades.[18] Cars are built to last a decade or more; power plants are built to last five or six decades. Replacing them more quickly than that, even when better or greener technology exists, does not always make economic sense. Second, human societies have been slow to politically accept climate change as a reality and figure out how they want to respond.[19] That lethargy is compounded by the decades-long delay between when emissions enter the atmosphere and when they have their most significant environmental effects. Third, there is usually some difficulty integrating new technologies with existing systems to displace old ones.[20] For instance, wind and solar energy typically create more variable electricity generation than conventional electrical plants do because the wind does not always blow and the sun does not always shine. The electrical grid, and the human systems that govern that grid, need to adapt to take full advantage of their potential. To compound the challenges, some businesses often oppose the change, making it even slower.[21] Not surprisingly, then, considerable uncertainty exists about the speed of the global energy transition.[22]

On the whole, the energy transition brings enormous benefits. It should be celebrated and sped up where possible. Inevitably, however, the transition also creates some negative distributional consequences. It will hurt some of those who make their livelihoods in ways related to fossil fuels.[23] If the transition is swift enough, it could also bring political instability and hard economic times for some states, especially coal- and oil-exporting states. Research suggests that

---

[17] There are some minor exceptions to this rule, but they are not exactly comforting. For instance, petroleum did replace whale oil as a fuel for lighting; but it did so only because humans hunted whales to near extinction. This is hardly salutary as an indicator of humans' ability to shift energy patterns to avoid an environmental problem!

[18] Aklin and Urpelainen 2018; Bernstein and Hoffmann 2019.

[19] Keohane and Victor 2011; Hayes and Knox-Hayes 2014; Allan 2018; Javeline and Kijewski-Correa 2018.

[20] Geels et al. 2017.

[21] Oreskes and Conway 2011; Brulle and Roberts 2017, 2020; Stokes 2020; Downie 2019.

[22] Sovacool 2016; Kern and Rogge 2016; Cherif et al. 2017; Fattouh et al. 2018; Van de Graaf and Bradshaw 2018.

[23] Van de Graaf 2018; Thurber 2019; Overland et al. 2019.

states with relatively high oil production costs, like Venezuela, Canada, and various African states, could face steep declines in the profitability of their oil exports—especially if electric cars rapidly take over the global car market.[24]

Subsystems theory can add to what is already known about the global energy transition by highlighting the interactions between energy, climate, and other issue areas like trade. For example, in 2020 the European Commission sought to enact a common climate policy for the EU that would include tariffs (BATs). The climate policy would raise the cost of products associated with GHG emissions through direct taxation and regulation (for producers inside the EU) and BATs (for producers outside the EU). At least in principle, the BATs would equalize the carbon costs of the product, regardless of where it was made. Ukrainian and Polish coal producers would face the same marginal increase in their costs. Yet that considers only the direct effects of the climate policy. As part of the political bargains to pass such policies, the EU would almost certainly offer billions of euros in transition funds and job creation programs for EU workers. Poland (an EU member) would presumably benefit from those funds,[25] but Ukraine (a non-EU member) would not. As this example illustrates, the impact of climate policies seeking to support the energy transition is complex, and it is not obvious that their effects will be only in proportion to states' marginal cost of production. If we ignore the interaction of subsystems, we will come to faulty conclusions.

The key insight from subsystems theory, though, is conceptual not empirical. Specifically, analysts should develop a broad empirical understanding of the whole energy transition, and only then seek to identify the key actors' behavior and decisions. That approach tends to surface the underlying structural forces and choices. It contrasts with conventional analysis that starts by disaggregating the world into fuel types (e.g., coal or gas) or institutions (e.g., the International Energy Agency, OPEC),[26] and only then considers evolving political dynamics. As we saw in the study of other issue areas, the subsystems approach tends to bring into view actors, behaviors, and tradeoffs that would otherwise be missed.

Adopting a subsystems perspective could help resolve a recurring analytical problem. As scholars point out, three different and sometimes incompatible perspectives on energy transitions are common: techno-economic, socio-technical, and political.[27] The first, rooted in economics, tends to focus on market equilibrium and efficiency; the second, rooted in sociology of science, focuses

---

[24] IRENA 2019.

[25] Ironically, Poland's opposition to EU climate change policies could render it ineligible to draw on the EU's transition resources (Rankin 2019). Presumably, Poland will find a way to tap such funds if the money becomes available to the rest of the EU.

[26] Some of my own research has this focus on institutions (Colgan et al. 2012; Van De Graaf and Colgan 2016). Studying the institutions is a natural starting point, of course, but it is not the only way to analyze.

[27] Cherp et al. 2018.

on technological lock-in and diffusion; and the third, rooted in political science, focuses on special interests, collective action problems, and punctuated equilibrium. Needless to say, different perspectives can lead to people talking past each other. Subsystems theory might help analysts from any one of these perspectives communicate with those coming from another perspective by drawing attention to the key questions of governance that guide how decisions and behavior actually occur.

In all probability, the energy transition will need to advance somewhat further before we have enough information to analyze it properly from a social science perspective. Subsystems theory is no more a crystal ball for forecasting the future than is any other social science theory. It can, however, offer a solid foundation for future analysis.

Crisis of Liberal International Order

The global energy transition and climate change are not the only factors emerging to challenge past patterns of international order. Many people now see the US-led postwar liberal international order facing a crisis.

Though I have argued throughout this book that there is no such thing as *the* international order, but rather multiple orders, I will use the conventional phrase "the liberal order" now. That phrase usefully refers to liberalism as a theme of international order. Actors are constantly contesting those themes. I described in chapter 6 how changes in subsystems aggregate up to changes in the themes themselves, by weakening or strengthening the consistency of an ordering theme across multiple subsystems. Realistically, there is never a perfect match between an order's theme and the behavior of all of the subsystems. However, the more there is a match among the most important governing arrangements, the stronger the theme is. After World War II, the governing arrangements in various subsystems made it possible, overall, to refer to a liberal order.

In recent years, two threats have undermined the liberal order, one internal and the other external. The internal threat is the loss of what John Ruggie referred to as "embedded liberalism," the social contract by which the gains of globalization and economic growth were distributed widely across society, to the rich and poor.[28] The liberal order's institutions became disconnected from ordinary people in the very countries that created them. Starting in the early 1980s, a neoliberal economic agenda eroded the social contract that had previously ensured political support for the liberal order. Many middle- and working-class voters in the United States, Britain, and elsewhere came to believe—with a good deal of

---

[28] Ruggie 1982; Mansfield and Rudra 2020.

justification—that the system was rigged.[29] In 2016, the bill for that broken social contract came due on both side of the Atlantic, as indicated by the Brexit referendum and the election of President Donald Trump. The politics of discontent continue to reverberate today.

The external threat to the liberal order came principally from illiberal states that participated only selectively in its institutions and often sought to undermine its norms, principles, and rules. China, for instance, flatly rejected a July 2016 ruling in a case the Philippines brought against it under the United Nations Convention on the Law of the Sea (UNCLOS). Despite being a treaty member of UNCLOS, China insisted on its claims in the South China Sea and refused to abide by the ruling. The United States and others also accuse China of violating the spirit and the letter of various economic agreements at the WTO. Similarly, Russia's incursion into Ukraine in 2014 and apparent efforts to undermine elections in various democracies threaten the principles of the liberal order. Cross-national information warfare is a rising concern for liberal democracies.[30]

We are likely to misunderstand the external threats facing the liberal order if we see them as monolithic. China, for instance, participates in many parts of the liberal order even as it resists other parts.[31] China has proven willing to engage on climate change, banning land mines, and many peacekeeping operations. Russia, too, values access to the WTO and other international organizations. In other words, participation varies by subsystem.

That partial engagement with liberal order points to the significance of subsystems. John Ikenberry, one of the great theorists of liberal internationalism, argues, "Liberal order is less like a castle with a drawbridge and walls and more like a shopping mall. It is easy for states to enter and exit and it is easier for them to resist or avoid its rules and institutions."[32] He adds that the liberal order is "less like a club and more like a public utility—a system of functional institutions and regimes to which states could variously attach themselves."[33] Though he does not use the language of subsystems, Ikenberry hints at the central role that they play. I would push his analogy further. At the international level, there is no central "public utility" or "shopping mall" at all – just a grabbag of ideas and principles that recur inconsistently across subsystems. Actors sustain the governing arrangements in each subsystem on its own, occasionally with overlap, but never from a central authority. International order exists at the level of those subsystems—it's all shops and no mall.

[29] Colgan and Keohane 2017.
[30] On cyber politics broadly, see Gartzke and Lindsay 2015; Poznansky and Perkoski 2018; Schneider 2019.
[31] Weiss and Wallace 2021.
[32] Ikenberry 2020: 282.
[33] Ikenberry 2020: 284.

One practical implication of seeing international order in this complex, fragmented fashion is that great powers like the United States and China are unlikely to simply compete or cooperate with each other over *the* international order. Instead, they will compete *and* cooperate.[34] In some subsystems, great powers will cooperate to pursue mutual interests, often at the expense of weaker states or non-state actors. In other subsystems, great powers will compete and perhaps form rival institutions to attract other states into their distinct subsystems.

Great powers have followed this pattern of competition and cooperation before. My research with Nicholas Miller studies the way the United States and the Soviet Union cooperated and competed during the Cold War to manage their spheres of influence, or what we called their rival hierarchies.[35] We identified three distinct mechanisms of interaction between the rival hierarchies: competitive *shaming*, where dominant states try to attract or retain subordinate states by drawing attention to abuses by a rival dominant state;[36] *outbidding*, where dominant states seek to attract or retain subordinates by providing more benefits than a rival dominant state;[37] and institutional *cooperation* between dominant states to enhance or maintain their position over subordinate states (e.g., working to restrict nuclear proliferation).[38] We expect that the United States, China, and perhaps others will use these same mechanisms as they compete and cooperate in the future.

Piloting International Order in the Twenty-first Century

What should scholars advise policymakers to do about international order? To answer that question, we have to know how much of yesterday's order we want to save, and how much to reform or replace. As a group, IR scholars find it strikingly difficult to answer those questions. For example, despite an almost universally negative reaction to the Trump administration and its use of US foreign

---

[34] Campbell and Sullivan 2019.

[35] Colgan and Miller 2019.

[36] Competitive shaming is different from "naming and shaming" in other policy areas, where at least the nominal goal of the shaming state is to compel the target state into changing its behavior (Hafner-Burton 2008; Murdie and Davis 2012; Hendrix and Wong 2013). Competitive shaming works differently: the shaming state aims not so much to compel different behavior as to make the target state look bad in front of world audiences.

[37] Bueno de Mesquita and Smith (2016) find outbidding operative among foreign aid donors. On outbidding between sub-state actors, see Crenshaw 1981; Snyder 2000; Kydd and Walter 2006; Toft 2007.

[38] Inter-hierarchy cooperation might even accomplish goals that each hierarchy would find it difficult to accomplish on its own (Carnegie and Carson 2019).

policy against the liberal order, IR scholars differed dramatically in their views about whether and how much of the liberal order is worth saving.[39]

The fact that the liberal order is an aggregation of many parts, rather than a single thing, is a crucial part of why scholars and analysts split on the question of whether to defend it. On one hand, liberal international order has helped preserve peace among the great powers, discouraged many countries from acquiring nuclear weapons, and helped lift billions of people out of crippling poverty. On the other hand, it has contributed to inequality and a loss of social cohesion in the United States and elsewhere, and has done little to limit the excesses of US military adventurism.

Perceiving the liberal order as made up of subsystems helps focus us on the task of picking and choosing which parts to save. For example, we might see that the trade system has generated valuable economic growth but also made it harder to adopt policies that mitigate climate change. We might keep the core elements of trade dispute resolution while modifying trade rules to facilitate carbon tariffs and other measures that accelerate decarbonization efforts.

Leaders looking to reform the liberal order should appreciate the difference between a pilot and an engine of change. Leaders are pilots. They can steer change, but are not usually its true cause. History's engine of change is structural shifts like decolonization or technological advancement. As I've highlighted in this book, decolonization fundamentally altered the global politics of oil. At best, a leader can navigate through structural shifts like that one. Leaders should strive to have a clear-eyed view of the strategic benefits and punishments for noncompliance available to them and others within an order, especially as it changes. Leaders with that clarity can design governing arrangements that match the instruments of coercion available to them, rather than unenforceable and unrealistic arrangements.

One motif running through my analysis of international order is about the hubris and intellectual blindness of leaders in great power states. Powerful actors often exaggerate their own legitimacy and staying power. They sometimes imagine that subordinate actors participate in an order because of it is strategic benefits, as opposed to the threat of punishment. Some of the Anglo-American oil companies had this kind of hubris, and got surprised in the 1970s. More broadly, many British-owned mining businesses got a rude awakening from decolonization. When the threat of imperial punishment lost its bite, former colonies decided to nationalize their assets and kick the British managers out of the country.[40] It is a lesson that policymakers in the United States should not ignore as they grapple with recent changes in their own global standing.

---

[39] Walt 2018.
[40] Stockwell 2000.

I hope this book provides insight into the analytic question of when and why international order changes or remains the same. I have focused on elements of *realpolitik*, like hegemony, strategic benefits, and punishments for noncompliance. Those elements bring about change and stability. Scholars should not lose sight, however, of an international order's normative content. As human beings, we should care not just about whether change or stability occurs, but also whether it is desirable.

E. H. Carr, one of the modern founders of realism in international relations, pointed out long ago that political analysis becomes insufficient if it offers no positive vision, no way to make things better. The quote from Carr that serves as this chapter's epigraph speaks to the need for realism *and* idealism.[41] If we care about things like peace, prosperity, self-determination, and environmental sustainability, we should study not only the conditions under which an order changes, but also how it might change for the better. In the end, this book is about how to create and sustain governing arrangements that actually work. Our world desperately needs them.

---

[41] Also: "Pure realism [analysis] can offer nothing but a naked struggle for power which makes any kind of international society impossible. Having demolished the current utopia with the weapons of realism, we still need to build a new utopia of our own." Carr 1946 [1964]: 93.

Bibliography

"A Different Agenda." 2012. *Nature* 487(7407): 271.

Aarts, Paul, and Gerd Nonneman, eds. 2006. *Saudi Arabia in the Balance*. London: Hurst and Company.

Abernethy, David B. 2002. *The Dynamics of Global Dominance: European Overseas Empires, 1415–1980*. New Haven: Yale University Press.

Acharya, Amitav. 2018. *Constructing Global Order: Agency and Change in World Politics*. Cambridge, UK: Cambridge University Press.

Acharya, Amitav, and Barry Buzan, eds. 2010. *Non-Western International Relations Theory: Perspectives on and beyond Asia*. London; New York: Routledge.

Acuto, Michele, and Simon Curtis. 2014. *Reassembling International Theory: Assemblage Thinking and International Relations*. London: Palgrave Macmillan.

Adelman, Morris Albert. 1982. "OPEC as a Cartel." In *OPEC Behaviour and World Oil Prices*, edited by James M. Griffin and David J. Teece, 37–63. London: George Allen and Unwin.

Adler, Emanuel. 2019. *World Ordering: A Social Theory of Cognitive Evolution*. Cambridge, UK: Cambridge University Press.

Adler, Emanuel, and Vincent Pouliot. 2011. *International Practices*. Cambridge, UK: Cambridge University Press.

Adler-Nissen, Rebecca. 2012. *Bourdieu in International Relations: Rethinking Key Concepts in IR*. New York: Routledge.

Aichele, Rahel, and Gabriel Felbermayr. 2015. "Kyoto and Carbon Leakage: An Empirical Analysis of the Carbon Content of Bilateral Trade." *Review of Economics and Statistics* 97(1): 104–15.

Aklin, Michaël, and Matto Mildenberger. 2020. "Prisoners of the Wrong Dilemma: Why Distributive Conflict, Not Collective Action, Characterizes the Politics of Climate Change." *Global Environmental Politics* 20(4): 4–27.

Aklin, Michaël, and Johannes Urpelainen. 2013. "Political Competition, Path Dependence, and the Strategy of Sustainable Energy Transitions." *American Journal of Political Science* 57(3): 643–58.

Aklin, Michaël, and Johannes Urpelainen. 2018. *Renewables: The Politics of a Global Energy Transition*. Cambridge, MA: MIT Press.

Aldy, Joseph E., and Robert N. Stavins. 2009. *Post-Kyoto International Climate Policy: Implementing Architectures for Agreement*. Cambridge, UK: Cambridge University Press.

Alfonsi, Christian. 2006. *Circle in the Sand: Why We Went Back to Iraq*. New York: Doubleday.

Alhajji, A. F., and David Huettner. 2000. "OPEC and Other Commodity Cartels: A Comparison." *Energy Policy* 28(15): 1151–64.

Alkon, Meir, and Audrye Wong. 2020. "Authoritarian Energy Transitions Undermined?: Environmental Governance Cycles in China's Power Sector." *Energy Research & Social Science* 68: 101531.

Allan, Bentley B. 2018. *Scientific Cosmology and International Orders*. Cambridge, UK: Cambridge University Press.

Allen, Susan Hannah, and Amy T. Yuen. 2014. "The Politics of Peacekeeping: UN Security Council Oversight across Peacekeeping Missions." *International Studies Quarterly* 58(3): 621–32.

Allison, Graham. 2017. *Destined for War: Can America and China Escape Thucydides's Trap?* Boston and New York: Mariner Books.

Alter, Karen J. 2014. *The New Terrain of International Law: Courts, Politics, Rights*. Princeton, NJ: Princeton University Press.

Alter, Karen J., and Sophie Meunier. 2009. "The Politics of International Regime Complexity." *Perspectives on Politics* 7(1): 13–24.

Andonova, Liliana B., Michele M. Betsill, and Harriet Bulkeley. 2009. "Transnational Climate Governance." *Global Environmental Politics* 9(2): 52–73.

Andonova, Liliana B., and Ronald B. Mitchell. 2010. "The Rescaling of Global Environmental Politics." *Annual Review of Environment and Resources* 35(1): 255.

Archer, Margaret S. 1988. *Culture and Agency*. Cambridge, UK: Cambridge University Press.

Aronoff, Kate, Alyssa Battistoni, Daniel Aldana Cohen, and Thea Riofrancos. 2019. *A Planet to Win: Why We Need a Green New Deal*. New York: Verso Books.

Ashford, Emma. 2018. "Unbalanced: Rethinking America's Commitment to the Middle East." *Strategic Studies Quarterly* 12(1): 127–48.

Astrasheuskaya, Nastassia, and Mehreen Khan. 2021. "Russian Businesses Start Counting Cost of EU Carbon Border Tax." *Financial Times*. https://www.ft.com/content/0fc621d1-675c-4768-814e-5863b172dd62 (May 21, 2021).

Autesserre, Séverine. 2014. *Peaceland: Conflict Resolution and the Everyday Politics of International Intervention*. New York: Cambridge University Press.

Auzanneau, Matthieu. 2018. *Oil, Power, and War: A Dark History*. White River Junction, Vermont: Chelsea Green Publishing.

Avant, Deborah D. 2005. *The Market for Force: The Consequences of Privatizing Security*. Cambridge, UK: Cambridge University Press.

Avant, Deborah D., Martha Finnemore, and Susan K. Sell. 2010. *Who Governs the Globe?* Cambridge, UK: Cambridge University Press.

Axelrod, Regina S., and Stacy D. VanDeveer. 2014. *The Global Environment: Institutions, Law, and Policy*. Washington, DC: CQ Press.

Axelrod, Robert M. 2006. *The Evolution of Cooperation*. New York: Basic Books.

Baccini, Leonardo, Veronica Lenzi, and Paul W. Thurner. 2013. "Global Energy Governance: Trade, Infrastructure, and the Diffusion of International Organizations." *International Interactions* 39(2): 192–216.

Bacevich, Andrew J. 2016. *America's War for the Greater Middle East: A Military History*. New York: Random House.

Bäckstrand, Karin. 2008. "Accountability of Networked Climate Governance: The Rise of Transnational Climate Partnerships." *Global Environmental Politics* 8(3): 74–102.

Bailey, Gavin. 2008. "The Narrow Margin of Criticality: The Question of the Supply of 100-Octane Fuel in the Battle of Britain." *The English Historical Review* 123(501): 394–411.

Baldwin, David A. 1971. "The Power of Positive Sanctions." *World Politics* 24: 19.

Baldwin, David A. 1989. *Paradoxes of Power*. Oxford and New York: Basil Blackwell.

Bapat, Navin A. 2019. *Monsters to Destroy: Understanding the War on Terror*. New York: Oxford University Press.

Barbieri, Katherine, and Jack S. Levy. 1999. "Sleeping with the Enemy: The Impact of War on Trade." *Journal of Peace Research* 36(4): 463–79.

Barkey, Karen, and Mark Von Hagen, eds. 1997. *After Empire: Multiethnic Societies and Nation-Building: The Soviet Union and the Russian, Ottoman, and Habsburg Empires.* Boulder, CO: Westview Press.

Barma, Naazneen, Kai Kaiser, Tuan Minh Le, and Lorena Viñuela. 2011. *Rents to Riches?: The Political Economy of Natural Resource-Led Development.* Washington, DC: World Bank Publications.

Barma, Naazneen, Ely Ratner, and Steven Weber. 2013. "The Mythical Liberal Order." *The National Interest* (124): 56–67.

Barnett, Michael, and Martha Finnemore. 2004. *Rules for the World: International Organizations in Global Politics.* Ithaca, NY: Cornell University Press.

Barnett, M. N., and M. Finnemore. 1999. "The Politics, Power, and Pathologies of International Organizations." *International Organization* 53(4): 699–732.

Barr, James. 2012. *A Line in the Sand.* London: Simon & Schuster.

Barr, James. 2018. *Lords of the Desert: The Battle between the United States and Great Britain for Supremacy in the Modern Middle East.* London: Simon & Schuster.

Barrett, Scott. 2006. "Climate Treaties and 'Breakthrough' Technologies." *American Economic Review* 96(2): 22–25.

Barrett, Scott. 2011. "Rethinking Climate Change Governance and Its Relationship to the World Trading System." *The World Economy* 34(11): 1863–82.

Barsky, R. B., and L. Kilian. 2004. "Oil and the Macroeconomy since the 1970s." *Journal of Economic Perspectives* 18(4): 115–34.

Bauerle Danzman, Sarah. 2019. *Merging Interests: When Domestic Firms Shape FDI Policy.* Cambridge, UK: Cambridge University Press.

Bauerle Danzman, Sarah, W. Kindred Winecoff, and Thomas Oatley. 2017. "All Crises Are Global: Capital Cycles in an Imbalanced International Political Economy." *International Studies Quarterly* 61(4): 907–23.

Bazilian, Morgan, et al. 2020. "Four Scenarios of the Energy Transition: Drivers, Consequences, and Implications for Geopolitics." *WIREs Climate Change*: e625.

Bazilian, Morgan, Smita Nakhooda, and Thijs Van de Graaf. 2014. "Energy Governance and Poverty." *Energy Research & Social Science* 1: 217–25.

Beber, Bernd, Michael J. Gilligan, Jenny Guardado, and Sabrina Karim. 2017. "Peacekeeping, Compliance with International Norms, and Transactional Sex in Monrovia, Liberia." *International Organization* 71(1): 1–30.

Bechtel, Michael M., Federica Genovese, and Kenneth F. Scheve. 2019. "Interests, Norms and Support for the Provision of Global Public Goods: The Case of Climate Co-Operation." *British Journal of Political Science* 49(4): 1333–55.

Beckley, Michael. 2012. "China's Century? Why America's Edge Will Endure." *International Security* 36(3): 41–78.

Bell, Mark S. 2017. "Examining Explanations for Nuclear Proliferation." *International Studies Quarterly* 60(3): 520–29.

Bellin, Eva. 2004. "The Robustness of Authoritarianism in the Middle East." *Comparative Politics* 36(2): 139–57.

Bentzen, J. 2007. "Does OPEC Influence Crude Oil Prices?: Testing for Co-Movements and Causality between Regional Crude Oil Prices." *Applied Economics* 39(11): 1375–85.

Bermeo, Sarah. 2018. *Targeted Development: Industrialized Country Strategy in a Globalizing World.* New York: Oxford University Press.

Bermeo, Sarah Blodgett, and David Leblang. 2015. "Migration and Foreign Aid." *International Organization* 69(03): 627–57.

Bernauer, Thomas, and Robert Gampfer. 2015. "How Robust Is Public Support for Unilateral Climate Policy?" *Environmental Science & Policy* 54: 316–30.

Bernstein, Steven, Michele Betsill, Matthew Hoffmann, and Matthew Paterson. 2010. "A Tale of Two Copenhagens: Carbon Markets and Climate Governance." *Millennium* 39(1): 161–73.

Bernstein, Steven, and Benjamin Cashore. 2012. "Complex Global Governance and Domestic Policies: Four Pathways of Influence." *International Affairs* 88(3): 585–604.

Bernstein, Steven, and Matthew Hoffmann. 2019. "Climate Politics, Metaphors and the Fractal Carbon Trap." *Nature Climate Change*: 1–7.

Bialos, Jeffrey P. 1989. "Oil Imports and National Security: The Legal and Policy Framework for Ensuring United States Access to Strategic Resources." *University of Pennsylvania Journal of International Business Law* 11: 235–300.

Blair, John Malcolm. 1976. *The Control of Oil*. New York: Pantheon.

Blair, Robert A. 2019. "International Intervention and the Rule of Law after Civil War: Evidence from Liberia." *International Organization* 73(2): 365–98.

Blair, Robert A. 2020. *Peacekeeping, Policing and the Rule of Law after Civil War*. Cambridge, UK: Cambridge University Press.

Blair, Robert A., Sabrina M. Karim, and Benjamin S. Morse. 2019. "Establishing the Rule of Law in Weak and War-Torn States: Evidence from a Field Experiment with the Liberian National Police." *American Political Science Review* 113(3): 641–57.

Blaydes, L. 2004. "Rewarding Impatience: A Bargaining and Enforcement Model of OPEC." *International Organization* 58(2): 213–37.

Blondeel, Mathieu, Jeff Colgan, and Thijs Van de Graaf. 2019. "What Drives Norm Success?: Evidence from Anti-Fossil Fuel Campaigns." *Global Environmental Politics* 19(4): 63–84.

Blyth, M. 2002. *Great Transformations: Economic Ideas and Institutional Change in the Twentieth Century*. Cambridge, UK: Cambridge University Press.

Blyth, Mark. 2013. *Austerity: The History of a Dangerous Idea*. Oxford: Oxford University Press.

Boiral, Olivier. 2007. "Corporate Greening through ISO 14001: A Rational Myth?" *Organization Science* 18(1): 127–46.

Bond, R. D. 1977. *Contemporary Venezuela and Its Role in International Affairs*. New York: New York University Press.

Bordoff, Jason, and Andrew W. Shoyer. 2008. "International Trade Law and the Economics of Climate Policy: Evaluating the Legality and Effectiveness of Proposals to Address Competitiveness and Leakage Concerns [with Comment]." *Brookings Trade Forum*: 35–68.

Börzel, Tanja A., and Thomas Risse. 2010. "Governance without a State: Can It Work?" *Regulation & Governance* 4(2): 113–34.

Borzyskowski, Inken von, and Felicity Vabulas. 2019. "Credible Commitments?: Explaining IGO Suspensions to Sanction Political Backsliding." *International Studies Quarterly* 63(1): 139–52.

Bosco, David. 2013. *Rough Justice: The International Criminal Court in a World of Power Politics*. New York: Oxford University Press.

Bourdieu, Pierre. 1984. *Distinction: A Social Critique of the Judgement of Taste*. Cambridge, MA: Harvard University Press.

Bove, Vincenzo, and Leandro Elia. 2011. "Supplying Peace: Participation in and Troop Contribution to Peacekeeping Missions." *Journal of Peace Research* 48(6): 699–714.

Brada, Josef C., Zdenek Drabek, and Ichiro Iwasaki. "Does Investor Protection Increase Foreign Direct Investment?: A Meta-Analysis." *Journal of Economic Surveys* n/a(n/a). https://onlinelibrary.wiley.com/doi/abs/10.1111/joes.12392 (November 2, 2020).

Brainard, Lael, and Isaac Sorkin, eds. 2009. *Climate Change, Trade, and Competitiveness: Is a Collision Inevitable?: Brookings Trade Forum 2008/2009*. Washington, DC: Brookings Institution Press.

Branch, Jordan. 2013. 127 *The Cartographic State: Maps, Territory, and the Origins of Sovereignty*. Cambridge University Press.

Brands, Hal. 2004. "George Bush and the Gulf War of 1991." *Presidential Studies Quarterly* 34(1): 113–31.

Brands, Hal, and Peter D. Feaver. 2016. "Should America Retrench?" *Foreign Affairs* (November/December 2016).

Brands, Hal, and David Palkki. 2012. "'Conspiring Bastards': Saddam Hussein's Strategic View of the United States." *Diplomatic History* 36(3): 625–59.

Braumoeller, Bear F. 2013. *The Great Powers and the International System: Systemic Theory in Empirical Perspective*. Cambridge and New York: Cambridge University Press.

Braumoeller, Bear F. 2019. *Only the Dead: The Persistence of War in the Modern Age*. New York: Oxford University Press.

Braut-Hegghammer, Målfrid. 2016. *Unclear Physics: Why Iraq and Libya Failed to Build Nuclear Weapons*. Ithaca: Cornell University Press.

Brémond, V., E. Hache, and V. Mignon. 2012. "Does OPEC Still Exist as a Cartel?: An Empirical Investigation." *Energy Economics* 34(1): 125–31.

Brew, Gregory. 2019. "The Collapse Narrative: The United States, Mohammed Mossadegh, and the Coup Decision of 1953." *Texas National Security Review* 2(4): 38–59.

Bronson, Rachel. 2006. *Thicker than Oil: America's Uneasy Partnership with Saudi Arabia*. New York: Oxford University Press.

Brooks, Risa A. 2008. *Shaping Strategy: The Civil-Military Politics of Strategic Assessment*. Princeton, NJ: Princeton University Press.

Brooks, Stephen, and William Wohlforth. 2016. *America Abroad: The United States' Global Role in the 21st Century*. New York: Oxford University Press.

Brown, Anthony Cave. 1999. *Oil, God, and Gold: The Story of Aramco and the Saudi Kings*. Boston: Houghton Mifflin.

Bueger, Christian. 2012. "From Epistemology to Practice: A Sociology of Science for International Relations." *Journal of International Relations and Development* 15(1): 97–109.

Brulle, Robert J., and J. Timmons Roberts. 2017. "Climate Misinformation Campaigns and Public Sociology." *Contexts* 16(1): 78–79.

Brulle, Robert J., and J. Timmons Roberts. 2021. "What Obstruction to Biden's Climate Initiative Will Look Like." *TheHill*. https://thehill.com/opinion/energy-environment/550037-what-obstruction-to-bidens-climate-initiative-will-look-like (May 13, 2021).

Bueger, Christian. 2018. "Territory, Authority, Expertise: Global Governance and the Counter-Piracy Assemblage." *European Journal of International Relations* 24(3): 614–37.

Bueno de Mesquita, Bruce, and Alastair Smith. 2016. "Competition and Collaboration in Aid-for-Policy Deals." *International Studies Quarterly* 60(3): 413–26.

Bukovansky, Mlada. 2009. *Legitimacy and Power Politics: The American and French Revolutions in International Political Culture*. Princeton, NJ: Princeton University Press.

Bulkeley, Harriet, et al. 2014. *Transnational Climate Change Governance*. Cambridge, UK: Cambridge University Press.

Bull, Hedley. 1977. *The Anarchical Society: A Study of Order in International Politics*. New York: Columbia University Press.

Burbank, Jane, and Frederick Cooper. 2010. *Empires in World History: Power and the Politics of Difference*. Princeton, NJ: Princeton University Press.

Busby, Joshua. 2018. "Warming World." *Foreign Affairs* 97(4): 49–55.

Busby, Joshua William. 2007. "Bono Made Jesse Helms Cry: Jubilee 2000, Debt Relief, and Moral Action in International Politics." *International Studies Quarterly* 51(2): 247–75.

Bush, George, and Brent Scowcroft. 1998. *A World Transformed*. New York: Knopf.

Bush, Sarah Sunn. 2015. *The Taming of Democracy Assistance*. Cambridge, UK: Cambridge University Press.

Büthe, Tim, and Walter Mattli. 2011. *The New Global Rulers: The Privatization of Regulation in the World Economy*. Princeton, NJ: Princeton University Press.

Buzan, Barry. 2004. *From International to World Society?* Cambridge and New York: Cambridge University Press.

Buzan, Barry, and George Lawson. 2015. *The Global Transformation: History, Modernity and the Making of International Relations*. Cambridge, UK: Cambridge University Press.

Byers, Michael, Kelsey Franks, and Andrew Gage. 2017. "The Internationalization of Climate Damages Litigation." *Washington Journal of Environmental Law & Policy* 7: 264.

Byman, D. L, and K. M. Pollack. 2001. "Let Us Now Praise Great Men: Bringing the Statesman Back In." *International Security* 25(4): 107–46.

Cameron, Maxwell A., Robert J. Lawson, and Brian W. Tomlin. 1998. *To Walk without Fear: The Global Movement to Ban Landmines*. Toronto: Oxford University Press.

Cammett, Melani, and Edmund Malesky. 2012. "Power Sharing in Postconflict Societies: Implications for Peace and Governance." *Journal of Conflict Resolution* 56(6): 982–1016.

Campbell, Kurt M., and Jake Sullivan. 2019. "Competition without Catastrophe." *Foreign Affairs* 98(5). https://www.foreignaffairs.com/articles/china/competition-with-china-without-catastrophe (September/October).

Cappella Zielinski, Rosella, Kaija Schilde, and Norrin Ripsman. 2020. "A Political Economy of Global Security Approach." *Journal of Global Security Studies* 6(1).

Carnegie, Allison. 2015. *Power Plays: How International Institutions Reshape Coercive Diplomacy*. New York: Cambridge University Press.

Carnegie, Allison, and Austin Carson. 2019. "The Disclosure Dilemma: Nuclear Intelligence and International Organizations." *American Journal of Political Science* 63(2): 269–85.

Carnegie, Allison, and Nikhar Gaikwad. 2017. "Public Opinion on Geopolitics and Trade: Theory and Evidence." Available at SSRN: https://ssrn.com/abstract=2909761 or http://dx.doi.org/10.2139/ssrn.2909761.

Caron, Justin, Sebastian Rausch, and Niven Winchester. 2015. "Leakage from Sub-National Climate Policy: The Case of California's Cap-and-Trade Program." *The Energy Journal* 36(2): 167–90.

Carr, Edward Hallett. 1964 [1946]. *The Twenty Years' Crisis, 1919–1939: An Introduction to the Study of International Relations*. New York: Harper Perennial.

Carson, Austin. 2018. *Secret Wars: Covert Conflict in International Politics*. Princeton, NJ: Princeton University Press.

Chalabi, Fadhil J. 2010. *Oil Policies, Oil Myths: Analysis and Memoir of an OPEC "Insider."* London: I. B.Tauris.

Chapman, Terrence L., and Stephen Chaudoin. 2013. "Ratification Patterns and the International Criminal Court." *International Studies Quarterly* 57(2): 400–9.

Chaudoin, Stephen. 2014. "Audience Features and the Strategic Timing of Trade Disputes." *International Organization* 68(4): 877–911.

Chaudoin, Stephen, Helen V. Milner, and Xun Pang. 2015. "International Systems and Domestic Politics: Linking Complex Interactions with Empirical Models in International Relations." *International Organization* 69(2): 275–309.

Chaudoin, Stephen, Helen V. Milner, and Dustin Tingley. 2017. "A Liberal International American Foreign Policy?: Maybe Down but Not Out." *H-Diplo/ISSF Policy Roundtable* 1(6).

Chenoweth, Erica, and Maria J. Stephan. 2011. *Why Civil Resistance Works: The Strategic Logic of Nonviolent Conflict*. New York: Columbia University Press.

Cherif, Reda, Fuad Hasanov, and Aditya Pande. 2017. *Riding the Energy Transition: Oil beyond 2040*. Washington, DC: International Monetary Fund.

Cherp, Aleh, et al. 2018. "Integrating Techno-Economic, Socio-Technical and Political Perspectives on National Energy Transitions: A Meta-Theoretical Framework." *Energy Research & Social Science* 37: 175–90.

Cherp, Aleh, Jessica Jewell, and Andreas Goldthau. 2011. "Governing Global Energy: Systems, Transitions, Complexity." *Global Policy* 2(1): 75–88.

Christensen, Thomas J. 2015. *The China Challenge: Shaping the Choices of a Rising Power*. New York: W. W. Norton.

Churchill, Winston S. 1923. *The World Crisis, 1911–1914*. New York: Charles Scribner's Sons.

Cirone, Alexandra E., and Johannes Urpelainen. 2013. "Trade Sanctions in International Environmental Policy: Deterring or Encouraging Free Riding?" *Conflict Management and Peace Science* 30(4): 309–34.

Ciută, Felix. 2010. "Conceptual Notes on Energy Security: Total or Banal Security?" *Security Dialogue* 41(2): 123–44.

Claes, Dag Harald. 2001. *The Politics of Oil-Producer Cooperation*. Boulder, CO: Westview Press.

Claes, Dag Harald. 2018. *The Politics of Oil: Controlling Resources, Governing Markets and Creating Political Conflicts*. Cheltenham: Edward Elgar Publishing.

Clayton, Blake, and Michael Levi. 2012. "The Surprising Sources of Oil's Influence." *Survival* 54(6): 107–22.

Cline, Howard F. 2013. *The United States and Mexico: Revised Edition*. Cambridge, MA: Harvard University Press.

Clinton, Bill. 2005. *My Life*. New York: Random House Digital, Inc.

Coe, Andrew J., and Jane Vaynman. 2015. "Collusion and the Nuclear Nonproliferation Regime." *The Journal of Politics* 77(4): 983–97.

Coggins, Bridget. 2014. *Power Politics and State Formation in the Twentieth Century: The Dynamics of Recognition*. Cambridge, UK: Cambridge University Press.

Cohen, Dara Kay. 2016. *Rape during Civil War*. Ithaca, NY: Cornell University Press.

Coleman, Katharina P. 2007. *International Organisations and Peace Enforcement: The Politics of International Legitimacy*. Cambridge, UK: Cambridge University Press.

Colgan, Jeff D. 2011. "Venezuela and Military Expenditure Data." *Journal of Peace Research* 48(4): 547–56.

Colgan, Jeff D. 2013a. "Domestic Revolutionary Leaders and International Conflict." *World Politics* 65(4): 656–90.

Colgan, Jeff D. 2013b. "Fueling the Fire: Pathways from Oil to War." *International Security* 38(2): 147–80.

Colgan, Jeff D. 2013c. "Oil, Conflict, and US National Interests." *Quarterly Journal: International Security* 4.

Colgan, Jeff D. 2013d. *Petro-Aggression: When Oil Causes War*. Cambridge, UK: Cambridge University Press.

Colgan, Jeff D. 2014. "The Emperor Has No Clothes: The Limits of OPEC in the Global Oil Market." *International Organization* 68(3): 599–632.

Colgan, Jeff D. 2015. "Oil, Domestic Conflict, and Opportunities for Democratization." *Journal of Peace Research* 52(1): 3–16.

Colgan, Jeff D. 2016. "Modern Energy and the Political Economy of Peace." Annual Meeting of the International Studies Association, Atlanta, GA.

Colgan, Jeff D. 2018. "The Market Is Valuing Climate Risk All Wrong." *Global Policy*. https://www.globalpolicyjournal.com/blog/06/07/2018/market-valuing-climate-risk-all-wrong (August 2, 2018).

Colgan, Jeff D. 2019. "American Perspectives and Blind Spots on World Politics." *Journal of Global Security Studies* 4(3): 300–9.

Colgan, Jeff D. 2020a. "Oil and Security: The Necessity of Political Economy." *Journal of Global Security Studies*, https://doi.org/10.1093/jogss/ogaa008.

Colgan, Jeff D. 2020b. "The Climate Case against Decoupling." *Foreign Affairs*. https://www.foreignaffairs.com/articles/united-states/2020-09-14/climate-case-against-decoupling (September 16, 2020).

Colgan, Jeff D., Jessica F. Green, and Thomas N. Hale. 2021. "Asset Revaluation and the Existential Politics of Climate Change." *International Organization* 75(2): 586–610.

Colgan, Jeff D., and Robert O. Keohane. 2017. "The Liberal Order Is Rigged: Fix It Now or Watch It Wither." *Foreign Affairs* 96: 36.

Colgan, Jeff D., Robert O. Keohane, and Thijs Van de Graaf. 2012. "Punctuated Equilibrium in the Energy Regime Complex." *Review of International Organizations* 7(2): 117–43.

Colgan, Jeff D., and Edward R. Lucas. 2017. "Revolutionary Pathways: Leaders and the International Impacts of Domestic Revolutions." *International Interactions* 43(3): 480–506.

Colgan, Jeff D., and Nicholas L. Miller. 2019. "Rival Hierarchies and the Origins of Nuclear Technology Sharing." *International Studies Quarterly* 63(2): 310–21.

Colgan, Jeff D., and Thijs Van de Graaf. 2015. "Mechanisms of Informal Governance: Evidence from the IEA." *Journal of International Relations and Development* 18: 455–81.

Colgan, Jeff D., and Thijs Van de Graaf. 2017. "A Crude Reversal: The Political Economy of the United States Crude Oil Export Policy." *Energy Research & Social Science* 24: 30–35.

Comin, Diego A., and Bart Hobijn. 2009. *The CHAT Dataset*. National Bureau of Economic Research. Working Paper. http://www.nber.org/papers/w15319 (August 21, 2018).

Conca, Ken, Joe Thwaites, and Goueun Lee. 2017. "Climate Change and the UN Security Council: Bully Pulpit or Bull in a China Shop?" *Global Environmental Politics* 17(2): 1–20.

Congressional Research Service. 1975. *Oil Fields as Military Objectives.* Washington, DC: United States Government Printing Office.

Conrad, Courtenay R., and Emily Hencken Ritter. 2013. "Treaties, Tenure, and Torture: The Conflicting Domestic Effects of International Law." *Journal of Politics* 75(2): 397–409.

Cooley, Alexander, and Daniel Nexon. 2020. *Exit from Hegemony: The Unraveling of the American Global Order.* New York: Oxford University Press.

Cooley, Alexander, and Jack Snyder. 2015. *Ranking the World.* Cambridge, UK: Cambridge University Press.

Cooley, Alexander, and Hendrik Spruyt. 2009. *Contracting States: Sovereign Transfers in International Relations.* Princeton, NJ: Princeton University Press.

Cooper, Frederick. 1996. *Decolonization and African Society: The Labor Question in French and British Africa.* Cambridge and New York: Cambridge University Press.

Cooper, Frederick, and Ann Laura Stoler. 1997. *Tensions of Empire: Colonial Cultures in a Bourgeois World.* Berkeley: University of California Press.

Copelovitch, Mark S. 2010. *The International Monetary Fund in the Global Economy: Banks, Bonds, and Bailouts.* Cambridge, UK: Cambridge University Press.

Cowhey, Peter F. 1985. *The Problems of Plenty: Energy Policy and International Politics.* Berkeley: University of California Press.

Cox, Robert W., and Timothy J. Sinclair. 1996. *Approaches to World Order.* Cambridge and New York: Cambridge University Press.

Crawford, Neta C. 2002. *Argument and Change in World Politics: Ethics, Decolonization, and Humanitarian Intervention.* Cambridge and New York: Cambridge University Press.

Crenshaw, Martha. 1981. "The Causes of Terrorism." *Comparative Politics* 13(4): 379–99.

Croco, Sarah E. 2015. *Peace at What Price?: Leader Culpability and the Domestic Politics of War Termination.* New York: Cambridge University Press.

Crystal, Jill. 1990. *Oil and Politics in the Gulf: Rulers and Merchants in Kuwait and Qatar.* Cambridge, UK: Cambridge University Press.

Cullenward, Danny, and David G. Victor. 2020. *Making Climate Policy Work.* Cambridge, UK: Polity Press.

Curtin, Joseph. "Climate Change Is Coming for Global Trade." *Foreign Policy.* https://foreignpolicy.com/2019/11/16/climate-change-disrupt-global-container-shipping-trade-policymakers-take-note/ (December 9, 2019).

Dafoe, Allan, Jonathan Renshon, and Paul Huth. 2014. "Reputation and Status as Motives for War." *Annual Review of Political Science* 17(1): 371–93.

Dahl, Carol, and Mine Yücel. 1991. "Testing Alternative Hypotheses of Oil Producer Behavior." *The Energy Journal* 12(4): 117–38.

Darden, K. 2009. *Economic Liberalism and Its Rivals.* Cambridge, UK: Cambridge University Press.

Dauvergne, Peter, and Kate J. Neville. 2009. "The Changing North-South and South-South Political Economy of Biofuels." *Third World Quarterly* 30(6): 1087–1102.

Davis, Christina L. 2012. *Why Adjudicate?: Enforcing Trade Rules in the WTO.* Princeton, NJ: Princeton University Press.

Dawisha, Karen, and Bruce Parrott. 1997. *The End of Empire?: The Transformation of the USSR in Comparative Perspective.* Armonk, NY: M. E. Sharpe.

De Búrca, Gráinne, Robert O. Keohane, and Charles Sabel. 2014. "Global Experimentalist Governance." *British Journal of Political Science* 44(3): 477–86.

De Onis, Juan. 1974. "A Multibillion Purchase of Treasury Issue Due." *New York Times.* http://select.nytimes.com/gst/abstract.html?res=F60F15FA3F59137B93C5A9178 2D85F408785F9 (October 6, 2009).

De Soto, Hernando. 2000. *The Mystery of Capital: Why Capitalism Triumphs in the West and Fails Everywhere Else.* New York: Basic Books.

Dean, Adam. 2016. *From Conflict to Coalition.* New York: Cambridge University Press.

Dellink, Rob, Hyunjeong Hwang, Elisa Lanzi, and Jean Chateau. 2017. "International Trade Consequences of Climate Change." Working Paper. Paris: OECD.

Demirer, R., and A. M. Kutan. 2006. "Does OPEC Matter after 9/11?: OPEC Announcements and Oil Price Stability." *Topics in Middle Eastern and African Economies* 9.

Deutch, J. M., J. R. Schlesinger, and D. G. Victor. 2006. *National Security Consequences of US Oil Dependency: Report of an Independent Task Force.* New York: Council on Foreign Relations Press.

Dietrich, Christopher R. W. 2017. *Oil Revolution.* Cambridge and New York: Cambridge University Press.

Dimitrov, Radoslav S. 2016. "The Paris Agreement on Climate Change: Behind Closed Doors." *Global Environmental Politics* 16(3): 1–11.

Donnelly, Jack. 2009. "Rethinking Political Structures: From 'Ordering Principles' to 'Vertical Differentiation'—and Beyond." *International Theory* 1(1): 49–86.

Doran, Charles F. 1977. *Myth, Oil, and Politics: Introduction to the Political Economy of Petroleum.* New York: Free Press.

Doran, Charles F. 1980. "OPEC Structure and Cohesion: Exploring the Determinants of Cartel Policy." *Journal of Politics:* 82–101.

Downie, Christian. 2019. *Business Battles in the US Energy Sector: Lessons for a Clean Energy Transition.* Abington and New York: Routledge.

Downs, G. W., D. M. Rocke, and P. N. Barsoom. 1996. "Is the Good News about Compliance Good News about Cooperation?" *International Organization* 50(3): 379–406.

Doyle, Michael W. 1986. *Empires.* Ithaca, NY: Cornell University Press.

Doyle, Michael W., and Nicholas Sambanis. 2006. *Making War and Building Peace: United Nations Peace Operations.* Princeton, NJ: Princeton University Press.

Drezner, D. W. 1999. *The Sanctions Paradox: Economic Statecraft and International Relations.* Cambridge, UK: Cambridge University Press.

Drezner, Daniel W. 2007. "The Trouble with Carrots: Transaction Costs, Conflict Expectations, and Economic Inducements." *Security Studies* 9(1–2): 188–218.

Drezner, Daniel W. 2014. *The System Worked: How the World Stopped Another Great Depression.* New York: Oxford University Press.

Drezner, Daniel W. 2019. "Can the United States Be the Global Rule-Maker Again?" *Washington Post.* https://www.washingtonpost.com/outlook/2019/11/27/can-united-states-be-global-rule-maker-again/ (December 3, 2019).

Drezner, Daniel W., and Kathleen R. McNamara. 2013. "International Political Economy, Global Financial Orders and the 2008 Financial Crisis." *Perspectives on Politics* 11(1): 155–66.

Duffield, John S. 1994. "NATO's Functions after the Cold War." *Political Science Quarterly* 109(5): 763–87.

Duffield, John S. 2007. *Over a Barrel: The Costs of U.S. Foreign Oil Dependence.* Stanford, CA: Stanford Law and Politics.

Edelstein, David M. 2017. *Over the Horizon: Time, Uncertainty, and the Rise of Great Powers.* Ithaca, NY: Cornell University Press.

Eilstrup-Sangiovanni, Mette, and Stephanie C. Hofmann. 2020. "Of the Contemporary Global Order, Crisis, and Change." *Journal of European Public Policy* 27(7): 1077–89.

Eisenhower, Dwight D. 1959. *Proclamation 3279—Adjusting Imports of Petroleum and Petroleum Products Into the United States.* https://www.presidency.ucsb.edu/documents/proclamation-3279-adjusting-imports-petroleum-and-petroleum-products-into-the-united (May 10, 2021).

El-Gamal, Mahmoud A., and Amy Myers Jaffe. 2010. *Oil, Dollars, Debt, and Crises: The Global Curse of Black Gold.* Cambridge, UK: Cambridge University Press.

Emmons, Alex. 2018. "Saudi Arabia Planned to Invade Qatar Last Summer. Rex Tillerson's Efforts to Stop It May Have Cost Him His Job." *The Intercept.* https://theintercept.com/2018/08/01/rex-tillerson-qatar-saudi-uae/ (August 2, 2018).

Everly, Steve. 2016. "The Top-Secret Cold War Plan to Keep Soviet Hands Off Middle Eastern Oil." *POLITICO Magazine.* http://politi.co/28Qu1iG (October 17, 2016).

Falkner, Robert. 2016. "A Minilateral Solution for Global Climate Change?: On Bargaining Efficiency, Club Benefits, and International Legitimacy." *Perspectives on Politics* 14(1): 87–101.

Farid, Mai, et al. 2016. "After Paris: Fiscal, Macroeconomic, and Financial Implications of Climate Change." *IMF Staff Discussion Note* 16(1).

Farrell, Henry, and Abraham L. Newman. 2010. "Making Global Markets: Historical Institutionalism in International Political Economy." *Review of International Political Economy* 17(4): 609–38.

Farrell, Henry, and Abraham L. Newman. 2015. "The New Politics of Interdependence: Cross-National Layering in Trans-Atlantic Regulatory Disputes." *Comparative Political Studies* 48(4): 497–526.

Farrell, Henry, and Abraham L. Newman. 2019. "Weaponized Interdependence: How Global Economic Networks Shape State Coercion." *International Security* 44(1): 42–79.

Farrell, Henry, and Abraham L. Newman. 2020. "The Folly of Decoupling from China." https://www.foreignaffairs.com/articles/china/2020-06-03/folly-decoupling-china (June 3, 2020).

Fattouh, Bassam, and Lavan Mahadeva. 2013. "OPEC: What Difference Has It Made?" *Annual Review of Resource Economics* 5(1): 427–43.

Fattouh, Bassam, Rahmat Poudineh, and Rob West. 2018. "The Rise of Renewables and Energy Transition: What Adaptation Strategy for Oil Companies and Oil-Exporting Countries?" Oxford Institute for Energy Studies.

Fazal, Tanisha M. 2007. *State Death: The Politics and Geography of Conquest, Occupation, and Annexation.* Princeton, NJ: Princeton University Press.

Fazal, Tanisha M., and Brooke C. Greene. 2015. "A Particular Difference: European Identity and Civilian Targeting." *British Journal of Political Science* 45(4): 829–51.

Feng, Huiyun, Kai He, and Xiaojun Li. 2019. *How China Sees the World: Insights from China's International Relations Scholars.* Singapore: Palgrave Macmillan.

Finnemore, Martha. 1993. "International Organizations as Teachers of Norms: The United Nations Educational, Scientific, and Cultural Organization and Science Policy." *International Organization* 47(4): 565–97.

Finnemore, Martha. 1996. *National Interests in International Society.* Ithaca, NY: Cornell University Press.

Finnemore, Martha. 2004. *The Purpose of Intervention: Changing Beliefs about the Use of Force.* Ithaca, NY: Cornell University Press.

Finnemore, Martha, and Michelle Jurkovich. 2020. "The Politics of Aspiration." *International Studies Quarterly* 64(4): 759–69.

Finnemore, Martha, and Kathryn Sikkink. 1998. "International Norm Dynamics and Political Change." *International Organization* 52(4): 887–917.

Fioretos, Orfeo. 2011. "Historical Institutionalism in International Relations." *International Organization* 65(2): 367–99.

Flavelle, Christopher, and Brad Plumer. 2019. "California Bans Insurers from Dropping Policies Made Riskier by Climate Change." *New York Times*. https://www.nytimes.com/2019/12/05/climate/california-fire-insurance-climate.html (December 9, 2019).

Fligstein, Neil, and Doug McAdam. 2012. *A Theory of Fields*. New York: Oxford University Press.

Flournoy, Michèle. 2020. "Treat China's Border Clash with India as a Clarion Call." *Financial Times* (June 9, 2019).

Fortna, Virginia Page. 2008. *Does Peacekeeping Work?: Shaping Belligerents' Choices after Civil War*. Princeton, NJ: Princeton University Press.

Fortna, Page. 2013. "Has Violence Declined in World Politics?" *Perspectives on Politics* 11(2): 566–70.

Fox-Penner, Peter. 2020. *Power after Carbon: Building a Clean, Resilient Grid*. Cambridge, MA: Harvard University Press.

Frankel, Jeffrey A. 2010. "Addressing the Leakage/Competitiveness Issue in Climate Change Policy Proposals." In *Climate Change, Trade, and Competitiveness: Is a Collision Inevitable?: Brookings Trade Forum 2008/2009*, edited by Lael Brainard and Isaac Sorkin, 69–91. Washington, DC: Brookings Institution Press.

Frech, H. E., and W. C. Lee. 1987. "The Welfare Cost of Rationing-by-Queuing across Markets: Theory and Estimates from the US Gasoline Crises." *Quarterly Journal of Economics* 102(1): 97.

Friedberg, Aaron L. 2011. *A Contest for Supremacy: China, America, and the Struggle for Mastery in Asia*. New York: W. W. Norton.

Frieden, Jeffry A. 1994. "International Investment and Colonial Control: A New Interpretation." *International Organization* 48(4): 559–93.

Friedman Lissner, Rebecca, and Mira Rapp-Hooper. 2018. "The Day after Trump: American Strategy for a New International Order." *Washington Quarterly* 41(1): 7–25.

FT editorial board. 2019. "How Central Banks Can Tackle Climate Change." *Financial Times*. https://www.ft.com/content/1eacda7e-fbd1-11e9-a354-36acbbb0d9b6 (December 2, 2019).

Fu, Diana. 2017. "Disguised Collective Action in China." *Comparative Political Studies* 50(4): 499–527.

Fuhrmann, Matthew. 2012. *Atomic Assistance: How "Atoms for Peace" Programs Cause Nuclear Insecurity*. Ithaca: Cornell University Press.

Fuhrmann, Matthew. 2020. "When Do Leaders Free-Ride?: Business Experience and Contributions to Collective Defense." *American Journal of Political Science* 64(2): 416–31.

Fung, Courtney J. 2019. *China and Intervention at the UN Security Council: Reconciling Status*. Oxford and New York: Oxford University Press.

Gallagher, John, and Ronald Robinson. 1953. "The Imperialism of Free Trade." *Economic History Review* 6(1): 1–15.

Gallagher, Kelly Sims, and Xiaowei Xuan. 2019. *Titans of the Climate: Explaining Policy Process in the United States and China*. Cambridge, MA: MIT Press.

Gallagher, Kevin P. 2015. *Ruling Capital: Emerging Markets and the Reregulation of Cross-Border Finance*. Ithaca, NY: Cornell University Press.

Gamson, William A. 1975. *The Strategy of Social Protest*. Homewood, IL: Dorsey Press.

Garavini, Giuliano. 2019. *The Rise and Fall of OPEC in the Twentieth Century*. Oxford and New York: Oxford University Press.

Gartzke, E., and D. J. Jo. 2009. "Bargaining, Nuclear Proliferation, and Interstate Disputes." *Journal of Conflict Resolution* 53(2): 209.

Gartzke, Erik, and Jon R. Lindsay. 2015. "Weaving Tangled Webs: Offense, Defense, and Deception in Cyberspace." *Security Studies* 24(2): 316–48.

Gartzke, Erik, and Dominic Rohner. 2011. "The Political Economy of Imperialism, Decolonization and Development." *British Journal of Political Science* 41(3): 525–56.

"Gauging the Iraqi Threat to Kuwait in the 1960s—Central Intelligence Agency." https://www.cia.gov/library/center-for-the-study-of-intelligence/csi-publications/csi-studies/studies/fall_winter_2001/article03.html (February 7, 2019).

Gause, F. Gregory, III. 2009. *The International Relations of the Persian Gulf*. Cambridge, UK: Cambridge University Press.

Gavin, Francis J. 2015. "Strategies of Inhibition: US Grand Strategy, the Nuclear Revolution, and Nonproliferation." *International Security* 40(1): 9–46.

Geels, Frank W., Benjamin K. Sovacool, Tim Schwanen, and Steve Sorrell. 2017. "Sociotechnical Transitions for Deep Decarbonization." *Science* 357(6357): 1242–44.

Gendzier, Irene L. 2015. *Dying to Forget: Oil, Power, Palestine, and the Foundations of US Policy in the Middle East*. New York: Columbia University Press.

Gerring, John. 2012. "Mere Description." *British Journal of Political Science* 42(4): 721–46.

Getachew, Adom. 2019. *Worldmaking after Empire: The Rise and Fall of Self-Determination*. Princeton, NJ: Princeton University Press.

Gewirtz, Julian. 2020. "The Chinese Reassessment of Interdependence." *China Leadership Monitor*. https://www.prcleader.org/gewirtz (June 1, 2020).

Ghadar, Fariborz. 1977. *The Evolution of OPEC Strategy*. Lexington, MA: Lexington Books.

Ghanem, Shukri M. 1986. *OPEC: The Rise and Fall of an Exclusive Club*. New York: Routledge.

Gheorghe, Eliza. 2019. "Proliferation and the Logic of the Nuclear Market." *International Security* 43(4): 88–127.

Gholz, Eugene, and Daryl Press. 2010a. "Footprints in the Sand." *American Interest* 5(4): 59–67.

Gholz, Eugene, and Daryl Press. 2010b. "Protecting 'The Prize': Oil and the US National Interest." *Security Studies* 19(3): 453–85.

Gilady, Lilach. 2018. *The Price of Prestige: Conspicuous Consumption in International Relations*. Chicago: University of Chicago Press.

Gilpin, Robert. 1975. *US Power and the Multinational Corporation*. New York: Basic Books.

Gilpin, Robert. 1981. *War and Change in World Politics*. Cambridge, UK: Cambridge University Press.

Glaser, Charles L. 2010. *Rational Theory of International Politics: The Logic of Competition and Cooperation*. Princeton, NJ: Princeton University Press.

Glaser, Charles L. 2019. "A Flawed Framework: Why the Liberal International Order Concept Is Misguided." *International Security* 43(4): 51–87.

Glaser, Charles L., and Rosemary Ann Kelanic, eds. 2016. *Crude Strategy: Rethinking the US Military Commitment to Defend Persian Gulf Oil*. Washington, DC: Georgetown University Press.

Global Climate Action from Cities, Regions and Businesses—2019. 2019. New Climate Institute. https://newclimate.org/2019/09/18/global-climate-action-from-cities-regions-and-businesses-2019/ (November 6, 2019).

Go, Julian. 2012. *Patterns of Empire: The British and American Empires, 1688 to the Present*. Illustrated edition. New York: Cambridge University Press.

Goddard, Stacie E. 2018. *When Right Makes Might: Rising Powers and World Order*. Ithaca, NY: Cornell University Press.

Goh, Evelyn. 2013. *The Struggle for Order: Hegemony, Hierarchy, and Transition in Post-Cold War East Asia*. Oxford: Oxford University Press.

Goh, Evelyn. 2019. "Contesting Hegemonic Order: China in East Asia." *Security Studies* 28(3): 614–44.

Goldgeier, James. 2018. "The Misunderstood Roots of International Order—And Why They Matter Again." *The Washington Quarterly* 41(3): 7–20.

Goldsmith, Benjamin E., and Baogang He. 2008. "Letting Go without a Fight: Decolonization, Democracy and War, 1900–94." *Journal of Peace Research* 45(5): 587–611.

Goldstein, J. L., D. Rivers, and M. Tomz. 2007. "Institutions in International Relations: Understanding the Effects of the GATT and the WTO on World Trade." *International Organization* 61(1): 37–67.

Goldstein, Judith, and Robert O. Keohane, eds. 1993. *Ideas and Foreign Policy: Beliefs, Institutions, and Political Change*. Ithaca, NY: Cornell University Press.

Goldstein, Judith, and Lisa L. Martin. 2000. "Legalization, Trade Liberalization, and Domestic Politics: A Cautionary Note." *International Organization* 54(3): 603–32.

Goldsworthy, D. 1994. *The Conservative Government and the End of Empire 1951–1957: Part I*. London: HM Stationery Office.

Goldthau, Andreas, and Nick Sitter. 2015. *A Liberal Actor in a Realist World: The European Union Regulatory State and the Global Political Economy of Energy*. Oxford: Oxford University Press.

Goldthau, Andreas, and Kirsten Westphal. 2019. "Why the Global Energy Transition Does Not Mean the End of the Petrostate." *Global Policy* 10(2): 279–83.

Goldthau, Andreas, and Jan Martin Witte. 2009. *Global Energy Governance: The New Rules of the Game*. Washington, DC: Brookings Institution Press.

Goldthau, Andreas, and Jan Martin Witte. 2011. "Assessing OPEC's Performance in Global Energy." *Global Policy* 2: 31–39.

Golombek, Rolf, Alfonso A. Irarrazabal, and Lin Ma. 2018. "OPEC's Market Power: An Empirical Dominant Firm Model for the Oil Market." *Energy Economics* 70: 98–115.

Gómez-Mera, Laura. 2015. "International Regime Complexity and Regional Governance: Evidence from the Americas." *Global Governance*: 19–42.

Goralski, Robert, and Russell W. Freeburg. 1987. *Oil & War: How the Deadly Struggle for Fuel in WWII Meant Victory or Defeat*. New York: William Morrow.

Gowa, Joanne. 1988. "Public Goods and Political Institutions: Trade and Monetary Policy Processes in the United States." *International Organization* 42(1): 15–32.

Graaff, Naná de. 2012. "Oil Elite Networks in a Transforming Global Oil Market." *International Journal of Comparative Sociology* 53(4): 275–97.

Grabel, Ilene J. 2017. *When Things Don't Fall Apart: Productive Incoherence and the New Development Finance*. Cambridge, MA: MIT Press.

Graham, Erin R., and Alexandria Serdaru. 2020. "Power, Control, and the Logic of Substitution in Institutional Design: The Case of International Climate Finance." *International Organization*: 1–36.

Gray, Julia. 2018. "Life, Death, or Zombie?: The Vitality of International Organizations." *International Studies Quarterly* 62(1): 1–13.

Green, Brendan Rittenhouse. 2020. *The Revolution That Failed: Nuclear Competition, Arms Control, and the Cold War*. Cambridge, United Kingdom; New York, NY: Cambridge University Press.

Green, Jessica F. 2013. *Rethinking Private Authority: Agents and Entrepreneurs in Global Environmental Governance*. Princeton, NJ: Princeton University Press.

Green, Jessica F. 2017. "The Strength of Weakness: Pseudo-Clubs in the Climate Regime." *Climatic Change* 144(1): 41–52.

Green, Jessica F. 2021. "Does Carbon Pricing Reduce Emissions? A Review of Ex-Post Analyses." *Environmental Research Letters* 16(4).

Green, Jessica F., and Jeff Colgan. 2013. "Protecting Sovereignty, Protecting the Planet: State Delegation to International Organizations and Private Actors in Environmental Politics." *Governance* 26(3): 473–97.

Griffin, J. M. 1985. "OPEC Behavior: A Test of Alternative Hypotheses." *American Economic Review* 75(5): 954–63.

Gruber, Lloyd. 2000. *Ruling the World*. Princeton, NJ: Princeton University Press.

Gulen, G. 1996. "Is OPEC a Cartel? Evidence from Cointegration and Causality Tests." *Energy Journal* 17: 43–58.

Gunitsky, Seva. 2013. "Complexity and Theories of Change in International Politics." *IT* 5: 35.

Gunitsky, Seva. 2017. *Aftershocks: Great Powers and Domestic Reforms in the Twentieth Century*. Princeton, NJ: Princeton University Press.

Gutner, Tamar, and Alexander Thompson. 2010. "The Politics of IO Performance: A Framework." *Review of International Organizations* 5(3): 227–48.

Haas, M. L. 2005. *The Ideological Origins of Great Power Politics, 1789–1989*. Ithaca, NY: Cornell University Press.

Haass, Felix, and Nadine Ansorg. 2018. "Better Peacekeepers, Better Protection?: Troop Quality of United Nations Peace Operations and Violence against Civilians." *Journal of Peace Research* 55(6): 742–58.

Haass, Richard N. 2018. "Liberal World Order, R.I.P." *Project Syndicate*. https://www.project-syndicate.org/commentary/end-of-liberal-world-order-by-richard-n--haass-2018-03 (July 3, 2020).

Hadden, Jennifer. 2015. *Networks in Contention: The Divisive Politics of Climate Change*. New York: Cambridge University Press.

Hafner-Burton, Emilie M. 2008. "Sticks and Stones: Naming and Shaming the Human Rights Enforcement Problem." *International Organization* 62(4): 689–716.

Hale, Thomas, David Held, and Kevin Young. 2013. *Gridlock: Why Global Cooperation Is Failing When We Need It Most*. Cambridge UK: Polity.

Hampson, Fen, and Paul Heinbecker. 2010. *Canada among Nations, 2009–2010: As Others See Us*. Montreal: McGill–Queen's Press.

Hancock, Kathleen J., and Vlado Vivoda. 2014. "International Political Economy: A Field Born of the OPEC Crisis Returns to Its Energy Roots." *Energy Research & Social Science* 1: 206–16.

Hang, Angel. 2019. "Already Cheaper than Gas, China's Renewables to Undercut Coal by 2026." *Green Tech Media*. https://www.greentechmedia.com/articles/read/chinas-renewables-cost-to-fall-below-coal-power-by-2026 (June 9, 2020).

Harrison, Kathryn, and Lisa McIntosh Sundstrom. 2007. "The Comparative Politics of Climate Change." *Global Environmental Politics* 7(4): 1–18.

Hayes, Jarrod, and Janelle Knox-Hayes. 2014. "Security in Climate Change Discourse: Analyzing the Divergence between US and EU Approaches to Policy." *Global Environmental Politics* 14(2): 82–101.

Hecht, Gabrielle. 2006. "Negotiating Global Nuclearities: Apartheid, Decolonization, and the Cold War in the Making of the IAEA." *Osiris* 21(1): 25–48.

Hegghammer, Thomas. 2010. *Jihad in Saudi Arabia: Violence and Pan-Islamism since 1979*. New York: Cambridge University Press.

Helleiner, Eric. 2014. *The Status Quo Crisis: Global Financial Governance after the 2008 Meltdown*. Oxford and New York: Oxford University Press.

Helveston, John, and Jonas Nahm. 2019. "China's Key Role in Scaling Low-Carbon Energy Technologies." *Science* 366(6467): 794–96.

Henderson, Errol A. 2009. "Disturbing the Peace: African Warfare, Political Inversion and the Universality of the Democratic Peace Thesis." *British Journal of Political Science*: 25–58.

Henderson, Errol A. 2013. "Hidden in Plain Sight: Racism in International Relations Theory." *Cambridge Review of International Affairs* 26(1): 71–92.

Henderson, Errol A., and J. David Singer. 2000. "Civil War in the Post-Colonial World, 1946–92." *Journal of Peace Research* 37(3): 275–99.

Hendrix, Cullen S. 2017. "Oil Prices and Interstate Conflict." *Conflict Management and Peace Science* 34(6): 575–96.

Hendrix, Cullen S., and Wendy H. Wong. 2013. "When Is the Pen Truly Mighty?: Regime Type and the Efficacy of Naming and Shaming in Curbing Human Rights Abuses." *British Journal of Political Science* 43(3): 651–72.

Henke, Marina E. 2019. *Constructing Allied Cooperation: Diplomacy, Payments, and Power in Multilateral Military Coalitions*. Ithaca, NY: Cornell University Press.

Henning, C. Randall. 2019. "Regime Complexity and the Institutions of Crisis and Development Finance." *Development and Change* 50(1): 24–45.

Henning, C. Randall, and Tyler Pratt. 2020. "Hierarchy and Differentiation in International Regime Complexes: A Theoretical Framework for Comparative Research."

Hertog, Steffen. 2010. *Princes, Brokers, and Bureaucrats*. Ithaca, NY: Cornell University Press.

Hill, Alice, and Leonardo Martinez-Diaz. 2020. "Adapt or Perish." *Foreign Affairs* 99(1): 107–17.

Hobson, John M., and George Lawson. 2008. "What Is History in International Relations?" *Millennium* 37(2): 415–35.

Hoffmann, Matthew J. 2020. "Why Climate Action Gets Stuck and What to Do about It." https://www.ted.com/talks/matthew_hoffmann_why_climate_action_gets_stuck_and_what_to_do_about_it?language=en (October 12, 2020).

Hooghe, Liesbet, and Gary Marks. 2003. "Unraveling the Central State, but How?: Types of Multi-Level Governance." *American Political Science Review* 97(2): 233–43.

Hook, Leslie, and Gillian Tett. 2019. "Hedge Fund TCI Vows to Punish Directors over Climate Change." *Financial Times*: 2.

Horowitz, Michael C., Sarah E. Kreps, and Matthew Fuhrmann. 2016. "Separating Fact from Fiction in the Debate over Drone Proliferation." *International Security* 41(2): 7–42.

Horowitz, Michael C., Allan C. Stam, and Cali M. Ellis. 2015. *Why Leaders Fight*. New York: Cambridge University Press.

Hough, Richard, and Denis Richards. 1989. *The Battle of Britain: The Jubilee History*. London: Hodder and Stoughton.

Hovi, Jon, Detlef F. Sprinz, Håkon Sælen, and Arild Underdal. 2016. "Climate Change Mitigation: A Role for Climate Clubs?" *Palgrave Communications* 2(1): 1–9.

Howard, Lise Morjé. 2019. *Power in Peacekeeping*. Cambridge, UK: Cambridge University Press.

Hudson, Valerie M. 2007. *Foreign Policy Analysis: Classic and Contemporary Theory*. Lanham, MD: Rowman & Littlefield.

Hufbauer, Gary Clyde, Jeffrey J. Schott, and Kimberly Ann Elliott. 2007. *Economic Sanctions Reconsidered*. Washington, DC: Peterson Institute.

Huff, Connor, and Joshua D. Kertzer. 2018. "How the Public Defines Terrorism." *American Journal of Political Science* 62(1): 55–71.

Hughes, Llewelyn. 2014. *Globalizing Oil*. Cambridge, UK: Cambridge University Press.

Hughes, Llewelyn, and Phillip Y. Lipscy. 2013. "The Politics of Energy." *Annual Review of Political Science* 16(1).

Hughes, Llewelyn, and Austin Long. 2014. "Is There an Oil Weapon?: Security Implications of Changes in the Structure of the International Oil Market." *International Security* 39(3): 152–89.

Hurd, Ian. 1999. "Legitimacy and Authority in International Politics." *International Organization* 53(02): 379–408.

Hurrell, Andrew. 2007. *On Global Order: Power, Values, and the Constitution of International Society*. Oxford University Press.

Hyam, Ronald, and William Roger Louis. 2000. *The Conservative Government and the End of Empire 1957–1964: Part I*. London: Stationery Office Books.

Hyde, Susan D. 2015. *The Pseudo-Democrat's Dilemma: Why Election Observation Became an International Norm*. Ithaca, NY: Cornell University Press.

Hyndman, K. 2008. "Disagreement in Bargaining: An Empirical Analysis of OPEC." *International Journal of Industrial Organization* 26(3): 811–28.

Ikenberry, G. John. 2000. *After Victory: Institutions, Strategic Restraint, and the Rebuilding of Order after Major Wars*. Princeton, NJ: Princeton University Press.

Ikenberry, G. John. 2018. "The End of Liberal International Order?" *International Affairs* 94(1): 7–23.

Ikenberry, G. John. 2020. *A World Safe for Democracy: Liberal Internationalism and the Crises of Global Order*. New Haven: Yale University Press.

Ikenberry, G. John, and Daniel H. Nexon. 2019. "Hegemony Studies 3.0: The Dynamics of Hegemonic Orders." *Security Studies* 28(3): 395–421.

Ikenberry, G. J. 1988. *Reasons of State: Oil Politics and the Capacities of American Government*. Ithaca, NY: Cornell University Press Ithaca.

International Renewable Energy Agency (IRENA). 2019. *A New World: The Geopolitics of the Energy Transformation*. Masdar City, UAE: IRENA.

"Iran Takes Credit for OPEC Decisions." 2011. *UPI.com*. http://www.upi.com/Business_News/Energy-Resources/2011/06/13/Iran-takes-credit-for-OPEC-decisions/UPI-13161307967060/ (November 6, 2011).

Jaffe, Amy Myers. 2018. "Green Giant." *Foreign Affairs* (March/April 2018). https://www.foreignaffairs.com/articles/china/2018-02-13/green-giant (November 26, 2018).

Jaffe, Amy Myers, and Ed Morse. 2013. "The End of OPEC." *Foreign Policy* (October 16).

Jamal, Amaney A. 2012. *Of Empires and Citizens: Pro-American Democracy or No Democracy at All?* Princeton, NJ: Princeton University Press.

Javeline, Debra. 2014. "The Most Important Topic Political Scientists Are Not Studying: Adapting to Climate Change." *Perspectives on Politics* 12(2): 420–34.

Javeline, Debra, and Tracy Kijewski-Correa. 2018. "Coastal Homeowners in a Changing Climate." *Climatic Change*. https://doi.org/10.1007/s10584-018-2257-4 (November 27, 2018).

Javeline, Debra, Tracy Kijewski-Correa, and Angela Chesler. 2019. "Does It Matter If You 'Believe' in Climate Change?: Not for Coastal Home Vulnerability." *Climatic Change* 155(4): 511–32.

Jentleson, Bruce W. 2018. "The Liberal Order Isn't Coming Back: What Next?" *Democracy* (48). https://democracyjournal.org/magazine/48/the-liberal-order-isnt-coming-back-what-next/ (March 4, 2019).

Jervis, Robert. 1976. *Perception and Misperception in International Politics*. Princeton, NJ: Princeton University Press.

Jervis, Robert. 1989. *The Meaning of the Nuclear Revolution: Statecraft and the Prospect of Armageddon*. Cornell University Press.

Jervis, Robert. 1997. *System Effects: Complexity in Political and Social Life*. Princeton, NJ: Princeton University Press.

Jinnah, Sikina. 2011. "Strategic Linkages: The Evolving Role of Trade Agreements in Global Environmental Governance." *Journal of Environment & Development* 20(2): 191–215.

Jinnah, Sikina. 2014. *Post-Treaty Politics: Secretariat Influence in Global Environmental Governance*. Cambridge, MA: MIT Press.

Jinnah, Sikina, Simon Nicholson, and Jane Flegal. 2018. "Toward Legitimate Governance of Solar Geoengineering Research: A Role for Sub-State Actors." *Ethics, Policy & Environment* 21(3): 362–81.

Jo, Hyeran, and Beth A. Simmons. 2016. "Can the International Criminal Court Deter Atrocity?" *International Organization* 70(3): 443–75.

Jones, Bart. 2008. *Hugo!: The Hugo Chavez Story from Mud Hut to Perpetual Revolution*. Hanover, NH: Steerforth.

Jones, Bruce D., Carlos Pascual, and Stephen John Stedman. 2009. *Power and Responsibility: Building International Order in an Era of Transnational Threats*. Washington, DC: Brookings Institution Press.

Jost, Tyler. Forthcoming. *Decision by Design: National Security Institutions and Interstate Politics*.

Kahler, Miles. 1984. *Decolonization in Britain and France*. Princeton, NJ: Princeton University Press.

Kalicki, Jan H., and David L. Goldwyn. 2005. *Energy and Security: Toward a New Foreign Policy Strategy*. Washington, DC: Woodrow Wilson Center Press.

Kalyanpur, Nikhil, and Abraham L. Newman. 2019. "Mobilizing Market Power: Jurisdictional Expansion as Economic Statecraft." *International Organization* 73(1): 1–34.

Kang, David C. 2010. "Hierarchy and Legitimacy in International Systems: The Tribute System in Early Modern East Asia." *Security Studies* 19(4): 591–622.

Karim, Sabrina, and Kyle Beardsley. 2017. *Equal Opportunity Peacekeeping: Women, Peace, and Security in Post-Conflict States*. New York: Oxford University Press.

Karl, Terry Lynn. 1997. *The Paradox of Plenty*. Berkeley: University of California.

Kastner, Scott L., Margaret M. Pearson, and Chad Rector. 2018. *China's Strategic Multilateralism: Investing in Global Governance*. New York: Cambridge University Press.

Katzenstein, J., and Lucia Seybert, eds. 2018. *Protean Power: Exploring the Uncertain and Unexpected in World Politics*. Cambridge, UK: Cambridge University Press.

Katzenstein, Peter J., ed. 1996. *The Culture of National Security: Norms and Identity in World Politics*. New York: Columbia University Press.

Kaufmann, R. K., et al. 2008. "Determinants of OPEC Production: Implications for OPEC Behavior." *Energy Economics* 30(2): 333–51.

Keck, Margaret E., and Kathryn Sikkink. 1998. *Activists beyond Borders: Advocacy Networks in International Politics*. Ithaca, NY: Cornell University Press.

Kelanic, Rosemary A. 2016. "The Petroleum Paradox: Oil, Coercive Vulnerability, and Great Power Behavior." *Security Studies* 25(2): 181–213.

Kelanic, Rosemary Ann. 2020. *Black Gold and Blackmail: Oil and Great Power Politics*. Ithaca, NY: Cornell University Press.

Kelley, Judith G., and Beth A. Simmons. 2015. "Politics by Number: Indicators as Social Pressure in International Relations." *American Journal of Political Science* 59(1): 55–70.

Kemp, Geoffrey. 2010. *The East Moves West: India, China, and Asia's Growing Presence in the Middle East*. 2nd ed. Washington, DC: Brookings Institution Press.

Kennard, Amanda. 2020. "The Enemy of My Enemy: When Firms Support Climate Change Regulation." *International Organization* 74(2): 187–221.

Kennedy, Paul. 1987. *The Rise and Fall of the Great Powers: Economic and Military Conflict from 1500 to 2000*. New York: Random House.

Keohane, Robert, and Helen Milner. 1996. *Internationalisation and Domestic Politics*. Cambridge, UK: Cambridge University Press.

Keohane, Robert O. 1984. *After Hegemony: Cooperation and Discord in the World Political Economy*. Princeton, NJ: Princeton University Press.

Keohane, Robert O., and Lisa L. Martin. 1995. "The Promise of Institutionalist Theory." *International Security* 20(1): 39–51.

Keohane, Robert O., and Joseph S. Nye. 1972. *Transnational Relations and World Politics*. Cambridge, MA: Harvard University Press.

Keohane, Robert O., and Joseph S. Nye. 1977. *Power and Independence*. Boston: Little Brown.

Keohane, Robert O., and David G. Victor. 2011. "The Regime Complex for Climate Change." *Perspectives on Politics* 9(1): 7–23.

Kern, Florian, and Karoline S. Rogge. 2016. "The Pace of Governed Energy Transitions: Agency, International Dynamics and the Global Paris Agreement Accelerating Decarbonisation Processes?" *Energy Research & Social Science* 22: 13–17.

Kertzer, Joshua D., and Brian C. Rathbun. 2015. "Fair Is Fair: Social Preferences and Reciprocity in International Politics." *World Politics* 67(4): 613–55.

Kim, Inwook. 2019. "A Crude Bargain: Great Powers, Oil States, and Petro-Alignment." *Security Studies* 28(5): 833–69.

Kim, Inwook, and Jackson Woods. 2016. "Gas on the Fire: Great Power Alliances and Petrostate Aggression." *International Studies Perspectives* 17(3): 231–49.

Kindleberger, Charles Poor. 1986. *The World in Depression, 1929–1939*. Berkeley, CA: University of California Press.

King, Charles. 2012. "Can There Be a Political Science of the Holocaust?" *Perspectives on Politics* 10(2): 323–41.

King, Gary, Robert O. Keohane, and Sidney Verba. 1994. *Designing Social Inquiry.* Princeton, NJ: Princeton University Press.

Kissinger, Henry. 2000. *Years of Renewal.* New York: Simon & Schuster.

Kissinger, Henry. 2015. *World Order.* New York: Penguin Books.

Klapp, Merrie Gilbert. 1987. *The Sovereign Entrepreneur: Oil Policies in Advanced and Less Developed Capitalist Countries.* Ithaca, NY: Cornell University Press.

Kleine, Mareike. 2013. *Informal Governance in the European Union: How Governments Make International Organizations Work.* Ithaca, NY: Cornell University Press.

Kohl, W. L. 2002. "OPEC Behavior, 1998–2001." *Quarterly Review of Economics and Finance* 42(2): 209–33.

Koremenos, Barbara, Charles Lipson, and Duncan Snidal. 2001. "Rational Design: Looking Back to Move Forward." *International Organization* 55(4): 1051–82.

Koubi, Vally, Tobias Böhmelt, Gabriele Spilker, and Lena Schaffer. 2018. "The Determinants of Environmental Migrants' Conflict Perception." *International Organization* 72(4): 905–36.

Krasner, Stephen D. 1974. "Oil Is the Exception." *Foreign Policy* (14): 68–84.

Krasner, Stephen D. 1978. *Defending the National Interest: Raw Materials Investments and U.S. Foreign Policy.* Princeton, NJ: Princeton University Press.

Krasner, Stephen D. 1983. *International Regimes.* Ithaca, NY: Cornell University Press.

Krasner, Stephen D. 1985. *Structural Conflict: The Third World Against Global Liberalism.* Berkeley: University of California Press.

Krasner, Stephen D. 1991. "Global Communications and National Power: Life on the Pareto Frontier." *World Politics* 43(3): 336–66.

Kratochwil, Friedrich, and John Gerard Ruggie. 1986. "International Organization: A State of the Art on an Art of the State." *International Organization* 40(4): 753–75.

Krauss, Clifford. 2011. "Mahmoud Ahmadinejad of Iran to Be Chairman at Next OPEC Meeting." *New York Times.* http://www.nytimes.com/2011/05/20/world/middleeast/20iran.html (November 6, 2011).

Kreps, Sarah E. 2011. *Coalitions of Convenience: United States Military Interventions after the Cold War.* New York: Oxford University Press.

Kring, William N. 2019. "Contesting the International Monetary Fund? Regional Battles for Global Liquidity." PhD diss., Brown University.

Kuhn, T. S. 1970. *The Structure of Scientific Revolutions.* 2nd ed. Chicago: University of Chicago Press.

Kuperman, Alan J. 2013. "A Model Humanitarian Intervention?: Reassessing NATO's Libya Campaign." *International Security* 38(1): 105–36.

Kurtz, Josh. 2012. "'Drill, Baby, Drill!' Almost Didn't Happen." *E&E News.* https://www.eenews.net/stories/1059969331 (July 3, 2020).

Kydd, Andrew H., and Barbara F. Walter. 2006. "The Strategies of Terrorism." *International Security* 31(1): 49–80.

Kyle, Jordan. 2014. "What Can We Learn from Oil Contracts?: Clarifying the Links between Transparency and Accountability." In *Transparency Governance in the Age of Abundance,* eds. Malaika Masson and Juan Cruz Vieyra. Washington, DC: Inter-American Development Bank.

Lakatos, Imre. 1976. "Falsification and the Methodology of Scientific Research Programmes." In *Can Theories Be Refuted?,* edited by S. G. Harding. Dordrecht: D.

Reidel. Available at http://link.springer.com/chapter/10.1007/978-94-010-1863-0_14 (April 30, 2015).

Lake, D. A. 2010. "Two Cheers for Bargaining Theory: Assessing Rationalist Explanations of the Iraq War." *International Security* 35(3): 7–52.

Lake, David A. 2009. "Open Economy Politics: A Critical Review." *Review of International Organizations* 4(3): 219–44.

Lake, David A. 2011. *Hierarchy in International Relations.* Ithaca, NY: Cornell University Press.

Lake, David A., Lisa L. Martin, and Thomas Risse. 2021. "Challenges to the Liberal Order: Reflections on International Organization." *International Organization* 75(2): 225–57.

Lake, David A., and Robert Powell. 1999. *Strategic Choice and International Relations.* Princeton, NJ: Princeton University Press.

Lake, Milli. 2014. "Organizing Hypocrisy: Providing Legal Accountability for Human Rights Violations in Areas of Limited Statehood." *International Studies Quarterly* 58(3): 515–26.

Lascurettes, Kyle. 2020. *Orders of Exclusion: Great Powers and the Strategic Sources of Foundational Rules in International Relations.* Oxford and New York: Oxford University Press.

Lawrence, Adria. 2013. *Imperial Rule and the Politics of Nationalism: Anti-Colonial Protest in the French Empire.* Cambridge, UK: Cambridge University Press.

Lawson, Fred H. 1989. "The Iranian Crisis of 1945–1946 and the Spiral Model of International Conflict." *International Journal of Middle East Studies* 21(3): 307–26.

Lawson, George. 2006. "The Promise of Historical Sociology in International Relations." *International Studies Review* 8(3): 397–423.

Layne, Christopher. 2007. *The Peace of Illusions: American Grand Strategy from 1940 to the Present.* Ithaca, NY: Cornell University Press.

Le Billon, Philippe. 2012. *Wars of Plunder: Conflicts, Profits and the Politics of Resources.* Columbia University Press New York.

Lee, Chia-yi. 2016. "Oil and Terrorism Uncovering the Mechanisms." *Journal of Conflict Resolution* 62(5).

Legro, Jeffrey. 1995. *Cooperation under Fire: Anglo-German Restraint during World War II.* Ithaca, NY: Cornell University Press.

Lenczowski, George. 1990. *American Presidents and the Middle East.* Durham, NC: Duke University Press.

Levi, Michael. 2013. *The Power Surge: Energy, Opportunity, and the Battle for America's Future.* New York: Oxford University Press.

Lewis, Joanna I. 2014. "The Rise of Renewable Energy Protectionism: Emerging Trade Conflicts and Implications for Low Carbon Development." *Global Environmental Politics* 14(4): 10–35.

Lieber, Keir A., and Daryl G. Press. 2020. *The Myth of the Nuclear Revolution: Power Politics in the Atomic Age.* Ithaca, NY: Cornell University Press.

Lieber, Robert J. 1992. "Oil and Power after the Gulf War." *International Security* 17(1): 155–76.

Lightfoot, Sheryl. 2016. *Global Indigenous Politics: A Subtle Revolution.* Abington: Routledge.

Lin, Jintai, et al. 2014. "China's International Trade and Air Pollution in the United States." *Proceedings of the National Academy of Sciences* 111(5): 1736–41.

Lind, Jennifer, and Daryl G. Press. 2018. "Markets or Mercantilism?: How China Secures Its Energy Supplies." *International Security* 42(4): 170–204.

Liou, Yu-Ming, and Paul Musgrave. 2013. "Refining the Oil Curse Country-Level Evidence from Exogenous Variations in Resource Income." *Comparative Political Studies* 47(11): 1584–1610.

Lipscy, Phillip Y. 2017. *Renegotiating the World Order: Institutional Change in International Relations.* Cambridge, UK: Cambridge University Press.

Lobell, Steven E., Norrin M. Ripsman, and Jeffrey W. Taliaferro. 2009. *Neoclassical Realism, the State, and Foreign Policy.* Cambridge, UK: Cambridge University Press.

Lujala, Päivi, and Siri Aas Rustad. 2012. *High-Value Natural Resources and Post-Conflict Peacebuilding.* Abington and New York: Routledge.

Luong, Pauline Jones, and Erika Weinthal. 2010. *Oil Is Not a Curse: Ownership Structure and Institutions in Soviet Successor States.* New York: Cambridge University Press.

Lutz, Catherine. 2009. *The Bases of Empire: The Global Struggle against US Military Posts.* New York: New York University Press.

Mahdavi, Paasha. 2020. *Power Grab: Political Survival through Extractive Resource Nationalization.* Cambridge and New York: Cambridge University Press.

Mahoney, James. 2000. "Path Dependence in Historical Sociology." *Theory and Society* 29(4): 507–48.

Mankiw, N. Gregory. 2011. *Principles of Economics.* Boston: Cengage Learning.

Mansfield, Edward, and Nita Rudra. 2020. "Embedded Liberalism in the Digital Era." *International Organization.* Available at SSRN: https://ssrn.com/abstract=3719975 or http://dx.doi.org/10.2139/ssrn.3719975.

Marcel, Valerie. 2006. *Oil Titans: National Oil Companies in the Middle East.* Baltimore and London: Brookings Institution Press and Chatham House.

Markowitz, Jonathan. 2014. "When and Why States Project Power." PhD thesis, University of California–San Diego.

Markowitz, Jonathan N. 2020. *Perils of Plenty: Arctic Resource Competition and the Return of the Great Game.* New York: Oxford University Press.

Martin, L. L., and B. A. Simmons. 1998. "Theories and Empirical Studies of International Institutions." *International Organization* 52(4): 729–57.

Martin, Lisa L. 1992. "Interests, Power, and Multilateralism." *International Organization* 46(4): 765–92.

Martin, Lisa L. 1993. *Coercive Cooperation: Explaining Multilateral Economic Sanctions.* Princeton, NJ: Princeton University Press.

Matanock, Aila M. 2017. "Bullets for Ballots: Electoral Participation Provisions and Enduring Peace after Civil Conflict." *International Security.* Available at SSRN: https://ssrn.com/abstract=2927319 or http://dx.doi.org/10.2139/ssrn.2927319.

Mathys, Nicole A., and Jaime de Melo. 2011. "Political Economy Aspects of Climate Change Mitigation Efforts." *The World Economy* 34(11): 1938–54.

Mattern, Janice Bially. 2005. *Ordering International Politics: Identity, Crisis, and Representational Force.* New York: Routledge.

Mattern, Janice Bially, and Ayşe Zarakol. 2016. "Hierarchies in World Politics." *International Organization* 70(3): 623–54.

Mattes, Michaela, Brett Ashley Leeds, and Royce Carroll. 2015. "Leadership Turnover and Foreign Policy Change: Societal Interests, Domestic Institutions, and Voting in the United Nations." *International Studies Quarterly* 59(2): 280–90.

Matthijs, Matthias. 2020. "Hegemonic Leadership Is What States Make of It: Reading Kindleberger in Washington and Berlin." *Review of International Political Economy* Online Preview: 1–28.

Maurer, Noel. 2013. *The Empire Trap: The Rise and Fall of U.S. Intervention to Protect American Property Overseas, 1893–2013*. Princeton, NJ: Princeton University Press.

Mazarr, Michael J., Miranda Priebe, Andrew Radin, and Astrid Stuth Cevallos. 2016. "Understanding the Current International Order." https://www.rand.org/pubs/research_reports/RR1598.html (March 25, 2021).

McCarthy, Kevin, Mac Thornberry, and Greg Walden. 2020. "Letter to Secretary of State Pompeo." https://republicanleader.house.gov/wp-content/uploads/2020/04/Pompeo-Letter.pdf (April 4, 2021).

McDermott, Rose. 2004. *Political Psychology in International Relations*. Ann Arbor: University of Michigan Press.

McDonald, Patrick J. 2015. "Great Powers, Hierarchy, and Endogenous Regimes: Rethinking the Domestic Causes of Peace." *International Organization*: 1–32.

McFarland, Victor. 2020. *Oil Powers: A History of the US-Saudi Alliance*. New York: Columbia University Press.

McFarland, Victor, and Jeff D. Colgan. 2018. "The Seven Sisters of the Global Oil Industry." In San Francisco.

McFarlane, Sarah, Summer Said, and Michael Amon. 2019. "Oil-Rich Saudi Arabia Barrels Into the Gas Business." *Wall Street Journal*. https://www.wsj.com/articles/oil-rich-saudi-arabia-barrels-into-the-gas-business-11558549343 (September 17, 2019).

McKenna, Phil. 2011. "Nuclear Power Is Safer than Fossil Fuels." *New Scientist* 209(2805): 10.

McNally, Robert. 2017. *Crude Volatility: The History and the Future of Boom-Bust Oil Prices*. New York: Columbia University Press.

McNamara, Kathleen R. 2002. "Rational Fictions: Central Bank Independence and the Social Logic of Delegation." *West European Politics* 25(1): 47–76.

McNamara, Kathleen R. 2010. "Constructing Europe: Insights from Historical Sociology." *Comparative European Politics* 8(1): 127–42.

Mearsheimer, John J. 1994. "The False Promise of International Institutions." *International Security* 19(3): 5–49.

Mearsheimer, John J. 2001. *The Tragedy of Great Power Politics*. New York: W. W. Norton.

Mearsheimer, John J. 2019. "Bound to Fail: The Rise and Fall of the Liberal International Order." *International Security* 43(4): 7–50.

Mearsheimer, John J., and Stephen M. Walt. 2016. "The Case for Offshore Balancing." *Foreign Affairs* (July/August 2016). https://www.foreignaffairs.com/articles/united-states/2016-06-13/case-offshore-balancing (August 17, 2017).

Meckling, Jonas. 2011. *Carbon Coalitions: Business, Climate Politics, and the Rise of Emissions Trading*. Cambridge, MA: MIT Press.

Meckling, Jonas, Nina Kelsey, Eric Biber, and John Zysman. 2015. "Winning Coalitions for Climate Policy." *Science* 349(6253): 1170–71.

Meckling, Jonas, Thomas Sterner, and Gernot Wagner. 2017. "Policy Sequencing toward Decarbonization." *Nature Energy* 2(12): 918–22.

Mehta, Rupal N., and Rachel Elizabeth Whitlark. 2017. "The Benefits and Burdens of Nuclear Latency." *International Studies Quarterly* 61(3): 517–28.

Meierding, Emily. 2020. *The Oil Wars Myth: Petroleum and the Causes of International Conflict*. Ithaca, NY: Cornell University Press.

Meunier, Sophie, and Kathleen R. McNamara. 2007. *Making History: European Integration and Institutional Change at Fifty*. Oxford and New York: Oxford University Press.

Meyer, J. W., and B. Rowan. 1977. "Institutionalized Organizations: Formal Structure as Myth and Ceremony." *American Journal of Sociology* 83(2): 340–63.

Meyer, Lorenzo. 2014. *Mexico and the United States in the Oil Controversy, 1917–1942.* Austin: University of Texas Press.

Milani, Abbas. 2011. *The Shah*. New York: St. Martin's Press.

Mildenberger, Matto. 2020. *Carbon Captured: How Business and Labor Control Climate Politics*. Cambridge, MA: MIT Press.

Mildenberger, Matto, and Dustin Tingley. 2017. "Beliefs about Climate Beliefs: The Importance of Second-Order Opinions for Climate Politics." *British Journal of Political Science* 49(4): 1279–1307.

Miller, Clark A., Jennifer Richter, and Jason O'Leary. 2015. "Socio-Energy Systems Design: A Policy Framework for Energy Transitions." *Energy Research & Social Science* 6: 29–40.

Miller, Nicholas L. 2014. "The Secret Success of Nonproliferation Sanctions." *International Organization* 68(4): 913–44.

Miller, Nicholas L. 2017. "Why Nuclear Energy Programs Rarely Lead to Proliferation." *International Security* 42(2): 40–77.

Milner, Helen V. 1997. *Interests, Institutions, and Information: Domestic Politics and International Relations*. Princeton, NJ: Princeton University Press.

Milner, Helen V., and Dustin Tingley. 2015. *Sailing the Water's Edge: The Domestic Politics of American Foreign Policy*. Princeton, NJ: Princeton University Press.

Mitchell, Ronald B., and Charli Carpenter. 2019. "Norms for the Earth: Changing the Climate on 'Climate Change.'" *Journal of Global Security Studies* 4(4): 413–29.

Mitchell, Timothy. 2002. "McJihad: Islam in the U.S. Global Order." *Social Text* 20(4): 1–18.

Mitchell, Timothy. 2011. *Carbon Democracy: Political Power in the Age of Oil*. Revised edition. London; New York: Verso.

Mobley, Richard A. 2001. "Gauging the Iraqi Threat to Kuwait in the 1960s." *Studies in Intelligence*. https://www.cia.gov/library/center-for-the-study-of-intelligence/csi-publications/csi-studies/studies/fall_winter_2001/article03.html (February 7, 2019).

Monteiro, Nuno P. 2014. *Theory of Unipolar Politics*. Cambridge, UK: Cambridge University Press.

Moran, Daniel, and James Avery Russell. 2009. *Energy Security and Global Politics: The Militarization of Resource Management*. New York: Taylor & Francis.

Moran, T. H. 1982. "Modeling OPEC Behavior: Economic and Political Alternatives." In *OPEC Behavior and World Oil Prices*, 94–130. London: George Allen and Unwin.

Moran, T. H. 1987. "Managing an Oligopoly of Would-Be Sovereigns: The Dynamics of Joint Control and Self-Control in the International Oil Industry Past, Present, and Future." *International Organization* 41(4): 575–607.

Morefield, Jeanne. 2014. *Empires without Imperialism: Anglo-American Decline and the Politics of Deflection*. New York: Oxford University Press.

Morin, Jean-Frédéric, and Sikina Jinnah. 2018. "The Untapped Potential of Preferential Trade Agreements for Climate Governance." *Environmental Politics* 27(3): 541–65.

Morrison, James Ashley. 2012. "Before Hegemony: Adam Smith, American Independence, and the Origins of the First Era of Globalization." *International Organization* 66(3): 395–428.

Morse, Julia C., and Robert O. Keohane. 2014. "Contested Multilateralism." *Review of International Organizations* 9(4): 385–412.

Moschella, Manuela, and Eleni Tsingou, eds. 2014. *Great Expectations, Slow Transformations: Incremental Change in Post-Crisis Regulation.* Colchester: ECPR Press.

Mosley, Layna. 2003. *Global Capital and National Governments.* Cambridge, UK: Cambridge University Press.

Mountford, Helen. 2019. "How Carbon Tax Backers Can Secure Public Support." *Financial Times*: 2.

Mukerjee, Madhusree. 2011. *Churchill's Secret War: The British Empire and the Ravaging of India during World War II.* New York: Basic Books.

Mukherjee, Janam. 2015. *Hungry Bengal: War, Famine and the End of Empire.* Oxford and New York: Oxford University Press.

Mukunda, Gautam. 2012. *Indispensable: When Leaders Really Matter.* Boston: Harvard Business Review Press.

Mulder, Nicholas. 2019. "Can 'Climate Sanctions' Save the Planet?" https://www.thenation.com/article/climate-green-new-deal/ (November 27, 2019).

Murdie, Amanda M., and David R. Davis. 2012. "Shaming and Blaming: Using Events Data to Assess the Impact of Human Rights INGOs." *International Studies Quarterly* 56(1): 1–16.

Musgrave, Paul, and Daniel H. Nexon. 2018. "Defending Hierarchy from the Moon to the Indian Ocean: Symbolic Capital and Political Dominance in Early Modern China and the Cold War." *International Organization* 72(3): 591–626.

Myers, Meghann. 2019. "Following Attacks, Pentagon Prepping to Send Troops to Saudi Arabia's Aid." *Military Times.* https://www.militarytimes.com/news/your-military/2019/09/20/following-attacks-pentagon-prepping-to-send-troops-to-saudi-arabias-aid/ (September 25, 2019).

Nance, Mark T., and M. Patrick Cottrell. 2014. "A Turn toward Experimentalism?: Rethinking Security and Governance in the Twenty-First Century." *Review of International Studies* 40(2): 277–301.

Narizny, Kevin. 2012. "Anglo-American Primacy and the Global Spread of Democracy: An International Genealogy." *World Politics* 64(2): 341–73.

National Academies of Sciences and Engineering. 2018. *Negative Emissions Technologies and Reliable Sequestration: A Research Agenda.* National Academies of Sciences. https://www.nap.edu/catalog/25259/negative-emissions-technologies-and-reliable-sequestration-a-research-agenda (November 5, 2019).

Nelkin, Dorothy. 1981. "Some Social and Political Dimensions of Nuclear Power: Examples from Three Mile Island." *American Political Science Review* 75(1): 132–42.

Nelson, Stephen, and David A. Steinberg. 2018. "Default Positions: What Shapes Public Attitudes about International Debt Disputes." *International Studies Quarterly* 62(3): 520–33.

Neumayer, Eric. 2003. "What Factors Determine the Allocation of Aid by Arab Countries and Multilateral Agencies?" *Journal of Development Studies* 39(4): 134–47.

Newell, Peter. 2008. "Civil Society, Corporate Accountability and the Politics of Climate Change." *Global Environmental Politics* 8(3): 122–53.

Newell, Peter, and Andrew Simms. 2020. "Towards a Fossil Fuel Non-Proliferation Treaty." *Climate Policy* 20(8): 1043–54.

Nexon, Daniel H., and Iver B. Neumann. 2017. "Hegemonic-Order Theory: A Field-Theoretic Account." *European Journal of International Relations* 24(3): 662–86.

Nexon, Daniel H., and Thomas Wright. 2007. "What's at Stake in the American Empire Debate." *American Political Science Review* 101(2): 253.

Nexon, Daniel, and Abraham L. Newman. "If the United States Doesn't Make The Rules, China Will." *Foreign Policy*. https://foreignpolicy.com/2019/11/17/beijing-washington-bernie-sanders-warren-american-market-power-can-serve-progressive-ends/ (November 22, 2019).

Nicolaidis, Kalypso A., Berny Sèbe, and Gabrielle Maas. 2015. *Echoes of Empire: Memory, Identity and the Legacy of Imperialism*. London and New York: I. B.Tauris.

Nielson, Daniel L., and Michael J. Tierney. 2003. "Delegation to International Organizations: Agency Theory and World Bank Environmental Reform." *International Organization* 57(2): 241–76.

Nitzan, Jonathan, and Shimshon Bichler. 2002. *The Global Political Economy of Israel*. London and Sterling, VA: Pluto Press.

Nordhaus, William. 2015. "Climate Clubs: Overcoming Free-Riding in International Climate Policy." *American Economic Review* 105(4): 1339–70.

Nordhaus, William. 2020. "The Climate Club." *Foreign Affairs* 99(3): 10–17.

Norrlof, Carla. 2010. *America's Global Advantage: US Hegemony and International Cooperation*. Cambridge, UK: Cambridge University Press.

Norrlof, Carla. 2020. "Global Monetary Order and the Liberal Order Debate." *International Studies Perspectives* 21(2): 109–53.

Nye, Joseph S. 2004. *Soft Power: The Means to Success in World Politics*. New York: Public Affairs.

Nyman, Jonna. 2014. "'Red Storm Ahead': Securitisation of Energy in US-China Relations." *Millennium* 43(1): 43–65.

Oatley, Thomas. 2011. "The Reductionist Gamble: Open Economy Politics in the Global Economy." *International Organization* 65(2): 311–41.

Oatley, Thomas. 2019. "Toward a Political Economy of Complex Interdependence." *European Journal of International Relations* 25(4): 957–78.

OFID Profile. 2018. Vienna: OFID.

Ong, Aihwa, and Stephen Collier, eds. 2005. *Global Assemblages: Technology, Politics and Ethics as Anthropological Problems*. Malden, MA: Blackwell.

Oreskes, Naomi, and Erik M. Conway. 2011. *Merchants of Doubt: How a Handful of Scientists Obscured the Truth on Issues from Tobacco Smoke to Global Warming*. New York: Bloomsbury Publishing.

Organization of Petroleum Exporting Countries. 1984. *OPEC Official Resolutions and Press Releases, 1960–1983*. 2nd ed. Oxford and New York: Pergamon Press.

Organski, A. F. K., and J. Kugler. 1981. *The War Ledger*. Chicago: University of Chicago Press.

O'Rourke, Lindsey A. 2018. *Covert Regime Change: America's Secret Cold War*. Ithaca, NY: Cornell University Press.

Osborne, D. K. 1976. "Cartel Problems." *The American Economic Review* 66(5): 835–44.

Ostrom, Elinor. 2010. "Polycentric Systems for Coping with Collective Action and Global Environmental Change." *Global Environmental Change* 20(4): 550–57.

O'Sullivan, Meghan. 2017. *Windfall: How the New Energy Abundance Upends Global Politics and Strengthens America's Power*. New York and London: Simon & Schuster.

O'Sullivan, Meghan L. 2014. *North American Energy Remakes the Geopolitical Landscape: Understanding and Advancing the Phenomenon*. Belfer Center, Harvard University. http://www.belfercenter.org/sites/default/files/legacy/files/North%20

American%20Energy%20Remakes%20the%20Geopolitical%20Landscape.pdf (February 22, 2017).

O'Sullivan, Meghan, Indra Overland, and David Sandalow. 2017. *The Geopolitics of Renewable Energy*. Cambridge, MA: Harvard Kennedy School. https://papers.ssrn.com/sol3/papers.cfm?abstract_id=2998305 (December 16, 2019).

Overland, Indra, et al. 2019. "The GeGaLo Index: Geopolitical Gains and Losses after Energy Transition." *Energy Strategy Reviews* 26: 100406.

Owen, John M. 2010. *The Clash of Ideas in World Politics: Transnational Networks, States, and Regime Change, 1510–2010*. Princeton, NJ: Princeton University Press.

Pachauri, R. K., et al. 2014. *Climate Change 2014: Synthesis Report. Contribution of Working Groups I, II and III to the Fifth Assessment Report of the Intergovernmental Panel on Climate Change*, edited by R. K. Pachauri and L. Meyer. Geneva: Intergovernmental Panel on Climate Change. https://epic.awi.de/id/eprint/37530/ (July 2, 2020).

Packer, G. 2005. *The Assassins' Gate: America in Iraq*. New York: Farrar, Straus & Giroux.

Painter, David S. 1986. *Oil and the American Century: The Political Economy of U.S. Foreign Oil Policy, 1941–1954*. Baltimore: Johns Hopkins University Press.

Painter, David S. 2009. "The Marshall Plan and Oil." *Cold War History* 9(2): 159–75.

Parent, Joseph M., and Emily Erikson. 2009. "Anarchy, Hierarchy and Order." *Cambridge Review of International Affairs* 22(1): 129–45.

Parra, Francisco. 2004. *Oil Politics: A Modern History of Petroleum*. London and New York: I. B. Tauris.

Parsons, Talcott, and Gerald M. Platt. 1973. *The American University*. Cambridge, MA: Harvard University Press.

Paul, Thazha V., Deborah Welch Larson, and William C. Wohlforth. 2014. *Status in World Politics*. New York: Cambridge University Press.

Paulson Jr., Henry M. 2019. "Remarks by Henry M. Paulson Jr., on the Delusions of Decoupling." Presented at the 2019 New Economy Forum, Beijing China. https://www.paulsoninstitute.org/press_release/remarks-by-henry-m-paulson-jr-on-the-delusions-of-decoupling/ (July 13, 2020).

Pelc, Krzysztof J. 2010. "Constraining Coercion?: Legitimacy and Its Role in US Trade Policy, 1975–2000." *International Organization* 64(1): 65–96.

Pepinsky, Thomas B. 2015. "Trade Competition and American Decolonization." *World Politics* 67(03): 387–422.

Perović, Jeronim, ed. 2017. *Cold War Energy: A Transnational History of Soviet Oil and Gas*. Cham: Palgrave Macmillan.

Peters, Margaret E. 2017. *Trading Barriers: Immigration and the Remaking of Globalization*. Princeton, NJ: Princeton University Press.

Pevehouse, Jon C. 2005. *Democracy from Above: Regional Organizations and Democratization*. Cambridge, UK: Cambridge University Press.

Phillips, Andrew. 2010. *War, Religion and Empire: The Transformation of International Orders*. Cambridge and New York: Cambridge University Press.

Phillips, Andrew, and Jason Campbell Sharman. 2015. *International Order in Diversity: War, Trade and Rule in the Indian Ocean*. Cambridge and New York: Cambridge University Press.

Phillips, Kevin. 1991. "Bush's Worst Political Nightmare: Banks and Oil Fields Shut on Same Day." *Los Angeles Times*. https://www.latimes.com/archives/la-xpm-1991-01-13-op-496-story.html (October 17, 2020).

Philpott, Daniel. 2001. *Revolutions in Sovereignty: How Ideas Shaped Modern International Relations*. Princeton, NJ: Princeton University Press.

Pistor, Katharina. 2019. *The Code of Capital: How the Law Creates Wealth and Inequality*. Princeton, NJ: Princeton University Press.

Poast, Paul. 2019. *Arguing about Alliances: The Art of Agreement in Military-Pact Negotiations*. Ithaca, NY: Cornell University Press.

Porter, Patrick. 2018. *A World Imagined: Nostalgia and Liberal Order*. Cato Institute. Policy Analysis. https://www.cato.org/publications/policy-analysis/world-imagined-nostalgia-liberal-order (October 25, 2019).

Porter, Patrick. 2020. *The False Promise of Liberal Order: Nostalgia, Delusion and the Rise of Trump*. Cambridge, UK, and Medford, MA: Polity Press.

Posen, Barry R. 2014. *Restraint: A New Foundation for U.S. Grand Strategy*. Ithaca, NY: Cornell University Press.

Poznansky, Michael. 2020. *In the Shadow of International Law: Secrecy and Regime Change in the Postwar World*. New York: Oxford University Press.

Poznansky, Michael, and Evan Perkoski. 2018. "Rethinking Secrecy in Cyberspace: The Politics of Voluntary Attribution." *Journal of Global Security Studies* 3(4): 402–16.

Prakash, Aseem, and Matthew Potoski. 2007. "Collective Action through Voluntary Environmental Programs: A Club Theory Perspective." *Policy Studies Journal* 35(4): 773–92.

Pratt, Tyler. 2018. "Deference and Hierarchy in International Regime Complexes." *International Organization* 72(3): 561–90.

Qaimmaqami, Linda, and Edward C. Keefer, eds. 2011. *Foreign Relations of the United States, 1969–1976, Volume XXXVI, Energy Crisis, 1969–1974*. Washington, DC: United States Government Printing Office.

Rajamani, Lavanya. 2016. "Ambition and Differentiation in the 2015 Paris Agreement: Interpretative Possibilities and Underlying Politics." *International & Comparative Law Quarterly* 65(2): 493–514.

Rankin, Jennifer. 2019. "European Green Deal to Press Ahead despite Polish Targets Opt-Out." *The Guardian*. https://www.theguardian.com/environment/2019/dec/13/european-green-deal-to-press-ahead-despite-polish-targets-opt-out (January 6, 2020).

Ratner, Ely, Daniel Kliman, and Susanna Blume. 2019. *Rising to the China Challenge*. Washington DC: Center for a New American Security. https://www.cnas.org/publications/reports/rising-to-the-china-challenge (July 13, 2020).

Raustiala, Kal, and David G. Victor. 2004. "The Regime Complex for Plant Genetic Resources." *International Organization* 58(02): 277–309.

Raval, Anjli. 2020. "OPEC Keeps Strategy under Wraps in Crude Stumble." *Financial Times* (September 22).

Raval, Anjli. 2021. "Dutch Court Orders Shell to Accelerate Emissions Cuts." *Financial Times* (May 26).

Reinker, Kenneth S. 2005. "NOPEC: The No Oil Producing and Exporting Cartels Act of 2004." *Harvard Journal on Legislation* 42: 285.

Renshon, Jonathan. 2017. *Fighting for Status: Hierarchy and Conflict in World Politics*. Princeton, NJ: Princeton University Press.

Reus-Smit, Christian. 2013. *Individual Rights and the Making of the International System*. Cambridge, UK: Cambridge University Press.

Reus-Smit, Christian. 2018. *On Cultural Diversity: International Theory in a World of Difference*. Cambridge and New York: Cambridge University Press.

Reynolds, D. B., and M. K. Pippenger. 2010. "OPEC and Venezuelan Oil Production: Evidence against a Cartel Hypothesis." *Energy Policy* 38(10): 6045–55.

Rich, Nathaniel. 2018. "Losing Earth: The Decade We Almost Stopped Climate Change." *New York Times*. https://www.nytimes.com/interactive/2018/08/01/magazine/climate-change-losing-earth.html (November 26, 2018).

Richardson, Bill. 2005. *Between Worlds: The Making of an American Life*. New York: Penguin.

Ripsman, Norrin M., Jeffrey W. Taliaferro, and Steven E. Lobell. 2016. *Neoclassical Realist Theory of International Politics*. Oxford and New York: Oxford University Press.

Roberts, Andrew. 2018. *Churchill: Walking with Destiny*. New York: Penguin.

Robinson, Stacy-ann, and D'Arcy Carlson. 2021. "A Just Alternative to Litigation: Applying Restorative Justice to Climate-Related Loss and Damage." *Third World Quarterly*. https://doi.org/10.1080/01436597.2021.1877128.

Rose, A.K. 2004. "Do We Really Know That the WTO Increases Trade?" *American Economic Review* 94(1): 98–114.

Rose, Gideon. 2019. "The Fourth Founding." *Foreign Affairs* 98(1): 10–21.

Rosenberg, Elizabeth. 2014. *Energy Rush: Shale Production and US National Security*. Washington, DC: Center for a New American Security.

Rosenberg, Elizabeth, Peter Harrell, and Ashley Feng. 2020. *A New Arsenal for Competition*. Center for a New American Security. https://www.cnas.org/publications/reports/a-new-arsenal-for-competition (June 1, 2020).

Rosenbloom, Daniel, Jochen Markard, Frank W. Geels, and Lea Fuenfschilling. 2020. "Opinion: Why Carbon Pricing Is Not Sufficient to Mitigate Climate Change—and How 'Sustainability Transition Policy' Can Help." *Proceedings of the National Academy of Sciences* 117(16): 8664–68.

Ross, Michael L. 2012. *The Oil Curse: How Petroleum Wealth Shapes the Development of Nations*. Princeton, NJ: Princeton University Press.

Ross, Michael L., Chad Hazlett, and Paasha Mahdavi. 2017. "Global Progress and Backsliding on Gasoline Taxes and Subsidies." *Nature Energy* 2(1): 16201.

Ross, Michael L., and Erik Voeten. 2015. "Oil and International Cooperation." *International Studies Quarterly* 60(1): 85–97.

Rossi, Carlos. 2014. "Introducing Public-Private Technology Pools to Address Climate Change." In *The Way Forward in International Climate Policy*, edited by Heleen de Coninck, R. Lorch, and A. D. Sagar, 37–43. London: Climate and Development Knowledge Network.

Rovner, Joshua, and Caitlin Talmadge. 2014. "Hegemony, Force Posture, and the Provision of Public Goods: The Once and Future Role of Outside Powers in Securing Persian Gulf Oil." *Security Studies* 23(3): 548–81.

Rudra, Nita, and Nathan M. Jensen. 2011. "Globalization and the Politics of Natural Resources." *Comparative Political Studies* 44(6): 639.

Ruggeri, Andrea, Han Dorussen, and Theodora-Ismene Gizelis. 2018. "On the Frontline Every Day?: Subnational Deployment of United Nations Peacekeepers." *British Journal of Political Science* 48(4): 1005–25.

Ruggie, John Gerard. 1982. "International Regimes, Transactions, and Change: Embedded Liberalism in the Postwar Economic Order." *International Organization* 36(2): 379–415.

Ruggie, John Gerard. 1983. "Continuity and Transformation in the World Polity: Toward a Neorealist Synthesis." *World Politics* 35(2): 261–85.

Ruggie, John Gerard. 1998. *Constructing the World Polity: Essays on International Institutionalisation*. London; New York: Routledge.

Sabatier, Paul A., ed. 2007. *Theories of the Policy Process*. 2nd ed. Boulder CO: Westview Press.

Sagan, Scott D. 1995. *The Limits of Safety: Organizations, Accidents, and Nuclear Weapons*. Princeton University Press.

Sagan, Scott D. 1997. "Why Do States Build Nuclear Weapons?: Three Models in Search of a Bomb." *International Security* 21(3): 54–86.

Salehyan, Idean. 2009. *Rebels without Borders: Transnational Insurgencies in World Politics*. Ithaca, NY: Cornell University Press.

Sampson, Anthony. 2009. *The Seven Sisters: The Great Oil Companies and the World They Shaped*. London: Pfd.

Sassen, Saskia. 2006. *Territory, Authority, Rights: From Medieval to Global Assemblages*. Princeton, NJ: Princeton University Press.

Sattler, Thomas, Gabriele Spilker, and Thomas Bernauer. 2014. "Does WTO Dispute Settlement Enforce or Inform?" *British Journal of Political Science* 44(4): 877–902.

Saunders, Elizabeth N. 2011. *Leaders at War*. Ithaca, NY: Cornell University Press.

Schake, Kori. 2017. *Safe Passage*. Cambridge, MA: Harvard University Press.

Schelling, Thomas C. 1997. "The Cost of Combating Global Warming: Facing the Tradeoffs." *Foreign Affairs*: 8–14.

Schelling, Thomas Crombie. 1966. *Arms and Influence*. New Haven: Yale University Press.

Scheve, Kenneth, and David Stasavage. 2012. "Democracy, War, and Wealth: Lessons from Two Centuries of Inheritance Taxation." *American Political Science Review* 106(1): 81–102.

Schneider, Jacquelyn. 2019. "The Capability/Vulnerability Paradox and Military Revolutions: Implications for Computing, Cyber, and the Onset of War." *Journal of Strategic Studies* 42(6): 841–63.

Schreurs, Miranda A., and Yves Tiberghien. 2007. "Multi-Level Reinforcement: Explaining European Union Leadership in Climate Change Mitigation." *Global Environmental Politics* 7(4): 19–46.

Schultz, Kenneth A. 2001. *Democracy and Coercive Diplomacy*. Cambridge, UK: Cambridge University Press.

Schwartz, John. 2017. "Exxon Mobil Lends Its Support to a Carbon Tax Proposal." *New York Times*. https://www.nytimes.com/2017/06/20/science/exxon-carbon-tax.html (October 11, 2018).

Schweller, Randall L. 2001. "The Problem of International Order Revisited: A Review Essay." *International Security* 26(1): 161–86.

Seabrooke, Leonard, and Eleni Tsingou. 2014. "Distinctions, Affiliations, and Professional Knowledge in Financial Reform Expert Groups." *Journal of European Public Policy* 21(3): 389–407.

Sending, Ole Jacob. 2015. *The Politics of Expertise: Competing for Authority in Global Governance*. Ann Arbor: University of Michigan Press.

Sending, Ole Jacob, Vincent Pouliot, and Iver B. Neumann. 2015. *Diplomacy and the Making of World Politics*. Cambridge, UK: Cambridge University Press.

Seto, Karen C., et al. 2016. "Carbon Lock-In: Types, Causes, and Policy Implications." *Annual Review of Environment and Resources* 41(1): 425–52.

Setzer, Joana, and Rebecca Byrnes. 2019. *Global Trends in Climate Change Litigation: 2019 Snapshot*. London: Grantham Institute, London School of Economics.

Seymour, Ian. 1980. *OPEC: Instrument of Change*. London: Macmillan.

Shaffer, Brenda. 2009. *Energy Politics*. Philadelphia: University of Pennsylvania Press.

Shaia, Fred, and Jeff D. Colgan. 2020. *Presidential Climate Action on Day One: A Foreign Policy Guide for the Next U.S. President*. Providence, RI: Climate Solutions Lab, Brown University. https://watson.brown.edu/files/watson/imce/news/explore/2020/Final%20CSL%20Report.pdf (October 17, 2020).

Shilliam, Robbie. 2010. *International Relations and Non-Western Thought: Imperialism, Colonialism and Investigations of Global Modernity*. Abington and New York: Routledge.

Simmons, Beth A. 2000. "International Law and State Behavior: Commitment and Compliance in International Monetary Affairs." *American Political Science Review* 94(04): 819–35.

Simmons, Beth A., Frank Dobbin, and Geoffrey Garrett. 2006. "Introduction: The International Diffusion of Liberalism." *International Organization* 60(4): 781–810.

Simons, Geoff. 2016. *Iraq: From Sumer to Saddam*. London: Palgrave Macmillan.

Simpson, J. 2008. "The Effect of OPEC Production Allocations on Oil Prices." In *21st Australasian Finance and Banking Conference 2008 Paper*, http://papers.ssrn.com/sol3/papers.cfm?abstract_id=1231602 (July 12, 2012).

Singer, David Andrew. 2007. *Regulating Capital: Setting Standards for the International Financial System*. Ithaca, NY: Cornell University Press.

Singer, J. David. 1961. "The Level-of-Analysis Problem in International Relations." *World Politics* 14(1): 77–92.

Sjoberg, Laura. 2013. *Gendering Global Conflict: Toward a Feminist Theory of War*. New York: Columbia University Press.

Skeet, Ian. 1988. *OPEC: Twenty-Five Years of Prices and Politics*. Cambridge and New York: Cambridge University Press.

Smith, James L. 2005. "Inscrutable OPEC?: Behavioral Tests of the Cartel Hypothesis." *Energy Journal* 26(1): 51–82.

Smith, James L. 2008. "Organization of the Petroleum Exporting Countries (OPEC)." In *The New Palgrave Dictionary of Economics*, edited by Steven N. Durlauf and Lawrence E. Blume, 229–31. Basingstoke: Nature Publishing Group.

Smith, James L. 2009. "World Oil: Market or Mayhem?" *Journal of Economic Perspectives* 23: 145–64.

Snell-Mendoza, Morice. 1996. "In Defence of Oil: Britain's Response to the Iraqi Threat towards Kuwait, 1961." *Contemporary British History* 10(3): 39–62.

Snyder, Jack L. 1991. *Myths of Empire: Domestic Politics and International Ambition*. Ithaca, NY: Cornell University Press.

Solingen, Etel. 1998. *Regional Orders at Century's Dawn*. Princeton, NJ: Princeton University Press.

Solingen, Etel. 2009. *Nuclear Logics: Contrasting Paths in East Asia and the Middle East*. Princeton: Princeton University Press.

Sovacool, Benjamin K. 2011. *The Routledge Handbook of Energy Security*. London: Routledge.

Sovacool, Benjamin K. 2016. "How Long Will It Take?: Conceptualizing the Temporal Dynamics of Energy Transitions." *Energy Research & Social Science* 13: 202–15.

Spruyt, Hendrik. 2005. *Ending Empire: Contested Sovereignty and Territorial Partition*. Ithaca, NY: Cornell University Press.

Staniland, Paul. 2018. "Misreading the 'Liberal Order': Why We Need New Thinking in American Foreign Policy." *Lawfare*. https://www.lawfareblog.com/misreading-liberal-order-why-we-need-new-thinking-american-foreign-policy (August 23, 2018).

Steinfeld, Edward S. 2010. *Playing Our Game: Why China's Rise Doesn't Threaten the West*. New York: Oxford University Press.

Stiglitz, Joseph. 2006. "A New Agenda for Global Warming." *The Economists' Voice* 3(7).

Stockwell, Sarah E. 2000. *The Business of Decolonization: British Business Strategies in the Gold Coast*. New York: Oxford University Press.

Stokes, Doug, and Sam Raphael. 2010. *Global Energy Security and American Hegemony*. Baltimore: Johns Hopkins University Press.

Stokes, Leah C. 2016. "Electoral Backlash against Climate Policy: A Natural Experiment on Retrospective Voting and Local Resistance to Public Policy." *American Journal of Political Science* 60(4): 958–74.

Stokes, Leah C., and Christopher Warshaw. 2017. "Renewable Energy Policy Design and Framing Influence Public Support in the United States." *Nature Energy* 2(8): 17107.

Stokes, Leah Cardamore. 2020. *Short Circuiting Policy: Interest Groups and the Battle over Clean Energy and Climate Policy in the American States*. New York: Oxford University Press.

Stone, Randall W. 2011. *Controlling Institutions: International Organizations and the Global Economy*. New York: Cambridge University Press.

Strange, Susan. 1996. *The Retreat of the State: The Diffusion of Power in the World Economy*. Cambridge, UK: Cambridge University Press.

Stulberg, Adam N. 2007. *Well-Oiled Diplomacy: Strategic Manipulation and Russia's Energy Statecraft in Eurasia*. Albany: State University of New York Press.

Stulberg, Adam N. 2012. "Strategic Bargaining and Pipeline Politics: Confronting the Credible Commitment Problem in Eurasian Energy Transit." *Review of International Political Economy* 19(5): 808–36.

Subotic, Jelena, and Ayşe Zarakol. 2013. "Cultural Intimacy in International Relations." *European Journal of International Relations* 19(4): 915–38.

Swidler, Ann. 1986. "Culture in Action: Symbols and Strategies." *American Sociological Review*: 273–86.

Szulecki, Kacper, and Kirsten Westphal. 2018. "Taking Security Seriously in EU Energy Governance: Crimean Shock and the Energy Union." In *Energy Security in Europe*, edited by Kacper Szulecki, 177–202. Cham: Springer.

Talmadge, Caitlin. 2008. "Closing Time: Assessing the Iranian Threat to the Strait of Hormuz." *International Security* 33(1): 82–117.

Tammen, R. L., et al. 2000. *Power Transitions: Strategies for the 21st Century*. New York: Chatham House.

Tang, Shiping. 2016. "Order: A Conceptual Analysis." *Chinese Political Science Review* 1(1): 30–46.

Tang, Shiping. 2018. "The Future of International Order(s)." *The Washington Quarterly* 41(4): 117–31.

Tannenwald, Nina. 2007. *The Nuclear Taboo: The United States and the Non-Use of Nuclear Weapons since 1945*. New York: Cambridge University Press.

Teece, David J. 1982. "OPEC Behavior: An Alternative View." In *OPEC Behaviour and World Oil Prices*, edited by James M. Griffin and David J. Teece. London: George Allen and Unwin.

Terzian, Pierre. 1985. *OPEC: The Inside Story*. London: Zed Books.

Tett, Gillian. 2019. "The Battle over Green Investment Is Hotting Up." *Financial Times*: 11.

"The Devil's Excrement—Economics Focus." 2003. *The Economist*. https://www.economist.com/finance-and-economics/2003/05/22/the-devils-excrement (August 14, 2018).

Thompson, Alexander. 2010. "Rational Design in Motion: Uncertainty and Flexibility in the Global Climate Regime." *European Journal of International Relations* 16(2): 269–96.

Thornhill, John. 2020. "Venture Capital Investors Seek Openings in Climate Tech to Save the Planet, and Make Money Too." *Financial Times*.

Thrall, A. Trevor, and Benjamin H. Friedman. 2018. *US Grand Strategy in the 21st Century: The Case for Restraint*. New York: Routledge.

Thurber, Mark C. 2019. *Coal*. Cambridge, UK and Medford, MA: Polity Press.

Tickner, Arlene B., and Ole Wæver, eds. 2009. *International Relations Scholarship around the World*. New ed. Abingdon and New York: Routledge.

"Tillerson, Mattis Call for Calming Tensions in Gulf Dispute." 2018. *Reuters*. https://www.reuters.com/article/us-usa-qatar/tillerson-mattis-call-for-calming-tensions-in-gulf-dispute-idUSKBN1FJ28U (October 26, 2018).

Tilly, Charles. 1992. *Coercion, Capital and European States: AD 990–1992*. Rev. ed. Cambridge, MA, and Oxford: Blackwell.

Tingley, Dustin, and Michael Tomz. 2019. "International Commitments and Domestic Opinion: The Effect of the Paris Agreement on Public Support for Policies to Address Climate Change." *Environmental Politics* 29(7): 1–22.

Toft, Monica Duffy. 2007. "Getting Religion?: The Puzzling Case of Islam and Civil War." *International Security* 31(4): 97–131.

Tomz, Michael. 2007. *Reputation and International Cooperation: Sovereign Debt across Three Centuries*. Princeton, NJ: Princeton University Press.

Tomz, Michael R., and Jessica L. P. Weeks. 2013. "Public Opinion and the Democratic Peace." *American Political Science Review* 107(4): 849–65.

Tooze, Adam. "Why Central Banks Need to Step Up on Global Warming." *Foreign Policy*. https://foreignpolicy.com/2019/07/20/why-central-banks-need-to-step-up-on-global-warming/ (November 22, 2019).

Toprani, Anand. 2012. "The French Connection: A New Perspective on the End of the Red Line Agreement, 1945–1948." *Diplomatic History* 36(2): 261–99.

Toprani, Anand. 2019. *Oil and the Great Powers: Britain and Germany, 1914 to 1945*. Oxford: Oxford University Press.

Towns, Ann E. 2010. *Women and States: Norms and Hierarchies in International Society*. Cambridge, UK: Cambridge University Press.

Trombetta, Maria Julia. 2018. "Fueling Threats: Securitization and the Challenges of Chinese Energy Policy." *Asian Perspective* 42(2): 183–206.

Tucker, Todd. 2019. "There's a Big New Headache for the Green New Deal." *Washington Post*. https://www.washingtonpost.com/politics/2019/06/28/theres-big-new-headache-green-new-deal/ (December 2, 2019).

Tucker, Todd, and Timothy Meyer. 2021. "Chapter 5: Reshaping Global Trade and Investment Law for a Green New Deal." In *Handbook on a Green New Deal*, eds. Kyla Tienhaara and Joanna Robinson. Abingdon, Oxon; New York: Routledge.

United Nations General Assembly Resolution 1803. 1962. https://legal.un.org/avl/ha/ga_1803/ga_1803.html (May 10, 2021).

Urpelainen, Johannes. 2013. "Can Strategic Technology Development Improve Climate Cooperation?: A Game-Theoretic Analysis." *Mitigation and Adaptation Strategies for Global Change* 18(6): 785–800.

US Department of Defense. 2018. "Operational Energy." https://www.acq.osd.mil/eie/OE/OE_index.html (July 3, 2020).

US Government. 1989. *Libya: A Country Study*. Washington, DC: United States Government Printing Office.

US Senate. 1975. *Multinational Oil Corporations and US Foreign Policy*.

Vabulas, Felicity, and Duncan Snidal. 2013. "Organization without Delegation: Informal Intergovernmental Organizations (IIGOs) and the Spectrum of Intergovernmental Arrangements." *Review of International Organizations* 8(2): 193–220.

Van de Graaf, Thijs. 2013. "Fragmentation in Global Energy Governance: Explaining the Creation of IRENA." *Global Environmental Politics* 13(3): 14–33.

Van de Graaf, Thijs. 2016. *The Palgrave Handbook of the International Political Economy of Energy*. New York: Springer.

Van de Graaf, Thijs. 2017. "Is OPEC Dead?: Oil Exporters, the Paris Agreement and the Transition to a Post-Carbon World." *Energy Research & Social Science* 23: 182–88.

Van de Graaf, Thijs. 2018. "Battling for a Shrinking Market: Oil Producers, the Renewables Revolution, and the Risk of Stranded Assets." In *The Geopolitics of Renewables*, edited by Daniel Scholten, 97–121. Cham: Springer

Van de Graaf, Thijs, and Michael Bradshaw. 2018. "Stranded Wealth: Rethinking the Politics of Oil in an Age of Abundance." *International Affairs* 94(6): 1309–28.

Van de Graaf, Thijs, and Jeff Colgan. 2016. "Global Energy Governance: A Review and Research Agenda." *Palgrave Communications* 2(15047): 1–12.

Van de Graaf, Thijs, and Dries Lesage. 2009. "The International Energy Agency after 35 Years: Reform Needs and Institutional Adaptability." *Review of International Organizations* 4(3): 293–317.

Van de Graaf, Thijs, Indra Overland, Daniel Scholten, and Kirsten Westphal. 2020. "The New Oil?: The Geopolitics and International Governance of Hydrogen." *Energy Research & Social Science* 70: 101667.

Van de Graaf, Thijs, and Aviel Verbruggen. 2015. "The Oil Endgame: Strategies of Oil Exporters in a Carbon-Constrained World." *Environmental Science & Policy* 54: 456–62.

VanDeveer, Stacy D., and Geoffrey D. Dabelko. 2001. "It's Capacity, Stupid: International Assistance and National Implementation." *Global Environmental Politics* 1(2): 18–29.

Vandewalle, Dirk. 2006. *A History of Modern Libya*. New York: Cambridge University Press.

Varadarajan, Tunku. 2018. "'Churchill: Walking with Destiny' Review: A Life at Full Pelt." *Wall Street Journal*: C7.

Verrastro, Frank, David Pumphrey, Alan Hegburg, and Marshall Nannes. 2011. *"NOPEC" Legislation and U.S. Energy Security*. Center for Strategic and International Studies. http://csis.org/publication/nopec-legislation-and-us-energy-security (November 5, 2011).

Victor, David G. 2001. *The Collapse of the Kyoto Protocol and the Struggle to Slow Global Warming*. Princeton NJ: Princeton University Press.

Victor, David G. 2008. "OPEC Is Irrelevant." *Newsweek*. http://www.thedailybeast.com/newsweek/2008/07/31/opec-is-irrelevant.html (October 18, 2011).

Victor, David G. 2011. *Global Warming Gridlock: Creating More Effective Strategies for Protecting the Planet*. Cambridge and New York: Cambridge University Press.

Victor, David G. 2015. *The Case for Climate Clubs*. Geneva: International Centre for Trade and Sustainable Development (ICTSD).

Victor, David G. 2017. *Three-Dimensional Clubs: Implications for Climate Cooperation and the G20*. Geneva: International Centre for Trade and Sustainable Development (ICTSD).

Victor, David G., Frank W. Geels, and Simon Sharpe. 2019. *Accelerating the Low Carbon Transition*. Washington, DC: Brookings Institution.

Victor, David G., David R. Hults, and Mark C. Thurber. 2012. *Oil and Governance: State-Owned Enterprises and the World Energy Supply*. Cambridge, UK: Cambridge University Press.

Villanger, Espen. 2007. "Arab Foreign Aid: Disbursement Patterns, Aid Policies and Motives." *Forum for Development Studies* 34(2): 223–56.

Vitalis, Robert. 2007. *America's Kingdom: Mythmaking on the Saudi Oil Frontier*. Palo Alto, CA: Stanford University Press.

Voeten, Erik. 2010. "Borrowing and Nonborrowing among International Courts." *Journal of Legal Studies* 39(2): 547–76.

Vogel, David. 1997. *Trading Up: Consumer and Environmental Regulation in a Global Economy*. Cambridge, MA: Harvard University Press.

Vonnegut, Kurt. 2005. *A Man without a Country*. Ed. Daniel Simon. New York: Seven Stories Press.

Vormedal, Irja, Lars H. Gulbrandsen, and Jon Birger Skjærseth. 2020. "Big Oil and Climate Regulation: Business as Usual or a Changing Business?" *Global Environmental Politics* 10(Y): 1–23.

Vreeland, James Raymond. 2003. *The IMF and Economic Development*. Cambridge, UK: Cambridge University Press.

Wæver, Ole. 1993. *Securitization and Desecuritization*. Copenhagen: Centre for Peace and Conflict Research.

Waghorn, Jonathan, Matthew Lanstone, Anthony Ling, and Mark Fletcher. 2006. *Global Energy: 125 Projects to Change the World*. New York: Goldman Sachs.

Wald, Ellen R. 2018. *Saudi, Inc.: The Arabian Kingdom's Pursuit of Profit and Power*. New York: Pegasus Books.

Wallander, Celeste A. 2000. "Institutional Assets and Adaptability: NATO after the Cold War." *International Organization* 54(04): 705–35.

Walt, Stephen M. 2018. "Why I Didn't Sign Up to Defend the International Order." *Foreign Policy*. https://foreignpolicy.com/2018/08/01/why-i-didnt-sign-up-to-defend-the-international-order/ (November 11, 2020).

Waltz, Kenneth N. 1979. *Theory of International Politics*. New York: McGraw-Hill.

Ward, Steven R. 2014. *Immortal: A Military History of Iran and Its Armed Forces*. Reprint edition. Washington, DC: Georgetown University Press.

Weaver, Catherine. 2008. *Hypocrisy Trap: The World Bank and the Poverty of Reform*. Princeton, NJ: Princeton University Press.

Weber, Max. 2004. *The Vocation Lectures*. Eds. David S. Owen and Tracy B. Strong. Indianapolis: Hackett.

Weber, Max. 2009. *From Max Weber: Essays in Sociology*. Abington and New York: Routledge.

"Weekly Review." 1964. *Middle East Economic Survey*.

"Weekly Review." 1966. *Middle East Economic Survey*.

"Weekly Review, Vol. VIII No.22." 1965. *Middle East Economic Survey*.

"Weekly Review, Vol. VIII No.23." 1965. *Middle East Economic Survey.*

"Weekly Review, Vol. X No.3." 1966. *Middle East Economic Survey.*

Weisiger, Alex, and Keren Yarhi-Milo. 2015. "Revisiting Reputation: How Past Actions Matter in International Politics." *International Organization* 69(2): 473–95.

Weiss, Jessica Chen. 2019. "A World Safe for Autocracy: China's Rise and the Future of Global Politics." *Foreign Affairs* (4): 92–108.

Weiss, Jessica Chen, and Jeremy L. Wallace. 2021. "Domestic Politics, China's Rise, and the Future of the Liberal International Order." *International Organization* 75(2): 635–64.

Wellhausen, Rachel L. 2015. *The Shield of Nationality: When Governments Break Contracts with Foreign Firms.* New York: Cambridge University Press.

Wenar, Leif. 2016. *Blood Oil: Tyrants, Violence, and the Rules That Run the World.* New York: Oxford University Press.

Wendt, A. 1999. *Social Theory of International Politics.* Cambridge, UK: Cambridge University Press.

Wheatcroft, Andrew. 1995. *The Habsburgs: Embodying Empire.* Penguin Books.

Whitlark, Rachel Elizabeth. 2017. "Nuclear Beliefs: A Leader-Focused Theory of Counter-Proliferation." *Security Studies* 26(4): 545–74.

Wight, Colin. 2006. *Agents, Structures and International Relations: Politics as Ontology.* Cambridge and New York: Cambridge University Press.

Wimmer, Andreas. 2013. *Waves of War: Nationalism, State Formation, and Ethnic Exclusion in the Modern World.* Cambridge and New York: Cambridge University Press.

Wimmer, Andreas, and Yuval Feinstein. 2010. "The Rise of the Nation-State across the World, 1816 to 2001." *American Sociological Review* 75(5): 764–90.

Winecoff, W. Kindred. 2017. "How Did American International Political Economy Become Reductionist?: A Historiography of a Discipline." *Oxford Research Encyclopedias.* http://politics.oxfordre.com/view/10.1093/acrefore/9780190228637.001.0001/acrefore-9780190228637-e-345 (October 5, 2017).

Winegard, Timothy C. 2016. *The First World Oil War.* Toronto: University of Toronto Press.

Wohlforth, William C. 1999. "The Stability of a Unipolar World." *International Security* 24(1): 5–41.

Wohlforth, William. C. 2009. "Unipolarity, Status Competition, and Great Power War." *World Politics* 61(1): 28–57.

Woods, Ngaire. 2006. *The Globalizers: The IMF, the World Bank, and Their Borrowers.* Ithaca, NY: Cornell University Press.

Wright, Thomas. 2017. *All Measures Short of War: The Contest for the Twenty-First Century and the Future of American Power.* New Haven: Yale University Press.

Yegorova, Natalia I. 1996. *The "Iran Crisis" of 1945–46: A View from the Russian Archives.* Washington, DC: Woodrow Wilson International Center for Scholars.

Yergin, Daniel. 2008. *The Prize: The Epic Quest for Oil, Money & Power.* New York: Free Press.

Yetiv, Steven A. 2004. *Crude Awakenings: Global Oil Security and American Foreign Policy.* Ithaca, NY: Cornell University Press.

Yetiv, Steven A. 2011. *The Petroleum Triangle: Oil, Globalization, and Terror.* Ithaca, NY: Cornell University Press.

York, Richard, and Shannon Elizabeth Bell. 2019. "Energy Transitions or Additions?: Why a Transition from Fossil Fuels Requires More than the Growth of Renewable Energy." *Energy Research & Social Science* 51: 40–43.

Young, Oran R. 1982. "Regime Dynamics: The Rise and Fall of International Regimes." *International Organization* 36(2): 277–97.

Zarakol, Ayşe, ed. 2017. *Hierarchies in World Politics*. Cambridge, UK: Cambridge University Press.

Zaum, Dominik, and Christine Cheng. 2011. *Corruption and Post-Conflict Peacebuilding: Selling the Peace?* London and New York: Routledge.

Zhou, Yue Maggie. "When Some US Firms Move Production Overseas, They Also Offshore Their Pollution." *The Conversation*. http://theconversation.com/when-some-us-firms-move-production-overseas-they-also-offshore-their-pollution-75371 (December 9, 2019).

Zürn, Michael. 2010. "Global Governance as Multi-Level Governance." In *Handbook on Multi-Level Governance*, edited by Henrik Enderlein, 80–102. Cheltenham: Edward Elgar.

Index

For the benefit of digital users, indexed terms that span two pages (e.g., 52–53) may, on occasion, appear on only one of those pages.

Abd al-Aziz Al Saud, King of Saudi Arabia, 137, 138
Abd al-Ilah, Regent to Faisal II (Iraq), 140
Abd al-Karim Qasim, prime minister of Iraq, 139
Abdullah, King of Saudi Arabia, 90
Abdullah Al-Salim Al-Sabah, Sheikh of Kuwait, 139
Abqaiq facility, attack on, 160
Abu Dhabi, 109n.46, 149–50
Abu Nidal group, 90
Acheson, Dean, 143–44
Achnacarry (or "As Is")
    Agreement, 61–62
actors, 47–48, 166
    in climate governance, 188, 189–90, 194–95, 212
    in energy transition subsystems, 219
    individuals' role, 16
    in nuclear politics, 172–73
    of strategic benefits, 57
    See also non-state actors; state actors; subsystems analysis guidelines
Adelman, Morris Albert, 97n.12
Adler, Emanuel, 177n.49
advantages to subsystems theory. *See* subsystems theory, advantages for applying
Afghanistan, 86–87, 151
Africa
    North African region, 123f, 123, 124–25
    peacekeeping operations in, 173
After Hegemony (Keohane), 7
"aha" moments, 214–15
aircraft, 121–22
air pollution, in China, 191
Ala Hussein, prime minister of Iran, 143

ALBA (Latin American Bolivarian Alternative), 89–90
Algeria
    as French colony, 123f, 123, 133–34, 147–48
    nationalization and, 66, 82–83
    oil-for-security deals, 146, 147f, 147–48
    OPEC membership, 71, 97, 101t, 102n.30
Allen, George V., 142
al Qaeda, 154
ambassadorial representation, 96
Amery, Leo, 129
Amin, Samir, 68
Anglo-American oil. *See* Britain; Seven Sister oil companies; United States
Anglo-Iranian Oil Company (later BP), 143, 145
    See also Anglo-Persian Oil Company (later BP)
Anglo-Iraq treaty (1920), 122
Anglo-Persian Oil Company (later BP), 61, 119–20
    See also Anglo-Iranian Oil Company (later BP); British Petroleum (BP)
Angola, 97, 101n.29, 116, 133–34
anticolonialism
    OPEC and, 87
    transnational group of anticolonial elites, 68–69
Arab Fund for Economic and Social Development, 88–89
Arabian American Oil Company (Aramco), 62, 67t, 69–70, 71–73, 141
    Saudi Aramco, 79–80, 84, 160
Arab Oil Congress, 69, 70
Argentina, 152

arms deals, 86–87
    religious associations, 87, 89, 90–91
    Saudi Arabia and, 86–87, 137–38, 155–
        56, 158, 215
    See also oil-for-security (OFS) deals
army. *See under* military
asset valuation and payments
    in climate change subsystems,
        188, 192–94
    in oil production subsystem, 84, 91–93
authority types, 38–39
    during decolonization, 45
    monarchy, 134, 135, 148
    nationalization changes, 82–83, 92*t*
    See also leadership selection;
        nationalization of oil companies
Azerbaijan, 105, 125, 141, 148

Baghdad Pact (CENTO, 1955), 140
Bahrain, 90
    as British territory, 122–23, 132–33,
        134, 150
    monarchy in, 134
    oil-for-security deals, 146, 147*f*,
        147n.101
    Suez Crisis and, 127
Baldwin, James, 186
Banco del Sur, 89–90
banks, 36, 47, 178–79
    assets-capital relationship and, 192
    Banco del Sur, 89–90
    climate governance and, 189, 193–94
    See also economic coercion; finance;
        World Bank
Barrett, Scott, 200, 205n.85
battery technology, 191
behavior patterns
    in international order definition, 23–24,
        24*t*, 32–34, 50
    observation step, in subsystems
        analysis, 164–65, 170, 173–74
    See also governing arrangements;
        instruments of coercion;
        punishments for noncompliance;
        strategic benefits
Belgium, 122
benefits for compliance. *See* punishments
    for noncompliance; strategic benefits

Betancourt, Romulo, 63–64
Biden administration, 202, 208
bilateral agreements and relationships,
        37n.31, 89, 90
    bilateral investment treaties
        (BITs), 166–67
    See also mutual gains
Black Panther Party, 87
boom and bust patterns, 84, 89–90
border adjustment taxes (BATs), 18–19,
        187, 196–97, 200–12, 213
    criticism, 200–1
    European Commission consideration
        of, 219
    monitoring climate policy through, 207
    rate setting, 202–4, 205, 206–7
    retaliatory tariff risk, 207–11
    trade goals *vs.* pro-climate policy
        goals, 205–7
    under WTO rules, 205–6, 216
    See also climate club; climate
        governance; taxes
boundaries of subsystems, 39–40
Bourdieu, Pierre, 40n.44
boycotts, 47
    of Iranian oil, 65–66, 143–44, 145, 159
    of Mexican oil, 65
    See also economic coercion;
        punishments for noncompliance
Brazil, 194
Brexit referendum, 180, 220–21
Britain, car ownership in, 77*f*
Britain, leadership selection
    Abu Dhabi, 149–50
    conceptual examples, 47
    Iraq, 139–40, 159, 184–85
    Oman, 66–67
    in post-independence governments, 134
    See also leadership selection;
        Seven Sisters era, instruments of
        coercion during
Britain, oil-for-security deals
    CENTO and, 140
    imperialist origins of, 12, 132–33, 135,
        136–37, 149–51
    Iran, 140, 141–42, 143, 150–51, 157
    Iraq, 139–41, 146, 157
    Iraq-Kuwait conflict and, 139, 151–53

Kuwait, 130, 138–39, 146, 149, 152,
154, 157
protectionism through, 56, 60, 130, 135
relationship with US and, 12, 136, 151–
52, 154
shift toward, after decolonization, 135,
150–51, 155
Thatcher and, 151–52, 154
See also oil-for-security (OFS) deals
British colonialism and imperial
expansion
final years of, 120, 121–24, 129, 132–
33, 149–51
in India, 43, 128–29
map, 123f
military cost analysis, 130–31
oil discoveries in British
territories, 122–23
See also colonialism and imperial
expansion; decolonization
British military, 66–67, 130–31
naval shift from coal to oil, 119–
20, 121–22
troops withdrawal after
decolonization, 150–51
WWII and, 124–25, 126
See also Britain, oil-for-security deals;
military coercion; oil-for-security
(OFS) deals
British oil companies. See Seven Sister oil
companies
British Petroleum (BP), 25, 52n.94, 61,
71, 145
Seven Sisters era market division, 61–62
See also Seven Sister oil companies
British pound, value of, 150
Brunei, 45, 132–33
Brzezinski, Zbigniew, 151
Bueno de Mesquita, Bruce, 222n.37
Bush, George H. W., 119, 120–21, 148–49,
151–53, 154
Bush, George W., 148–49
Byrd-Hagel resolution, 191n.23, 209

Canada
climate club membership, 204–5
G7 membership, 86
NAFTA membership, 46

oil imports to US, 6
oil production in, 24–25, 122
cap-and-trade system, 187, 196
capital controls, 178f, 178–79, 192
See also climate-related capital
subsystem
capitalist societies, asset valuation in, 192
capital turnover cycle, 218
carbon pricing, 18–19, 200–2, 207–9, 211–12
carbon tariffs. See border adjustment
taxes (BATs)
carbon taxing, 187, 196, 197, 208
Cárdenas, Lázaro, 65
car ownership, 76, 77f, 127, 218
electric cars, 218–19
Carr, E. H., 214, 224
cartel definitions, 94, 95, 99, 112
See also OPEC, cartel reputation
Carter, Jimmy, 151
Carter Doctrine, 151, 157
Castro, Fidel, 143–44
causal inference, 11, 39, 163–64, 166–67,
173–75, 184
central banks, climate governance and,
189, 193–94
See also banks; World Bank
Central Command military task force
(US), 151
Central Intelligence Agency (CIA), 137–
38, 141, 143–44, 148–49
Central Treaty Organization
(CENTO), 140
Chávez, Hugo, 89–90, 110
cheating on production quotas. See OPEC,
production quotas, cheating on
Cheney, Dick, 152
Chevron, 25, 52n.94
See also Seven Sister oil companies
China
hegemonic rise, 1–2
liberal international order participation
of, 221, 222
oil-for-security deals and, 156
oil production in, 24–25, 126
China, climate change and, 221
emissions rates, 190–91, 196, 208
energy technology development,
191, 195

China, climate change and (*cont.*)
  intellectual property law and, 195–96
  venture capitalist investment in Chinese
    companies, 195
China, climate club membership, 201, 202,
    212, 216
  as essential, 18–19, 187, 209–11, 213
Churchill, Winston, 119–20, 121–22,
    129, 144–45
Cirone, Alexandra E., 199n.62
climate change events and effects
  asset valuation and, 188, 192–94
  climate adaptation responses, 193
  pace and urgency of, 189–90, 204
  trade disruptions through, 196–97
  See also energy transition, global
climate club, 26–27, 201–11
  decoupled economies and, 19, 187,
    210–11, 213
  domestic costs for joining, 201–4,
    203f, 204f
  outsider states, 201–5, 206–9
  requirements and encouragements for
    joining, 201, 202–3
  retaliatory tariff risk, 207–11
  size considerations, 18–19, 187,
    203–4
  See also border adjustment taxes
    (BATs); China, climate club
    membership; EU, climate club
    membership; United States, climate
    club membership
climate governance
  banks and, 189, 193–94
  defining actors in, 188, 189–90, 194–
    95, 212
  designing, 4–5, 27–28
  free-riding concerns, 187, 200–1, 202,
    209, 212
  governance fragmentation, 191–92
  information sharing in, 187, 195–
    96, 198
  instruments of coercion and, 188–
    89, 197
  international deficit of, 187n.3
  regime complex, 188, 198
  subsystems advantages, 198
  unilateral mitigation policy, 187

  See also border adjustment taxes
    (BATs); United States, climate
    change and
climate laggards, 195, 198–99, 206–7
climate leaders, 191, 195
  domestic politics and, 203, 209, 211
  willingness to assume leader role, 200–
    1, 203
  See also climate club
climate policies
  cap-and-trade system, 187, 196
  carbon pricing, 18–19, 200–2, 207–
    9, 211–12
  carbon taxing, 187, 196, 197, 208
  domestic implementation, 202, 212
  global energy transition and, 219
  strength of punishments in current, 18,
    191, 198–99, 205n.85
  threat of sanctions in absence of, 205
  See also border adjustment taxes (BATs)
climate politics, subsystems identification,
    26–27, 189–90, 197–98, 212
  subsystems' overlap, 193–94, 196–
    97, 212
  See also climate-related capital
    subsystem; climate-trade nexus
    subsystem; emissions reductions
    subsystem; negative-emissions
    technologies subsystem
climate-related capital subsystem, 26–27,
    186–87, 192–94, 216
  actors involved in, 194
  assets-capital relationship, 192
  emissions reductions subsystem
    and, 193–94
  insurers' role in, 193
  punishments for noncompliance in, 194
  strategic benefits in, 194
climate-trade nexus subsystem, 26–27,
    186–87, 196–97, 216
  BATs and, 199–200
  emissions reductions subsystem
    and, 196
  trade network positioning, 204–5
Clinton, Bill, 114
club goods, 76, 80t, 187
  Ikenberry on, 21–22
  See also climate club; strategic benefits

coal
    British naval move away from, 119–
        20, 121–22
    consumption levels, 18, 217–18
    depreciation allowances for coal
        plants, 192
    electricity generated by, 134, 217
    Marshall Plan and, 127
coercion, instruments of. See instruments
    of coercion
Cold War, 120, 151, 164–65, 222
    oil-for-security origins and, 134, 135–36
colonialism and imperial expansion
    anticolonialism, 68–69, 87
    as background to oil production
        subsystem changes, 91
    Falklands War, 152
    hegemonic actors overestimate strategic
        benefits from, 48–49
    nationalization and, 64
    oil fields' legal ownership during, 63
    oil-for-security origins in, 135
    punishments for noncompliance
        during, 178f, 178–79
    Seven Sisters era, country
        comparisons, 67t
    See also British colonialism and
        imperial expansion; decolonization
communism, 86–87, 137–38, 192
    communist threat as pretext for
        leadership selection, 143
communitarian strategic benefits,
    defined, 42
    See also strategic benefits
Compagnie française des pétroles (CFP,
    now Total), 61
competition and cooperation, patterns
    of, 222
competitive shaming, 27, 172–73, 194, 222
complexity and adaptability, 50, 113
concessionaires, 61, 63, 66, 72–73, 139–
    40, 142
concession fees, 60, 64, 75–76, 81–82
Conference of the Parties (COP)
    meetings, 188
Congo, 97
constructivism, 21, 23–24, 24t, 33–34
consumption levels

civilian fuel consumption, 6
    of coal, 18, 217–18
    of renewable energy, 18
    See also oil consumption
contextual analysis, 164
Coolidge, Calvin, 59
cooperation and collaboration, climate
        governance and, 195–96
    hegemonic stability theory and, 189
    See also climate club
cooperation and collaboration, OPEC
        member states. See OPEC,
        cooperation among members
cooperation with international order,
        incentives. See punishments for
        noncompliance; strategic benefits
Council on Foreign Relations, 5
coup d'etats
    in Iran, 75, 144–45
    in Iraq, 140
    in Venezuela, 63–64
    See also leadership selection
court cases, climate-related, 189–90
covert operations, 14, 41–42, 47–48, 65–
        66, 144
Covid-19 pandemic, 6n.19, 7
Cowhey, Peter, 78
Cox, Robert, 168, 184
credit, 47
    See also economic coercion
Creole Petroleum Company, 81
crude oil, 79, 83–84, 125
    prices, 17–18, 69, 73
    Venezuelan reserves, 81
Cullenward, Danny, 202n.81
currency
    British pound devaluation, 150
    US dollar, oil priced in, 157–58
Curzon, George, 121–22

Dannenberg, Astrid, 200
debt, 93
decarbonization, 187, 188, 193, 201–2,
        204, 208–9, 223
decolonization aftermath, instruments of
        coercion affected by
    assessment of, 54–57, 91
    economic coercion, 15–16, 32, 54, 55t

decolonization aftermath, instruments of coercion affected by (*cont.*)
  leadership selection, 15–16, 51–52, 54, 55*t*, 56–57, 64–65, 134
  military coercion, 54, 55*t*
  new governing arrangements and ordering shifts, 45, 48–49, 149
  oil-for-security deals, context, 121–24, 128–34, 135–37, 149–51, 155, 158
  punishments for noncompliance, 15–16, 32, 51–52, 54, 55*t*, 60–61
  strategic benefits, 16
  See also nationalization of oil companies; oil-for-security (OFS) deals
decolonization process
  anticolonial elites and, 68–69
  conflict during, 133–34
decolonization timing, 51, 128–34
  colonialism resurgence, 129
  in petro-colonies, 120, 129–34
  statistical analysis, 131–33, 131*t*, 133*t*, 158
decoupled economies, 19, 187, 210–11, 213
deductive reasoning, 165
deep cooperation, 27–28, 34–35, 177, 198–99
defection from international order, 44–45
depletion rates, 102–8, 104*t*, 112
  See also oil production levels
descriptive inference, 20n.67, 39, 166–67, 168, 184
Designing Social Inquiry (King et al.), 167
developing nations
  anticolonialism efforts in, 87
  China claims status, 190–91
  climate negotiations and, 191
  Green Lend Lease and, 195
  oil prices and, 87–88
diamond market, 17–18
diplomatic benefits to OPEC member states, 110–12
dollar, as global reserve currency, 137–38, 157–58
domestic politics
  international order affected by hegemons', 41–42

oil-for-security deals and revolutions, 146
domestic politics, climate governance and, 187, 211–12
  asset valuation importance, 188
  climate club membership and, 201–4, 203*f*, 204*f*
  emissions reductions subsystem, 189–90
  Green New Deal, 195
  leakage risks, 196
  local economic benefits, 197
  Paris Agreement and, 198–99
  See also China, climate club membership; climate governance; EU, climate club membership; United States, climate club membership
dominant-partner trade situation, 204–5
dominant producer hypothesis, 105–6
Doyle, Michael, 51n.87

Eagleburger, Lawrence, 152
earnings potential, 84
economic aid, oil revenue and, 17–18, 86–91
  Marshall Plan, 127–28
  See also finance; oil-for-security (OFS) deals; oil revenue
economic and military hegemony, commingling of, 8
economic coercion
  boycotts, 47, 65–66, 143–44, 145, 159
  conceptual overview, 4, 8, 14, 47
  decolonization's effect on, 15–16, 32, 54, 55*t*
  embargoes, 47, 52–53, 83, 85, 109, 126
  sanctions, 47, 53, 107, 199–200, 205
  See also arms deals; banks; border adjustment taxes (BATs); instruments of coercion
economic growth variable in OPEC cartel analysis, 103
economic influence, definitions, 95
  See also OPEC, cartel reputation
economic strategic benefits, defined, 42
  See also strategic benefits
economic subsystems, 11–12

See also climate-related capital
subsystem; climate-trade nexus
subsystem; oil production subsystem
The Economist, 116
economy, global. *See* global market
Ecuador, 97, 101n.29, 105, 110–11
Eden, Anthony, 143–44
Egypt
  Libya and, 147–48
  monarchy in, 134
  oil-for-security deals and, 135–36
  Saudi Arabia and, 89, 138, 157
  war and conflict involving, 83, 124, 138
Eisenhower, Dwight D., 71
Eisenhower administration, 69
electricity production, 134, 217
embargoes, 47, 52–53, 83, 85
  safeguards against, 109
  US imposes on Japan, WWII, 126
  See also economic coercion; 1973
    oil shock
embedded liberalism, 220–21
emissions rates, 4–5, 217–18
  China, 190–91, 196, 208
  EU, 208
  US, 208
emissions reductions subsystem, 26–27,
    186–87, 189–92, 216
  climate leaders in, 201
  climate-related capital subsystem
    and, 193–94
  climate-trade nexus subsystem
    and, 196
  governance fragmentation in, 191–92
  leakage risks, 196
  punishments for noncompliance
    in, 191–92
  strategic benefits in, 190–92
  See also climate politics, subsystems
    identification; negative-emissions
    technologies subsystem
empire, definition, 51
empirical inference, 52n.93, 165
empirical patterns
  in nuclear politics, 170
  observation of, 164–65, 166–68,
    169, 219
endogeneity, 98–99

energy independence, 215
  defined, 5–7
  See also energy security
energy security, 5–8
  defined, 5
  as political rhetoric, 5–7
  See also oil-for-security (OFS) deals; oil
    security subsystem; renewable energy
    technology
energy transition, global, 217–20
  conventional focus of analysis, 219
  energy transitions, defined, 217
  historical consumption patterns, 18, 217–18
  impact of climate policy relating to, 219
  multiple perspectives problem, 219–20
  oil's significance throughout, 17–18
  pace of, 218
  scale of, 217–18
  strategic benefits of, 218–19
  subsystems theory insight into,
    27, 219–20
  See also climate change
enforceability of punishments. *See*
    strength and enforceability of
    punishments
England. *See* Britain
environmental issues. *See* climate change
Equatorial Guinea, 97
Europe, and EU
  car ownership in, 76, 77*f*, 127
  China and, 209–11
  climate subsystems and, 189–90
  emissions rates, 208
  IEA proposal response by, 85–86
  Marshall Plan and, 127–28
  oil-for-security deals, 136
  oil politics response after 1973 shocks, 85
  oil sources for, 127–28
  OPEC legal challenges in, 112
  See also Britain; colonialism and
    imperial expansion
European Central Bank (ECB), 193
European Commission, 219
EU, climate club membership, 18–19,
    187, 208
  BATs and, 202, 212, 216, 219
  China and, 19, 201, 209–11
  retaliatory tariffs and, 208

Evian Accords (1962), 133–34
exports. *See* border adjustment taxes
    (BATs); imports and exports
Exxon (later ExxonMobil), 61–62,
    81, 136
ExxonMobil, 25, 52n.94
    See also Seven Sister oil companies

Fahd, King of Saudi Arabia, 86, 153–54
Faisal, Crown Prince of Saudi Arabia,
    137, 138
Faisal, King of Iraq, 64–65, 122–23,
    135, 139–40
Faisal, King of Saudi Arabia, 83, 89, 168
Faisal II, King of Iraq, 140
Falklands War (1982), 152
Feinstein, Yuval, 131–32
fields, oil. *See* oil fields, geopolitical
    distribution of
fields (in sociology), limits of, 40n.44
50/50 profit agreements, 63–64, 72–73,
    74, 77–78
    See also oil revenue
finance
    climate change effects on practices,
        189, 197
    development finance, 186–87, 197
    global economic and political influence,
        86–91, 127–28, 137–38
    hegemonic stability theory and, 19
    IMF capital controls and developing
        nations, 178f, 178–79, 184
    Marshall Plan and, 127–28
    See also banks; economic aid, oil
        revenue and; global market; issue
        areas; oil revenue
financial crisis (2008), 180
Financial Times, 195
firms and states relationship, 52–53
fiscal strength variable in OPEC cartel
    analysis, 103
Flournoy, Michèle, 31
Ford, Gerald, 85–86
foreign aid. *See* economic aid, oil revenue
    and; economic coercion; oil revenue
fossil fuel replacement. *See* climate change;
    energy transition, global; renewable
    energy technology

fossil fuels
    asset valuation, 192–93
    industry employment, 218–19
    See also coal; emissions; oil
        consumption; oil prices
fracking, 155, 215
France
    car ownership in, 77f
    OECD membership of, 85–86
    oil companies and, 61, 62, 145
    oil-for-security deals with, 136
    Suez Crisis involvement, 127
Frankel, Jeffrey A., 205n.87
free-riding, climate governance concerns
    about, 187, 200–1, 202, 209, 212
French colonialism, 45, 120, 122, 123f
    Algeria, 123f, 123, 133–34, 147–48
    decolonization conflicts, 133–34
Fridays for Future, 211
Fund for International Development
    (OFID, OPEC), 88–89
Furtado, Celso, 68

G7 (Group of Seven, and various
    iterations), 86
Gabon, 45, 97, 110–11
game theory, 44–45, 200–1
Geertz, Clifford, 168
geostrategic benefits, defined, 42
Germany, 77f, 140
    WWII and, 49, 124–25
GHG. *See* emissions
Glaspie, April, 153
globalization, neopositivism on, 166–67
global market, 11–12
    climate change and, 187, 193
    decoupled global economy, 210–
        11, 213
    loose oil market, 60, 91
    Marshall Plan and, 127–28
    oil fields distribution and, 52
    oil production comparisons, 97, 122,
        134, 217–18
    oil value in, 17–18
    one-world open economy, 210n.106
    OPEC era changes in, 60–61
    price stability/volatility metric, 32–33
    during Seven Sisters era, 60, 61–62, 92t

tight oil market, 76, 79, 91
US expectations of Saudi involvement
    in, 155–56
See also cartel definitions; finance;
    OPEC, cartel reputation
global warming. *See* climate change
governance questions, identification step
    in subsystems analysis, 4, 163–64
    in climate politics, 188–89
    empirical particulars identification,
        relationship to, 166, 167
    governance questions, defined, 36–38,
        39, 165–66
    guidelines, 37–38, 40n.43, 164, 165–66,
        167, 169, 175, 188–89
    in nuclear politics, 170
    in oil politics, 52
    in peacekeeping operations, 173
governing arrangements, climate
    subsystems. *See* climate governance
governing arrangements, compliance
    incentives. *See* instruments
    of coercion; punishments for
    noncompliance; strategic benefits
governing arrangements, defined, 9–
    10, 34–35
    contemporary IR scholarly views, 22–
        23, 24t, 27, 34, 38–39
    contemporary IR scholars overlook,
        19–20, 21, 27
    hegemony, relationship to, 3–4, 14–15
    Ikenberry's definition, 34
    international order, relationship to, 19–
        21, 27, 31–35, 45–46, 181–84
    issue areas, relationship to, 9, 11f,
        11, 15f
    multiplicity of, 3–4, 9, 19–20, 21
    ordering themes, relationship to,
        9–10, 11f, 15f, 15, 19–20, 34–35,
        39, 181–84
    subsystems, relationship to, 9–10, 11f,
        15f, 36, 37, 175
governing arrangements, oil subsystems.
    See international oil companies
    (IOCs); nationalization of oil
    companies; oil production
    subsystem; oil security subsystem;
    OPEC; Seven Sister oil companies

governing arrangements, variables
    affecting change, 15f, 39, 50,
        56f, 177–79
    contemporary IR scholars on, 11, 33–34
    decolonization, 15–16, 32, 136–37
    hegemonic actors, 3–4, 14, 15, 35, 57
    institutional actors, 49–50
    instruments of coercion, 13–15, 31–32,
        45, 168–69
    nuclear politics, 164–65, 171
    ordering themes' independence, 9–10,
        39, 44–45, 181–84, 182f
    peacekeeping operations, 173–75
    rival collective images, 168–69, 171, 184
    social movement theory, 168–69, 184
Great Britain. *See* Britain
Green, Jessica F., 202n.78
greenhouse gases (GHG). *See under*
    emissions
green industrial policy, 208–9, 211–12
Green Lend Lease, 195
Green New Deal, 195, 197
green protectionism, 197, 205
green sanctions, 199–200
Group of Seven (G7, and various
    iterations), 86
Gulf Oil Corporation, 25, 141
Gulf Wars. *See* Iraq-Kuwait conflict

Hamas, 87
Hashemite dynasty (Iraq), 140–41
Heath, Edward, 152
hegemon
    defined, 2–3
    pure and partial, differences, 2–3, 14–
        15, 19
    relation to subsystems, 32, 41–42, 46–49
hegemonic actors
    China's rise, 1–2
    domestic politics of, international order
        affected by, 41–42
    imposing punishments upon, 46, 177
    instruments of coercion, access to, 14–
        15, 47–48
    strategic benefits overestimated by, 48–49
    See also United States as hegemon
hegemonic decline, 14–15, 46–49, 57
    of US, 1–2, 3, 7–8, 19, 189

hegemonic stability theory, 3–4, 7, 8, 32, 35–189

Hezbollah, 87, 90

historicism, 164, 166–67, 168

Hitler, Adolf, 124, 125–26

Holland/the Netherlands, 83, 122, 133–34, 189–90

Hussein, Saddam, 79, 152, 153–54

Hyndman, K., 98

ideational shifts, 43

IEA (International Energy Agency), 56–57, 85–86

Ikenberry, John, 1–2n.1, 20n.66, 21–22, 34, 221

imperialism/colonialism. *See* colonialism and imperial expansion; decolonization

imports and exports, 138–39
 BATs and, 199, 207
 Eisenhower administration quota system, 69
 export bans, 6n.20
 global fluctuations, 134, 155
 monitoring, 207
 See also border adjustment taxes (BATs); OPEC

incentive-response changes, 50

independence movements, 128–29, 150
 petrostates and non-petrostates, compared, 131–32, 131t, 133t
 sovereign state creation, 45, 48–49, 60, 149
 See also colonialism and imperial expansion; decolonization; nationalization of oil companies

India
 as British territory, 43, 128–29
 nuclear politics and, 171

individual actors' role, 16
 climate action, 187
 See also actors, defining

Indonesia, 36, 105, 126
 decolonization, 133–34
 OPEC membership, 71, 97

industrial production, emissions leakage risks, 196

information sharing
 among OPEC members, 75–76, 79, 80–81, 80t, 187, 198
 climate governance and, 187, 195–96, 198
 IEA requirements, 86
 through competitive shaming, 172–73

institutional change, 20, 54, 55t

institutions, role of, 22–23, 35, 49–50
 See also actors, defining

instrumental interconnection of subsystems, 184–85, 196–97

instruments of coercion, defined, 4, 13–16, 31–32, 46–49
 assessing changes in, 53–57
 availability and ability to use, 9, 14–15, 48–49
 in climate subsystems, 188–89, 197
 contemporary IR scholarship on, 21–22
 cost-effectiveness, 14–15, 31–32, 46–47, 51–52
 hegemonic access to, 14–15, 47–48
 selection criteria for research focus, 14
 types, 14, 47–48
 See also decolonization aftermath, instruments of coercion affected by; economic coercion; leadership selection; military coercion; punishments for noncompliance; Seven Sisters era, instruments of coercion during

insurance, climate risks and, 193

intellectual property rights, 195–96

Inter-American Development Bank, Venezuelan funding of, 89

Intermediate-range Nuclear Treaty, 172

International Atomic Energy Agency (IAEA), 171

International Civil Aviation Organization, 189–90

international climate order, 27, 211–12
 weakness of, 187n.3, 188
 See also climate governance; domestic politics, climate governance and

International Energy Agency (IEA), 56–57, 85–86

International Monetary Fund (IMF), 36, 89, 178–79, 180
 capital controls by, 178f, 178–79, 184

international oil companies (IOCs)
    majors and independents divisions,
        72–73, 78
    as oligopsony, 73
    See also Seven Sister oil companies
international order, defined, 9, 19–
        21, 31–40
    behavior patterns and, 23–24, 24*t*, 32–
        34, 50
    de facto vs. de jure rules, 23–24, 33n.6
    hegemon in IR theory of, 2–3
    input/output distinction, 23–24,
        24*t*, 32–34
    See also liberal international order
international order, analyzing changes, 25,
        32–35, 40–46, 163, 214–15, 224
    aggregate levels, 36, 163, 179–80
    deep cooperation and, 177n.49
    exogenous variables, 15*f*, 15–16
    explanatory variables, 40–43
    governing arrangements, relationship
        to, 19–21, 27, 32–35, 45–46, 181–84
    hegemonic decline, 14–15, 46–49
    hegemonic stability theory, 35
    institutions' role, 35, 49–50
    IR theories, limitations of, 10–11, 35,
        41, 49, 181
    punishments and benefits relationship,
        27, 43–46, 44*f*, 149–50, 177
    war and, 20, 35
    See also actors, defining; instruments of
        coercion; international relations (IR)
        theory; issue areas; punishments for
        noncompliance; strategic benefits;
        subsystems theory
international organizations, climate
        and, 211
international political economy (IPE)
        scholarship, 7
international relations (IR) theory, 19–24
    constructivist analysis, 21, 23–24,
        24*t*, 33–34
    hegemonic stability theory, 3–4, 7, 8,
        32, 35–189
    international rules design, 97, 163
    liberal institutional analysis, 21–22,
        24*t*, 35
    ordering themes, 10

realist analysis, 21–23, 24*t*, 57–58
    regime theory, 35
international relations (IR) theory,
        limitations, 19–24
    analysis of OPEC as cartel, 108–9, 113,
        114, 116, 117–18
    approach to hegemony, 19
    causal inference, 39, 163–64, 166–67
    change variations overlooked, 10–11,
        19–20, 35, 180, 181
    complexity arguments, 50, 113
    governing arrangements overlooked,
        19–20, 21, 27
    issue areas focus, 4, 27
    liberal international order crisis
        debates, 214, 222–23
    oil politics, intertwined dimensions
        overlooked, 25
    oil security subsystem overlooked, 7, 11
    punishments and benefits overlooked,
        21, 41, 216
    security competition focus, 38–39
    systemic level focus, 19–20, 27, 180–81
    war focus, 3, 20, 35, 49
International Renewable Energy Agency,
        217n.11
international systems, term, 11*f*
international trade, exogenous easing of,
        54n.103
intrinsic interconnection of subsystems,
        184–85, 196–97
investment, venture capitalism and climate
        change, 194–95
investment risk variable in OPEC cartel
        analysis, 103, 104*t*
IOCs. *See* international oil companies
        (IOCs); Seven Sister oil companies
IPE (international political economy)
        scholarship, 7
Iran
    armed groups funded by, 87, 90
    British imperial influence of, 122, 123,
        134, 135
    coup d'etat, 75, 144–45
    domestic politics and, 110, 143–44
    Iraq invasion of, 1979, 84
    leadership selection, 47, 64–65, 75, 134,
        135, 141, 144–45, 146

Iran (*cont.*)
  nuclear politics and, 12, 164–
    65, 170–71
  oil reserves discovery in, 61, 119–20
  Seven Sisters control in, 61, 65–66, 67*t*,
    143–44, 145, 159
Iran, oil-for-security deals, 146
  Anglo-American, 141–42, 145
  British, 140, 141–42, 150–51, 152–
    53, 157
  punishments for noncompliance, 136–
    37, 142–45
  rejection of, 56*f*, 120–21, 147*f*, 147–48,
    151, 158
  Soviet, 141–42
  US, 142, 144–45, 146
Iran, OPEC membership, 97
  cartel myth perpetuated, 110
  domestic politics and, 110
  formation involvement, 66, 67*t*, 70, 71
  1973 oil shock, 82, 84–85
  as original signatory, 71
  posted price negotiations and, 77–78
  production levels and, 101–2nn.29–30,
    101*t*, 109n.46
  profit negotiations, 74–75, 77–78
  sanctions on, 107
Iran, punishments for
    noncompliance, 80*t*
  nationalization attempts and, 64–66,
    67*t*, 75, 78–79, 82–83, 142–45, 159
  oil boycotts, 65–66, 143–44, 145, 159
Iran-Contra deal, 137–38
Iran Crisis (1946), 141–42
Iranian Revolution, 84
Iraq
  British imperial influence of,
    119, 122–23
  coup d'etat, 140
  independence granted, 1932, 122–23,
    130, 132–33, 139–40
  Iran invasion by, 1979, 84
  leadership selection in, 64–65, 66, 122–
    23, 134, 139–41, 159, 184–85
  Seven Sisters era, 61, 63–64, 66, 67*t*
Iraq, oil-for-security deals, 139–41,
    146, 159
  British, 139–41, 146, 157

Kuwait invasion and, 153
  punishments for
    noncompliance, 136–37
  rejection of, 147*f*, 147–48, 151, 158
  US, 140–41
Iraq, OPEC membership, 97
  as original signatory, 71
  production levels, 109n.46, 143–44
  production quotas, 101n.29, 101*t*
Iraq, punishments for
    noncompliance, 136–37
  nationalization attempts and, 65n.16,
    66, 67*t*, 78–80, 82–83
Iraq-Kuwait conflict
  British involvement, 139, 151–53
  decolonization border demarcations,
    122–23, 130
  US involvement, 7–8, 41–42, 47, 120–
    21, 137, 139, 151–54, 157
Iraq Petroleum Company, 61, 79, 139–40
Irish Republican Army (IRA), 87
Islam
  Islamic movements, funding for, 87,
    88–89, 90–91, 92*t*
  Muslim petrostates, oil-for-security
    variable, 148
Islamic Revolutionary Guard (Qods
    force), 87, 90
Islam/Muslim bias, foreign aid from Saudi
    Arabia and, 89
Israel, 83, 90, 128, 155; 171
issue areas
  behavior definitions within, 163–64
  defining, 4, 9, 11*f*, 36
  regime theory and, 35, 36
  simultaneous change and
    continuity in, 39
  subsystems theory relating to empirics
    of, 164, 166–68, 169
Italy, 77*f*, 123*f*, 123, 124–25

Japan, 85–86, 120, 126–27
jihad, 89, 90
Johnson, Lyndon Baines, 139, 150–51
Jordan, 134, 140
jurisdiction and sovereignty over
    oil, 11–12
  See also oil security subsystem

Katzenstein, Peter J., 176n.48
Kazakhstan, 105
Kellogg-Briand Pact (1928), 23–24
Kennedy, John F., 137, 138
Keohane, Robert O., 7, 8, 54n.103
Khomeini, Ruhollah, 84
Kindleberger, Charles P., 7
Kissinger, Henry, 31, 83, 85–86
Krasner, Stephen, 97
Kurita Takeo, 126–27
Kuwait
    arms purchases from US, 158
    British imperial influence of, 122–23,
        132–33, 138–39
    decolonization and independence of,
        66, 130, 132–33, 139
    economic aid by, 88–89
    monarchy in, 134
    nationalization in, 66, 67t, 80, 82–83
    oil discovered in, 122–23, 138–39
    OPEC membership, 71, 97, 101t,
        102n.30, 109n.46, 143–44
    Seven Sisters era, 63–64, 66, 67t
    See also Iraq-Kuwait conflict
Kuwait, oil-for-security deals
    acceptance of, 147f
    Britain, 130, 138–39, 146, 149, 152,
        154, 157
    Iraq invasion and, 153
    US, 153, 159
Kuwait Oil Company, 84, 141
Kyoto Protocol (1997), 190–91, 205n.83
    failure of, 191, 198–99

Latin American Bolivarian Alternative
    (ALBA), 89–90
Latin American Economic
    System (Sistema Económico
    Latinoamericano y del Caribe, or
    SELA), 89
leaders, hubris of, 223
leadership selection, 4, 47, 66–67
    climate change and, 189
    conceptual overview, 14
    cost-effectiveness of, 32, 149
    coup d'etats, 63–64, 75, 140, 144–45
    decolonization's effect on, 15–16, 51–52,
        54, 55t, 56–57, 64–65, 134

    in Iran, 47, 64–65, 75, 134, 135, 141,
        144–45, 146
    in Iraq, 64–65, 66, 122–23, 134, 139–41,
        159, 184–85
    oil-for-security deals and, 135,
        138, 140–41
    Operation Ajax, 65–66, 144, 149, 159
    pretexts for, 143
    in Saudi Arabia, 138
    in Venezuela, 63–64
    See also Britain, leadership selection;
        instruments of coercion;
        punishments for noncompliance;
        United States, leadership selection
Lebanon, 87, 148, 153
legitimacy, perception of, 43
Lend Lease program (WWII), 195
level of analysis, 9–11, 20, 26, 35, 36,
    166, 179–84
liberal institutionalism, 21–22, 24t, 35
liberal international order, 183–84, 222–24
    crisis of, 1–2, 180, 214, 220–22, 223
    defined, 1–2n.1, 9–10, 20n.64, 180
    Ikenberry's analogies of, 221
    internal and external threats, 220–21
    partial participation, 221
    See also international order; United
        States, liberal international order and
Liberia, 173
Libya
    armed groups funding by, 87
    decolonization and independence of,
        66, 123, 134
    as Italian colony, 123f, 123
    nationalization in, 66, 67t, 80, 82–83
    oil-for-security deals, 146, 147f, 147–48,
        151, 154, 157, 158, 159
    OPEC membership, 71, 77–78, 97, 101t,
        102n.30
    size, 148
    WWII and, 124–25
lobby groups, climate policy and, 208
low-carbon technology, 217

Maadi (Mehdi) Pact, 70–71
MacArthur, Douglas, 126–27
Macmillan, Harold, 129
Maghribi, Mahmood, 66, 68, 80

majlis (parliament, Iran), 143, 145
Malaysia, 36
Mankiw, N. Gregory, 99
market allocations. *See* OPEC,
 production quotas
market conditions. *See* economic coercion;
 finance; global market; oil prices; oil
 production subsystem; OPEC, cartel
 reputation
Marshall, George, 127
Marshall Plan, 127–28
Mattis, James, 156
McCain, John, 7
McCarthy, Kevin, 7
Mearsheimer, John, 2n.4, 9n.30,
 21n.71, 38–39
Mercosur, 89–90
Mesopotamian Campaign, 122
Mexico, 46, 105, 122
 nationalization in, 65, 78–79
MI6, 144
Middle East region, defined, 12n.36
 See also under oil-for-security (OFS)
 deals; OPEC; individual country
military, oil as fuel in, 119–20, 121–22,
 124–27, 131
military and economic hegemony,
 commingling of, 8
military coercion, 4, 8
 climate change and, 189
 conceptual overview, 14, 47
 decolonization's effect on, 54, 55t
 See also British military;
 instruments of coercion;
 oil-for-security (OFS) deals; oil
 security subsystem
Miller, Clark A., 217n.8
Miller, Nicholas L., 27, 172–73, 222
Milner, Helen V., 54n.103
Mobil (later ExxonMobil), 61–62
modern oil era, 25–26, 91–93, 92t
 historical overview, 1, 60–61
 See also nationalization of oil
 companies; 1973 oil shock; oil-for-
 security (OFS) deals; OPEC, cartel
 reputation
Mohammed bin Salman, Crown Prince of
 Saudi Arabia, 155

monarchical rule, 134, 135, 148
 See also colonialism and imperial
 expansion; leadership selection
monitoring imports and exports, 207
 See also border adjustment taxes
 (BATs); climate governance; imports
 and exports
monopolies, oil subsystems and, 52, 122
Montreal Protocol, 205n.85
Mossadegh, Mohammad, 65–66, 75, 143–
 45, 159
mujahedin, 86–87
Muslim petrostates, oil-for-security
 variable, 148
 See also Islam; individual countries
Mussolini, Benito, 124–25
"Mutual Defense Agreement" between US
 and Saudi Arabia (1951), 137
mutual gains, 12, 24t, 42, 46
 See also bilateral agreements and
 relationships; OPEC, cooperation
 among members; strategic benefits

Naimi, Ali al-, 96n.6
naming and shaming, 222n.36
Nasser, Abdel Gamal, 89, 147–48
National Iranian Oil Company,
 82n.88, 143
nationalization attempts
 conditions leading to, 60–61, 64–71,
 75–76, 223
 Iran, 64–66, 67t, 75, 78–79, 82–83, 142–
 45, 159
 Iraq, 65n.16, 66, 67t, 78–80, 82–83
 Kuwait, 66, 67t, 80, 82–83
 Libya, 66, 80, 82–83
 Mexico, 65, 78–79
 obstacles and risks, 64–65, 66–69, 67t,
 78–80, 91
 OPEC solidarity, 75–76, 78–82
 profit incentives, 64, 66, 78–79
 Saudi Arabia, 65, 67t, 79–80, 82–83
 Venezuela, 65, 67t, 82–83, 84
nationalization attempts, Seven Sister
 responses, 60, 91
 Iran oil boycott, 65–66, 143–44,
 145, 159
 leadership selection in Iran, 65–66, 144

Libya, 66
Mexico, 65
nationalization of oil companies, 25, 52–
    53, 55t, 157–58
    authority structure changes, 82–83, 92t
    employees' experience of transition, 84
    government costs and asset valuation,
        84, 91–93
    marketing issues, 83–84, 91
    See also OPEC
national security, securitization and, 6
    See also domestic politics; energy
        security
natural gas, 134
Nature magazine, 163
negative-emissions technologies
        subsystem, 26–27, 186–87, 194–96,
        216, 217
    See also climate politics, subsystems
        identification; emissions reductions
        subsystem; renewable energy
        technology
neoliberalism, 220–21
    See also liberal international order
neopositivism, 164, 166–68
the Netherlands/Holland, 83, 122, 133–
    34, 189–90
New International Economic Order
    (NIEO), 87
Newman, Abraham, 199–200
Nexon, Daniel, 199–200
Nicaraguan Contras arms deals, 137–38
Nigeria, 66, 82–83, 108
    OPEC membership, 71, 97, 101t,
        102n.30
1973 oil shock, 73, 82–85, 169
    contemporary IR theory and, 8, 10–
        12, 35
1973 oil shock, aftermath, 55t, 85–91
    global response, 85
    IPE scholarship development, 7
    oil revenue distribution, 82, 84, 92t, 93
    OPEC cartel reputation, 108–9
1979-1980 oil shock, 84
1997 financial crisis of Southeast
    Asia, 36
Niskanen Center, 208
Nixon administration, 83, 157–58

noncompliance punishment. See
    punishments for noncompliance
non-petro-colonies and -states, 54n.106,
    131–32, 135–36, 158
non-state actors, 3n.8, 13–14, 49–50
    authority of, 38n.36
    climate change and, 189
    international order definition, 34–
        35, 56–57
    subsystems definition, 4, 9, 36
    See also actors, defining; state actors
Nordhaus, William, 199, 202n.81
North Africa, 123f, 123, 124–25
North American Free Trade Agreement
    (NAFTA), 46
North Atlantic area, 22n.76, 134
    See also Britain; Europe, and EU;
        United States
North Korea, 53, 170–71
North Sea, 119n.2
Norway, 24–25, 119n.2
Nuclear Nonproliferation Treaty (NPT),
    12, 171, 172
nuclear politics, 163–65, 170–73,
    194, 216
    defining actors in, 172–73
    nuclear proliferation and
        nonproliferation, 12, 170, 171–72,
        178f, 179
    sanctions, 53
    strength of benefits and punishments,
        21, 178f, 179
    weapons management vs. proliferation
        topics, 172
    weapons variable in diplomatic
        representation analysis, 111
Nyerere, Julius, 68

Occidental (independent oil
    company), 77–78
OECD (Organization for Economic Co-
    operation and Development), 85–
    86, 88–89
OFS. See oil-for-security (OFS) deals
oil consumption
    levels of, 17n.53, 18, 127–28
    military importance, 119–20, 121–22,
        124–27, 131

oil fields, geopolitical distribution of, 11–12, 52
  concessions and legal rights for, 61, 63, 66, 72–73, 139–40, 142
  Seven Sisters era divisions, 61–63
oil fields, ownership and management experiments, 75–76
Oil-for-Food program, 154
oil-for-security (OFS) deals, 56–58, 60, 120–21, 215
  acceptance or rejection of, 12, 56f, 56–57, 120–21, 146–48, 147f, 158
  basic structure of, 135, 159–60
  departures from, 121, 146–48, 151
  as deterrence strategy, 153, 157
  as evidence for oil security subsystem, 157–58
  leadership selection and, 135, 138, 140–41
  Libya, 146, 147f, 147–48, 151, 154, 157, 158, 159
  locals' opinion and effects on, 124, 135, 149
  monarchical regimes assist, 135
  for non-petrostates, 135–36
  policymakers and, 215–16
  protectionism through, 26, 129–30, 135, 150–51
  punishments for noncompliance, 136–37, 142–43, 152, 153
  See also Britain, OFS deals; Iran, OFS deals; Iraq, OFS deals; Kuwait, OFS deals; oil security subsystem; Saudi Arabia, OFS deals; United States, OFS deals
oil-for-security (OFS) deals, origins of, 12, 26, 120–21, 134–37
  Cold War and, 134, 135–36
  decolonization and, 121–24, 128–34, 135–37, 149–51, 155, 158
  imports and exports rates, 134, 155
  Marshall Plan and, 127–28
  shift from British to US dominance, 136, 148–51, 155
  WWII and, 124–28
"Oil Is the Exception" (Krasner), 97
oil politics, subsystems of. See oil subsystems

oil prices
  boom and bust patterns, 84, 89–90
  crude, 17–18, 69, 73
  effect on developing world, 87–88
  embargoes' influence on, 52–53
  OPEC cooperation in, 76–79, 80–81, 80t, 99
  OPEC's founding affected by, 69, 70, 71
  posted and market, 70, 73, 76, 77–78, 80t, 82, 91
  short-term changes vs. long-term averages, 84, 95
  subsystems, distinguishing, 52–53
  supply and demand influence, 52–53, 61–62, 67–68, 76, 77f
  Texas Railroad Commission and, 69
  US dollar as global reserve currency, 137–38, 157–58
  See also global market; 1973 oil shock; OPEC, cartel reputation; Seven Sister oil companies, price setting by
oil production authority. See nationalization of oil companies; OPEC; Seven Sister oil companies
oil production costs
  depletion rates and lift costs, 103, 105–6
  petrostates with high costs, 218–19
  Seven Sisters era, 62, 63–64, 74
oil production levels
  energy security rhetoric and, 7
  global comparisons, after WWI, 122
  global comparisons, after WWII, 134
  global comparisons, against OPEC members, 97
  global comparisons, to other fuels, 217–18
  in Iran, during and after boycott, 143–44
  in Mexico, 65, 122
  of new OPEC members, 99–100, 100f
  Saudi Arabian influence on, 7, 96, 97, 105, 112, 137–38
  Seven Sisters era, 52, 61–63, 67–68, 81, 95, 143–44
  See also depletion rates; OPEC, production quotas
oil production subsystem, 25, 215
  analysis, 91–93, 92t, 95

asset valuation and payments in, 84, 91–93
conceptual and historical overview, 52–53, 60
defined, 11–12
independent and dependent variables, 55t
oil security subsystem intertwined with, 124, 149
order variations over time, 56f, 177
retail marketing, 83–84
strength of punishments, eras compared, 66–67, 91, 92t
See also modern oil era, 1970s to present; 1973 oil shock; OPEC, production quotas; punishments for noncompliance, oil production subsystem; Seven Sisters era; subsystems; United States, oil production subsystem

oil revenue
global market value, 17–18
Marshall Plan encourages, 127–28
See also finance; oil-for-security (OFS) deals; oil prices

oil revenue, to OPEC members
accounting tricks in, 74–75
cooperation in profit negotiations, 60–61, 74–75, 77–78, 80t
distribution since 1973 shocks, 82, 84, 92t, 93
50/50 profit agreements, 63–64, 72–73, 74, 77–78
global economic and political influence through, 86–91, 127–28, 137–38
nationalization and, 64, 66, 78–79
See also arms deals

oil security subsystem, 25, 119–60, 215
contemporary IR scholars overlook, 7, 11
defined, 11–12
G7 and, 86
IEA, 56–57, 85–86
independent and dependent variables, 55t
oil production subsystem intertwined with, 124, 149
order variations over time, 56f, 177

strategic benefits assessment, 54n.106, 157–58
See also oil-for-security (OFS) deals; oil production subsystem; punishments for noncompliance, oil security subsystem; subsystems

oil security subsystem, statistical analysis, 156–59
decolonization timing and, 158
punishments for noncompliance, 124, 136–37, 142–45, 152, 159
strategic benefits, 159

oil subsystems, analysis overview, 15–16, 51–57
changes variables, assessment of, 53–57, 60–61, 91
selection logic, 52–53
See also oil production subsystem; oil security subsystem; subsystems

oligopsony, oil companies as, 73

Oman, 66–67, 129–30n.35, 134, 146, 147f, 148

Omar al-Sayyid, Ahmad, 80

OPEC, cartel reputation, 16–17, 52, 95–96, 97–98
active perpetuation of, 109–12
among government analysts, 109, 112, 113–14
among journalists, 94, 109, 113
among market analysts, 112
among policymakers and politicians, 94, 96, 108–9, 112, 114, 115–16
cartel aims of members, 16–17, 81, 83, 85–86, 97
cartel definitions, 94, 95, 99, 99n.25, 112
cognitive dissonance in beliefs about, 112
consequences of beliefs, 114–16
diplomatic and other political benefits to member states, 95–96, 108–12, 115–16
market influence, perceptions about, 94, 95, 96, 108–16, 118
"rational myth" concept in, 17, 95–96, 108, 112, 116
in scholarship, 94, 97, 98, 105–6, 108–9, 113, 114–15, 116, 117–18

OPEC, cartel reputation, statistical analysis of, 98–108, 101t, 104t
cheating variable, 25–26, 94–95, 101–2, 116
data used in, 103n.34
depletion rates variable, 103–8
diplomatic benefits, 111
dominant producer hypothesis, 105–6
findings, 94–95, 96, 99, 100, 103–8
market impact, 94, 95, 96, 108–12
production restriction tests, 94–95, 96, 98–108, 99n.24
research methods, 98–108
OPEC, cooperation among members, 68, 72–73, 74–75, 97, 179
as cheating deterrence, 73, 74, 81
gradual harmonization and virtuous circle, 78, 80t
nationalization support, 75–76, 78–82
policy experimentation and information sharing, 75–76, 79, 80–81, 80t, 187, 198
political benefits as true organizational function, 95–96, 108–12, 115–16
price setting, 76–79, 80–81, 80t
profit negotiations, 60–61, 74–75, 77–78, 80t
semi-collaboration, 72–73, 76, 77–78
tax codes, 74–75, 77–78, 80–81, 80t, 198
weakness of benefits, 95, 108
OPEC, formation of, 1, 25, 54–56, 55t, 60–61
Arab Oil Congress and, 69, 70
conditions leading to, 60–61, 66–71, 91–93
oil prices and, 69, 70, 71
original signatories, 71
Pérez Alfonzo and Tariki's reflections on, 63, 72, 76, 93, 94
public announcement, 70
Seven Sisters' initial reactions, 71–72
See also nationalization of oil companies; Pérez Alfonzo, Juan Pablo; Tariki, Abdullah
OPEC, production quotas, 52, 94, 97, 101t
depletion rates, 102–8, 104t
economic impact, endogeneity in logic, 98–99

impact tests, 101–3
setting, 81, 97n.8, 98–99
See also oil production subsystem; OPEC, cartel reputation
OPEC, production quotas, cheating on, 96
in cartel reputation analysis, 25–26, 94–95, 101–2, 116
inability to enforce punishments, 25–26, 95, 107–8, 109, 116, 187, 198
strategic cooperative benefits to deter, 73, 74, 81
OPEC era, 25, 60
historical overview, 10, 52
subsystems analysis, 91–93, 92t
See also nationalization of oil companies; 1973 oil shock; oil-for-security (OFS) deals; OPEC, cartel reputation; Seven Sisters era
OPEC Fund for International Development (OFID), 88–89
OPEC member states
imperialist control of, 123f, 123
listed, 71, 97, 102n.30, 110–11
new members' production levels, 99–100, 100f
OPEC as shorthand for, 113
See also under individual member
Operation Ajax, 65–66, 144, 149, 159
Operation Desert Shield, 137, 154
Operation Desert Storm, 137, 154
Operation Vantage, 139
ordering themes, 179–80
defining, 11f
governing arrangements, relationship to, 9–10, 11f, 15f, 15, 19–20, 34–35, 39, 181–84, 182f
liberal international order context, 220
subsystem theory advantages, 39
See also international order
Organization of Arab Petroleum Exporting Countries (OAPEC), 83
Organization of the Islamic Conference, 89
Organization of the Petroleum Exporting Countries (OPEC)
See nationalization of oil companies; 1973 oil shock; OPEC; Seven Sister oil companies; individual member state

Ostrom, Elinor, 181, 207
outbidding, 172–73, 194, 222
overlap between subsystems, 124, 149,
  184–85, 196–97
ozone depletion, 205n.85

Pachachi, Nadim, 63
Page, Howard, 81
Pakistan, 140, 171
Palestine, 87, 90
Palestinian Liberation Organization
  (PLO), 87
Pan Am Flight 103, 87
pan-Arabism and -Islamism, 89
papal authority, 38n.36
Paris Agreement (2015), 18, 190–
  91, 198–99
Parra, Francisco, 68, 81–82
partial and pure hegemony, differences,
  2–3, 14–15, 19
Paulson, Henry, 210n.106
peacekeeping operations, 163–64, 169–70,
  173–75, 216
peacetime subsystems change, 49
Pérez Alfonzo, Juan Pablo, 25, 59,
  68, 69–71
  cartel aims, 81
  political career, 59, 63–64, 69, 72
  reflections on OPEC's formation,
    63, 72, 93
  Texas Railroad Commission as OPEC
    inspiration, 69, 81
  See also OPEC, formation of; Tariki,
    Abdullah
Persia. See Iran
Persian Gulf states
  . See under oil-for-security (OFS) deals;
    individual country
persuasion, 43
PetroAmérica, 89–90
Petroandino, 89–90
Petrocaribe, 89–90
petrochemical industry, 82
petro-colonies and petrostates.
  See decolonization; independence
    movements; nationalization of oil
    companies; individual state
petrodollar recycling, 86, 158

Petróleos de Venezuela (PDVSA), 84
Petroleum Law of 1943 (Venezuela), 63–64
Petrosur, 89–90
the Philippines, 126–27, 221
Poland, 124, 219
policy experimentation and information
    sharing
  among OPEC members, 75–76, 79, 80–
    81, 80t, 187, 198
  in climate governance, 187, 195–96, 198
policymaking, 36, 83, 86, 198, 215–16
  in empire definition, 51n.87
political contestation, 168–69, 171, 173–74
political influence, funded by oil revenue,
    86–91, 127–28
  See also oil-for-security (OFS) deals; oil
    revenue; OPEC, cartel reputation;
    Saudi Arabia, influence of
Portugal, 122, 133–34
posted prices. See oil prices
pound, value of, 150
power asymmetries, 46, 171, 172
practice theory, 23–24, 33
Pratt, Tyler, 20n.63
Prebisch, Raúl, 68
price influence, definitions, 95
  See also OPEC, cartel reputation
price of oil. See oil prices
price stability/volatility metric, 32–33
production costs, fossil fuels and, 196
  See also oil production
profit. See oil revenue
prorationing. See oil production levels;
    OPEC, production quotas
prospective analysis, 177
protectionism, 56, 60, 129–30,
    135, 150–51
  See also oil-for-security (OFS) deals
public and private spheres, climate politics
    and, 194
  See also actors, defining; climate
    governance
punishments for noncompliance, climate
    change subsystems, 188–89, 216
  BATs, 187, 199–200, 202
  climate club operations, 26–27, 201–2
  climate-related capital subsystem, 194
  climate-trade nexus subsystem, 197

punishments for noncompliance, climate change subsystems (*cont.*)
emissions reductions subsystem, 191–92
Kyoto Protocol failure, 191, 198–99
See also climate governance
punishments for noncompliance, conceptual overview, 4, 9, 12–13, 31–32, 40–42, 43–44
assessing changes in oil politics subsystems, 53–57, 60–61
contemporary IR scholarship and, 21, 41, 216
decolonization's effect on, 15–16, 32, 51–52, 54, 55*t*, 60–61
deep cooperation hypothesis, 177
disproportionate, 46
hegemonic actors avoid, 46, 177
identifying, subsystems analysis guidelines, 166, 168
instruments of coercion, relationship to, 13–14, 15–16
international order shifts away, 149–50
liberal international order, 13, 27, 221
nuclear politics, 171, 178*f*
rival collective images and, 184
strategic benefits, distinction from, 41, 42, 44*f*, 177
tariffs, 37–38n.33
See also boycotts; instruments of coercion; strategic benefits; strength and enforceability of punishments
punishments for noncompliance, oil production subsystem
as calculated risk, 66, 75, 78–79
military occupation as implication, 60, 66–67
OPEC's inability to impose, 95, 107–8, 109, 178*f*
Seven Sisters era, 60, 65–67, 75, 124
See also nationalization attempts; oil production subsystem
punishments for noncompliance, oil security subsystem, 124, 142–45, 159
Marshall Plan and, 128
oil-for-security deals, 136–37, 140–41, 142–43, 152, 153

See also oil-for-security (OFS) deals; oil security subsystem
pure and partial hegemony, differences, 2–3, 14–15, 19

Qaddafi, Muammar, 87
Qasim, Iraq ruler, 146
Qatar, 122–23, 132–33, 134, 150, 155–56
oil-for-security deals, 146, 147*f*
OPEC membership, 71, 97, 101*t*, 102n.30, 109n.46
Qods force, 87, 90
quotas. *See* oil production levels; OPEC, production quotas

racial equality, decolonization and, 51–52, 128–29
racism
of Churchill, 129
by oil companies toward local workers, 66, 124, 143
railroads
oil transport by, 69
US discourages Western European use, 127, 128
Rashid Ali, prime minister of Iraq, 140
rates of change, 11
oil subsystems, compared, 11–12
See also international order, analyzing changes
"rational myth" of OPEC as cartel, 17, 95–96, 112, 116
concept defined, 108
See also OPEC, cartel reputation
realism, 21–23, 24*t*, 57–58
realpolitik elements, 224
Red Line Agreement, 61–62
reductionism, 39, 183
regime complexity, 35, 36, 37, 188, 198
regimes, defined, 36
regime theory, 9, 35, 36
regime types
monarchical rule, 134, 135, 148
See also authority types; leadership selection
religion, 148
See also Islam

renewable energy standards (RES),
    217n.11
renewable energy technology, 214
    China's development of, 191, 195
    climate-trade nexus subsystem and, 197
    consumption levels, 18
    economic cost of, 217n.11
    negative-emissions technologies
        subsystem, 26–27, 186–87, 194–96,
        216, 217
    solar and wind energy, 18, 191, 217, 218
    systems integration variables, 218
rentier politics, 147–48
Republican Party, 208
resource curse, 147–48
resource nationalism, 66, 91–93
retaliatory tariffs, climate club and, 207–11
    See also border adjustment taxes (BATs)
retrospective analysis, 177
Reus-Smit, Christian, 22n.80
Reza Pahlavi, Mohammad, Shah of Iran,
        64–65, 67t, 85, 122, 141, 150–51
    Mossadegh and Iranian
        Revolution, 144–45
    nationalization issues, 75, 143, 144–45
    OPEC formation and, 70, 71, 81
    profit negotiations by, 74–75, 82
Reza Pahlavi, prime minister of Iran, 75,
        122, 141
Richardson, Bill, 114
risk assessment of punishments for
        noncompliance, 12, 22, 40–41,
        54n.105, 169
    decolonization and declining risk,
        32, 60–61
    nationalization, 66, 67–68, 78–82
    OPEC cooperation, 73, 74–75, 76, 78,
        80t, 81
    rival collective images, 45–46, 168–69,
        171, 172–73, 174, 179, 184
    constructivism and, 21, 24t
rival hierarchies, 27, 135–36, 172–73, 222
road construction, 127
Rockefeller, John D., 122
Rommel, Erwin, 124–25
Roosevelt, Franklin D., 137
Roosevelt, Kermit, Jr., 144
Roosevelt, Theodore, 144

Rose, Andrew, 99–100
Rosenbloom, Daniel, 202n.78
Rostow, Walt, 150n.105
Rouhani, Fuad, 68, 71, 74–75
Royal Dutch-Shell, 25, 61–62, 65, 145
Royal Navy (Britain), 119–20, 122
    See also British military
royalties, 63
    expensing, 74–75
    See also oil revenue; taxes
Ruggie, John, 220–21
Rusk, Dean, 150–51
Russia/Soviet Union/USSR, 7, 24–25, 86–
        87, 120, 151, 221
    Cold War and, 134, 222
    Iran and, 141–42
    joins G8, 86
    nuclear politics and, 170–71, 172–73
    WWII and, 49, 125

Sadat, Anwar, 83
sanctions, 47, 53, 107, 199–200, 205
    See also boycotts; economic coercion
Saudi Arabia
    Egypt conflict, 89, 138, 157
    monarchy in, 134
    nationalization in, 65, 67t, 79–80, 82–83
    oil prices during Covid-19 pandemic, 7
    oil reserves discovery in, 62
    punishments for noncompliance with
        climate politics, 194
    Seven Sisters era, 61, 62, 63–64, 67t
    size, 148
    Yom Kippur War financing by, 83
    See also Tariki, Abdullah
Saudi Arabia, influence of, 47–48, 112
    Bahrain and, 147n.101
    cartel reputation, 96
    political influence funded by oil
        revenue, 88–89
    production, 7, 96, 97, 105, 112, 137–38
    in US relations, 86, 137–38, 153–54, 215
Saudi Arabia, oil-for-security deals, 60,
        138–39, 141, 146
    acceptance of, 147f
    arms deals, 137–38, 155–56, 158, 215
    Iraq invasion of Kuwait and, 153–54
    leadership selection and, 138

Saudi Arabia, oil-for-security deals (*cont.*)
  public opinion of US in, 155
  as template, 159–60
  See also oil-for-security (OFS)
    deals; United States, OFS deals,
    Saudi Arabia
Saudi Arabia, OPEC membership, 95, 97
  depletion rates, 104*t*, 105–6, 112
  influence on cartel reputation, 96
  1973 oil shock and, 82
  as original signatory, 71
  production quotas, 101*t*, 102n.30
  profit negotiations and, 74–75
  See also Tariki, Abdullah
Saudi Aramco, 79–80, 84, 160
  See also Arabian American Oil
    Company (Aramco)
Schwarzkopf, Norman, 154
Schwinn, Walter, 66–67
scope conditions changes, 50
Scowcroft, Brent, 152
securitization, 6
selection bias, 106–7
September 11, 2001 terrorist attacks,
    89, 154
Seven Sister oil companies, 10, 25, 54–56,
    55*t*, 60–61
  governing arrangements' variations
    over time, 56*f*
  locals' experience of US-owned, 135
  production setting by, 52, 61–63, 81,
    95, 143–44
  See also nationalization of oil
    companies; oil-for-security (OFS)
    deals; OPEC
Seven Sister oil companies, price setting
    by, 52, 61–63, 69, 136
  as context for OPEC's founding,
    69, 70, 71
  cooperation in, 62–63, 177
  Maadi Pact circumvents, 70–71
  strength of enforceable punishments
    in, 198
  See also oil prices
Seven Sister oil companies, profit
    agreements with petrostates, 63–64,
    72–73, 91, 157–58
  accounting tricks, 74–75

50/50 agreements, 63–64, 72–73,
    74, 77–78
  Marshall Plan and, 127–28
  oil production costs, 62, 63–64, 74
  OPEC cooperates in negotiations, 60–
    61, 74–75, 77–78, 80*t*
  tax codes and royalty expensing in, 74–
    75, 77–78
  See also OPEC, cooperation among
    members
Seven Sisters era, 10, 61–69, 122
  Anglo-American relations during, 136
  market behavior in, 60, 61–62
  Marshall Plan and, 127–28
  political behavior in, 60, 63, 66–67
  response to OPEC formation, 71–72
  subsystems analysis, 91–93, 92*t*
  See also colonialism and imperial
    expansion; nationalization of oil
    companies; OPEC, formation of
Seven Sisters era, instruments of coercion
    during, 120
  leadership selection, 60, 66–67, 144
  strategic benefits, 60–61, 62–63, 66–67,
    72, 91, 92*t*, 157–58
  See also nationalization attempts, Seven
    Sister responses
Seybert, Lucia, 176n.48
Shakhbut, ruler of Abu Dhabi, 149–50
Shell, 52n.94, 69
  See also Seven Sister oil companies
Smith, Adam, 187
Smith, James L., 102n.30, 222n.37
social contradictions, 168–69, 173–74, 184
soft power, 14
solar and wind energy, 18, 191, 217, 218
  See also renewable energy technology
solidarity of OPEC member states. *See*
    OPEC, cooperation among members
South Africa, 171
Southeast Asia, 36
South Korea, 36
sovereign state creation, 45, 48–49, 60, 149
  See also decolonization; independence
    movements; nationalization of oil
    companies
Soviet Union. *See* Russia/Soviet Union/
    USSR

Standard Oil (and various iterations), 25, 65, 122
state actors, 9, 12, 40, 41n.48, 49–50, 60–61
    authority of, 38n.36
    domestic politics of, 41–42
    subsystems definition and, 37–38
    See also actors, defining; non-state actors
state-run oil industry. *See* nationalization of oil companies
strategic benefits, climate change subsystems, 42, 188–89
    climate club operations, 201–2, 203–4
    climate-related capital subsystem, 194
    emissions reductions subsystem, 190–92
    Kyoto Protocol failure, 191
    strength and weakness of, 190–91
    See also climate governance
strategic benefits, conceptual overview, 9, 12–13, 31–32, 42–43
    contemporary IR scholarship on, 21, 216
    decolonization's effects on, 16
    deep cooperation hypothesis, 177
    defining actors, 57
    disproportionate, 46, 78–79
    to global energy transition, 218–19
    hegemonic actors overestimate benefits, 48–49
    identifying, subsystems analysis guidelines, 166, 168–69
    instruments of coercion, relationship to, 13–14, 15–16, 46–47
    international order shifts and, 27, 43–46, 44f, 149–50, 177–79
    mutual gains, 12, 24t, 42, 46
    nuclear politics, 21, 172–73, 179
    punishments for noncompliance, distinction from, 41, 42, 44f, 177
    See also instruments of coercion; punishments for noncompliance; strength of benefits
strategic benefits, oil production subsystem
    assessing changes in oil politics subsystems, 53–57, 91
    nationalization and loss of benefits, 65, 67–68, 78–79, 91

OPEC era, 76, 78–79, 92t
OPEC formation and loss of benefits, 60–61, 70
Seven Sisters era, 60–61, 62–63, 66–67, 72, 91, 92t, 157–58
Venezuelan foreign aid and, 89–90
See also oil production subsystem; OPEC, cartel reputation; OPEC, cooperation among members
strategic benefits, oil security subsystem
    Marshall Plan and, 127–28
    See also oil-for-security (OFS) deals
strength and enforceability of punishments
    in current climate policy, 18, 191, 198–99, 205n.85
    in future climate policy design, 187, 189
    necessity of, 18, 21, 198, 216
    oil production subsystem, eras compared, 66–67, 91, 92t
    OPEC cheating, 25–26, 95, 107–8, 109, 116, 187, 198
    overview, 13, 21, 40–42, 43–45, 46, 56f, 177–79, 178f
    See also punishments for noncompliance
strength of benefits, 56f, 60–61, 66–67, 177–79, 178f
    climate subsystems, 190–91
    OPEC membership benefits as weak, 95, 108
    overview, 13, 21, 43–45, 46
    See also strategic benefits
strikes, Iranian oil workers, 145
structural changes, 54
structural realists, 41n.48, 58n.109
Subsystem A. *See* oil production subsystem
Subsystem B. *See* oil security subsystem
subsystems, defined, 4, 9–10, 11f, 31–32, 36, 37–38
    See also governing arrangements; instruments of coercion; international order; issue areas; regime theory
subsystems analysis guidelines, 26, 37–38, 163, 164–69
    accuracy in evaluating, 175–77, 197–98

subsystems analysis guidelines (*cont.*)
behavior patterns observation step, 164–65, 170, 173–74
breadth in evaluating, 175–77, 197–98
causal analysis and, 184
for competing analyses, 175–77
descriptive inference and, 184
empirical pattern observation, 164–65, 166–68, 169, 219
governance questions identification, 37–38, 40n.43, 164, 165–66, 167, 169, 175, 188–89
overlap and interconnection, 184–85, 196–97
parsimony in evaluating, 175–77, 191–92, 192n.27, 197–98
political and social contradictions examination, 168–69
relating subsystem theory to issue areas' empirics, 164, 166–68, 169
reliability and validity and, 175–77
See also governance questions, identification step in subsystems analysis; nuclear politics; peacekeeping operations
subsystems theory, advantages for applying, 38–39
to climate change policy, 198
disadvantages, 39–40
to global energy transition, 27, 219–20
to liberal international order crisis, 221–22, 223
to nuclear politics, 171
to peacekeeping operations, 174–75
subsystems theory, overview, 36–40, 49–50
contemporary IR scholarship comparisons, 19–24
defined, 4, 9–10, 11*f*, 31–32, 36, 37–38
empirical inference for identification, 52n.93
governing arrangements, relationship to, 9–10, 11*f*, 15*f*, 36, 37, 175
leading actors' role, 47–48
multiplicity of paths to changes in, 49, 58n.108
ordering themes within, 9–10

See also governing arrangements; instruments of coercion; international order; issue areas; punishments for noncompliance; strategic benefits
Suez Canal, 124–25
Suez Crisis (1956), 127
Sunni Muslims, 148
Syria, 140, 148

tanks, 121–22, 125
tariff agreements, 37–38n.33
retaliatory tariff risk of BAT use, 207–11
See also border adjustment taxes (BATs)
Tariki, Abdullah, 25, 59, 68, 70–71, 72
cartel aims, 81
political career, 59–60
reflections on OPEC's formation, 76, 93, 94
reflections on Pérez Alfonzo, 69–70
Yamani succeeds, 81, 138
See also OPEC, formation of; Pérez Alfonzo, Juan Pablo
taxes, 63–64
Marshall Plan and, 127
royalty expensing before, 74–75
tax codes and cooperation among OPEC member states, 74–75, 77–78, 80–81, 80*t*, 198
See also border adjustment taxes (BATs)
technology, 40
as engine of change, 223
IEA policy on, 86
military, 119–20, 121–22, 124
punishments for noncompliance affected by, 41
See also renewable energy technology
territorial conquest, rules of, 21, 177, 178*f*
terrorism, 87, 89, 154
Texaco, 25
Texas, 69
Texas Railroad Commission, 69, 81
Thailand, 36
Thatcher, Margaret Roberts, 119, 120–21
Bush and, 151–52, 154
Tierzan, Pierre, 130
Tillerson, Rex, 156

trade dispute-resolution tribunals
    (WTO), 205–6
transportation industry, 82, 127–28
Treaty on the Prohibition of Nuclear
    Weapons (2017), 171, 179
Trudeau, Justin, 205n.83
Truman, Harry S., 142n.85
Trump, Donald J., 46, 180, 220–21
Trump administration, 155–56, 170–
    71, 208
Turkey, 140

Ukraine, 219, 221
UNFCCC, 188, 191
unilateral climate change mitigation
    policy, 187
United Arab Emirates (UAE), 88–89, 90
    British imperial influence of, 122–23,
        132–33, 134, 150
    oil-for-security deals, 146, 147f, 158
    OPEC membership, 71, 97, 101t,
        102n.30
United Kingdom, car ownership in, 77f
    See also Britain
United Nations, 154, 179
    General Assembly, 87
    international climate order and,
        211, 212
    See also climate governance
United Nations Convention on the Law of
    the Sea (UNCLOS), 221
UN Resolution on the Permanent
    Sovereignty over Natural
    Resources, 68
UN Security Council, 142, 143
United States, climate change and
    BATs adoption, 199–200
    carbon pricing and, 208–9
    emissions rates, 208
    Green New Deal, 197
    hegemonic stability theory and, 189
    venture capitalist investment in US
        companies, 195
    See also climate governance
United States, climate club membership,
    18–19, 187, 201, 202, 208–11,
    212, 216
    Canada and, 204–5

    China and, 209–11, 213
    retaliatory tariffs and, 208
    See also climate club
United States, foreign policy
    Biden administration, 202, 208
    Eisenhower administration, 69
    Nixon administration, 83, 157–58
    Trump administration, 155–56, 170–
        71, 208
    See also oil-for-security (OFS) deals;
        Seven Sister oil companies
United States, leadership selection, 48
    Iran, 47, 144–45
    Saudi Arabia, 138
    See also leadership selection
United States, liberal international order
    and, 220
    Cold War and, 222
    complexity of competition and
        cooperation, 222, 223
    public goods or club goods provision
        by, 21–22
    punishments for noncompliance, 13,
        27, 221
    strategic benefits, 27
    See also liberal international order
United States, nuclear politics and, 164–
    65, 170–71, 172–73
    See also nuclear politics
United States, OFS deals, defense
    deployment
    Afghanistan invasion, 151
    after decolonization, 15–16
    Iraq (2003), 154
    Iraq-Kuwait conflict, 7–8, 41–42, 47,
        120–21, 137, 139, 151–54, 157
United States, OFS deals, Saudi Arabia,
    153–54, 155–56, 158, 215
    Iraq-Kuwait conflict and, 137, 153–54
    origins of, 86–87, 137–38, 159–60
    Qatar conflict and, 155–56
    US defense in Saudi Arabia, 137, 153–
        54, 157, 160
    See also Saudi Arabia
United States, oil-for-security deals, 7–8
    current doubts about ongoing,
        27, 155–56
    as de facto imperialism, 120

United States, oil-for-security deals (*cont.*)
　Iran, 142, 144–45, 146
　Iraq, 140–41
　Kuwait, 139, 159
　locals' opinion of US, 135, 155
　protectionism through, 60,
　　135, 150–51
　relationship with Britain and, 12, 136,
　　151–52, 154
　subsystems theory analysis, 11
　See also oil-for-security (OFS) deals
United States, oil production subsystem
　IEA and, 56–57, 85–86
　imports and exports, and domestic
　　production rates, 6, 69, 122, 134, 155
　1973 oil shock and, 83, 85–86
　OPEC cartel reputation, beliefs about,
　　113–14, 115, 118
　OPEC legal challenges in, 112
　OPEC underestimated, 71
　See also nationalization attempts; oil
　　production subsystem; Seven Sister
　　oil companies
United States, oil security subsystem
　Cold War, 134, 135–36
　energy security rhetoric, 5–7
　Marshall Plan and, 127–28
　WWII and, 126–27
　See also oil-for-security (OFS) deals; oil
　　security subsystem
United States as hegemon
　as benign hegemon, 21–22
　hegemonic decline, 1–2, 3, 7–8, 19, 189
　nuclear politics, 172
　as partial hegemon, 47–48
　punishments for noncompliance
　　against, 46, 177
　WWII, importance of, 49
　See also hegemonic actors
US dollar, as global reserve currency, 137–
　38, 157–58
US Energy Information Agency, 101–2
United States military. *See* military
　coercion; oil-for-security (OFS)
　deals; United States, OFS deals
US National Academies of
　Sciences, 194–95
Universal Postal Union, 178

Urpelainen, Johannes, 199n.62
USSR. *See* Russia/Soviet Union/USSR

Venezuela, 59
　coup d'etat, 63–64
　foreign aid by, 89–90
　nationalization in, 65, 67*t*, 82–83, 84
　oil production in, 65, 122
　political changes in, 63–64, 69
　royalty expensing and, 74–75
　Seven Sisters control in, 63–64
　See also Pérez Alfonzo, Juan Pablo
Venezuela, OPEC membership, 93, 97
　cartel myth perpetuated in, 110
　as original signatory, 71
　production quotas, 101*t*, 102n.30
venture capitalism, climate change
　and, 194–95
Victor, David G., 202n.81
Vietnam, 15–16, 51–52
Vonnegut, Kurt, 186, 187
von Rundstedt, Gerd, 126

Waltz, Kenneth N., 58n.108
war
　close-neighbor aggression after
　　decolonization, 51n.92
　Cold War, 120, 134, 135–36, 151, 164–
　　65, 222
　contemporary IR scholars' focus on, 3,
　　20, 35, 49
　energy security rhetoric, 6
　Falklands War, 152
　hegemonic stability theory and, 3–4
　oil revenue funds armed
　　violence, 86–87
　territorial conquest distinction, 177n.50
　WWI, 119–20, 121–22
　WWII, 49, 120, 124–28, 195
　Yom Kippur War, 83
　See also Iraq-Kuwait conflict; military
　　coercion
Waxman-Markey bill (2009), 208
weak benefits and punishments. *See*
　strength and enforceability of
　punishments; strength of benefits
weapons management, 172
　See also nuclear politics

whale oil, 218n.17
Williams, Eric, 68
Wilson, Harold, 150
Wimmer, Andreas, 131–32
wind and solar energy, 18, 191, 217, 218
    See also renewable energy technology
Wodajo, Kifle, 68
Wohlforth, William, 22n.77
World Bank, 3, 23–24, 180
    China and, 191n.18
    "Ease of Doing Business" index, 207
    Venezuela and, 89–90
World Muslim League, 89
World Trade Organization (WTO), 107–8,
    180, 205–7, 213
    climate club and, 205–6, 216

environmental exemption
    provisions, 206
trade dispute rules of, 205–6
World War I, 119–20, 121–22
World War II, 49, 120, 124–28, 195
    fuel's importance in, 124–27

Yamani, Ahmed, 81, 82, 138
Yemen, 137, 155
Yom Kippur War (1973), 83

Zahedi, Fazlollah, 144
Zapata Petroleum Company, 148–
    49, 152–53
Zayed bin Sultan Al Nahyan, ruler of Abu
    Dhabi, 149–50